The Domestic Savings Shortfall in Sub-Saharan Africa

The United Nations University World Institute for Development Economics Research (UNU-WIDER) was established by the United Nations University as its first research and training centre and started work in Helsinki, Finland, in 1985. The mandate of the institute is to undertake applied research and policy analysis on structural changes affecting developing economies; to provide a forum for the advocacy of policies leading to robust, equitable, and environmentally sustainable growth; and to promote capacity strengthening and training in the field of economic and social policy-making. Its work is carried out by staff researchers and visiting scholars in Helsinki and via networks of collaborating scholars and institutions around the world.

United Nations University World Institute for
Development Economics Research—UNU-WIDER
Katajanokanlaituri 6B, 00160 Helsinki, Finland
www.wider.unu.edu

The Domestic Savings Shortfall in Sub-Saharan Africa

What Can Be Done About It?

Edited by

ROSE NGUGI

KUNAL SEN

UNU WIDER

A study prepared by the United Nations University World Institute for Development Economics Research—(UNU-WIDER)

OXFORD
UNIVERSITY PRESS

OXFORD
UNIVERSITY PRESS

Great Clarendon Street, Oxford, OX2 6DP,
United Kingdom

Oxford University Press is a department of the University of Oxford.
It furthers the University's objective of excellence in research, scholarship,
and education by publishing worldwide. Oxford is a registered trade mark of
Oxford University Press in the UK and in certain other countries

Published in the United States of America by Oxford University Press
198 Madison Avenue, New York, NY 10016, United States of America

British Library Cataloguing in Publication Data

Data available

Library of Congress Control Number: 2024950778

ISBN 9780198932482

DOI: 10.1093/oso/9780198932482.001.0001

Printed and bound by
CPI Group (UK) Ltd, Croydon, CR0 4YY

Foreword

Domestic financing plays a crucial role in the revenue collection efforts of developing countries. Countries with high domestic savings rates tend to experience higher economic growth rates than others. The greater the domestic savings, the greater is the much-needed flexibility to implement homegrown policies to confront growth and development challenges. Furthermore, a high savings rate reduces vulnerability to sudden shifts in international capital flows.

However, efforts to increase domestic savings rates have not met with much success in low-income countries, especially in Sub-Saharan Africa, despite financial liberalization and sound macroeconomic policies. We need to know more about the ways to increase domestic financing in these countries.

To address the knowledge gap, the United Nations University World Institute for Development Economics Research (UNU-WIDER) has conducted the project 'The Domestic Savings Shortfall in Developing Countries—What Can Be Done about It?' in collaboration with the Kenya Institute for Public Policy Research and Analysis (KIPPRA). Four years of research efforts are now distilled within this book. I sincerely thank the chapter authors for their scholarly contributions and my fellow editor, Rose Ngugi, for her editorial skills in bringing this rich research to publication.

This research project was undertaken with special financial support from the Norwegian Agency for Development Cooperation (Norad), for which all parties are most grateful. UNU-WIDER gratefully acknowledges the support and financial contribution to its work programme by the institute's core donors of the governments of Finland and Sweden. Without this vital funding, our research and policy advisory work would be impossible.

Kunal Sen
Director, UNU-WIDER
Helsinki
January 2025

Acknowledgements

This book is an outcome of the UNU-WIDER project 'The Domestic Savings Shortfall in Developing Countries—What Can Be Done about It?', conducted in collaboration with the Kenya Institute for Public Policy Research and Analysis (KIPPRA). We wish to thank the Norwegian Agency for Development Cooperation (Norad) for its specific contribution to UNU-WIDER's Domestic Revenue Mobilization programme.

We acknowledge the comments of the anonymous reviewers of the manuscript and the invaluable support and guidance of the commissioning editor Adam Swallow at Oxford University Press.

Rose Ngugi
Kunal Sen
January 2025

Acknowledgements

Contents

PART III. COUNTRY STUDIES

PART IV. CONCLUSION

List of Figures

List of Tables

List of Abbreviations

4IR	Fourth Industrial Revolution
AADFI	Association of African Development Finance Institutions
AARP	American Association of Retired Persons
ADB	Asian Development Bank
ADF	augmented Dickey–Fuller
AELP	African Exchanges Linkage Project
AERC	African Economic Research Consortium
AES	African Economic Society
AfDB	African Development Bank Group
AI	artificial intelligence
AIC	Akaike information criterion
AIH	absolute income hypothesis
AltX	alternative exchange
AML	anti-money laundering
ANG	Angola
ARDL	autoregressive distributed lag
ASEA	African Securities Exchanges Association
ATM	automated teller machine
BBUA	Barico Bilbao Vizcaya Argentina
BCEAO	Banque Centrale des États de l'Afrique de l'Quest
BEAC	Banque des États de l'Afrique Centrale
BIC	Baysian information criterion
BIDF	Bangladesh Infrastructure Development Fund
BOT	Botswana/Bank of Tanzania
BRICS	Brazil, Russia, India, China, and South Africa
BRVM	*Bourse Régionale des Valeurs Mobilières*
BUGDPC	Boston University Global Development Policy Center
CAEMU	Central African Economic and Monetary Community Union
CAGR	compound annual growth rate
CAMPOST	Cameroon Postal Service
CBK	Central Bank of Kenya
CCUS	carbon capture, usage, and storage
CEMAC	Economic Community of Central African States
CFA	chartered financial analyst/Communauté Financière Africaine
CFT	countering the financing of terrorism
CI	composite indicator
CIC	China Investment Corporation
CMA	Common Monetary Area

COBAC	Central African Banking Commission
CPI	consumer price index/corruption perceptions index
CPIA	country policy and institutional assessment
CUSUM	cumulative sum chart
CUSUMSQ	cumulative sum chart squared
DB	defined benefits
DC	defined contribution
DDE	distressed debt exchange
DDEP	Domestic Debt Exchange Programme
DERG	Development Economics Research Group
DFE	dynamic fixed effects
DFI	development finance institution
DFS	digital financial services
DLT	distributed ledger technology
DRC	Democratic Republic of the Congo
DRM	domestic resource mobilization
DSA	debt sustainability assessment
DSF	Debt Sustainability Framework
DSSI	Debt Service Suspension Initiative
DW	Durbin–Watson
EAP	East Asia and the Pacific
ECF	equity crowdfunding
ECM	error correction model
ECOWAS	Economic Community of West African States
ERP	Economic Recovery Programme
ERS	Economic Recovery Strategy
ETF	exchange-traded fund
FDI	foreign direct investment
FGFSRs	first-generation financial-sector reforms
FINSAP I and II	Financial Sector Adjustment Programmes I and II
FLI	financial liberalization index
FSD	Financial Sector Deepening
GAB	Gagon
GAX	Ghana Alternative Market
GDP	gross domestic product
GEMS	Growth Enterprise Market Segment
GFC	global financial crisis
GIZ	Deutsche Gesellschaft für Zusammenarbeit
GMM	generalized method of moments
GNI	gross national income
GPDI	gross personal disposable income
GSIA	Ghana Securities Industry Association
GSMA	Global System for Mobile Communications Association
HIPCs	Heavily Indebted Poor Countries
ICRG	International Country Risk Guide

IDA	International Development Association
IDPM	Institute of Data Processing Management
IDS	Institute of Development Studies
IFC	International Finance Corporation
IFSWF	International Forum of Sovereign Wealth Funds
IIFM	International Islamic Financial Market
ILO	International Labour Organization
IMF	International Monetary Fund
IMR	infant mortality rate
IOPS	International Organisation of Pension Supervisors
IoT	internet of things
IPD	Initiative for Policy Dialogue
IPO	initial public offering
IRC	interest rate control
IRF	impulse response function
ISSA	International Social Security Association
IWG	International Workplace Group plc
JSE	Johannesburg Stock Exchange
KCB	Kenya Commercial Bank
KIAP	*Key Indicators of Asia and the Pacific*
KIHBS	Kenya Integrated Household Budget Survey 2015–16
KIPPRA	Kenya Institute for Public Policy Research and Analysis
KNBS	Kenya National Bureau of Statistics
LAC	Latin America and the Caribbean
LCH	life cycle hypothesis
LCM	life-cycle model
LIC	low-income country
LM	Lagrange multiplier
LMIC	lower-middle-income country
LSE	London School of Economics
MAC	market access country
MDRI	Multilateral Debt Relief Initiative
MENA	Middle East and North Africa
MFI	microfinance institution
MG	mean group
MIC	middle-income country
ML	machine learning
MNO	mobile network operators
MSME	micro, small, and medium enterprises
MVNO	mobile virtual network operator
NAM	Namibia
NBER	National Bureau of Economic Research
NBFIRA	Non-Bank Financial Institutions Regulatory Authority
NBS	National Bureau of Statistics
NDB	national development bank

NEPAD	New Partnership for Africa's Development
NIIF	National Investment and Infrastructure Fund (India)
NMP	national microfinance policy
Norad	Norwegian Agency for Development Cooperatives
NSE	Nairobi Securities Exchange
NSGRP	National Strategy for Growth and Reduction of Poverty
NSIA	Nigeria Sovereign Investment Authority
ODI	Overseas Development Institute
OECD	Organisation for Economic Co-operation and Development
OLS	ordinary least squares
P2P	peer to peer
PAYG	pay as you go
PEP	Partnerships for Economic Policy/politically exposed persons
PIF	public investment fund
PIH	permanent income hypothesis
PMA	Palestine Monetary Authority
PO—RALG	President's Office Regional Administration and Local Government
PP	Phillips–Perron
PPP	purchasing power parity
PSR	payment systems regulator
R&D	research and development
REIT	real estate investment trust
RIR	real interest rate
ROSCA	rotating savings and credit association
RTGS	real-time gross settlement system
SACCO	savings and credit cooperative
SAHO	South African History Online
SAP	structural adjustment programme
SBC	Schwarz Bayesian criterion
SBIC	Schwarz Bayesian information criterion
SDF	sovereign development fund
SDG	Sustainable Development Goal
SDR	special drawing rights
SEI	Stockholm Environment Institute
SGFSRs	second-generation financial-sector reforms
SHG	self-help group
SMEs	small and medium-sized enterprises
SMR	statutory minimum reserve
SOAS	School of Oriental and African Studies, University of London
SSA	Sub-Saharan Africa
SSP	social security payment
SUERF	
SWF	sovereign wealth fund
TCDC	Tanzania Cooperative Development Commission
TI	Transparency International

TMCD	Oxford Technology and Management Centre for Development
ToT	terms of trade
TWF	Turkey Wealth Fund
TZS	Tanzanian shilling
UNCDF	United Nations Capital Development Fund
UNDP	United Nations Development Programme
UNICEF	United Nations Children's Fund
UNU	United Nations University
URBRA	Uganda Retirement Benefits Regulatory Authority
VaR	value at risk
VAT	value-added tax
V-Dem	Varieties of Democracy
VSLA	village savings and loan associations
WAEMU	West Africa Economic and Monetary Union
WDI	World Development Indicators
WFE	World Federation of Exchanges
WGI	World Governance Indicators
WIDER	World Institute for Public Policy Research and Analysis
WIEGO	Women in Informal Employment: Globalizing and Organizing

Notes on Contributors

Charles Godfred Ackah is a development economist and Associate Professor at the Institute of Statistical, Social and Economic Research, University of Ghana. His research is in the microeconomics of development with a focus on both household and firm behaviour. He has published widely in the areas of trade policy, industrial organization, and household and firm dynamics in developing countries.

Tony Addison was a professor of economics in the University of Copenhagen's Development Economics Research Group (DERG), and formerly Chief Economist and Deputy Director of the United Nations University World Institute for Development Economics Research (UNU-WIDER) in Helsinki. He was previously Professor of Development Studies, Manchester University. He has undertaken many advisory assignments for governments and for agencies such as the International Labour Organization, the United Nations Children's Fund (UNICEF), and the World Bank. His most recent books are *Resources Matter: Ending Poverty While Protecting Nature* and *Extractive Industries: The Management of Resources as a Driver of Sustainable Development*, both with Alan Roe and both published by Oxford University Press for UNU-WIDER.

Elizabeth Asiedu is a professor of economics at Howard University, Washington, DC. Her research focuses on issues related to foreign direct investment, foreign aid, and gender. She has published in peer-reviewed journals and consulted for several international organizations.

Fafanyo Asiseh is an associate professor in the Department of Economics at North Carolina Agricultural and Technical State University. Her research specializes in development economics, gender economics, and health economics. She has authored agricultural and health economics publications that analyse individual and household behaviours in developed and developing countries.

Prema-chandra Athukorala is an emeritus professor of economics at Arndt-Corden Department of Economics, Australian National University. His research is in trade and development, and development macroeconomics. His publications in these subject areas include twelve books, six edited volumes, and over 200 papers in scholarly journals and multi-author volumes.

Samuel Gachanja is Senior Researcher with Capital Markets Authority (Kenya). He previously worked with the National Treasury and Economic Planning as a policy analyst. His interest is in policy and applied research in fields of capital markets and Islamic finance.

Cornel Joseph is a distinguished lecturer of economics at Mkwawa University College of Education, part of the University of Dar es Salaam in Tanzania. He specializes in development economics, labour economics, and public finance, where he has made significant contributions through his extensive research. His published works delve into critical topics such as gender disparities in the labour market, human capital development, public debt management, and strategies for inclusive growth across sub-Saharan Africa.

Monica Lambon-Quayefio is an applied microeconomist and senior lecturer at the Department of Economics, University of Ghana. Her research broadly focuses on gender and labour markets, social protection, education, and digital technologies in agriculture. She has published in the areas of poverty and inequality, unpaid care work, child labour, and social protection.

Amir Lebdioui is an associate professor of the political economy of development at the University of Oxford, and the director of the Oxford Technology and Management Centre for Development (TIDE). Before joining Oxford, Amir was a lecturer at the School of Oriental and African Studies, University of London and was a research fellow at the London School of Economics (LSE). His research has focused on industrial policy, economic diversification, resource-based development, and biodiversity-based innovation models. His book, *Survival of the Greenest: Economic Transformation in a Climate-Conscious World*, was recently published by Cambridge University Press for UNU-WIDER.

Josphat Machagua is a policy analyst specializing in trade, fintech, debt, investment, finance, innovation, and green energy. He holds an MA in Economics from the University of Nairobi and has a certificate in development economics from LSE. He has previously worked with the Kenya Institute for Public Policy Research and Analysis (KIPPRA).

Theresa Mannah-Blankson is a clinical professor of economics at the University of North Carolina at Charlotte. She obtained her PhD in Economics from the University of Massachusetts at Amherst in 2016. Her research spans development economics, macroeconomics, and gender. Theresa has published widely in peer-reviewed journals and policy reports, contributing significantly to economics with a particular focus on development issues.

Rodgers Musamali is a policy analyst at the Private Sector Development Department, KIPPRA. He is passionate about sustainable economic development and designing pro-poor policies in developing countries. His research is in firm operations and performance, financial-sector developments, entrepreneurship, and gender mainstreaming. He has published in peer-reviewed journals and discussion papers.

Cecilia Mutia is an economist at the National Treasury of Kenya, with a keen interest in financial inclusion and public finance management for sustainable growth and development. She has published with KIPPRA, the University of Nairobi, and Partnerships for Economic Policy (PEP).

Njuguna Ndung'u is the former cabinet secretary, National Treasury and Economic Planning. Prior to his current appointment, he served as the executive director of the African Economic Research Consortium (AERC) and the immediate former governor, Central Bank of Kenya. Professor Ndung'u has been a member of the Global Advisory Council of the World Economic Forum, Brookings Africa Growth Initiative, and the Advisory Committee of the Alliance for Financial Inclusion and also Senior Advisor for the United Nations Capital Development Fund (UNCDF)-based Better Than Cash Alliance. He holds a PhD in economics from the University of Gothenburg, Sweden.

Rose Ngugi is Fellow of the African Economic Research Consortium (Nairobi) and Chairperson of the Southern Voice. Previously, she was Executive Director at KIPPRA, where she managed research and capacity-building activities at the institute. Her research interests include financial-sector developments, macroeconomic issues, and sustainable development. She has published widely in peer-reviewed journals and discussion papers.

Githinji Njenga is a principal policy analyst with KIPPRA. He has over 20 years of experience in public policy research and analysis. He has also lectured part-time at the University of Nairobi, School of Economics, and worked as an economist with the Government of Kenya. His research interests are in applied economics, focusing mainly on financial economics.

Owen Nyang'oro is a lecturer at the Department of Economics and Development Studies, University of Nairobi. He previously worked as a policy analyst at KIPPRA and as an economic analyst at the Communications Authority of Kenya. His research interests are in applied economics, with a focus on financial economics, household finance, trade finance, and monetary policy.

Jones Arkoh Paintsil is a PhD (economics) student at Howard University, Washington, DC and a graduate assistant in the Department of Economics. He specializes in applied econometrics, development economics, and data science. Jones has co-authored six publications on child health, women's empowerment, and intimate partner violence in sub-Saharan Africa.

Desiree Sama-Lang is a PhD candidate at the Pan African University of Governance, Cameroon. Her research interests lie in the field of governance and economic development, with a specific focus on how governance and regional integration interact to solve Africa's challenges.

Kunal Sen is Director of UNU-WIDER and a professor of development economics at the Global Development Institute, University of Manchester. His has over three decades of experience in academic and applied development economics research. He has performed extensive research on the political economy of development, international finance, the determinants of savings, the political economy determinants of inclusive growth, the dynamics of poverty, social exclusion, female labour force participation, and the informal sector in developing economies. His research has focused on India, East Asia, and sub-Saharan Africa. Kunal's recent authored books are *The Political Economy of India's Growth Episodes* (Palgrave Macmillan) and *Out of the Shadows? The Informal Sector in Post-Reform India* (Oxford University Press India). He has published over 100 journal articles, publishing in the *Journal of Development Economics*, *Journal of Development Studies*, and *World Development*. He was awarded the Sanjaya Lall Prize in 2006 and the Dudley Seers Prize in 2003 for his publications.

Wanissa Suanin is an assistant professor of economics in the Faculty of Economics at Thammasat University, Thailand. Her research is in international trade and development macroeconomics. She has published in scholarly journals, including the *Journal of Agricultural Economics* and *European Review of Agricultural Economics*.

Abrams Tagem is a tax research specialist with the African Tax Administration Forum (ATAF), Pretoria. He previously worked as a consultant with the United Nations Development Programme Tax for Sustainable Development Goals (UNDP Tax for SDGs) Initiative and research associate with UNU-WIDER. His experience and interests are at the nexus of research, policy, and practice in domestic resource mobilization—that is, tax revenue mobilization, sovereign debt, and domestic savings. He completed his PhD in Economics at the University of Nottingham and has worked as a consultant with the African Development Bank, the Overseas Development Institute (ODI), and the World Bank. He has published in various international journals, including *International Tax and Public Finance*, the *Journal of Institutional Economics*, and the *South African Journal of Economics.*

Maureen Were is a senior economist and Acting Deputy Director, Real Sector Analysis Division in the Research Department, Central Bank of Kenya. She has over 20 years of experience in macroeconomic policy, research, and economic analysis. She previously worked for UNU-WIDER as a research fellow, where she was seconded to UONGOZI Institute in Tanzania (2018–21). Before joining the Central Bank of Kenya, she worked as a policy analyst at KIPPRA and assistant lecturer at Egerton University, Njoro, Kenya. She has published widely, including in refereed journals, on various macroeconomic and socio-economic development issues. These include a co-edited book on *Sustaining Tanzania's Economic Development: A Firm and Household Perspective.*

PART I
INTRODUCTION

1

The domestic savings shortfall in sub-Saharan Africa

What are the key issues?

Rose Ngugi and Kunal Sen

1. Introduction

The vast empirical literature on economic growth has found that investment is a key determinant (Barro 1998). At the same time, the cross-country literature has established that investment rates are primarily determined by domestic savings (Thirlwall 1974). These two 'stylized facts' imply that gross domestic savings is a crucial determinant of economic growth (Athukorala and Sen 2004). Countries that have high savings rates tend to grow faster on average. Furthermore, a high domestic savings rate that is broadly in line with the country's investment rate reduces vulnerability to sudden shifts in international capital flows that are unrelated to macroeconomic fundamentals and more influenced by herd behaviour or self-fulfilling investor expectations (Loayza et al. 2000).

One of the distinguishing features of sub-Saharan Africa's (SSA) economic development has been the low rate of savings in the region, as compared to most other regions in the world. In the period 2000–17, the average savings rate in SSA was 22%, compared to 34% in East Asia and 27% in South Asia. Of more concern is the fact that the savings rate in SSA has fallen from a high of 27% in 2006 to 19% in 2017 (Figure 1.1). For economic growth to increase in the region, a major policy impetus should be to increase domestic savings rates.

From a policy perspective, the available evidence does not clearly indicate the size—or even the sign—of the effects of policy variables on savings rates. For example, what is the role of fintech in promoting savings in Africa? Can pension funds augment domestic savings in Africa, as they have done in East Asia? How can capital markets be developed, and what is the role of sovereign wealth funds in mobilizing savings? Does financial liberalization—by increasing interest rates and increasing financial depth—inhibit or encourage savings? What are the emerging debt challenges that African countries face as they borrow abroad to make up for

Rose Ngugi and Kunal Sen, *The domestic savings shortfall in sub-Saharan Africa*. In: *The Domestic Savings Shortfall in Sub-Saharan Africa*. Edited by: Rose Ngugi and Kunal Sen, Oxford University Press. © UNU-WIDER (2025).
DOI: 10.1093/oso/9780198932482.003.0001

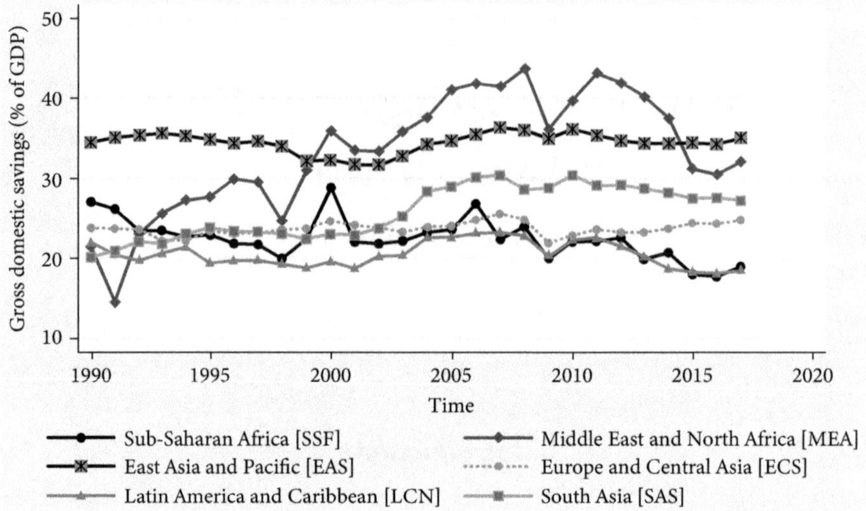

Figure 1.1 Domestic savings around the world

Source: authors' illustration based on World Development Indicators, the World Bank.

the shortfall in savings for investment purposes? What can SSA learn from the experience of Asia?

This volume aims to increase knowledge about (i) the key drivers of domestic savings rates in SSA; (ii) whether alternative approaches, such as pension funds or fintech, could provide new solutions to increase domestic savings; (iii) lessons learnt from the experiences so far in different countries in SSA; and (iv) what SSA can learn from the experience of other regions that have been more successful in raising savings rates.

To address these questions, the volume has several thematic chapters on specific issues that are of relevance in the SSA context, such as the role of fintech, capital markets, and pension systems in mobilizing savings; the role of sovereign wealth funds in Africa; the emerging public debt challenge in the continent; the effects of financial liberalization on private saving; and lessons from the savings experience in the Asian region. This is followed by four in-depth country studies of the determinants of savings, using a common conceptual framework and econometric methodology. The countries studied are Kenya, Tanzania, Ghana, and Cameroon.

An important objective of the volume is to provide concrete policy findings that can contribute to the Addis Ababa Action Agenda of the United Nations on financing for development, which provides a new global framework for financing sustainable development by aligning all financing flows and policies with economic, social, and environmental priorities.

In the rest of this introductory chapter, we first describe the theoretical literature on the determinants of savings rates. This is followed by a discussion of the key policy issues in the SSA context. We then set out the outline of the book, including a discussion of the selection criteria used in the choice of countries in the volume.

2. What determines savings rates?

This section begins with a discussion of the life-cycle model (LCM), which is the workhorse theory of the determinants of private savings rates and provides the analytical framework for the country studies in the volume.[1] We also consider modifications/extensions to reflect structural features that are prevalent in developing countries (for more detailed discussion, see Athukorala and Sen 2002, 2004).

In the LCM, accumulation for retirement is the prime motive for saving (Modigliani 1970; Deaton 1989). The model is built around the consumption/saving behaviour of a representative agent, who is assumed to maximize the present value of lifetime utility, subject to a budget constraint. The budget constraint is equal to the current net worth plus the present value of expected labour income over the remaining working life of the agent. Under the simplifying assumptions of perfect capital markets and perfect foresight of the agent about the 'true' income generation process, the model predicts that consumption in a particular period depends on expectations about lifetime income (*not* on the income in that period, as postulated by the Keynesian model). As income tends to fluctuate systematically over the course of a person's life, saving behaviour is crucially determined by one's stage in the life cycle (Modigliani 1986). Individuals smoothen consumption over their lifetime and are consequently net savers during their working years and dis-savers during retirement (see Athukorala and Sen 2002 for an extended discussion of the model).

At the aggregate level, the major determinants of the saving rate (over time in each country or across countries) are the rate of growth of per capita income and the age structure of the population (Grigoli et al. 2018). With respect to the rate of growth of per capita income, the simplest version of the LCM predicts that an increase in the latter will unambiguously increase the aggregate saving rate, because it increases the lifetime resources (and saving) of younger age groups relative to older age groups. The age structure of the population is uniquely related to population growth under the assumption of 'balanced population growth' (Modigliani 1986). With an increase in the population growth rate, age-specific

[1] For details on the LCM and its advantages over other approaches, see Modigliani (1970, 1986, 1993), Gersovitz (1988), and Deaton (1989). For the empirical literature on the determinants of savings, see Collins (1989), Hussein and Thirlwall (1999), and Grigoli et al. (2018).

fertility rates increase and so does the number of savers relative to the number of dis-savers. Therefore, if all the individual households in two given economies have the same saving profile over their life cycles, the economy with the faster population growth may show a higher aggregate saving rate.

The other key determinants of private saving suggested by the LCM is the real interest rate on bank deposits (Deaton and Paxson 2000). The net effect of the interest rate on saving/consumption is ambiguous. A higher interest rate increases the present price of consumption relative to the future price (the substitution effect) and thus provides an incentive to increase saving. However, if the household is a net lender, the interest rate rise also raises lifetime income and thus tends to increase consumption and decrease saving (the income effect). Thus, saving responds positively to interest rate increases only if the substitution effect is stronger than the income effect. In the case of a typical developing economy, it could be argued that the impact of a change in real interest rate on saving is expected to be positive (McKinnon 1973; Shaw 1973). Here, portfolio choices are limited, and the saving process tends to be highly *money intensive*. Therefore, the substitution effect tends to be much larger than the income effect of an interest rate change. In addition to the real interest rate, wealth can influence household saving, as accumulated wealth lessens a household's dependence on current income sources, enabling them to save less.

There are six other issues that we need to consider when applying the LCM to developing countries. The first issue is to do with the key proposition of the life-cycle hypothesis that the saving rate is related to the growth of per capita income, *not* the level of per capita income. The absence of a link between current saving and current income in the LCM theory of consumption is an implication of the assumption that individuals are forward-looking and therefore base their saving decisions on lifetime income rather than current income. However, the validity of this premise is in doubt for low-income countries. As Modigliani (1993: 210) himself notes,

> For at least that portion of the population that lives at, or near, the starvation level, may find it impossible or too burdensome to set aside resources now to provide for later consumption. People in that predicament may tend to live more from hand-to-mouth, skipping retirement or being supported by the extended family. It is thus conceivable that, for a sufficiently low value of per capita income, the saving–income ratio for given growth would tend to rise with income.

The country studies use *both* the level and the growth of per capita income as explanatory variables for the saving rate.

A second issue is the presence of liquidity constraints in developing countries, which implies that households cannot borrow at the desired level to smoothen consumption over time (Liu and Woo 1994). The level of financial development, measured by the ratio of private credit to gross domestic product (GDP) (or alternately, M2[2] over GDP) is usually taken as a proxy for the presence of liquidity constraints in the literature.

A third issue relates to the economic shocks that households in developing countries face on a regular basis, along with a high level of uncertainty (Kimball 1990). Uncertainty of the economic environment is particularly true for rural households, who are likely to face large weather-related shocks to their incomes. This leads to precautionary saving on the part of the household to smoothen consumption over time (Deaton 1977). As is standard in the literature, we capture uncertainty in the economic environment by the inflation rate, with the expectation that the inflation rate and saving will be positively related.

A fourth issue relates to the effect of terms of trade changes on saving behaviour. Terms of trade shocks can lead to large real income changes, leading to changes in savings. A large empirical literature has documented the effect of terms of trade shocks on savings (Dayal-Gulati and Thimann 1997). In line with this literature, terms of trade are considered as an additional determinant of saving.

Fifth, public saving is often considered as an additional determinant of private saving and has been extensively studied in relation to the impact of the fiscal policy stance on savings (Corbo and Schmidt-Hebbel 1991; Loayza et al. 2000). One strand of the literature has argued that public saving can be a perfect substitute for private saving (Barro 1974; Bernheim 1987). However, if public saving leads to the creation of infrastructure, which leads to a higher return on private saving, the volume of private saving may increase.

Finally, institutional quality may also matter for private saving—higher institutional quality would lead to increases in the savings rate (Freytag and Voll 2013). This is for two reasons. First, better institutions would imply lower uncertainty about the future for households with respect to economic and political risk and lead to higher savings. Second, stronger contract enforcement laws would enable households to trust banking institutions with their deposits and channellize their disposal income to financial savings.

The country studies in this volume examine the determinants of savings in each country context, drawing from the expanded LCM model (as discussed above) as the common analytical framework. They also use a common econometric methodology—the autoregressive distributed lag (ARDL) model—to estimate the determinants of savings (Hendry 1996). The ARDL approach uses a general to specific modelling procedure, which aims to minimize the possibility of estimating spurious relations while retaining long-run information. The equation to be estimated is embedded within a sufficiently complex dynamic specification, including lagged dependent and independent variables so that a parsimonious specification of the model can be uncovered (see this chapter's appendix for the econometric methodology).

[2] M2 is a measure of the money supply that includes cash, checking deposits, and other deposits readily convertible to cash, such as certificates of deposits.

3. Policy issues in the African context

Mobilizing adequate and appropriate domestic resources is a policy priority in financing sustainable development. Without adequate savings, it is difficult to boost investment and therefore achieve strong sustainable economic growth. SSA made significant milestones in the reform agenda with the structural adjustment and stabilization programmes, but a lot more is required for financial deepening, fiscal stability, and a robust saving culture.

Multiple shocks complicate the economic recovery path. In addition to the effects of the COVID-19 pandemic, Africa has felt the devastating effects of subsequent shocks including drought conditions and the disruption of the global supply chain. This affects the enabling environment for a thriving private sector. Economic transformation therefore remains a key policy priority in achieving sustainable growth and development. For example, this will allow export diversification, which will serve to cushion the continent from external shocks and enhance productivity across the sector, boosting income level.

Technology advancement has revolutionized financial services, especially with the fintech products. That said, fintech is yet to significantly fulfil its potential role in boosting saving. Fintech platforms are facilitating transactions, and therefore financial inclusion, but may have limited effect in increasing savings. It requires financial literacy and consumer protection to build trust and a strong saving culture. In addition, promoting financial deepening with the use of technology is necessary for effective savings mobilization.

Long-term financing is a priority given the significant demand for long-term investments. Capital markets are still shallow, pension schemes have low coverage with a focus on the formal sector, and sovereign wealth funds are yet to play a key role in mobilizing savings for investment in SSA. The national development banks are not adequately capitalized. Strengthening the policy, legislative, and institutional framework; incentivizing private sector participation; and developing appropriate products for households and the mushrooming micro and small enterprises—the majority of which are informal and engaging the youth—will go a long way in building confidence and ensuring that the market players receive their expected returns.

Fiscal stability remains critical in promoting saving. Savers expect that their returns on savings are secured and the future is certain on their expected income. Thus, addressing the growing debt burden becomes a priority in securing fiscal stability.

4. Outline of the book

The book consists of two parts: (i) thematic studies and (ii) country studies.

The *thematic studies* examine the implications of new developments in African financial markets on savings behaviour (Chapter 2), capital market development

(Chapter 3), the role of pensions in generating investible funds (Chapter 4) and of sovereign wealth funds in mobilizing investible funds (Chapter 5), public debt challenges in Africa (Chapter 6), the implications of financial liberalization for private saving in SSA (Chapter 7), and lessons on how to increase savings rates from East and South Asia (Chapter 8).

In addition, the volume contains four *country studies*—Kenya (Chapter 9), Tanzania (Chapter 10), Ghana (Chapter 11), and Cameroon (Chapter 12). The countries are selected based on their performance on both the growth of their savings rates and their level of savings, which translates into the following criteria: (i) high versus low growth rate in savings and (ii) high versus low level of savings (see Table 1.1 and Figures 1.2–1.5). Tanzania has performed well on both criteria, Ghana and Cameroon on one criterion but not both, and Kenya has not performed well on both criteria. Thus, the choice of countries is such that the country studies capture the diversity of savings performance in SSA.

Table 1.1 Selection criteria

		Savings rate	
		High savings rate	**Low savings rate**
Growth in savings	High growth in savings	Tanzania	Ghana
	Low growth in savings	Cameroon	Kenya

Source: authors' illustration.

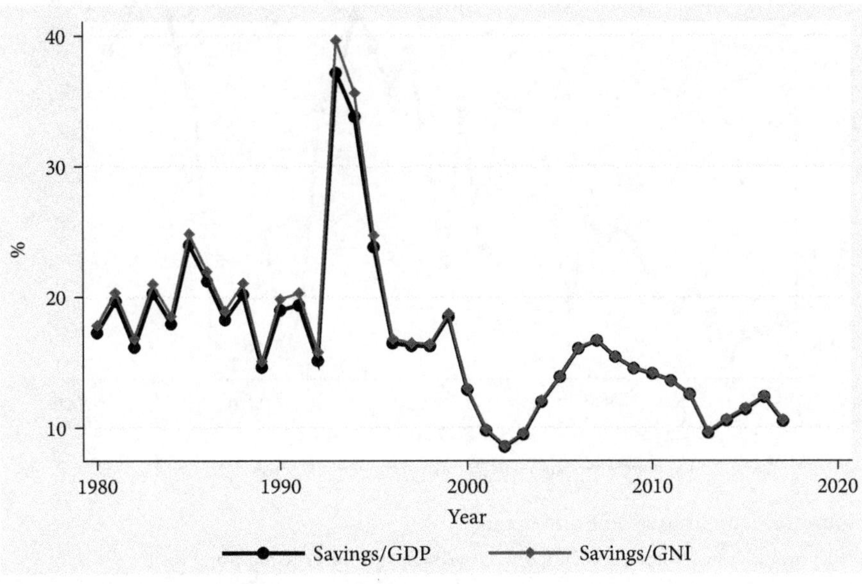

Figure 1.2 Domestic savings in Kenya

Source: authors' illustration based on World Development Indicators, the World Bank.

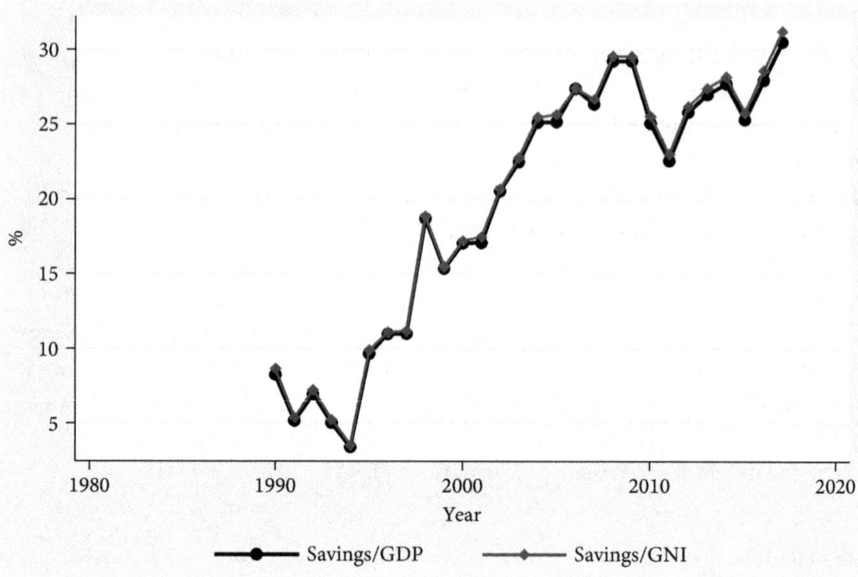

Figure 1.3 Domestic savings in Tanzania

Note: GNI: gross national income.
Source: authors' illustration based on World Development Indicators, the World Bank.

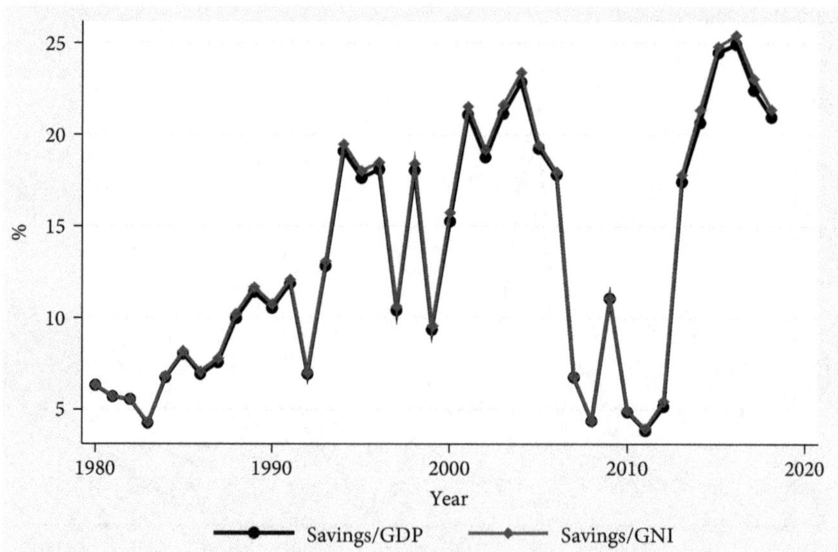

Figure 1.4 Domestic savings in Ghana

Source: authors' illustration based on World Development Indicators, the World Bank.

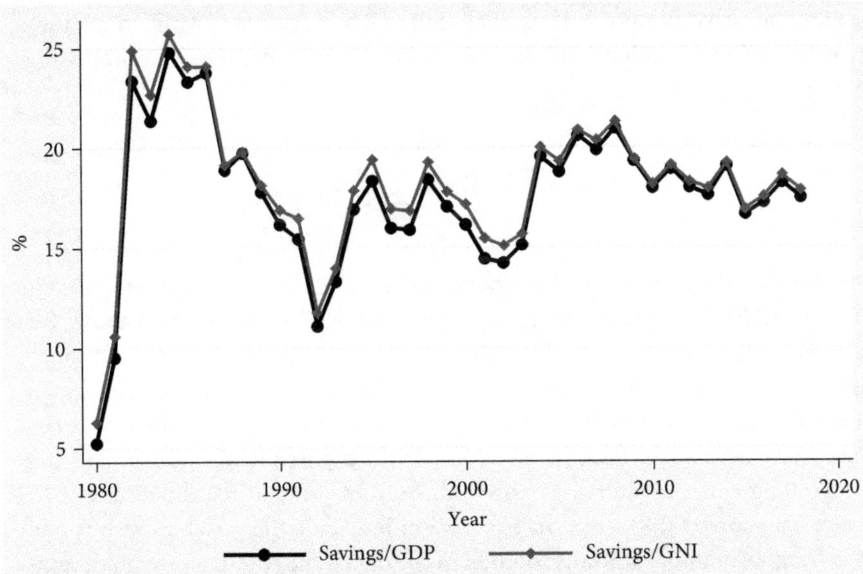

Figure 1.5 Domestic savings in Cameroon

Source: authors' illustration based on World Development Indicators, the World Bank.

The volume concludes with a set of key findings and policy implications (Chapter 13).

Appendix: The econometric methodology

The econometric methodology for the country studies is the autoregressive distributed lag (ARDL) approach, which is suitable for linear time-series data modelling (see Ang and Sen 2011 and Body 2011 for applications of the ARDL model to the determinants of savings). It is a suitable method for estimating the long-run relationship between savings aggregates and their determinants. The generalized ARDL (p, q) model with k explanatory variables is specified as follows:

$$Y_t = \gamma + \beta_1 Y_{t-1} + \ldots + \beta_p Y_{t-p} + \alpha_0 X_t + \alpha_1 X_{t-1} + \ldots + \alpha_q X_{t-q} + \varepsilon_t \qquad \text{(A1)}$$

where Y_t is the private savings rate, X_t is a $(k \times 1)$ vector of independent variables, γ is the constant term, and ε_t is the error term with standard *i.i.d* properties. The dependent variable is explained by lags of itself as well as current and lagged values of the independent variables. The number of lags of the dependent variable (the autoregressive component) is included up to lag order, while the number of lags of independent variables is included up to order q.[3] Compressing equation (A1) yields

$$Y_t = \gamma_0 + \sum_{i=1}^{p} \beta_i Y_{t-i} + \sum_{i=0}^{q} \alpha_i' X_{t-i} + \varepsilon_t \tag{A2}$$

where the notations are defined as above, and β and α are coefficients to be estimated. The ARDL is appealing for two main reasons. First, the method allows for a mixture of I(0) and I(1) variables, that is stationary in levels or, at most, first-differenced stationary, respectively. For example, the growth rate of per capita income is typically stationary, while its level tends to be non-stationary (first-differenced stationary). Second, it allows for the possibility of distinguishing between long-run and short-run effects. Instead of using a first difference ordinary least squares (OLS)—by construction, differencing the variables results in a loss of long-term information embodied in the data—the ARDL allows for a mixture of long-run and short-run estimates through an unrestricted error correction model (ECM) of the form:[4]

$$\Delta Y_t = \gamma_0 + \sum_{i=1}^{p} \delta_i \Delta Y_{t-i} + \sum_{i=0}^{q} \delta_i \Delta X_{t-i} + \lambda (Y_t - \theta X_t) + \varepsilon_t \tag{A3}$$

where $\lambda = \left(1 - \sum_{i=1}^{p} \delta_i\right)$ is the speed of adjustment to equilibrium, the expression in brackets is the long-run relationship between variables, and $\theta = \frac{\sum_{i=0}^{q} \pi_i}{\left(1 - \sum_{i=1}^{p} \delta_i\right)}$ is the long-run parameter. If $\lambda = 0$, then there is no evidence of a long-run relationship between private savings and its determinants. The parameter is expected to be significantly negative under the prior assumption that following a deviation, the variables return to their long-run equilibrium (co-integration). In addition to the above, the method is more efficient for samples with small to moderate time-series properties and allows for post-estimation diagnostics to be carried out.[5]

[3] The lags are determined by information criteria. The default in STATA (statistical software for data science) is the Bayesian information criterion (BIC), but STATA also allows for the analyst to select the Akaike information criterion (AIC).

[4] For this ARDL to be reparametrized as an ECM, there must be co-integration (existence of an equilibrium long-term relationship between the variables). The co-integration test draws on the ARDL bounds approach of Pesaran et al. (2001).

[5] Standard post-estimation diagnostics include normality tests, first- and second-order serial correlation, heteroskedasticity, model mis-specification, and model stability tests (see Cameron and Trivedi 2010 for details).

References

Ang, J. B., and K. Sen (2011). 'Private Saving in India and Malaysia Compared: The Roles of Financial Liberalization and Expected Pension Benefits'. *Empirical Economics*, 41(2): 247–67.

Athukorala, P., and K. Sen (2002). *Saving, Investment and Growth in India*. Delhi: Oxford University Press.

Athukorala, P., and K. Sen (2004). 'The Determinants of Private Saving in India'. *World Development*, 32(3): 491–503.

Barro, R. J. (1974). 'Are Government Bonds Net Worth?' *Journal of Political Economy*, 82: 1095–117.

Barro, R. J. (1998). *Determinants of Economic Growth: A Cross-Country Empirical Study*. Cambridge, MA: MIT Press.

Bernheim, B. D. (1987). 'Ricardian Equivalence: An Evaluation of Theory and Evidence'. *NBER Macroeconomics Annual*, 2: 263–304. https://doi.org/10.1086/ma.2.4623723

Body, Y. (2011). 'Long-Run Determinants of Savings Rates in WAEMU Countries: An Empirical Assessment from ARDL Bounds Testing Approach'. *South African Journal of Economics*, 79(3): 312–29.

Cameron, A. C., and P. K. Trivedi (2010). *Microeconometrics Using Stata*. New York: Stata Press.

Collins, S. (1989). 'Saving Behaviour in Ten Developing Countries'. In B. Douglas Bernheim and J. B. Shoven (eds), *National Saving and Economic Performance*, pp. 349–76. Washington, DC: NBER.

Corbo, V., and K. Schmidt-Hebbel (1991). 'Public Policies and Saving in Developing Countries'. *Journal of Development Economics*, 36: 89–115.

Dayal-Gulati, A., and C. Thimann (1997). ' Saving in Southeast India and Latin America Compared: Searching for Policy Lessons'. IMF Working Paper WP/97/110. Washington, DC: International Monetary Fund.

Deaton, A. (1977). 'Involuntary Saving through Unanticipated Inflation'. *American Economic Review*, 67(5): 899–910.

Deaton, A. (1989). 'Saving in Developing Countries: Theory and Review'. In *Proceedings of the World Bank Annual Conference on Development Economics*, pp. 61–108. Washington DC: World Bank.

Deaton, A., and C. H. Paxson (2000). 'Growth and Saving among Individuals and Households'. *Review of Economics and Statistics*, 82: 212–25.

Freytag, A., and S. Voll (2013). 'Institutions and Savings in Developing and Emerging Economies'. *Public Choice*, 157(3/4): 475–509.

Gersovitz, M. (1988). 'Saving and Development'. In H. B. Chenery and T. N. Srinivasan (eds), *Handbook of Development Economics*, Vol. 1, pp. 381–424. Amsterdam: North Holland.

Grigoli, F., A. Herman, and K. Schmidt-Hebbel (2018). 'Saving in the World'. *World Development*, 104(1): 257–70.

Hendry, D. F. (1996). *Dynamic Econometrics*. Oxford: Oxford University Press.

Hussein, K. A., and A. P. Thirlwall (1999). 'Explaining Differences in the Domestic Savings Ratio Across Countries: A Panel Data Study'. *Journal of Development Studies*, 36: 31–52.

Kimball, M. (1990). 'Precautionary Saving in the Small and the Large'. *Econometrica*, 58: 53–73.

Liu, L.-Y., and W. T. Woo (1994). 'Saving Behaviour under Imperfect Capital Markets and the Current Account Consequences'. *Economic Journal*, 104: 512–27.

Loayza, N., K. Schmidt-Hebbel, and L. Serven (2000). 'What Drives Private Saving around the World?' *Review of Economics and Statistics*, 82: 165–81.

McKinnon, R. I. (1973). *Money and Capital in Economic Development*. Washington, DC: Brooking Institute.

Modigliani, F. (1970). 'The Life Cycle Hypothesis of Saving and Inter-Country Differences in the Saving Ratio'. In W. A. Eltis, M. F. Scott, and J. N. Wolfe (eds), *Induction, Growth and Trade*, pp. 197–225. Oxford: Clarendon Press.

Modigliani, F. (1986). 'Life Cycle, Individual Thrift, and the Wealth of Nations'. *American Economic Review*, 76: 297–313.

Modigliani, F. (1993). 'Recent Declines in the Savings Rate: A Life Cycle Perspective'. In M. Baldassarri, L. Paganetto, and E. S. Phelps (eds), *World Saving, Prosperity, and Growth*, pp. 249–86. London: Macmillan.

Pesaran, M. H., Shin, Y., and Smith, R. J. (2001). 'Bounds Testing Approaches to the Analysis of Level Relationships'. *Journal of Applied Econometrics*, 16(3): 289–326.

Shaw, E. (1973). *Financial Deepening in Economic Development*. Oxford: Oxford University Press.

Thirlwall, A. P. (1974). *Inflation, Saving and Growth in Developing Countries*. London: Macmillan.

PART II
THEMATIC STUDIES

2

Fintech, savings, and financial inclusion in sub-Saharan Africa

Njuguna Ndung'u

1. Introduction

Technology and innovation are revolutionizing the financial sector the world over. They have changed several sectors of the economy in terms of how they operate and their resource management. The world has witnessed the development of diverse instruments and processes, such as mobile phones, artificial intelligence (AI)/machine learning (ML) and big data analytics, blockchain/distributed ledger technology (DLT), and cloud computing, which have stimulated the development of fintech (financial technology)—technology-enabled solutions that are disrupting traditional financial services and challenging incumbent service providers (Disrupt Africa 2021).

These developments stem from the roll-out of physical infrastructure that has allowed the development of, and investment in, the core digital infrastructure. For example, fibre-optic cables have enabled the growth of internet and mobile phone services. This, in turn, has enabled fintechs[1] to innovate and roll out products that are considered disruptive but shape the way financial services are offered and created electronic payment platforms that are effective, efficient, and real-time.

The first fintech disruption was witnessed with the development of mobile phone-based retail electronic payments that were effective, efficient, transparent, and safe. This all-inclusive, real-time retail electronic payments platform was an easy entry point for financial services navigating across all market segments, including informal markets. It was operated by commercial banks, which were able to increase their level of retail activity. In the process, this made banking services accessible and important to African economies. Once an effective electronic payments platform is operational, it becomes transformative.

In the past 20 years, fintechs have changed the way banking services are provided; the way banks work; how capital is raised; and how payments, including

[1] Fintechs are firms that combine innovative business models and technology to enable, enhance, and disrupt financial services. Fintechs can be classified into two categories: those that provide financial services (core fintechs) and those that enable such services (enabling fintechs) (Ernst & Young 2019).

Njuguna Ndung'u, *Fintech, savings, and financial inclusion in sub-Saharan Africa*. In: *The Domestic Savings Shortfall in Sub-Saharan Africa*. Edited by: Rose Ngugi and Kunal Sen, Oxford University Press. © UNU-WIDER (2025).
DOI: 10.1093/oso/9780198932482.003.0002

retail payments, are conducted. They have also redefined knowledge of money and its form through the rise of mobile money, with consequences on the design of monetary policy frameworks. The increased use of fintech is viewed as a catalyst to innovation, promoting savings and investment, driving economic activity, and increasing access to financial services at different levels. Increased access to financial services is likely to lead to economic vibrancy and a drive to inclusive growth for sub-Saharan Africa (SSA).

In the next decade, it is expected that fintech development will be driven by AI, DLT, cloud computing, the internet of things, 'open-source software, serverless architecture and software as a service', 'no code and low code development', and process automation (Fong et al. 2021). These developments will lead to massive investment by firms in technology to facilitate innovations and remain competitive in the market.

This chapter traces the development of fintech in SSA and its role in future. It outlines the benefits of fintech in promoting financial inclusion by increasing access to financial services, especially among underserved and unserved populations. Other major benefits of fintech include digitization of government processes such as tax collection, revenue administration, social transfers, and public financial management, leading to savings of cost and time for both citizens and government. It also examines the fintech regulation and provides policy suggestions for SSA countries seeking to balance potential fintech benefits and risks.

The rest of the chapter is organized as follows. Section 2 outlines the evolution of fintech and financial inclusion in SSA. Section 3 discusses how fintech is providing solutions to the binding constraints on financial services. Section 4 examines the adoption and development of fintech in SSA. Section 5 explores fintech regulatory challenges, while Section 6 discusses the possibilities of fintech propelling the Fourth Industrial Revolution. Section 7 concludes.

2. Fintech evolution, savings, and financial inclusion in SSA

The evolution of digital financial services (DFS) in Africa provided a means of managing bank accounts at minimal cost, thus enabling commercial banks to reach more customers and grow deposits. Recall the years when banks used to set minimum balances for deposit and savings accounts, which meant those with low or irregular flow of income remained unbanked. A trip to the bank was an expensive exercise. The digital banking platform solved these financial service access constraints. Consequently, commercial banks have used digital platforms to increase their base of micro-accounts, deposit taking, and credit extension to populations that were previously unbanked (Misati et al. 2022).

In Kenya, Gubbins and Totolo (2018) showed that it took several days for customers to access credit facilities within traditional banking. The 2016 Kenya

Integrated Household Budget Survey found on average, across all loan types, that borrowers needed 11 days to secure a short-term loan. If it was a long-term loan that required formal security, other than the employer's details, it could take months for the collateral to be registered, credit committees to meet, and lawyers to perfect the collateral charge.[2] In addition to high interest rates and collateral requirements, application for a bank loan involved out-of-pocket costs such as physical travel to the point of service, valuing the collateral, legal fees to perfect the collateral applications, and (once the loan was disbursed) a component of insurance. Some consumers, especially small businesses, could not meet the collateral requirements to access bank loans. This led to a significant use of informal sources of funding such as moneylenders ('shylocks'), credit terms from suppliers, *chamas*,[3] friends, and family. These informal financial outlets for entrepreneurs were costly, risky, and not conducive to business development, but above all, they robbed the formal banking system of a huge potential proportion of customers. The fintech evolution appears to be solving this problem as the digital platform of virtual banking services is developing independently of physical bank branches.

Africa is ranked among the lowest regions in terms of access to financial services. For example, only 23% of adults in Africa have an account with a formal financial institution, compared with 89% in high-income regions and 55% in East Asia & Pacific (IMF 2019). Lack of access to accounts with a formal financial institution excludes whole populations from the security and reliability provided by these institutions. This low financial inclusion profile can also be related to low savings in the region. A savings culture emerges with secure saving products and available avenues for secure investment.

Evidence is emerging that the success of financial inclusion in African economies, especially among women and low-income earners, is driven by the fintech evolution. Among the constraints that sustained financial exclusion in Africa were low levels of income, irregular flows of income, physical distance from a bank branch or financial service point, and the collateral requirements to access credit (Ndung'u and Oguso 2021b). At a stroke, the fintech evolution has removed these constraints and turned financial exclusion into financial inclusion. Ndung'u (2018) affirmed that financial transactions using a digital platform or electronic banking services are the first step to greater financial inclusion and a pathway to a broader range of financial services provided by stronger and more diverse financial institutions.

In the case of Kenya, the fintech journey began with the development of the M-Pesa technological platform in March 2007. M-Pesa was developed as a bank product in partnership with a telecommunications company. Over the years, the

[2] That is, register and effect the charge on a security (e.g. title deed) used to secure a loan.

[3] This refers to a group or an informal cooperative society through which members pool savings and borrow money for their personal use as well as for individual or group investments.

uptake of M-Pesa has seen market, product, and fintech development in six major stages, as outlined by Ndung'u (2018) and has created opportunities for raising the level of savings in SSA.

Figure 2.1 shows the financial inclusion trends in selected SSA countries and other comparator countries that have conducted demand-side financial inclusion surveys in the past two decades. It shows that in South Africa, financial inclusion increased from 62% in 2004 to 90% in 2018. In Kenya, the 2021 FinAccess Household Survey showed that financial inclusion had increased from 26.7% in 2006 to 83.7% in 2021. However, in Nigeria, despite the uptake of fintechs, financial inclusion remained below 50% in 2018, on account of limited banking-sector partnerships with telecommunications operators, reflected also in low mobile money accounts and digital payments of 6% and 30%, respectively (Financial Technology

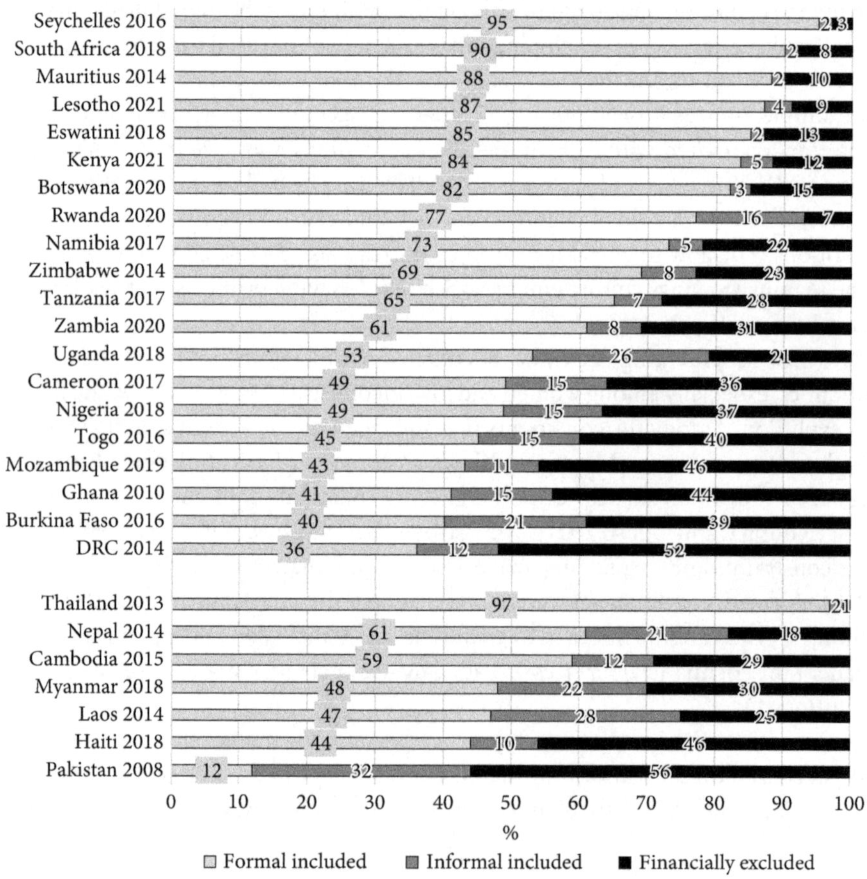

Figure 2.1 Financial inclusion: Regional comparison

Source: author's construction based on financial inclusion survey reports

Partners 2019). Seychelles, a small island country with a small population, had almost 100% financial inclusion by 2021, while countries that had lagged in adopting fintechs, such as the Democratic Republic of the Congo (DRC), Burkina Faso, and Ghana, had low financial inclusion.

3. How fintechs are providing solutions to constraints on financial services

In Africa, there seems to be an increase in market information flow, which has come with other benefits such as formalized capital investment, increased productivity, and more efficient financial services and e-government services. These results are driven by the evolution of a retail electronic payments system that is effective, efficient, transparent, and safe, but above all real-time. This was a game changer in providing easier entry into the financial services sector and a platform for the development of new products across all sectors of the economy.

Taking Kenya as an example, Suri and Jack (2016) pointed out that when M-Pesa was launched, the average distance to the nearest bank was 9.2 kilometres; eight years later (in 2015), the average distance to the nearest M-Pesa agent was a mere 1.4 kilometres. An earlier study by Suri and Jack (2014) showed that the safety and certainty of using mobile phone-based (M-Pesa) money transfers substantially reduced the risks and costs of sending and receiving money as well as of making payments.

The commercial banks have adopted this technological platform to manage micro-accounts and reach customers cost-effectively. Additionally, women, who are considered efficient savers, are now able to save in instruments that are safe, confidential, and tailored to their needs, thus lowering the gender financial inclusion gap. In addition, fintechs have rolled out sustainable business models mostly for underserved and unserved populations. The new business models have been adopted across various sectors of the economy. Examples are M-Kopa in the solar energy sector;[4] the One Acre Fund, which has focused on smallholder farmers, thus increasing their productivity, crop insurance, and activity in the agriculture sector;[5] M-Tiba virtual health insurance products; water vending machines for poor urban households; and Kenya's M-Akiba, a retail infrastructure bond issued by the government to encourage investment in government securities using mobile phones, among other products (Ndung'u 2018). The fintech evolution has also allowed monitoring of financial transactions, improved

[4] See https://www.m-kopa.com/newsroom/m-kopa-releases-the-2023-impact-report.
[5] See https://www.oneacrefund.org/library.

the anti-money-laundering/countering-the-financing-of-terrorism (AML/CFT) regime, and enabled central banks to design forward-looking monetary policy.

Governments have also developed e-government services, tax policy designs, tax payment platforms, and revenue administration systems that minimize leakages, enhancing domestic resource mobilization and increasing the tax base. Digital payments have reduced paperwork and ensured direct payments of money from accounts at the consolidated fund to the intended recipients (Ndung'u 2019). Governments have also designed and developed targeted social protection programmes, especially during the COVID-19 pandemic lockdowns.

4. The fintech landscape in SSA

The uptake of fintechs in SSA was propelled by increased usage of mobile phones, which has spurred innovation around mobile money. The mobile internet penetration rate in SSA was 46% in 2020 and projected to grow to 50% by 2025, compared with the global average penetration rate of 51% in 2020, which is expected to grow to 60% by 2025 (GSMA 2021).

The mobile phone is used to solve communication and information flow/search problems and has become a useful technological tool in the development discourse. The mobile telephony industry's contribution to SSA's gross domestic product (GDP) was estimated at 8% (US$130 billion of economic value added) in 2020 compared with 5.7% in MENA and 5.1% of global GDP (GSMA 2021). In addition, the mobile telephony industry has also created growth in employment opportunities (directly and indirectly), thereby generating significant global economic value added. This has led to significant growth in public funding, with more than US$410 billion raised through taxes on the mobile phone industry. These shows the huge potential for this sector to contribute to economic vibrancy and development.

Table 2.1 and Figure 2.2 show that the number of people without access to mobile internet services is higher in SSA, at 24%, than in the Middle East and North Africa (MENA) or globally, at 9% and 8%, respectively. However, World Bank data show that the use of mobile phones to make payments and send remittances has particularly gained importance in SSA compared with other world regions. Remittances sent via mobile phone increased by 6.5 percentage points in SSA, while they grew in other regions by an average 1.9 percentage points from 2014 to 2017 (Figure 2.2, panel iv). The use of mobile phones increased in SSA from 3.1% in 2014 to 7.4% in 2017, while in the Europe and Central Asia region, the usage grew from 2.5 to 8.6% (Figure 2.2, panel iii).

The use of digital payments is also rising as rapidly in SSA, increasing from 24.1 to 33.1% in 2014 and 2017, respectively, as compared to an increase from 58.7 to 67.1% in Europe and Central Asia (Figure 2.2, panel i). In the selected

Table 2.1 Fintech and financial development indicators

Indicator			
	SSA	**Low- and middle-income countries**	**High-income countries**
Mobile cellular subscription (per 100 people) (2017)	73	96	126
ATMs (per 100,000 adults) (2017)	6	27	68
Fixed broadband subscriptions (per 100 people) (2017)	1	9	31
Bank or mobile money account (% of population aged 15+) (2017)	43	63	94
GDP per capita, PPP (current international $) (2017)	3,730	10,345	45,789
	SSA	**MENA**	**Global**
Mobile industry contribution to GDP (%) (2020)	8.0	5.7	5.1
Mobile internet penetration rate (%) (2020)	46	65	51
People without access to mobile internet services (% of total population) (2020)	24	9	8
Mobile internet subscribers (% of total population) (2020)	48	46	41

Source: author's construction based on World Bank and IMF data; GSMA (2021).

African countries,[6] the number of registered mobile money accounts per 1,000 adults has continuously increased over the years, with Kenya leading, followed by Ghana and South Africa (Figure 2.2, panel ii)—a clear indication of the great strides being achieved in Kenya as well as in other countries in SSA.

The fintech evolution has been successful in developing core infrastructure with immediate application and uptake and seems to ride on the available physical infrastructure. In the case of communications, the spread of fibre-optic networks has allowed fintechs to flourish. The fintech revolution in Africa is primarily driven by the three main hubs of South Africa, Kenya, and Nigeria. These areas have more advanced fintech ecosystems than the rest of Africa. Ernst & Young (2019) showed that, in 2018, the fintech sector in SSA comprised over 260 active companies, with both local (80%) and international (20%) players. Figure 2.3 shows the number and growth of fintechs in the SSA region from 2007 to 2018.

Despite the COVID-19 pandemic, Disrupt Africa (2021) showed that fintech start-ups in Africa grew by 17.3% from the 491 reported in 2019 to 576 in 2021.

[6] The selected countries are leaders in mobile money in SSA, ranked in that order, based on International Monetary Fund (IMF) and World Bank financial access data.

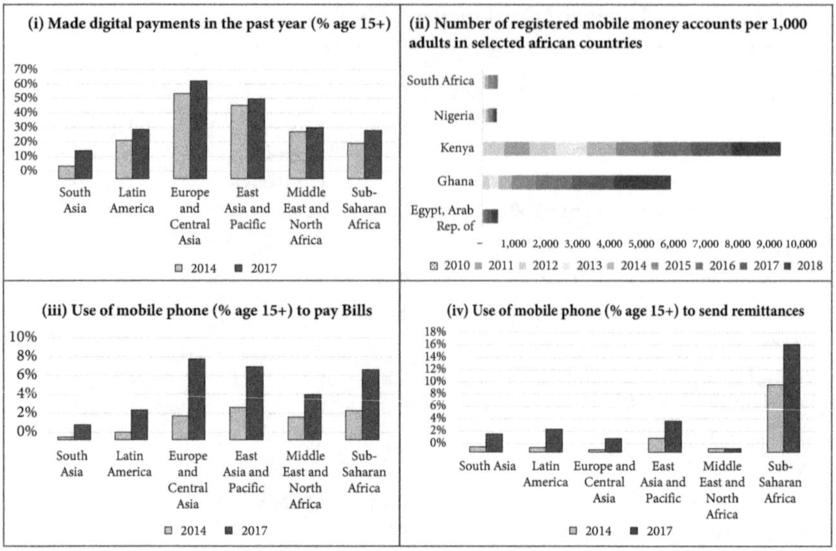

Figure 2.2 Uptake of use of mobile phone and mobile money accounts

Source: author's construction based on IMF data, FinAccess surveys, and the World Bank Global Financial Development database.

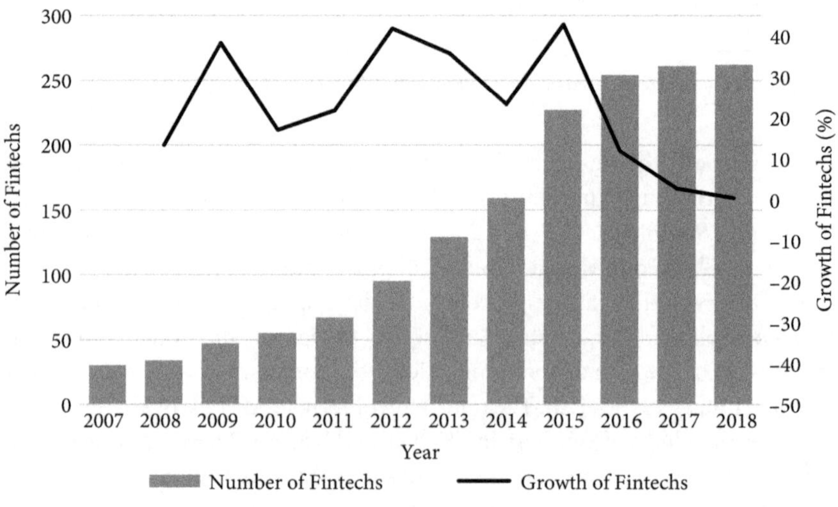

Figure 2.3 Growth of fintechs in SSA

Source: author's construction based on Ernst & Young (2019).

However, this was a slower growth than the 63.1% recorded between 2017 and 2019. According to Ernst & Young (2019), the number of fintechs had grown at a compound annual growth rate (CAGR) of 24% over the 10-year period to 2018, as shown in Figure 2.3. Disrupt Africa (2021) reported that the top six countries—South Africa, Nigeria, Kenya, Egypt, Ghana, and Uganda—performed particularly well, contributing 85.4% of start-ups (492 companies) in 2021. This was up from 81.7% in 2019 after a peak of 88.4% in 2017.

The three main fintech hubs in SSA include South Africa, Kenya, and Nigeria (Figure 2.4). In addition, there are encouraging signs of fintech growth in Ghana, Uganda, Cameroon, and Rwanda. South Africa, arguably the epicentre of SSA fintechs, harbours about one-third of the firms, predominantly located in Cape Town and Johannesburg. As the most diversified hub, South Africa exhibits great similarities to more developed markets. Its focus is strategically placed on the enabling fintech segment, making the country one of the main contributors to the growth of fintechs across the continent (Ernst & Young 2019). Kenya, the second largest fintech hub, hosting around 20% of the entire SSA fintech landscape, has a stronger focus on the payments segment (Ernst & Young 2019). Nigeria's fintech sector is the third-largest hub, with most of its fintechs based in Lagos. Like Kenya, the Nigerian fintech sector is dominated by the payments segment.

The increasing demand for investments in Africa has provided a ground for the development of segments of fintechs such as investment technologies (Investtech), which, like the insurance segment (Insurtech), is revolutionizing the assets management subsector by helping to raise expected risk-adjusted net returns for investors. Investtech enhances the capabilities of investment firms to increase the speed of acquiring and executing transactions, as well as inferential depth (profoundness and durable accuracy of investment insights). Disrupt Africa (2021) shows that Investtech start-ups in Africa grew by 18.5% from 2019 to 2021, when there were 77 start-ups, accounting for 13.4% of fintech companies in Africa.

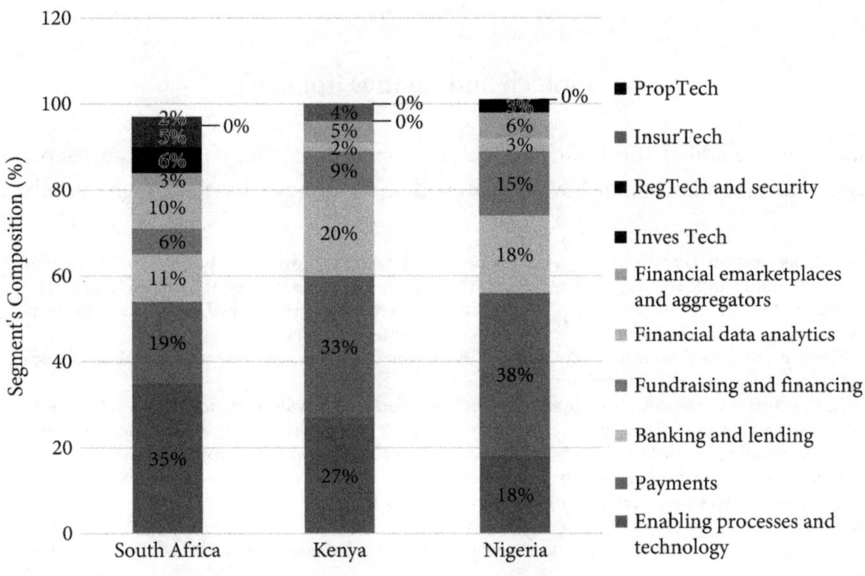

Figure 2.4 Fintech segments in the main SSA regional hubs

Source: author's construction based on Ernst & Young (2019).

This, however, was a much slower growth rate than the 242% increase recorded between 2017 and 2019.

The Cambridge Centre for Alternative Finance (CCAF 2020) showed that online alternative finance models are developing in Africa. The models include donation-based[7] crowd funding, crowd-led[8] microfinance, revenue-share, real estate[9] crowd funding, peer-to-peer (P2P) business lending,[10] reward-based[11] crowd funding, equity-based[12] crowd funding, and balance sheet[13] business lending. CCAF (2020) showed that in 2018, P2P consumer lending was the dominant model across the African continent, with a 53% market share, followed by balance sheet business lending at 22%. Figure 2.5a shows the trend in total alternative finance market volume in the African regions from 2016 to 2018, while Figure 2.5b shows the region's market share in 2018.

As shown in Figure 2.5a, CCAF (2020) the alternative finance market across Africa raised US$209.1 million in 2018, which represented a substantial increase of 102% from the 2017 volume of U$103.8 million. There was sporadic improvement from US$44.4 million in 2013 to US$181.6 million in 2016 before the drop reported in 2017 (CCAF 2020). This growth is partially due to the continued growth of African platforms, which CCAF (2020) attributed to an improved regulatory environment for domestic fintech ecosystems and growth and expansion of existing firms. Figure 2.5b shows that East Africa was the overall regional leader in the total online alternative finance market in 2018, with a 57.8% market share—an 18-percentage point increase from its 40% market share in 2017. Southern Africa (led by South Africa) had the second largest market share, at 20.6%, followed by West Africa (led by Nigeria) at 14.1%. In contrast, Central Africa had a market share of just 7.1%, while North Africa reported a negligible share of only 0.5%.

4.1 Fintech and savings uptake

Fintech has enabled the financial sector to catalyse savings into more usable forms. Commercial banks have broadened their deposit base through mobile

[7] In donation-based crowd funding, donors provide funding to individuals, projects, or companies based on philanthropic or civic motivations with no expectation of monetary or material return.
[8] In crowd-led microfinance, crowd-lenders provide micro-loans to unbanked/low-income borrowers via an online microfinance platform, for zero or low-interest returns.
[9] In real estate crowd funding, individuals or institutional funders provide equity or subordinated-debt financing for real estate purchases.
[10] In P2P business lending, individuals or institutional funders provide a loan to a business borrower. In P2P consumer lending, individuals or institutional funders provide a loan to a consumer borrower.
[11] In reward-based crowd funding, backers provide finance to individuals, projects, or companies in exchange for non-monetary rewards or products.
[12] In equity-based crowd funding, individuals or institutional funders purchase equity issued by a company.
[13] In balance sheet business lending, the platform entity provides a loan directly to a business borrower.

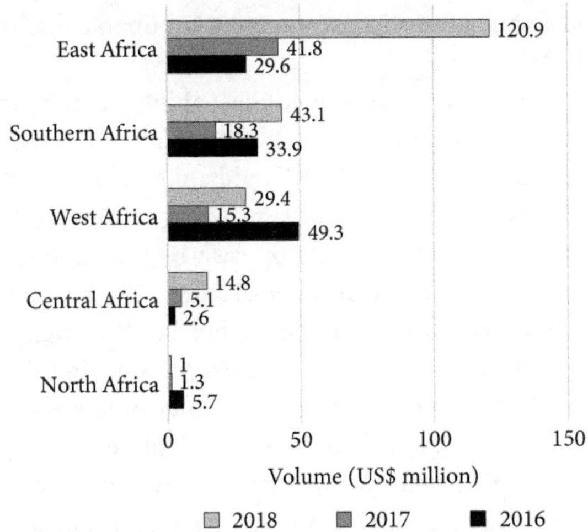

Figure 2.5a Total online alternative finance market volume by region in Africa, 2016–18 (US$ million)

Source: author's construction based on CCAF (2020).

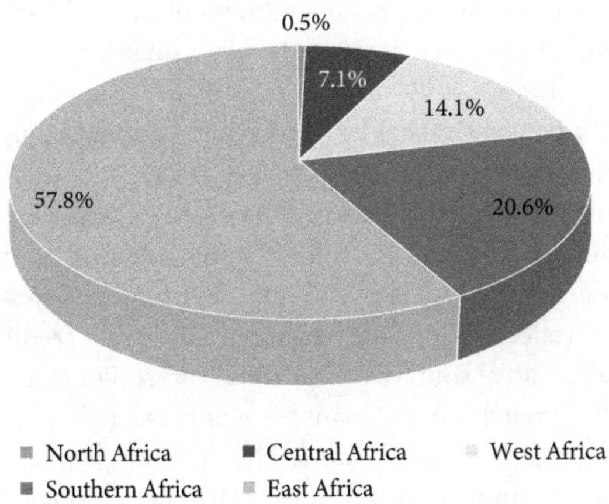

Figure 2.5b Market share, 2018

Source: author's construction based on CCAF (2020).

banking and agency banking, tapping into low-income households and collecting even low-value deposits. These developments encourage micro-savers to increase their deposits/savings in commercial banks, and the variety of mobile financial products and services has expanded considerably (IMF 2016). Subsequently, growth in deposits has provided banks with the capacity to intermediate and grow, leading to the emergence of strong banks leveraging the digital platform to manage micro-accounts, build deposits that provide them with intermediation capacity, and extend financial services to previously unbanked and underserved populations (CCAF 2020).

Since 2012, when M-Shwari demonstrated the viability of moving from a transactions platform to a virtual savings and credit supply platform, partnerships between mobile network operators (MNOs) and banks have multiplied (Ndung'u and Oguso 2021a).[14] The development of similar digital financial products has taken place across Africa, including M-Co-op cash by the Co-operative Bank of Kenya, KCB M-Pesa by the Kenya Commercial Bank, Timiza by Barclays Bank (now ABSA Bank) and Eazzy loans by the Equity Bank in Kenya, M-Pawa in Tanzania, Mokash in Uganda and Rwanda, and MoMoKash in Côte d'Ivoire.

Ndung'u and Oguso (2021a) pointed out that other unregulated, application-based fintech products also emerged in response to the increasing demand for short-term micro credit provided on the digital lending platform. Application-based (app-based) fintech lenders in Kenya include Tala, Branch, Saida, Haraka, Okash, Pesa Pata, Pesa na Pesa, Zidisha, and Kiva. Tala was the first instant mobile loans app launched in Kenya, as Mkopo Rahisi (Easy Loan), in 2014. These app-based virtual credit supply platforms were not previously regulated and did not report to the credit reference bureaus like the telco-facilitated bank virtual savings and credit products. However, the Amendment of Central Bank of Kenya Act in 2021 brought app-based virtual credit providers under Central Bank of Kenya regulation.

Table 2.2 shows there are similarities among the various savings products in the five SSA countries under study. Less than seven years after their launch, these products were already serving over 28.8 million customers in Kenya, 8.6 million in Tanzania, 5.5 million in Uganda, 1.3 million in Rwanda, and 2.1 million in Côte d'Ivoire. There was a general increase in digital savings and deposits in most of the countries, which reflects the important role that virtual credit supply products are playing as alternative sources of finance in Africa. For example, as of June 2019 in Kenya, approximately 16,333 loans were approved per day, with an average loan of US$35 repayable within 27 days. The picture is similar across the five countries; small amounts and a short turnaround time are characteristic of digital lending.

The development of DFS products has especially benefited the young population, which is technologically savvy, and the unbanked (mostly women). Ndung'u and Oguso (2021a) have shown that both urban and rural dwellers, retailers and artisans (who earn low daily incomes and seek a safe and profitable way to save and borrow money to expand their businesses), and poor households (who must deal with urgent family situations and attempt to smooth consumption) have benefited

[14] One of the innovative resource management styles adopted by small businesspeople is pushing back to a virtual savings account from a transactions account and transferring from the virtual savings account to the transactions account when payments are required. This can happen several times in a single business day. It is costless to push back and to withdraw. In this way, the businesses keep fewer funds in the transactions account. They also tend to open several virtual savings accounts.

Table 2.2 Characteristics of fintech savings and credit products in Africa

	M-Shwari (Kenya)	M-Pawa (Tanzania)	MoKash (Uganda)	MoKash (Rwanda)	MoMoKash (Ivory Coast)
Launched	November 2012	May 2014	August 2016	February 2017	January 2018
Number of customers (June 2019)	28.8 million	8.6 million	5.5 million	1.3 million	2.1 million
Interest on savings (per annum, %)	6.65	5	5	5	7
Loan qualification	Have had an active M-Pesa account for at least six months	Have had an active M-Pesa account for at least six months, save on M-Pawa, and actively use M-Pawa services	Have been an MTN mobile money subscriber for at least six months, save on MoKash, and actively use other MTN services	Have been an MTN mobile money subscriber for at least six months, save on MoKash, and actively use other MTN services	Have an MTN MoMo account, are well identified, and actively use MoMoKash
Loan limit	Based on the M-Pesa transactions history, savings, and past loan repayments	–	UGX 1,000,000	Rwf 300,000	100,000 CFA francs
Repayment duration (days)	30	30	30	30	30

Continued

Table 2.2 *Continued*

	M-Shwari (Kenya)	M-Pawa (Tanzania)	MoKash (Uganda)	MoKash (Rwanda)	MoMoKash (Ivory Coast)
Facilitation fee (%)	7.5	9	9	9	—
Total deposits at June 2018 (US$ million)	140.20	8.04	1.48	0.51	—
Total deposits at June 2019 (US$ million)	166.60	7.79	1.98	1.06	7.84
Average savings at June 2018 ($)	5.97	1.09	—	0.65	—
Average savings at June 2019 ($)	5.82	0.91	0.36	0.81	2.51
Total loan amount disbursed at June 2018 (US$ million)	2,771.63	56.43	19.81	4.11	—
Total loan amount disbursed at June 2019 (US$ million)	3,749.71	69.52	50.27	13.46	6.87
Average usage per day in June 2019 (number of customers)	16,333	2,953	6,189	1,399	9,037

Source: author's own data.

from digital financial products and platforms. Poor households can now enlarge their asset base through savings and investments to escape cycles of poverty. Thus, micro-savers and micro-borrowers can benefit from fintech-driven financial services and increase financial inclusion, thereby fighting poverty sustainably.

5. Regulation of fintech

5.1 Fintech and the regulatory space

Fintechs have emerged as not only major competitors but also enablers in the provision of financial services. They have, in some places, collaborated with existing providers to scale up financial services, while in some cases, fintechs have launched financial services products in direct competition with traditional providers. Their disruptive effect is also evident in recent changes to the way in which services are provided by banks and by insurance, pension, and payments providers (Ndung'u 2019).

Overall, in comparison with traditional banks, fintechs have been able to offer customers the precise financial product they need, at the right price, within the shortest possible time. But in pushing the frontiers of financial services, fintechs have moved to sectors in which no specific regulations have been developed, which has raised concerns, especially regarding cybersecurity. Moreover, ease of access, particularly to credit apps, has in some cases led to over-indebtedness and welfare losses among poor, vulnerable, and financially illiterate populations (MicroSave Consulting 2019). Among the activities considered especially risky are digital lending and digital betting. Yet the regulators of betting and gambling in Kenya, for example, do not seem concerned about these developments and have been under political pressure not to impose regulations.

Thus, maximizing the benefits of fintech while minimizing the risks for the financial system is the major challenge that financial regulators must deal with. The introduction of more and stricter regulations to minimize likely risks and vulnerabilities resulting from the adoption of fintech may stifle further financial innovation. The ideal approach for policymakers would therefore be to adopt regulation that continuously identifies emerging risks and vulnerabilities while at the same time strengthening the incentives for prudent behaviour among the fintech players in a particular market segment. Such regulation requires a financial system that is stable, efficient, and innovative (Erik et al. 2021). However, policymakers in SSA continue to face difficulty in striking the right balance between adopting regulations that support growth-enhancing fintech innovations and implementing effective risk-based regulations across different sectors.

The regulation of fintech is in its infancy in SSA and several challenges persist. The first is that mobile payments still require the use of an electronic signature or PIN to authorize transactions. The legality of electronic signatures, however, still relies on old national laws and regulations that typically verify individuals based on an official identity document and their physical address.[15] Additionally, international AML/CFT regulations requiring customer due diligence to identify suspicious transactions also rely largely on old national laws. Given that only 22% of African households have postal addresses and many of the adult population lack official identification documents (African Development Bank 2013), this limits the reach of technology-based solutions. This calls for a clear regulatory framework for fintech and other technology-based solutions, especially regarding electronic identification and legality issues.

A second challenge is limited interoperability of technology-based platforms and products in SSA countries. As these products were developed separately, the first-mover advantage is prevalent. But optimizing fintech requires interoperability of different platforms at various levels so that, for example, customers can access a single point of sale to perform various transactions across different platforms. The World Bank 2010 Global Payment Systems Survey (World Bank 2011) shows that less than 20% of technology-based products are fully or partially interoperable, which limits the attractiveness and usage of fintech solutions. Limited interoperability has largely been driven by the lack of a clear regulatory framework covering, for example, termination costs for mobile money, pricing, and fair competition among the players. Interoperable platforms would increase innovation in the market, enlarge the market, and lower unit costs.

Third, there are challenges on market conduct issues. The low levels of financial literacy and income in SSA limit the ability of a large population to optimally use and understand fintech-based solutions. This has raised market conduct issues regarding consumer protection against exploitation, high indebtedness, and other undesirable behaviours. The problem calls for a clear market conduct regulatory framework that guides and governs the provision and operation of technology-based financial services. Additionally, there is need for a clear regulatory framework aimed at promoting financial literacy.

Fourth, challenges exist on market development issues such as supportive infrastructure, including internet connectivity, fair competition practices, safety, and security. This has led to calls for an adequate regulatory framework to eliminate entry and exit barriers for fintech solutions development with the aim of promoting general market development. Such a regulatory framework should also seek to address security and safety issues in relation to the use of technology-based solutions.

[15] One of the legal amendments in Kenya in 2006 that supported the roll-out of M-Pesa was the recognition of an electronic signature and of electronic units of money. That, in a sense, legitimized the retail electronic payments platform.

The fifth challenge to regulation is policy trade-offs. The upsurge of digital innovations largely fuelled by fintech's diverse development and coverage has led to complex policy trade-offs in four broad areas.

1. **Balancing 'traditional' financial stability and competition**: SSA's central banks' traditional role has been to promote financial system stability through appropriate regulation and financial institution supervision. The call for central banks to take a lead in promoting the adoption of fintech may conflict with their traditional objective of promoting financial stability. To address the traditional financial stability versus market integrity regulation trade-off, the authorities (including central banks) should adopt a risk-proportionality objective. Therefore, traditional financial stability and market integrity become complementary regulatory and policy objectives.
2. **Balancing efficiency and risks**: despite its benefits in enhancing efficiency, fintech brings new risks such as lack of infrastructure interconnectedness. Fintech-led innovations have supported digital finance to reach a level where market failure potentially raises systemic risks in some countries. For example, P2P lending by fintechs reached significant levels in China, necessitating a regulatory crackdown in 2017 (Erik et al. 2021). This means that authorities should develop a regulatory environment that balances efficiency and risks in fintech adoption.
3. **Balancing fintech adoption and control of new risks to data privacy and consumer protection**: the proliferation of fintech services increases the risks of compromising data privacy, exploitative costs, abusive practices, fraud, and errors of which customers may not be aware. This raises the question of how policymakers can adopt policies promoting the adoption of fintech solutions without compromising consumer protection (Erik et al. 2021). Bearing in mind that many consumer protection regulatory policies in SSA focus on the traditional provision of financial services, any shortcoming emanating from fintech customers' interactions may lead to undetected consumer protection risks. This calls for delicate policy balancing to ensure data privacy and consumer protection while spurring fintech adoption.
4. **Shifting from quantity- to price-based monetary policy**: fintech innovations have led to a decline in cash held outside the banking system, increasing inside money. The velocity of money is no longer constant and the relationship between base and broad money is not predictable. These factors have led to a shift from a quantity- to a price-based monetary policy framework. Thus, new and efficient indicators of monetary policy and monetary policy instruments need to be developed to create an efficient signalling environment.

5.2 Emerging issues in regulation

Technology is ever-changing, developing, and dynamic, constantly raising new issues and challenges, such as that posed by recent advances in DLT. Whereas emerging technologies are still facing significant challenges, such as scalability, security, and high energy consumption, the utilization of DLT offers potential solutions, including enhanced transparency, security, and efficiency for SSA payment platforms, hence lowering trading costs and increasing interoperability across platforms, countries/jurisdictions, and time (IMF 2019). Ultimately, regional payments will facilitate intra-Africa trade.

An emerging practice in fintech regulation is the adoption of regulatory sandboxes to facilitate entry into markets, as already practised in Kenya, South Africa, and the United Kingdom. Regulatory sandboxes allow regulators to support product development by fintechs by providing a secure testing environment for innovative products, ultimately catalysing disruptive innovations. The original idea of a regulatory sandbox made M-Pesa the most successful fintech product in Kenya, revolutionizing DFS.

High-powered networks such as 5G offer significant opportunities for increasing efficiency and speed, but SSA is lagging in the adoption of 5G technologies, which is projected to be 3% in 2025 for the SSA region compared with 7% in MENA, 21% globally, and 53% in East Asia and the Pacific (GSMA 2021). While Kenya, Togo, Seychelles, Madagascar, and South Africa have begun to deploy 5G networks for commercialization, Mali, Uganda, Zambia, Nigeria, and Ethiopia are still in the early stages of 5G network deployment (GSMA 2021). SSA governments should ensure the adoption and availability of this high-powered spectrum to realize high-performance networks and services and should support their digital connectivity goal by having effective spectrum pricing models to ensure affordable, high-quality mobile technology services.

For the effective adoption of 5G technologies, SSA governments and other players should first ensure that users have access to affordable and quality networks. This involves providing high-quality and affordable handsets, tariffs, data, and services. Second, they must seek to improve users' digital skills and knowledge. Increased digital literacy enhances awareness of mobile technology benefits. Third, they must ensure the safety and security of users' data and devices. This can be achieved through addressing data privacy, theft, harassment, and fraud, with the aim of building users' trust. Fourth, they must see to it that users are constantly provided with relevant and appropriate services, content, and product to meet customers' ever-changing tastes and preferences.

Finally, effective regulation of fintech will create a platform for regulator collaboration. The success of M-Pesa in Kenya was attributed to the regulatory coordination between the central bank and the Communication Authority. Other collaborations might be between industry-specific regulators, such as those in insurance and pensions sectors, and service providers; different government sectors (Agriculture, Energy, Health, Communication, and Technology); and competition and telco regulators.

5.3 Suggested solutions to fintech development challenges

To enhance fintech development and financial inclusion in Africa, several policy and institutional reforms are required. First, Africa needs to create a competitive ecosystem and infrastructure that facilitate entry. Second, robust consumer protection regulations are needed to create an enabling and innovative environment. Third, state capacity needs to be enabled to develop institutions that protect the market and foster innovation. Fourth, since most African countries lack a comprehensive legal framework for addressing cybercrime, there is need to build capacity to monitor and prevent cybercrime, especially in terms of office-level surveillance.

Despite improvements in the ICT infrastructure across the continent, there are still several technological bottlenecks that are restricting the spread of digital infrastructure. Mahnkopf (2019) points to limited fibre-optic networks, lack of a standardized application programming interface or common data language, poor integration of largely autonomous systems, and exposure to the danger of cyberattacks. Successful fintech applications must operate on a reliable electrical grid that permits large numbers of participants to connect via mobile phones or the internet, and the products must be designed with simplicity and low cost in mind (Yermack 2018). There is a need to address the key enablers of mobile and internet connectivity, particularly around network quality, affordability for low-income users, digital skills, and the creation of content in more local languages (Ndung'u 2018). If these issues are not adequately addressed, the exclusion resulting from connectivity challenges is likely to further widen the digital divide in Africa.

Deficiencies in the interoperability of MNOs and transparency in the pricing of services are still concerns for telecommunication regulators and financial institutions (Ndung'u 2019). The retail electronic payments platforms were developed individually but should now move towards an interoperable platform that would facilitate leasing agreements to enlarge the market, lower unit costs, and provide room for more innovative solutions and scalability, while at the same time allowing seamless and transformative regulatory technology to emerge. There is a need to enhance MNOs' and mobile virtual network operators' (MVNOs') interoperability, agent network interoperability, and regional payments interoperability across Africa.

Another requirement is improvement in the personal identity system (e-ID system) to cope with market innovations and secure the market. One of the major impediments to credit and other types of borrowing in Africa is the lack of collateral—not because of insufficient assets but rather due to inefficient registration systems (Dahou et al. 2009). There is a need for Africa to leverage digital technology to generate comprehensive databases of all citizens (where they are, what they do, their physical addresses) and the services they use or require. A new e-ID system, including a machine-readable card with a microchip that contains comprehensive details of the holder, will make it easier to transmit transaction and other data in real time and minimize risks (Ndung'u and Oguso 2021a).

Deficits in education and vocational training also represent a great obstacle for developing countries, including those in SSA, especially regarding the key technology of AI, which is based on four components: algorithms or computer programs, computing power, huge amounts of data, and people to develop programs and applications (Mahnkopf 2019). There is a need to enhance research and capacity in these areas across SSA to increase the uptake of fintech products and to encourage innovation.

Finally, in conjunction with the banking sector, capital markets are a central component of efficient financial markets and resource mobilization. However, they remain largely underdeveloped in Africa and therefore further discourage investors (Dahou et al. 2009). Thus, there is a need for African governments to support the development of capital markets to enhance resource mobilization, intra-Africa trade, and opportunities for both domestic and foreign investors (Dahou et al. 2009). Pooling resources and investors at the regional level will also help to build economies of scale in terms of financial infrastructure and regulatory capacity, while providing both domestic and foreign investors with a diversified set of opportunities (Dahou et al. 2009; Ndung'u and Oguso 2021b).

6. Fintech and the Fourth Industrial Revolution

Fintech innovations have heralded a Fourth Industrial Revolution (4IR), where automation and the internet of things (IoT) now apply to almost all aspects of life. The digital revolution being experienced across Africa could allow countries to create their own unique development path by taking the lead in innovation and technologies of the 4IR. The historical narrative of developing 'smokestack industries' has traditionally been regarded as the key driver of structural transformation in Africa. However, 'industries without smokestacks' such as services, agro-processing, and horticulture, have benefited from technological change to achieve productivity growth.

Small-scale manufacturing in Africa may also become more competitive and efficient thanks to emerging technologies (Naudé 2017). Prisecaru (2016) notes that innovative producers have rapid access to digital platforms for research and development (R&D), marketing, and distribution and so can quickly improve the quality, price, and availability of their products/services. Further, consumers are increasingly involved in production and distribution chains and can easily connect to suppliers by means of digital technological platforms. Naudé (2017) argues that additive manufacturing (3D-printing) has potential to open opportunities for entrepreneurs to enter manufacturing and has promising implications for agricultural industrialization in Africa. A recent project that piloted additive manufacturing is the 3D4AgDev project, funded by the Bill and Melinda Gates Foundation and the Deutsche Gesellschaft für Internationale Zumammenarbeit (GIZ) and supported by the University of Galloway. This project provides women smallholder farmers with 3D-printing technology to design labour-saving agricultural tools, producing plastic prototypes for local tool manufacturers (artisans, blacksmiths) to copy or modify.

The 4IR in Africa will increase its participation in global value chains, a significant driver of labour productivity, mainly in the agro-industrial and horticultural, tourism, business, and trade services sectors (Newfarmer et al. 2018). This will allow countries to industrialize at a much earlier stage of development, as lead firms choose to offshore fragments of the production value chain to countries where labour is cheaper or where locational criteria confer a competitive cost advantage (Newfarmer et al. 2018). The 4IR may also allow suppliers in developing countries to meet standards and regulations that allow access to rich country markets, permit imports under privileged tariff treatment for intra-firm trade, or facilitate the use of network technology that would not otherwise be available (Newfarmer et al. 2018). This vibrancy will allow fintechs to roll out new products to cover the space and increase efficiency.

The service industry is becoming increasingly important in African economies. Much of manufacturing is undergoing a process of servicification, while services-sector firms have become larger, providing a range of specialized services such as engineering design, legal advice, and accounting (Newfarmer et al. 2018). Evidently, services in African markets are fast becoming the primary source of within-sector productivity growth, already accounting for more than 50% of labour productivity growth in several African countries.

7. Conclusions

In summary, the fintech evolution is defining the growth and development path of financial sector in SSA.

1. Fintech has revolutionized the retail payments ecosystem, which has spilled over to other sectors and navigated across different market segments. The retail electronic payments system operated by commercial banks that has emerged is effective, efficient, transparent, and safe. Retail electronic

payments are easier entry points for financial services, with the capacity to formalize informal market transactions, thanks to their ability to navigate between formal and informal markets.

2. Fintechs have rolled out new products across all sectors, including the financial sector (which has benefited from a wide range of innovations) and the agriculture, manufacturing, health, energy, and education sectors.
3. Fintech has enhanced both financial-inclusion and financial-sector development. Commercial banks and microfinance institutions now have a technological platform for managing micro-accounts and reaching out to customers cost-effectively. With the creation of retail electronic payment systems, banks have been able to upgrade their banking infrastructure so that virtual savings and credit supply platforms have emerged, along with increased investment in government instruments. Strong banks with intermediation capacity have also emerged in Africa.
4. Fintech has enabled the formulation of effective price-based monetary policy, supportive of market development and innovation. In addition, DFS have allowed an efficient surveillance system to be developed and thus have enabled improvements in the AML/CFT regime.
5. Low-income earners are enabled to save in instruments that are safe and secure. Women, in particular, who tend to be efficient savers, have been enabled to escape from cycles of poverty.
6. Fintech is supporting e-government services platforms. Perhaps the most significant driver of future economic management is the development of tax payment platforms and revenue administration. This increases efficiency, resolves governance issues, supports the mobilization of domestic resources, and minimizes revenue leakages. Fintechs are designing platforms for e-government services that are effective and easy to access, as well as targeted government social protection programmes.
7. The fintech revolution is pushing African economies towards the 4IR, propelling the continent forwards in savings, investment, and growth.

References

African Development Bank (2013). 'Financial Inclusion in Africa.' African Development Bank Group. Available at: https://www.afdb.org/fileadmin/uploads/afdb/Documents/Project-and-Operations/Financial_Inclusion_in_Africa.pdf (accessed 2 September 2022).

CCAF (Cambridge Centre for Alternative Finance) (2020). 'The Global Alternative Finance Market Benchmarking Report: Trends, Opportunities and Challenges for Lending, Equity, and Non-Investment Alternative Finance Models.' Cambridge: Cambridge Centre for Alternative Finance. Available at: https://www.jbs.cam.ac.uk/wp-content/uploads/2020/08/2020-04-22-ccaf-global-alternative-finance-market-benchmarking-report.pdf (accessed 2 September 2022).

Dahou, K., H. I. Omar, and M. Pfister (2009). 'Deepening African Financial Markets for Growth and Investment'. Background paper for official documentation for the Ministerial and Expert Roundtable of the New Partnership for Africa's Development (NEPAD)/Organisation for Economic Co-operation and Development (OECD) Africa Investment Initiative on 11–12 November. Available at: https://www.oecd.org/investment/investmentfordevelopment/43966839.pdf (accessed 2 September 2022).

Disrupt Africa (2021). 'Finnovating for Africa 2021: Reimagining the African Financial Services Landscape'. Available at: https://disruptafrica.gumroad.com/l/razjs (accessed 2 September 2022).

Erik, F., F. Jon, N. Harish, and R. Tara (2021). 'What Does Digital Money Mean for Emerging Market and Developing Economies?' BIS Working Paper 973. Basel: Bank for International Settlement. Available at: https://www.bis.org/publ/work973.pdf (accessed 2 September 2022).

Ernst & Young (2019). 'Fintechs in Sub-Saharan Africa: an Overview of Market Developments and Investment Opportunities'. London: Ernst & Young Global.

Financial Technology Partners (2019). 'Fintech in Africa: Leapfrogging Legacy Straight to Mobile'. San Francisco, CA: Financial Technology Partners. Available at: https://www.ftpartners.com/fintech-research/fintech-in-africa (accessed 2 September 2022).

Fong, D., F. Han, L. Liu, J. Qu, and A. Shek (2021). 'Seven Technologies Shaping the Future of Fintech'. McKinsey & Company, 9 November. Available at: https://www.mckinsey.com/cn/our-insights/our-insights/seven-technologies-shaping-the-future-of-fintech (accessed 2 September 2022).

GSMA (Global System for Mobile Communications Association) (2021). 'State of the Industry Report on Mobile Money. The GSMA's Mobile Money Programme'. London: GSM Association. Available at: https://www.gsma.com/sotir/wp-content/uploads/2022/03/GSMA_State_of_the_Industry_2022_English.pdf (accessed 2 September 2022).

Gubbins, P., and E. Totolo (2018). 'Digital Credit in Kenya: Evidence from Demand-Side Surveys'. Nairobi: Financial Sector Deepening Trust Kenya.

IMF (International Monetary Fund) (2016). 'Financial Development in Sub-Saharan Africa—Promoting Inclusive and Sustainable Growth'. Washington, DC: IMF.

IMF (2019). 'Fintech: The Experience So Far'. IMF Policy Paper 2019/024. Washington, DC: IMF, 27 June. Available at: https://www.imf.org/en/Publications/Policy-Papers/Issues/2019/06/27/Fintech-The-Experience-So-Far-47056 (accessed 2 September 2022).

Mahnkopf, B. (2019). 'The 4th Wave of Industrial Revolution—a Promise Blind to Social Consequences, Power and Ecological Impact in the Era of Digital Capitalism'. EuroMemo Group Discussion Paper 01/2019. Available at: http://www2.euromemorandum.eu/uploads/01_2019_mahnkopf_the_4th_wave_of_industrial_revolution.pdf (accessed 2 September 2022).

MicroSave Consulting (2019). 'Making Digital Credit Truly Responsible—Insights from Analysis of Digital Credit in Kenya'. Nairobi: MicroSave Consulting, 18 September. Available at: https://www.microsave.net/2019/09/18/11310 (accessed 2 September 2022).

Misati, R., J. Osoro, M. Odongo, and F. Abdul (2022). 'Does Digital Financial Innovation Enhance Financial Deepening and Growth in Kenya?' *International Journal of Emerging Markets*, 19(3): 679–705. https://doi.org/10.1108/IJOEM-09-2021-1389 (accessed 2 September 2022).

Naudé, W. (2017). 'Entrepreneurship, Education and the Fourth Industrial Revolution in Africa'. IZA Discussion Paper 10855, 10 July. Bonn: Institute of Labour Economics. https://doi.org/10.2139/ssrn.2998964.

Ndung'u, N. (2018). 'Next Steps for the Digital Revolution in Africa: Inclusive Growth and Job Creation Lessons from Kenya'. Working Paper 20. Washington, DC: Africa Growth Initiative, Brookings Institution.

Ndung'u, N. (2019). 'Digital Technology and State Capacity in Kenya'. CGD Policy Paper 154. Washington, DC: Center for Global Development, 6 August. Available at: https://www.cgdev.org/publication/digital-technology-and-state-capacity-kenya (accessed 2 September 2022).

Ndung'u, N., and A. Oguso (2021a). 'Fintech Revolutionizing Financial Services: The Case of Virtual Savings and Credit Supply Technological Platforms in Africa'. In R. Rau, R. Wardrop, and L. Zingales (eds), *The Palgrave Handbook of Technological Finance*, pp. 189–215. Basingstoke: Palgrave Macmillan. https://doi.org/10.1007/978-3-030-65117-6_8.

Ndung'u, N., and A. Oguso (2021b). 'Financial Sector Development and Financial Inclusion in Africa: Gaps, Challenges and Policy Options'. In A. H. Ahmad, D. T. Llewellyn, and V. Murinde (eds), *Inclusive Financial Development*, pp. 28–51. Cheltenham: Edward Elgar. https://doi.org/10.4337/9781800376380.00008.

Newfarmer, R. S., J. Page, and F. Tarp (2018). 'Industries without Smokestacks and Structural Transformation in Africa: Overview'. In R. S. Newfarmer, J. Page, and F. Tarp (eds), *Industries without Smokestacks: Industrialization in Africa Reconsidered*, pp. 1–26. United Nations University World Institute for Development Economics Research, 20 December. Oxford: Oxford University Press. https://doi.org/10.1093/oso/9780198821885.001.0001.

Prisecaru, P. (2016). 'Challenges of the Fourth Industrial Revolution'. *Knowledge Horizons—Economics*, 8(1): 57–62.

Suri, T., and W. Jack (2014). 'Risk Sharing and Transactions Costs: Evidence from Kenya's Mobile Money Revolution'. *American Economic Review*, 104(1): 183–223. https://doi.org/10.1257/aer.104.1.183.

Suri, T., and W. Jack (2016). 'The Long-Run Poverty and Gender Impacts of Mobile Money'. *Science*, 354(6317): 1288–92. https://doi.org/10.1126/science.aah5309.

World Bank (2011). 'Payment Systems Worldwide—a Snapshot: Outcomes of the Global Payment Systems Survey 2010'. Financial Infrastructure Series. Washington, DC: World Bank. Available at: https://openknowledge.worldbank.org/handle/10986/12813 (accessed 2 September 2022).

Yermack, D. (2018). 'Fintech in Sub-Saharan Africa: What Has Worked Well, and What Hasn't'. NBER Working Paper 25007. Cambridge, MA: National Bureau of Economic Research. https://doi.org/10.3386/w25007.

3

Accelerating capital markets development in sub-Saharan Africa

Githinji Njenga, Josphat Machagua, and Samuel Gachanja

1. Introduction

Capital markets are organized, highly interconnected, and regulated financial markets in which long-term debts such as bonds, preference shares, equity shares, mutual funds, public deposits, derivatives, foreign exchange, and commodities are traded (Laeven 2014). The primary role of capital markets is to channel surplus funds or the savings of companies and households into long-term productive use by making long-term investments through the issuance and trading of long-term securities (Fama 2021). Governments also utilize the capital markets to raise funds for various investment projects through the issuance of long-term bonds. Hence, capital markets facilitate capital growth by mobilizing savings and converting them into investments, and therefore are a stimulant of economic growth. Africa Union (2015) indicates that the development of Africa's capital markets is a key priority for Africa to take full responsibility in financing its development. Further, Nnyanzi et al. (2018) are of the view that capital markets are essential facilitators of economic growth in sub-Saharan Africa (SSA).

There is evidence that countries with high savings rates tend to grow faster on average. South and East Asian countries have experienced high economic growth mainly due to the high level of domestic savings (Figure 3.1). Over the past 30 years, the domestic savings rate (percentage of gross domestic product, GDP) and the GDP growth rate in South and East Asian countries have averaged 33 and 4.8%, respectively. In the same period, the domestic savings rate (percentage of GDP) and GDP growth rate in SSA averaged 22.4 and 3.4%, respectively. Hence, the mobilization of domestic savings through capital markets is critical for economic development in SSA.

Therefore, developing capital markets is of great importance to SSA economies. The financial sector in SSA countries, except for South Africa, is bank dominated (Allen et al. 2011). Over the past few decades, significant advances have been made in the banking sector in SSA with the introduction of mobile banking platforms,

Githinji Njenga, Josphat Machagua, and Samuel Gachanja, *Accelerating capital markets development in sub-Saharan Africa*. In: *The Domestic Savings Shortfall in Sub-Saharan Africa*. Edited by: Rose Ngugi and Kunal Sen,
Oxford University Press. © UNU-WIDER (2025). DOI: 10.1093/oso/9780198932482.003.0003

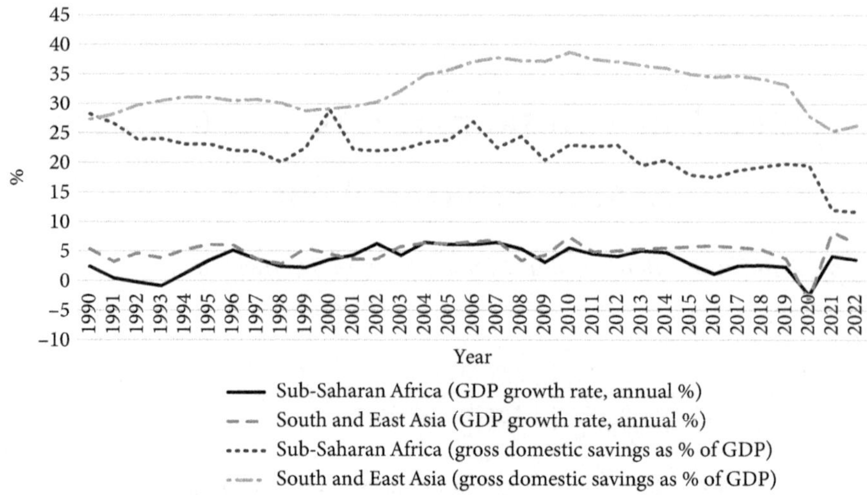

Figure 3.1 Gross domestic savings and GDP growth rate
Source: authors' compilation based on data from World Bank (2024).

enabling unbanked populations to have access to banking services. However, the banking industry remains characterized by high interest rate margins, which reduce financial intermediation and thus investment levels. Hence, developing the capital markets in SSA economies can facilitate diversification of the financial sector, complement the banking sector through risk-sharing financial instruments, and provide long-term financing to the private and public sectors.

Further, the development of capital markets as a source of funding in SSA can help in managing foreign currency and refinancing risks. This is because, in SSA, funds are mainly sourced from abroad and are denominated in foreign currency. Local capital markets can also complement the gradual reductions in concessional funding from donors, often with stringent conditionalities (Nega and Schneider 2011; Osano 2016). Hence, when fully developed, capital markets can serve as an alternative source of funding for SSA (Osano 2016; Calderón and Zeufack 2020). Capital markets additionally play a significant role in enhancing corporate governance standards (Haque et al. 2008). The need to create regulatory and legal frameworks to increase the level of transparency, corporate governance, and dissemination of information boosts investor confidence (Samaha et al. 2012).

Capital markets are also critical in tapping into foreign remittances. Remittances have become a significant source of foreign capital for many countries, at times exceeding other private capital inflows (Lartey 2013). The remittances in SSA averaged US$43.9 billion in the 2015–22 period compared to US$4.8 billion in 2000 (World Bank 2021). The African Capacity Building Foundation (2016) notes that the tremendous growth in remittances offers a promising and stable potential for increasing domestic savings and fostering long-term domestic investment, especially in the underdeveloped infrastructure in priority areas such as physical infrastructure (communication and transport), health care, housing, education, energy, agriculture, and micro, small, and medium enterprises (MSMEs). Osano (2016) estimates the funding deficit for MSMEs, agri-business, housing, and infrastructure in Africa to be approximately US$300 billion per annum. Capital markets can therefore narrow these funding gaps in infrastructure for economic take-off. Kodongo and Ojah (2016) note that there is a strong correlation between investment in infrastructure and robust economic development.

To enlarge the prevailing literature on developing capital markets in SSA countries, this study explores two areas: (i) the evolution, structure, and products and (ii) the performance of capital markets in SSA countries. We employ a literature review and secondary data to identify the issues that require interventions in developing capital markets in SSA countries. The remainder of the study is organized in three sections. Section 2 reviews the evolution, structure, and products in capital markets, while Section 3 analyses the performance of the markets. The conclusion and policy implications are provided in Section 4.

2. Evolution, structure, and products

2.1 Evolution

The developed world's major stock markets emerged in the nineteenth and twentieth centuries, led by the London Stock Exchange and the New York Stock Exchange (Raubenheimer 2019). The stock exchange concept also spread rapidly to SSA after colonial occupation and the discovery of minerals (Karekwaivenani 2003). During the colonial period, financial systems in most SSA countries were underdeveloped. Banks dominated the financial sector, with a few countries such as Zimbabwe and South Africa dominated by colonial settlers having capital markets (Gakunu 2007).

The Johannesburg Stock Exchange and Zimbabwe Stock Exchange were established in 1887 and in 1894, respectively, to facilitate the exploitation of trade sparked by the discovery of natural resources (Karekwaivenani 2003). The discovery of gold in 1886 in Witwatersrand, South Africa led to the formation of mining and financial companies by investors who needed a central facility to access primary capital (JSE 2021; SAHO 2021). The Zimbabwe Stock Exchange was formed to meet the capital needs of the gold-mining industry, whose rapid expansion was fuelled by prospects of gold in Zimbabwe (then Southern Rhodesia). During this period the Johannesburg and London Stock Exchanges also had new listings of Zimbabwe enterprises, which sought to raise capital for their mining activities.

In 1954, the Nairobi Securities Exchange (then Nairobi Stock Exchange) was the third exchange to be established as a voluntary association of the European community stockbrokers and registered under the Societies Act. The exchange was charged with developing the securities market and regulating trading activities in British Kenya (NSE 2013). The Nigerian Exchange Group (NGX Group), formerly known as the Nigerian Stock Exchange, was established in 1961 primarily as a securities market (Nigeria Exchange Group 2019). In 1988, the Stock Exchange of Mauritius was the fifth exchange to be established (ASEA 2021a). Other capital markets in SSA were established after the financial crises in the 1990s caused recessions in these economies. Thus, to restore economic growth, many SSA countries initiated broader stabilization and adjustment programmes to reform the financial system by rehabilitating the formal banking system, removing financial repression, and establishing capital markets (Gakunu 2007).

Thus, most exchanges in SSA are young, 32 years and younger except for the Johannesburg Stock Exchange, Zimbabwe Stock Exchange, Nairobi Securities Exchange, and Nigerian Stock Exchange. South Africa, Nigeria, and Zambia have more than one exchange. There are two regional exchanges serving several countries. The *Bourse Régionale des Valeurs Mobilières*, established in 1998, is situated in Abidjan and serves seven countries in West Africa. The *Bourse des Valeurs Mobilières de l'Afrique Centrale*, serving Central Africa countries, was established in 2003 and initially located in Libreville before moving to Douala (Table 3.1).

2.2 Structure: Institutional and legal framework

The players in SSA capital markets mainly include financial intermediaries, market regulators, and local and foreign investors. The role of financial intermediaries is to reduce information asymmetries, extend corporate control, manage investment risks, and mobilize savings. This includes exchanges, underwriting firms, stock brokerage firms, and investment banks (Mahdi 2008). The underwriting firms administer the public issuance and distribution of securities during initial public offers (IPOs), evaluating investors' risks and insuring them against contingencies. Stock brokerage firms connect the buyers and sellers of stocks and securities and facilitate their transactions. Investment firms offer financial advice and invest on behalf of their clients as well as administering mergers and acquisitions (Soumare et al. 2021).

The existence of an effective and robust institutional governance mechanism to offer services, enforce rules and regulations, and uphold investors' rights is a crucial component of the legal and institutional environment needed for the development of capital markets. In SSA, the regulators in capital markets include local central banks, capital market authorities, and securities and exchange commissions. The regulators, through various laws, rules, and regulations, guide the

Table 3.1 List of exchanges in SSA countries

Region	Country	Exchange	Location	Year established
East Africa	Kenya	Nairobi Securities Exchange	Nairobi	1954
	Mauritius	Stock Exchange of Mauritius	Port Louis	1988
	Uganda	Uganda Securities Exchange	Kampala	1997
	Tanzania	Dar es Salaam Stock Exchange	Dar es Salaam	1998
	Somalia	Somali Stock Exchange	Mogadishu	2015
	Rwanda	Rwanda Stock Exchange	Kigali	2011
	Seychelles	Merj Exchange Limited	Victoria	2012
Southern Africa	South Africa	Johannesburg Stock Exchange Limited	Johannesburg	1887
		A2X Markets	Johannesburg	2017
		4 Africa Exchange	Johannesburg	2017
		ZAR X	Johannesburg	2016
		Equity Express Securities Exchange	Johannesburg	2017
	Eswatini (formerly Swaziland)	Eswatini Stock Exchange	Mbabane	1990
	Zambia	Lusaka Stock Exchange	Lusaka	1994
		Africa Digital Stock Exchange Ltd	Zambia	2018
	Zimbabwe	Zimbabwe Stock Exchange	Harare	1894
	Namibia	Namibia Stock Exchange	Windhoek	1992
	Mozambique	Bolsa de Valores de Mozambique	Maputo	1999
	Malawi	Malawi Stock Exchange	Blantyre	1995
	Lesotho	Maseru Securities Exchange	Maseru	2016
	Angola	Angola Stock Exchange and Derivatives	Luanda	2016
	Botswana	Botswana Stock Exchange	Gaborone	1989

Continued

Table 3.1 *Continued*

Region	Country	Exchange	Location	Year established
West Africa	Nigeria	Nigerian Stock Exchange	Lagos	1960
		Abuja Securities and Commodities Exchange	Abuja	1998
	Ghana	Ghana Stock Exchange	Accra	1990
	Côte d'Ivoire, Benin, Burkina Faso, Guinea-Bissau, Mali, Niger, Senegal, Togo	Bourse Régionale des Valeurs Mobilières (Regional Securities Exchange in English) The stock market is for eight countries in the West Africa Economic and Monetary Union (WAEMU)	Abidjan	1998
	Cameroon	Douala Stock Exchange (joined Bourse des Valeurs Mobilières de l'Afrique Centrale in 2019)	Douala	2001
	Cape Verde	Bolsa de Valores de Cabo Verde	Mindelo	2005
Central Africa	Gabon, the Central African Republic, Republic of Congo, Equatorial Guinea, Chad	Bourse des Valeurs Mobilières de l'Afrique Centrale (Stock Exchange of Central Africa)	Libreville (now in Douala)	2003

Source: authors' compilation based on data from ASEA (2021a), Maseru Securities Market (2019), and Somali Stock Exchange (2022).

day-to-day trading activities in the capital markets (see Njenga et al. 2022: Table A1). They also conduct supervisory and regulatory oversight to protect the interests of investors and issuers by ensuring that the players in capital markets operate seamlessly and that contracts and agreements are settled on time. Capital markets therefore play a significant role in enhancing the institutional governance and legal standards in an economy (Haque et al. 2008; Samaha et al. 2012).

The African Securities Exchanges Association (ASEA), established in 1993, fosters capital mobilization, promotes sustainability, and enhances financial inclusion for the benefit of Africa's economic development. It hosts 27 exchanges in 37 African countries. The organization makes concerted efforts in lobbying for and promoting the position of African capital markets as drivers of economic growth in the region (Raubenheimer 2019). It does so by championing the exchanges' common areas of interest, such as capacity building, market development, and cross-border trading of securities. In 2018, the African Development Bank and ASEA launched the African Exchanges Linkage Project, whose aim is to create linkages between capital markets in SSA by developing laws, regulations, and procedures that enable seamless operation and trade coordination in the SSA capital markets (ASEA 2021b).

Some of the exchanges in SSA are also signatories to international associations such as the World Federation of Exchanges. This organization promotes and encourages capital markets to adhere to internationally accepted standards of best practice by developing appropriate, broadly accepted guidelines, rules, recommendations, and standards documentation aimed at maintaining and enhancing the framework of cross-border issuing, trading, and investing capital market instruments (WFE 2021).

Despite the presence of the legal and regulatory framework in SSA countries, uncertainty in the capital markets remains. In the Global Competitiveness Index compiled by the World Economic Forum, most regulators in SSA have an average score for ensuring the stability of the financial market. In the Global Competitiveness Report 2017–18, Guinea-Bissau, Namibia, Rwanda, South Africa, Botswana, Kenya Mauritius, Nigeria, Eswatini, and Zambia scored highly, at above 4.1 out of 7, in the indicator for the regulation of securities exchanges (Schwab 2019). The other countries had a low score, an indication of uncertainty in the stability of the markets. Similarly, in the Global Competitiveness Report 2016–17, only a few countries scored highly. These were South Africa, Namibia, Rwanda, Nigeria, Botswana, Kenya, Mauritius, Uganda, Zambia, and Cape Verde, who had a score of above 4.1 (Schwab 2018). Indeed, Chimpango (2019) shows that many capital markets in SSA remain undeveloped and sluggish due to the high risks and uncertainty in enforcing standard financial market agreements. Hence, alignment with internationally recognized contractual and legal frameworks can help to mitigate such risks and uncertainty to enhance the accountability and dissemination of information and increase the level of transparency and corporate governance in capital markets, which boosts investor confidence.

In the Global Competitiveness Reports 2017–18 and 2016–17, Singapore and Malaysia ranked highly in ensuring the stability of financial markets, with a score of 6.4 and 5.3, respectively, in the indicator of regulation of securities exchanges. Singapore and Malaysia have strengthened their institutional governance to promote efficiency and effectiveness in both the public and private sectors. Singapore's robust economic fundamentals include prudent government policies, good corporate governance, the credibility of policymakers, and a sound financial system that has seen many high-net-worth individuals choose Singapore as the financial centre for managing their wealth. The depth and breadth of institutions in Singapore also give them ready access to global and regional financial markets while, at the same time, providing a full suite of wealth management services to meet their holistic needs (Monetary Authority of Singapore 2021).

To remedy poor corporate governance, widely seen as one of the causes of the 1997 Asian financial crisis, the Malaysian government initiated corporate governance reforms in 1998. These included making corporate boards more responsive to shareholders; better training, education, and laws to enhance the protection of minority shareholders (Singh and Yusof 2005); improving disclosure and transparency, including guidelines on prospectus regulation; and enabling civil lawsuits for insufficient or misleading disclosure (Securities Commission of Malaysia 2001). The Capital-Market Master Plan (2000–10) further strengthened minority shareholders' rights and disclosure requirements. The Malaysian government passed additional corporate governance legislation, including the Anti-Corruption Commission Bill in 2008 and the Witness Protection Bill in 2004 (Woodsome 2016).

2.3 Products

Exchanges in SSA have limited diversity of products available for trading, likely because many are still at their early developmental stage. Most exchanges only offer plain vanilla (unsophisticated) products in equities and bonds; a limited number of commodities in the form of agricultural products (tea, coffee, beans, sugar, wheat, groundnuts, sunflower, sorghum, and maize); and a few metals such as gold, platinum, and diamonds (Soumare et al. 2021).

There are only a few exchanges with diversified products (see Njenga et al. 2022: Table A2). South Africa's Johannesburg Stock Exchange offers a variety of exotic (sophisticated) products in equities, bonds, derivatives, investment funds, securitized derivatives, real estate investment trusts (REITs), and exchange-traded funds (ETFs). The Nairobi Securities Exchange, which has a derivatives market that was established in 2019, trades in equity index futures (these are derivatives instruments that give investors exposure to price movements on an underlying index made up of a certain group of shares or stocks) and single stock futures (derivative instruments that give investors exposure to price movements on a particular underlying stock) (NSE 2021). Other products in the Nairobi Securities Exchange are investment funds, REITs, and ETFs. The Seychelles (Merj Exchange Limited) also has a derivatives market of stocks and currency. The Meri Exchange also offers investment funds and ETFs. Although the Stock Exchange of Mauritius, Dar es Salaam Stock Exchange of Tanzania, Uganda Securities Exchange, Eswatini Stock Exchange, Lusaka Stock Exchange of Zambia, Zimbabwe Stock Exchange, Namibia Stock Exchange, Botswana Stock Exchange, Nigeria Stock Exchange, and Ghana Stock Exchange offer investment funds, REITs, and ETFs, they are yet to establish derivatives markets.

3. Performance of capital markets

3.1 Equity market

3.1.1 Initial public offerings (IPOs)

Primary capital markets allow firms to raise capital from the public by issuing new stocks through IPOs. Despite the increased liberalization and integration of financial markets with the rest of the world, the SSA region's equity capital markets still lag far behind in performance in terms of the capital raised through IPOs (see Njenga et al. 2022: Table 2 and Table A1). In 2010, there were 14 IPOs in SSA, which raised US$1.8 billion, compared to 1,258 IPOs across the globe, which raised US$299.1 billion. The number of IPOs across the globe increased to 1,415 in 2020, raising US$331.3 billion. However, the number of IPOs in SSA fell to three in 2020, raising US$514 million (PwC 2021). The US$13.6 billion raised in SSA in the period from 2010 to 2020 compares unfavourably with South Korea, Singapore, and Malaysia, which raised a total of US$84.9 billion. In the same period, Malaysia had a total of 203 IPOs compared to 148 IPOs in SSA.

Figure 3.2 shows the top SSA countries by number of IPOs and share of amount raised. South Africa and Nigeria are top both in the number of IPOs issued and the subsequent amounts raised, followed by Ghana, Mauritius, Botswana, and Tanzania. Except for Mauritius, which is a tourism-dependent economy, these are oil-exporting or resource-intensive economies. The non-resource-intensive economies, including Kenya, Rwanda, and Uganda, are other countries where IPOs are active. In the 2010–20 period, there were only three IPOs in Kenya, which raised a total of Ksh7.77 billion. One IPO was oversubscribed at 764%, with the other two IPOs being undersubscribed at 60 and 28.96% (Capital Markets Authority, 2020).

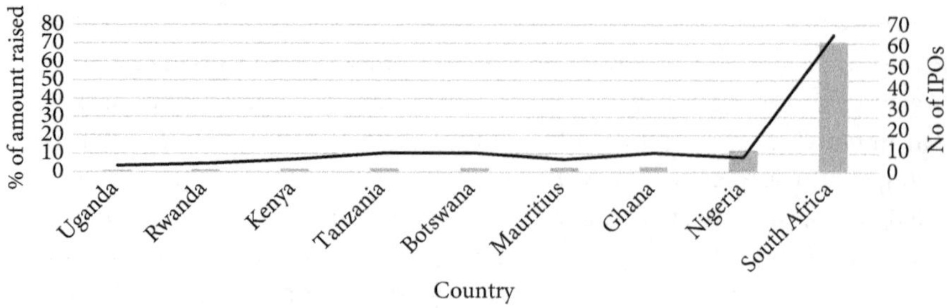

Figure 3.2 IPOs in selected SSA countries (2010–20)

Source: authors' compilation based on data from PwC (2019, 2021).

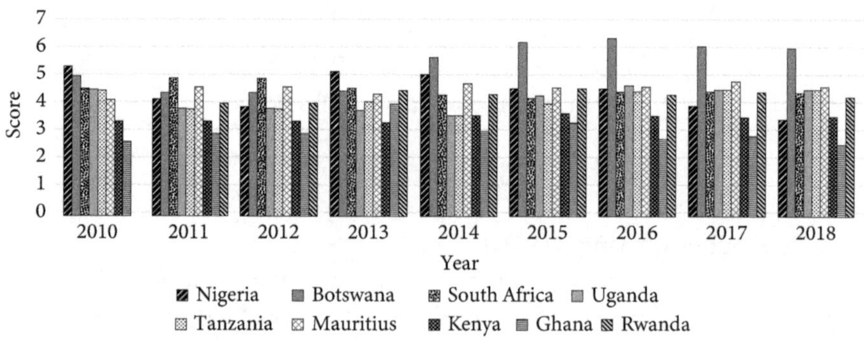

Figure 3.3 Global Competitiveness Index: Macroeconomic environment for selected SSA countries

Source: authors' compilation based on various World Economic Forum Global Competitiveness reports.

The condition of an economy's macroeconomic environment is important as it affects firms' investment decisions and the subsequent raising of funds. Some of the indicators of a macroeconomic environment include inflation, government debt-to-revenue ratio, and public debt dynamics. Thus, a conducive macroeconomic environment is likely to influence firms to make favourable investment decisions and hence the issuance of IPOs.

Figure 3.3 shows the macroeconomic environment scores in the Global Competitiveness Index for selected SSA countries where IPOs are active. Generally, at the time of the issue of IPOs, the selected countries had a conducive macroeconomic environment. For example, Nigeria, which had high macroeconomic environment scores in 2010, 2013, and 2014 at 5.43, 5.25, and 5.17, respectively, managed to raise a total of USD828 million (see Njenga et al. 2022: Table A3). This implies that there is a relationship between the macroeconomic environment and IPO issues.

3.1.2 Listed firms

There are a small number of listings across all exchanges in SSA. South Africa leads with over 250 firms, followed by Nigeria, which has slightly over 150 firms. Other countries, including Ghana, Kenya, Mauritius, Namibia, and Seychelles, have fewer than 100 firms. Further, there is low listing of foreign firms and cross-listing in SSA. Domestic firms comprise over 80% of listings in the selected SSA countries. Domestic firm listings also dominate in South Korea and Malaysia, at about 99%. However, in Singapore, the share of foreign firms listed averages about 40% for the 2010–20 period. The main reason for this is that Singapore has an extremely open trade and capital flow policy, which attracts foreign investment (see Njenga et al. 2022: Figures 4, 5, and 6).

Openness to foreign investment, including restriction on capital flows, affects foreign participation in capital markets. Using the Global Competitiveness Index's prevalence of foreign companies indicator to assess the attractiveness of foreign investment in SSA countries, we can deduce that there are friendly capital flow policies in these countries. Most SSA countries have a score of above 4 out of 7 (Figure 3.4). This indicates that, despite the efforts of SSA countries to attract foreign investment, the participation of these foreign firms in stocks/securities remains low, likely due to other factors such as the macroeconomic environment.

To boost listings, some SSA countries have set up over-the-counter markets and boards with less strict listing requirements to attract indigenous firms, which are largely informal. The Johannesburg Stock Exchange has developed the AltX (alternative exchange) board, which is a division of the Johannesburg Stock Exchange Limited. This board focuses on high-growth small and medium-sized enterprises (SMEs). The AltX, currently with 130 listed firms, offers small firms a springboard onto the main board of the Johannesburg Stock Exchange, with a clear growth path and access to capital (JSE 2022). The Nairobi Securities Exchange also developed the Growth Enterprise Market Segment (GEMS) board in 2013 for SMEs. It enables SMEs to raise substantial capital within a regulatory environment that is designed to meet their specific needs. The board also offers the SMEs flexible listing requirements in line with their growth phase (NSE 2022a). The GEMS has so far listed only five firms.

The Nigeria Exchange Group has a Growth Board that targets fast-growth firms such as SMEs operating in various sectors, including technology companies, and connects them with an extensive pool of investors. Growth Board firms enjoy a reduced fee structure, relaxed entry criteria, and reduced post-listing obligations. They also enjoy an increased turnaround time for approvals (Nigeria Exchange Group 2020). To boost listings, the Ghana Stock Exchange has established the Ghana Alternative Market (GAX) to encourage the listing of SMEs whose advisory and regulatory fees are lower than that of the main market (GSIA 2022).

Despite the efforts to boost listings of MSMEs in SSA, they remain unattractive for listing, mainly because they are associated with low returns. One of

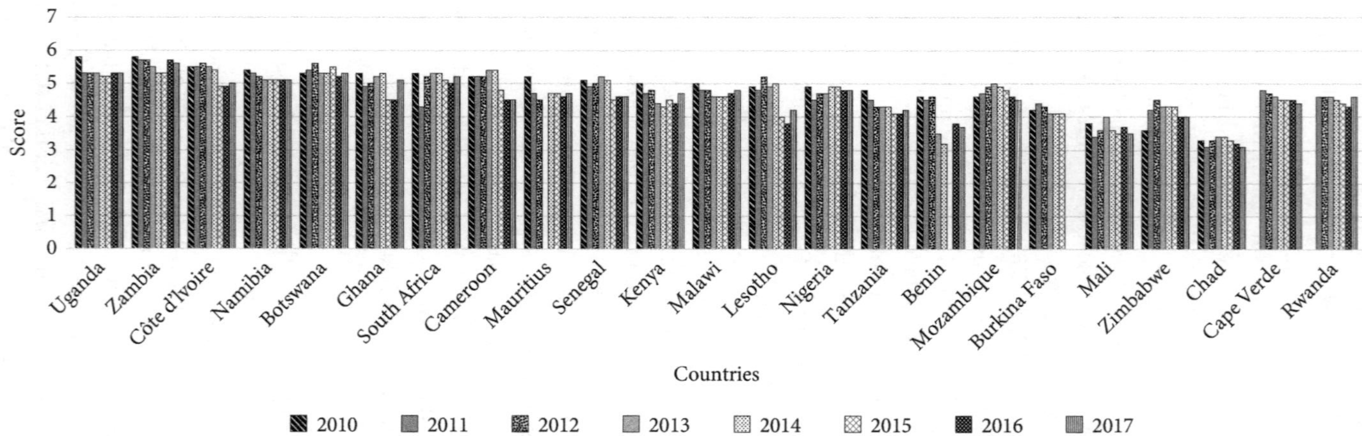

Figure 3.4 Global Competitiveness Index: Prevalence of foreign ownership of companies

Source: authors' compilation based on various World Economic Forum Global Competitiveness reports.

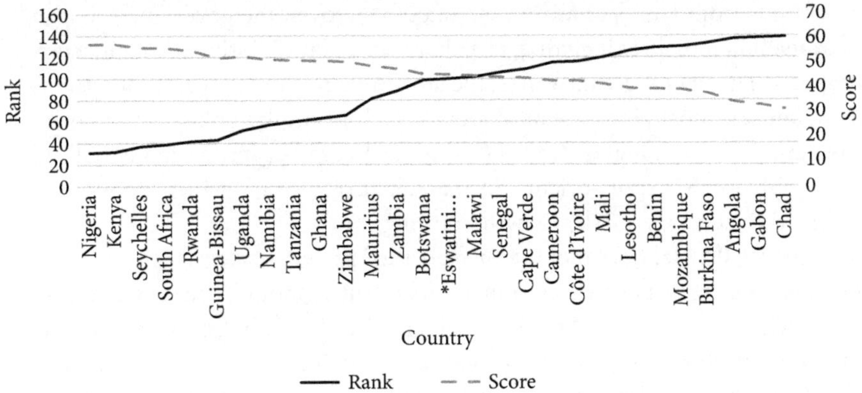

Figure 3.5 Global Competitiveness Index: Entrepreneurial culture for selected SSA countries

Source: authors' compilation based on Schwab (2019).

the constraints that MSMEs face is the entrepreneurial culture, which affects their development. The entrepreneurial culture in most SSA countries is weak. The Global Competitiveness Index report 2019 (Schwab 2019) indicates that, except for a few countries, the score for entrepreneurial culture attitudes towards entrepreneurial risk, willingness to delegate authority, growth of innovative companies, and companies embracing disruptive ideas in SSA is below 50 out of 100 (Figure 3.5). In the same period, South Korea, Singapore, and Malaysia scored 52.1, 64.2, and 70.4, respectively.

Platforms that cater to the unique requirements of MSMEs have been successful in South East Asian countries. In 2015, for example, the Malaysia Securities Commission introduced two alternative financing platforms via equity crowdfunding (ECF) and peer-to-peer lending to promote alternative avenues for raising capital. These platforms were intended to ease funding for companies or ventures. The two platforms connect issuers with traditionally untapped pools of investors through cheaper, faster, and more convenient delivery channels. The number of ECF platforms has increased to 10 and they have facilitated 106 fruitful fundraising (crowdfunding) campaigns, raising a total of MYR110.26 million through issuing equity, mainly preference shares, for 102 private limited companies (CFA Institute Research Foundation 2021).

Further, the governments of South Korea, Malaysia, and Singapore have sought to promote indigenous firms, thus making them attractive for listing. The South Korean government, under its import-substitution industrialization policy, selected indigenous industrial firms known as *Cheobols*, which are large-scale, family-run conglomerates owned by a single family (Gupta and Sharma 2014; Kim 2017) in focused industries, allowing them to buy foreign currencies and to borrow funds from banks at favourable rates. Moreover, the government put in place protection measures including tariff barriers and prohibition of manufacturing imports. Through these measures, the government wanted to give indigenous firms an opportunity to increase productivity via learning-by-doing and importation of superior technologies (Cha 2008). South Korea became an industrialized country with many export-orientated manufacturing firms, which boosted its capital market development by growth in listings.

From the 1970s, Malaysia adopted an export-led growth strategy, which focused on moving away from a primary product-dependent economy (rubber and tin) to one in which the manufacturing industry emerged as the leading growth sector. As a result, the country created robust, private-sector-driven industries starting with textiles, electrical and electronic products, rubber products, and a service-sector economy with a major focus on financial markets (Woodsome 2016).

After independence, Singapore embarked on a comprehensive programme of industrialization, with a focus on labour-intensive industries. The state's neoliberal policies, a conducive business environment, and an expansive and efficient financial sector opened it to trade and capital flows, enabling multinational enterprises to set up bases there and transfer capital, which jumpstarted manufacturing. By 1972, seven years after gaining independence, 25% of Singapore's manufacturing firms were foreign-owned or joint-venture companies, with Japan and the United States as major investors. These firms primarily exported textiles, garments, and basic electronics. However, by the 1990s, the country had transitioned into export promotion in water fabrication, pharmaceuticals, biotech research, aerospace engineering, and integrated circuit design products and had become a major logistics and financial hub in the region (Zhou 2021).

3.1.3 Equity turnover and market capitalization

Equity turnover in selected SSA and Asian countries for the 2010–20 period is given in Figure 3.6.

In SSA countries, South Africa ranks first, with an average turnover of 74%. Other countries, such as Namibia, Ghana, Nigeria, Kenya, and Mauritius, have a turnover of below 50%. South Korea has an average turnover of about 140%, which is higher than that of Singapore and Malaysia, at 74 and 43%, respectively. Except for Nigeria and Kenya, which have a substantive proportion of foreign investors, there is generally a low proportion of foreign investors in the trading of securities in most SSA countries (see Njenga et al. 2022: Figure 10).

The trading of equities affects market capitalization, which is a measure of the size of the stock market. South Africa has a huge market capitalization of above 200%, which is higher than that of Singapore, Malaysia, and South Korea. Other SSA countries have a market capitalization of below 100% (Figure 3.7).

Exchanges in SSA are gradually adopting the electronic systems of trading, clearance, and settlement (Table 3.A1 in the appendix). This has enhanced the

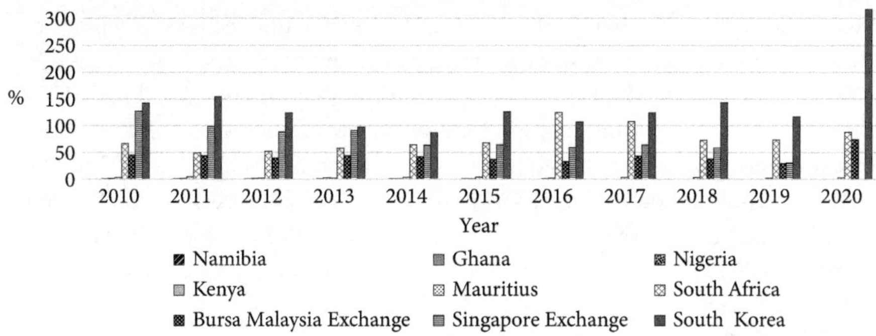

Figure 3.6 Equity turnover (% of GDP) in selected SSA and Asian countries
Source: authors' compilation based on data from World Bank (2024).

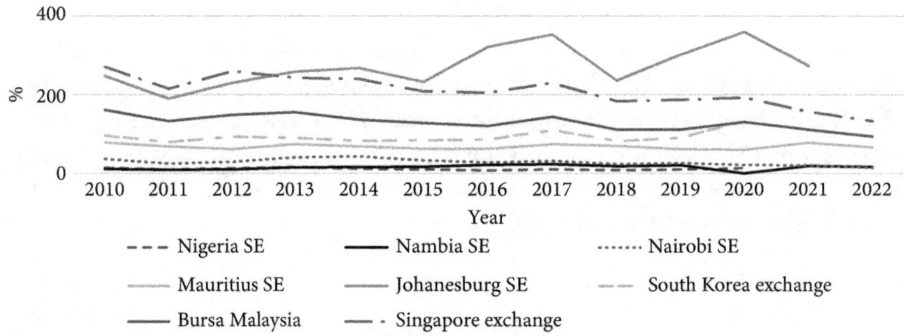

Figure 3.7 Market capitalization (% of GDP) in selected SSA and Asian countries
Source: authors' compilation based on data from World Bank (2024).

transparency and efficiency in the trading of securities, with most SSA countries reducing their settlement cycles after trade from a T + 5 (settlement after five business days) to a T + 3 basis (JSE 2016; NSE 2022b). There are, however, a few exchanges, such as the Rwanda Stock Exchange and Maseru Securities Exchange in Lesotho, which trade manually and/or use manual clearing and settlement (Maseru Securities Market 2022; Rwanda Stock Exchange 2022). Similarly, several exchanges do not have a central depository system. In South Korea, Malaysia, and Singapore, the exchanges are fully automated, making the clearing and settlement of transactions two days after the trade date, that is T + 2 (Bursa Malaysia 2022; Korea Exchange 2022; Singapore Exchange 2022).

The adoption of technology has helped to lower transaction costs in many exchanges in SSA. However, the transaction costs in most SSA exchanges are relatively high when compared with the transaction costs in developed and emerging markets around the world. In some exchanges, such as the *Bourse Régionale des Valeurs Mobilières* (BRVM), which serves the francophone countries in West

Africa, and the Stock Exchange of Mauritius, the transaction fee is a percentage of the entire transaction value (except for the government securities in Mauritius). At the Stock Exchange of Mauritius, the fees for a transaction not exceeding MUR3 million is 1.25%, decreasing to 0.9% for any transaction above MUR10 million. However, there is no upper limit for the fees paid in a transaction at the BRVM. The transaction commission to the BRVM and to the Central Depository/Settlement Bank (DC/BR) is 0.3% of the transaction amount (BRVM 2022; Stock Exchange of Mauritius 2022).

3.1.4 Rights issues

Rights issues are an important means through which listed firms raise equity capital by giving existing shareholders an opportunity to buy additional new shares. Thus, a firm can raise additional capital to expand its operations much more cheaply than it would if it used debt capital. Capital increase from rights issues enhance a firm's reputation and strengthen its financial structure (Corporate Finance Institute 2020). There are a few rights issues in SSA countries. Nigeria is the leader in rights issues, followed by Mauritius and Uganda (see Njenga et al. 2022: Figure 12). As in the case of IPOs, the macroeconomic environment can affect rights issues. This compares unfavourably with Malaysia, which had 650 rights issues between 2010 and 2019.

3.2 Bonds market

The development of the local debt capital markets in SSA is of significant interest given the relatively low levels of bank credit that are available to the private sector. Domestic credit to the private sector is estimated to range between 17 and 54% of GDP on average for the key SSA economies, compared to well over 100% of GDP in developed capital markets (World Bank 2021). In most SSA countries, however, corporate bonds constitute a tiny part of the bond markets. In Kenya, for example, treasury bonds continue to dominate the market at 99%. It is only in South Africa and Nigeria that the corporate bonds market dominates in terms of the number of issuances. The public-sector bonds listed in many SSA countries dominate mainly because these countries do not have a vibrant private sector, which is dominated by very few large private corporations and many MSMEs in the informal sector (Soumare et al. 2021).

The total capital raised from corporate bonds in SSA in the 2011–19 period was US$1.2 billion. In some countries, no corporate bonds were issued (see Njenga et al. 2022: Table A5). About 85% of corporate bonds listed on the SSA capital markets have an average maturity of 11 years, while 81% of public bonds have an average maturity of about 8 years. Only 9 countries in SSA issue long-term bonds (bonds with a maturity of more than 20 years) in the domestic market. These are South Africa, Nigeria, Kenya, Mauritius, Angola, Botswana, Ghana, Namibia, and Tanzania. This can be explained by the fact that these countries have a larger pool of investors than their counterparts in SSA. These countries also have better macroeconomic fundamentals and a bigger GDP. However, they are also limited by a lack of depth in the local capital markets and a benchmark yield curve that can provide pricing signals to potential corporate issuers, which impedes the development of corporate bond markets (Soumare et al. 2021).

As most SSA countries do not have well-established and liquid capital markets, external debt has become the only source of capital. External debt is driven by low revenues and high expenditure needs, particularly in infrastructure development. The countries in SSA that have issued Eurobonds on the international capital markets include South Africa, Nigeria, Angola, Ethiopia, Zambia, Ghana, Kenya, Senegal, Gabon, Cameroon, Mozambique, Namibia, Rwanda, and Seychelles (see Njenga et al. 2022: Table A6). In the 2011–19 period, over US$391.7 billion was raised from non-local currency public bonds, out of which US$120 billion were Eurobond issues, for which the largest issuers were South Africa and Nigeria. The appetite for Eurobonds has been supported by sustained GDP growth over the past two decades in most SSA countries; portfolio diversification strategies in mature capital markets, where investors are looking for additional yields; and prolonged low global interest rates (Van der Wansem et al. 2019; Soumare et al. 2021). In addition, the lack of conditionalities, such as those imposed by the International Monetary Fund (IMF), the World Bank, and other bilateral and multilateral lenders, and the drive to signal financial strength are the two pull-factors that make Eurobond funding a source of capital for many SSA countries. However, the Eurobonds issued by SSA countries in the international markets attract relatively high interest rates when compared to concessional financing and the concentrated principal payments at maturity. The average coupon rate varies from 5% in Mozambique to 10.14% in Zambia (Cbonds 2021; Soumare et al. 2021).

In addition to the relatively high interest rates, other indirect fees, such as the hedging cost and cost-of-carry, are added to the direct costs of the Eurobonds. All of these are considered when evaluating the total cost of borrowing from the international markets. As a result, a few SSA countries have defaulted while others are experiencing difficulties in servicing foreign currency denominated debt. In December 2020, 6 countries in SSA were in debt distress while 14 others were at a high risk of debt distress (AfDB 2021). This is particularly profound in rentier states, such as Zambia and Angola, where volatile commodity prices and depreciation in local currencies have exacerbated the balance-of-payment deficits and reduced government revenues, increasing the budget deficits. Since the onset of the COVID-19 pandemic, Zambia has been unable to make a $42.5 million Eurobond repayment, becoming the first SSA economy to default on its debt (Soumare et al.

2021). Other emerging risk factors include fast-growing interest expenses as a share of government revenue, debt rollover risks due to shorter debt maturities, narrowing of the differential between real interest rates and GDP growth, debt collateralization with limited transparency, and expanding contingent liabilities (AfDB 2021).

In Asia, South Korea has one of the largest bond markets (see Njenga et al. 2022: Table 3). All fixed-income instruments in South Korea are available to both local and foreign investors. In South Korea, a corporate bond issuer is rated by at least two credit-rating agencies before the issue of bonds at the South Korean exchange. The treasury bonds are issued on a regular basis with maturities of 3, 5, and 10 years, with the 3-year bond being the most liquid (Cbonds 2022). Between 2010 and 2020, the number of bonds listed in South Korea grew from 3,764 to 4,951 bonds. The capital raised from the bonds listed also grew from US$985.6 billion in 2010 to US$1.04 trillion in 2020 (Korea Exchange 2021).

The Singapore Exchange is also Asia's most internationally connected exchange, with over 40% of listed firms and over 80% of listed bonds originating from outside the country (Singapore Exchange 2021). Singapore's bond market has become one of the most developed and fastest growing in Asia. Between 2010 and 2020, the number of bonds listed in Singapore grew from 164 to 1,032. The capital raised from the bonds listed also grew from US$72.9 billion in 2010 to US$452.1 billion in 2020. The bond market is made up of Singapore Government Securities, quasi-government bonds, corporate bonds, and structured securities. The bond market is also fully accessible to all issuers and investors across the globe, with no hedging restrictions, capital controls, or withholding taxes, making the bond market's profile international in nature, with foreign countries and firms accounting for more than 25% of bond issuances. The state, through its regulatory agencies, also fine-tuned the bond listing requirements in 2009 to qualify high-grade securities issued by foreign entities as regulatory liquid assets. Since then, there has been an increase in issuances by well-established AAA-rated foreign issuers such as the International Bank for Reconstruction and Development, African Development Bank, and International Finance Corp (Monetary Authority of Singapore 2021).

The continuous measures by the Malaysian government and regulatory authorities have positioned Malaysia as a hub for Islamic financial market activities, particularly in sukuk (CFA Institute Research Foundation 2021). Between 2010 and 2020, the number of bonds listed in Malaysia grew from 19 to 23. The capital raised from the bonds listed also grew from US$27.7 billion in 2010 to US$32.8 billion in 2019. The Malaysian bond market is one of the most developed and dynamic bond markets in the region, with its domestic market share of the total global sukuk issuances accounting for 40.6% of the total US$132.2 billion sukuk issuances in 2020 (IIFM 2021).

4. Conclusions and policy implications

Most SSA countries recognize the importance of local capital markets and have made efforts to develop them. However, these efforts have not fully reaped the expected benefits from these markets, particularly in mobilization of the substantial domestic savings necessary to facilitate high economic growth in these countries. To identify what could be done to raise domestic savings in SSA through the capital markets, this chapter explored two areas: (i) the evolution, structure, and products and (ii) the performance of capital markets in SSA countries. The key findings indicate that

- although there is a legal and regulatory framework that governs capital markets in most SSA countries, uncertainty in ensuring the stability of the markets remains;
- a conducive macroeconomic environment is critical as it influences firms' investment decisions, hence the raising of capital through IPOs and rights issues;
- MSMEs in SSA countries remain unattractive for listing due to constraints such as a weak entrepreneurial culture;
- although there are friendly capital flow policies in most SSA countries, the participation of foreigners in the capital markets is low, likely due to other underlying factors such as the macroeconomic environment; and
- due to the presence of underdeveloped capital markets in most SSA countries, external debt has become the only source of capital, and this is likely to plunge the countries into external debt crises because of high interest rates and other associated indirect fees, especially on Eurobonds.

Several interventions could support developing capital markets in SSA countries to facilitate the mobilization of domestic savings:

- The stability of the capital markets is crucial for building investor confidence. This calls for strict enforcement of the enacted laws, regulations, and rules governing capital markets. Enhancing the professionalism of public officers could strengthen regulatory oversight;
- A continuous, stable, and conducive macroeconomic environment will incentivize investments, thus spurring growth of the capital markets. Some of the indicators of a macroeconomic environment include inflation, government debt-to-revenue ratio, and public debt dynamics;
- The development and implementation of focused policies for supporting MSMEs are necessary to ameliorate constraints such as the weak

entrepreneurial culture, which hinders their growth and thus their attractiveness for listing. Entrepreneurial culture entails values, beliefs, mindsets, and behaviour that promote successful businesses;

- Reflecting on prudent and comprehensive policies that support the development of capital markets is crucial and includes timely review of such policies; and
- Designing effective approaches to exploit the anticipated benefits from trade agreements such as the African Continental Free Trade Area is key to growing the vibrant private sector necessary to support the development of capital markets in SSA countries.

Appendix

Table 3.A1 Infrastructural and institutional development indicators in SSA exchanges

Country	Market regulator	Government law	Exchange control	Clearing and settlement	Settlement cycle	International custodian	Foreign participation	Trading system	Central depository	Trading days	Reporting system
Southern Africa											
South Africa	Yes	Yes	None	Electronic	T + 3	Yes	Yes	Electronic	Yes	5	International
Botswana	Yes	Yes	None	Electronic	T + 3	Yes	Yes	Electronic	Yes	5	International
Zimbabwe	Yes	Yes	None	Electronic	T + 3	Yes	Yes	Electronic	None	5	International
Namibia	Yes	Yes	None	Electronic	T + 5	Yes	Yes	Electronic	Yes	5	International
Eswatini	Yes	Yes	None	Electronic	T + 5	Yes	Yes	Electronic	Yes	5	International
Zambia	Yes	Yes	None	Electronic	T + 3	Yes	Yes	Electronic	Yes	5	International
Lesotho	Yes	Yes	None	Electronic	T + 2	No	Yes	Manual	Yes	5	International
Malawi	Yes	Yes	None	Electronic	T + 5	Yes	Yes	Electronic	Yes	5	International
Mozambique	Yes	Yes	None	Electronic	T + 3	Yes	Yes	Electronic	Yes	5	International
Angola	Yes	Yes	None	Electronic	T + 2	No	Yes	Electronic	Yes	5	International
Eastern Africa											
Kenya	Yes	Yes	None	Electronic	T + 3	Yes	Yes	Electronic	Yes	5	International
Tanzania	Yes	Yes	None	Electronic	T + 3	Yes	Yes	Electronic	Yes	5	International

Continued

Table 3.A1 *Continued*

Country	Market regulator	Government law	Exchange control	Clearing and settlement	Settlement cycle	International custodian	Foreign participation	Trading system	Central depository	Trading days	Reporting system
Uganda	Yes	Yes	None	Electronic	T + 3	Yes	Yes	Electronic	Yes	5	International
Mauritius	Yes	Yes	None	Electronic	T + 3	Yes	Yes	Electronic	Yes	5	International
Rwanda	Yes	Yes	None	Electronic	T + 2	Yes	Yes	Manual	Yes	5	International
Somalia	N/A	N/A	N/A	N/A	N/A	N/A	N/A	N/A	N/A	N/A	N/A
Seychelles	Yes	Yes	None	Electronic	T + 3	Yes	Yes	Electronic	Yes	5	International
West Africa											
Nigeria	Yes	Yes	None	Electronic	T + 3	Yes	Yes	Electronic	Yes	5	International
Ghana	Yes	Yes	None	Electronic	T + 3	Yes	Yes	Electronic	Yes	5	International
Côte d'Ivoire	Yes	Yes	Yes	Electronic	T + 3	Yes	Yes	Electronic	Yes	5	Local
Cape Verde	Yes	Yes	None	Electronic	T + 3	Yes	Yes	Electronic	Yes	5	Local
Gabon	Yes	Yes	Yes	Electronic	T + 3	Yes	Yes	Electronic	Yes	5	International

Source: authors' compilation based on data from the various stock exchanges in SSA.

References

African Capacity Building Foundation (2016). 'Infrastructure Development and Financing in Sub-Saharan Africa: Toward a Framework for Capacity Enhancement'. Africa Portal, 1 January. Available at: https://www.africaportal.org/publications/infrastructure-development-and-financing-in-sub-saharan-africa-toward-a-framework-for-capacity-enhancement (accessed September 2022).

AfDB (African Development Bank Group) (2021). 'African Economic Outlook 2021. From Debt Resolution to Growth: The Road Ahead from Africa. African Development Bank', 12 March. Available at: https://www.afdb.org/en/documents/african-economic-outlook-2021 (accessed September 2022).

Africa Union (2015). 'Goals and Priority Areas of Agenda 2063'. Available at: https://au.int/en/agenda2063/goals (accessed September 2022).

Allen, F., I. Otchere, and L.W. Senbet (2011). 'African Financial Systems: A Review'. *Review of Development Finance*, 1(2): 79–113. https://doi.org/10.1016/j.rdf.2011.03.003.

ASEA (African Securities Exchanges Association) (2021a). 'Membership. African Securities Exchanges Association—the Premier Association of 25 Securities Exchanges in Africa'. Available at: https://african-exchanges.org/membership (accessed September 2022).

ASEA (2021b). 'The African Exchanges Linkage Project (AELP): Phase 1'. Available at: https://africanexchangeslink.com/wp-content/uploads/2021/08/brochure210420_AELP_updated_FINAL-compressed.pdf (accessed September 2022).

BRVM (*Bourse Régionale des Valeurs Mobilières*) (2022). 'What Are the Applicable Fees?' Available at: https://www.brvm.org/en/what-are-applicable-fees# (accessed September 2022).

Bursa Malaysia (2022). 'Trading Procedures'. Available at: https://www.bursamalaysia.com/trade/trading_resources/equities/trading_procedures (accessed September 2022).

Calderón, C., and A. G. Zeufack (2020). 'Borrow with Sorrow? The Changing Risk Profile of Sub-Saharan Africa's Debt'. Policy Research Working Paper 9137. Washington, DC: World Bank. Available at: http://documents1.worldbank.org/curated/en/370721580415352349/pdf/Borrow-with-Sorrow-The-Changing-Risk-Profile-of-Sub-Saharan-Africas-Debt.pdf (accessed September 2022).

Capital Markets Authority (2020). *Quarterly Statistical Bulletin December 45/2020*. Nairobi: Capital Markets Authority.

Cbonds (2021). 'Africa: Domestic and International Bond Search'. Cbonds.com—Financial Market Data. Available at: https://cbonds.com/bonds (accessed September 2022).

Cbonds (2022). 'Republic of Korea Bonds'. Available at: https://cbonds.com/country/Korea-bond (accessed September 2022).

CFA Institute Research Foundation (2021). 'Capital Markets: Malaysia'. Available at: rfbr-apac-capital-markets-malaysia.ashx (cfainstitute.org) (accessed September 2022).

Cha, M. S. (2008). 'The Economic History of Korea'. In R. Whaples (ed.), *EH.Net Encyclopedia*. Available at: https://eh.net/encyclopedia/the-economic-history-of-korea (accessed September 2022).

Chimpango, B. W. (2019). 'The Development of African Capital Markets: A Legal and Institutional Approach'. PhD thesis. Nottingham: Nottingham Trent University. Available at: https://core.ac.uk/download/pdf/30624139.pdf (accessed September 2022).

Corporate Finance Institute (2020). 'Rights Issue'. Available at: https://corporatefinanceinstitute.com/resources/knowledge/finance/rights-issue (accessed September 2022).

Fama, E. F. (2021). 'Efficient Capital Markets a Review of Theory and Empirical Work'. In E. F. Fama (ed.), *The Fama Portfolio*, 76–121. Chicago, IL: University of Chicago Press. https://doi.org/10.7208/9780226426983-007.

Gakunu, P. (2007). 'Reforming the Financial System in Sub-Saharan Africa: The (Long) Way Ahead'. *Finance & Bien Commun*, 3(28–29): 139–46. Available at: https://www.cairn.info/revue-finance-et-bien-commun-2007-3-page-139.htm (accessed 18 December 2024).

GSIA (Ghana Securities Industry Association) (2022). 'Custodian Banks'. Available at: https://gsiaonline.org/members/13/0 (accessed September 2022).

Gupta, P., and A. M. Sharma (2014). 'A Study of the Impact of Corporate Governance Practices on Firm Performance in Indian and South Korean Companies'. *Procedia—Social and Behavioral Sciences*, 133: 4–11.

Haque, F., T .G. Arun, and C. Kirkpatrick (2008). 'Corporate Governance and Capital Markets: a Conceptual Framework'. *Corporate Ownership and Control*, 5(2): 264–76. Available at: https://papers.ssrn.com/sol3/papers.cfm?abstract_id=3037927 (accessed September 2022).

IIFM (International Islamic Financial Market) (2021). *IIFM Sukuk Report 2021 (10th Edition)*. Available at: https://www.iifm.net/sukuk-reports (accessed September 2022).

JSE (Johannesburg Stock Exchange) (2016). 'Johannesburg Stock Exchange Switches to T+3 Settlement Cycle on 11 July'. African Markets, 22 June. Available at: https://www.african-markets.com/en/stock-markets/jse/johannesburg-stock-exchange-switches-to-t-3-settlement-cycle-on-11-july (accessed September 2022).

JSE (2021). 'History & Company Overview'. Available at https://www.jse.co.za/our-business/history-%26-company-overview (accessed September 2022).

JSE (2022). 'Firms Listed on AltX. Johannesburg Stock Exchange (JSE)'. Available at: https://www.jse.co.za/altx-small-cap-trading-fee (accessed September 2022).

Karekwaivenani, G. (2003). 'A History of the Rhodesian Stock Exchange: The Formative Years, 1946–1952'. Available at: https://ir.uz.ac.zw/jspui/bitstream/10646/507/1/02-Kare.pdf (accessed September 2022).

Kim, J. (2017). 'Corporate Financial Structure of South Korea after Asian Financial Crisis: The Chaebol Experience'. *Journal of Economic Structures*, 6(1): 1–14.

Kodongo, O., and K. Ojah (2016). 'Does Infrastructure Really Explain Economic Growth in Sub-Saharan Africa?' *Review of Development Finance*, 6(2): 105–25. Available at: https://www.sciencedirect.com/science/article/pii/S1879933716301798 (accessed 18 December 2024).

Korea Exchange (2021). 'KOSDAQ Market'. Global KRX. Available at: https://global.krx.co.kr/contents/GLB/02/0201/0201010301/GLB0201010301.jsp (accessed 9 February 2021).

Korea Exchange (2022). 'Basic Facts about Trading System: General Procedures of Trading'. Global KRX. Available at: https://global.krx.co.kr/contents/GLB/06/0602/0602010201/GLB0602010201.jsp#826f2bceb71bdd795d4f782fda605cb1=1 (accessed September 2022).

Laeven, L. (2014). 'The Development of Local Capital Markets: Rationale and Challenges'. IMF Working Paper 2014/234. Available at: https://www.imf.org/en/Publications/WP/Issues/2016/12/31/The-Development-of-Local-Capital-Markets-Rationale-and-Challenges-42551 (accessed September 2022).

Lartey, E. K. (2013). 'Remittances, Investment, and Growth in Sub-Saharan Africa'. *Journal of International Trade and Economic Development*, 22(7): 1038–58. https://doi.org/10.1080/09638199.2011.632692.

Mahdi, S (2008). 'The Role of Financial Intermediaries in Capital Market'. *Zagreb International Review of Economics and Business*, 11(1): 97–109.

Maseru Securities Market (2019). 'Background. URL'. Available at: https://www.msm.org.ls/background (accessed September 2022).

Maseru Securities Market (2022). 'Trading Method'. Available at: https://www.msm.org.ls/trading-method (accessed September 2022).

Monetary Authority of Singapore (2021). 'Capital Markets'. Available at: https://www.mas.gov.sg/regulation/capital-markets (accessed September 2022).

Nega, B., and G. Schneider (2011). 'International Financial Institutions and Democracy in Africa: The Case for Political Conditionality and Economic Unconditionality'. *Journal of Economic Issues*, 45(2): 421–30. https://doi.org/10.2753/JEI0021-3624450219.

Nigeria Exchange Group (2019). 'About Us'. Available at: https://ngxgroup.com/about-us (accessed September 2022).

Nigeria Exchange Group (2020). 'Growth Board'. Available at: https://ngxgroup.com/exchange/raise-capital/growth-board (accessed September 2022).

Njenga, G., J. Machagua, and S. Gachanja (2022). 'Capital Markets in Sub-Saharan Africa'. WIDER Working Paper Series 2022/112. Helsinki: United Nations University-World Institute for Public Policy and Analysis (UNU-WIDER). https://doi.org/10.35188/UNU-WIDER/2022/246-1.

Nnyanzi, J. B., J. M. Bbale, and B. Yawe (2018). 'Capital Markets and Growth in Selected Sub-Saharan African Countries: A Sectoral Analysis'. ResearchGate, September. Available at: https://www.researchgate.net/publication/327745936_CAPITAL_MARKETS_AND_GROWTH_IN_SELECTED_SUBSAHARAN_AFRICAN_COUNTRIES_A_SECTORAL_ANALYSIS (accessed March 2021).

NSE (Nairobi Securities Exchange) (2013). 'History of NSE'. Available at: https://www.nse.co.ke/our-story (accessed September 2022).

NSE (2021). 'Annual Reports'. Available at: https://www.nse.co.ke/annual-reports (accessed September 2022).

NSE (2022a). 'Growth Enterprise Market Segment'. Available at: https://www.nse.co.ke/growth-enterprise-market-segment (accessed September 2022).

NSE (2022b). 'Our Story'. Available at: https://www.nse.co.ke/our-story (accessed September 2022).

Osano, E. (2016). 'Five Reasons Why Capital Markets Matter in Africa'. FSD Africa. Available at: https://www.fsdafrica.org/news/five-reasons-why-capital-markets-matter-in-africa (accessed September 2022).

PwC (PricewaterhouseCoopers) (2019). '2019 Africa Capital Markets Watch'. Available at: https://www.pwc.com/ng/en/assets/pdf/africa-capital-markets-watch-2019.pdf (accessed September 2022).

PwC (2021). 'Africa Capital Markets Watch 2020'. Available at: https://www.pwc.co.za/en/publications/africa-capital-markets-watch.html (accessed September 2022).

Raubenheimer, H. (ed.) (2019). 'African Capital Markets: Challenges and Opportunities'. CFA Institute Research Foundation Brief. Available at: https://rpc.cfainstitute.org/sites/default/files/-/media/documents/article/rf-brief/rf-african-capital-markets.pdf (accessed September 2022).

Rwanda Stock Exchange (2022). 'Rwanda Stock Exchange Trading System'. Available at: https://www.rse.rw/product-and-services/Trading-System (accessed September 2022).

SAHO (South African History Online) (2021). 'The Johannesburg Stock Exchange Is Established'. Available at: https://www.sahistory.org.za/dated-event/johannesburg-stock-exchange-established (accessed September 2022).

Samaha, K., K. Dahawy, K. Hussainey, and P. Stapleton (2012). 'The Extent of Corporate Governance Disclosure and Its Determinants in a Developing Market: The Case of Egypt'. *Advances in Accounting*, 28(1): 168–78.

Schwab, K. (ed.) (2018). *The Global Competitiveness Report 2018*. Geneva: World Economic Forum.

Schwab, K. (ed.) (2019). *The Global Competitiveness Report 2019*. Geneva: World Economic Forum.

Securities Commission of Malaysia (2001). 'Capital Market Masterplan: Malaysia'. Available at: https://www.sc.com.my/resources/publications-and-research/capital-market-masterplan-1 (accessed September 2022).

Singapore Exchange (2021). 'Annual Reports and Shareholders' Meetings'. Available at: https://investorrelations.sgx.com/financial-information/annual-reports (accessed September 2022).

Singapore Exchange (2022). 'Clearing Information at Singapore Exchange'. Available at: https://www.sgx.com/securities/clearing-information (accessed September 2022).

Singh, R. A., and Z. A. Yusof (2005). 'Development of the Capital Market in Malaysia'. In D. Vandenbrink and D. Hew (eds), *Capital Markets in Asia: Changing Roles for Economic Development*. Tokyo: Tokyo Club Foundation for Global Studies.

Somali Stock Exchange (2022). 'About Us'. Available at: https://www.sse.so/about-us (accessed September 2022).

Soumare, I., D. Kanga, J. Tyson, and S. Raga (2021). 'Capital Market Development in Sub-Saharan Africa: Progress, Challenges, and Innovations'. ODI Research Series for Financial Development in Africa. Working Paper 2. Available at: https://cdn.odi.org/media/documents/ODI_Working_Paper_2_Capital_markets_development_in_SSA_FINAL_clean.pdf (accessed September 2022).

Stock Exchange of Mauritius (2022). 'Regulations and Governance: Transaction Fees'. Available at: https://www.stockexchangeofmauritius.com/regulations-governance/transaction-fees (accessed September 2022).

Van der Wansem, P. B., L. Jessen, and D. Rivetti (2019). 'Issuing International Bonds: A Guidance Note'. MTI Global Practice Discussion Paper 13. Washington, DC: World Bank. Available at: https://openknowledge.worldbank.org/handle/10986/31569 (accessed September 2022).

Woodsome, J. (2016). 'Malaysia's Capital Market Masterplan, 2001–2010: A Case Study'. Milken Institute Center for Financial Markets Working Paper, February. Available at: https://milkeninstitute.org/sites/default/files/reports-pdf/Malaysia-Case-Study-FORMATTED.pdf (accessed September 2022).

World Bank (2021). 'World Development Indicators. Personal Remittances Received (Current US $): Sub-Saharan Africa'. Available at: https://data.worldbank.org/indicator/BX.TRF.PWKR.CD.DT?locations=ZG (accessed September 2022).

World Bank (2024). 'World Development Indicators'. Available at: https://databank.worldbank.org/source/world-development-indicators (accessed April 2024).

WFE (World Federation of Exchanges) (2021). 'Korea Exchange- Bonds Market'. Available at: https://statistics.world-exchanges.org/ReportGenerator/Generator (accessed September 2022).

Zhou, P. (2021). 'The History of Singapore's Economic Development'. Available at: https://www.thoughtco.com/singapores-economic-development-1434565 (accessed September 2022).

4

Old-age savings in sub-Saharan Africa

Owen Nyang'oro and Githinji Njenga

1. Introduction

Resource mobilization and social protection are a major concern in developing countries. Low levels of economic development in these countries call for mobilization of resources to finance development activities so as to facilitate production and improve living standards. Social pensions are important in providing social protection for the elderly by ensuring they have some level of basic income, redistributing income among generations, and providing insurance to the elderly (Juergens and Galvani 2020). Social protection is important for meeting the 2030 Agenda for Sustainable Development, although over 50% of the world's population is without any social protection (Durán-Valverde et al. 2019; ILO 2021), which raises policy concerns. Pensions for the elderly are the most common form of social protection in the world, with 77.5% of people above retirement age receiving some form of old-age pension (ILO 2021).

Social old-age pensions provide an alternative source of income for elderly people not covered by contributory schemes (World Bank 2018). In sub-Saharan Africa (SSA), however, not everyone who qualifies is covered by an old-age pension, mainly because of the contributory nature of most pension schemes in the region. Only 32.5% of the working-age population contribute to a pension scheme globally, and the labour force contribution is 53.7% globally compared with only 6.1 and 8.9%, respectively in SSA (ILO 2021).

Social pension schemes in SSA are characterized by low coverage and high costs and are regressive, focusing mainly on formal sector employees (Stewart and Yermo 2009; Sy 2017; Guven 2019). The contributory model of the social safety net excludes informal workers, making it unsuccessful in most developing countries due to the large size of their informal economies (World Bank 2019b; ILO 2021)—for instance, in Africa, the informal economies are large and heterogeneous (Guven 2019). It is estimated that fewer than 10% of the older population in SSA have a contributory pension, as the majority of workers are in the informal sector or agriculture and are not covered by pension schemes (Stewart and Yermo 2009; ILO 2010a; Bloom and McKinnon 2013; Dorfman 2015). People

Owen Nyang'oro and Githinji Njenga, *Old-age savings in sub-Saharan Africa*. In: *The Domestic Savings Shortfall in Sub-Saharan Africa*. Edited by: Rose Ngugi and Kunal Sen, Oxford University Press. © UNU-WIDER (2025).
DOI: 10.1093/oso/9780198932482.003.0004

in the informal sector are highly susceptible to shocks, both local and global, the effects of which are greater for the older population (see Alfers et al. 2021).

The need for improved social protection mechanisms is dictated by the demographic structures in these economies; where the majority of the population are young with low dependency ratios, there is a small but increasing ageing population, and fertility rates are high. Most of these countries have multigenerational households, with active members of the household being responsible for the care of extended family members, particularly the young and the old. Most older people depend on family support systems[1] due to the scarcity of work opportunities and the limited availability of pensions (ILO 2017, 2018; Juergens and Galvani 2020), while at the same time, household composition is gradually changing to smaller families and household types (United Nations 2020), increasing household dependency levels. The number of poor older people in developing countries is also projected to increase (ILO 2010a) as the population structure changes, further complicating the need for social support. In 2010, the Yaoundé Tripartite Declaration committed African countries to achieving a secure minimum income for the elderly through old-age pensions;[2] however, this has been elusive.

The state of the pension sector and the need to offer adequate social protection to the elderly in SSA calls for reforms to the pension system. Early reforms to the pension sector focused on pension privatization, motivated by policy advice proposed by the World Bank in 1994. The initial success of the adoption of a multi-pillar pension system was short-lived as most countries faced a myriad of challenges such as increased fiscal burdens and a decline in active contributors; hence falling short of meeting the objectives with regard to social pensions, leading to a reversal of pension reforms in some countries (Gill et al. 2004). The approach also failed to meet the needs of those in informal/temporary work (Bloom and McKinnon 2013). A different approach to reforms by the International Labour Organization (ILO), based on parametric reforms and involving minor changes to the existing pension system rather than an overhaul of the entire system, has led to favourable outcomes (Ortiz et al. 2018). This has ensured that the pension system maintains the core objective of meeting the welfare needs of people in old age. SSA countries can learn from these experiences when reforming their pension systems, although they are starting from a worse position, especially as regards meeting the needs of the older population given their social structures and economic conditions.

[1] This may not be the case with older people living in informal urban settlements, who are more likely to live as single-person households (Ezeh et al. 2006).

[2] The Yaoundé Tripartite Declaration on the Implementation of the Social Protection Floor was adopted on 8 October 2010 at the Second African Decent Work Symposium, held in Yaoundé, Cameroon. African member states committed 'to adopt the principles, main elements and practical aspects of the Social Protection Floor, in synergy with the AU Social Policy Framework for Africa' (ILO 2010b).

Pension funds are savings that provide the main source of livelihood for the elderly, enabling them to meet basic needs by providing income security, addressing social inequality, consumption smoothing, insurance (or risk-sharing), poverty relief, redistribution, and addressing social inequality (Stewart and Yermo 2009; ILO 2017; Juergens and Galvani 2020). Low and uncertain incomes limit access to private insurance and savings products (Bloom and McKinnon 2013), leaving the elderly vulnerable. Poverty rates tend to be higher in elderly-headed households and among elderly people with dependants compared with the average population. Pension programmes lead to significant reductions in the poverty gap ratio among the elderly (Kakwani and Subbarao 2005) and are also important in protecting against the socio-economic risks and vulnerabilities associated with older age (Juergens and Galvani 2020). Given the multigenerational nature of households, pensions received by older people are shared with secondary beneficiaries (Casey and McKinnon 2009).

The extent of the need for social protection in SSA among the elderly can be inferred from the pensions received among this category of the population. In SSA, 19.8% of the population above statutory pensionable age receive a pension (ILO 2021), the lowest proportion among all regions. Inferring from household data in Kenya, the 2015–16 Kenya Integrated Household Budget Survey reported that 17.4% of households received a regular income from a pension as another source of income, with the monthly average pension being KES2,106 (approximately US$20). The 2021 Kenya Financial Access Household Survey found that 10.6% of the adult population (about 2.9 million) used pension schemes. The main barriers to participation in pension schemes in Kenya were unaffordability (48.7%) and lack of knowledge about pensions (21.3%) (FinAccess 2021). In Zambia, the Finscope Survey reported that the pensions uptake was at 8.2% in 2020 (Bank of Zambia 2020). The main barriers to the use of pension services identified in Zambia were unemployment (66.6%) and a lack of money to contribute (12.2%). In Uganda, the pension coverage is 18% of the working population (URBRA 2021).

The challenge in most developing countries is the low rate of savings, which may be attributed to a number of factors, such as levels of financial literacy, inadequate financial inclusion in some countries, and huge numbers of informal-sector workers, coupled with low income levels and high dependency rates. Enhancing the provision of pension services as a way of providing support in old age may also be good for the development of these economies. More developed countries are likely to have high social protection benefits (see Nyang'oro and Njenga 2022: Figure 4.1), but a more developed pension system may also spur economic development through the provision of financing for infrastructure development. Given the dynamics of SSA countries, pension funds can play a major role in providing social protection and mobilizing much-needed resources for development; however, the potential of pension funds is yet to be fully exploited.

2. Pension funds and resource mobilization

Pension funds are useful for mobilizing long-term funds to support infrastructure development (Stewart and Yermo 2009; Commonwealth Secretariat 2014; Sy 2017). SSA economies have low levels of development, characterized by inadequate or poor-quality infrastructure; hence the need to mobilize resources to finance development activities so as to facilitate production and improve living standards. Infrastructure has a direct effect on productivity and output and is an input to the production process (AfDB 2018). Infrastructure gaps can be addressed by governments through the mobilization of domestic and external financing resources. The annual infrastructure funding gap in Africa is estimated between US$68 billion and US$108 billion (AfDB 2018), and it is expected to widen over the medium term (Juvonen et al. 2019). SSA countries spent about US$60 billion on infrastructure development in 2012, against an estimated need of US$93 billion (Sy 2017).

The financing gap in Africa widened during the COVID-19 pandemic following the withdrawal of international banks and the reduction in multilateral and bilateral lending (Baker McKenzie 2021). However, these countries face capacity constraints on lending to infrastructure projects. The need for resource mobilization to meet the infrastructure gap provides an opportunity for pension funds, which are currently underutilized in SSA (Sly 2017; Juvonen et al. 2019). Pension funds, among other institutional investors such as insurance companies and sovereign wealth funds, can be a source of long-term investment resources given their long-term investment horizons (AfDB 2021).

Allocation of pension funds to infrastructure has been limited by governance, regulatory obstacles, and a lack of adequate financial instruments (Arezki and Sy 2016). Increasing availability of financial instruments provides opportunity for institutional investors to fill the gap left by conventional investors (ICA 2018). Infrastructure investment provides an avenue for diversification and protects institutional investors against inflation and interest rates (Suzuki et al. 2016). Pension funds are also important for the development of capital markets and the improvement of liquidity (Enache et al. 2015; United Nations 2019). Institutional investors can invest in infrastructure directly by investing in projects and infrastructure funds or project/infrastructure bonds or indirectly through listed equity, debt, and co-investments (Arezki and Sy 2016; Sy 2017). Most institutional investors invest in infrastructure indirectly (Suzuki et al. 2016). The disparities in pension investment in infrastructure are related to the type of pension scheme in place, which determines the preference for liquid or relatively illiquid investments (Sy 2017).

Pension funds impact on economic growth through various channels—fiscal, labour market, and financial (Figure 4.1). In the financial transmission channel, pension funds lead to the development of domestic capital markets, from which

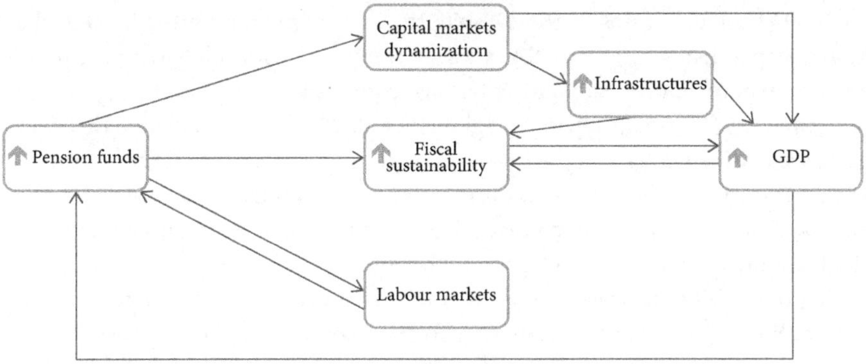

Figure 4.1 Pension funds and infrastructure: The theoretical virtuous circle

Source: BBVA research, Figure 3 in Alonso et al. (2016: (5); reproduced here with permission. Original available at: https://www.bbvaresearch.com/wp-content/uploads/2016/11/WP_16-19.pdf.

funds for infrastructure development can be raised through the backing of these funds. Economic growth and improved labour markets provide more resources to pension funds, thus improving fiscal sustainability. The development of pension funds improves fiscal sustainability by reducing public borrowing, thus boosting growth through the fiscal channel (Alonso et al. 2016). In the labour market channel, improved pension funds create incentives for the formalization of labour markets and lead to improved labour market efficiencies, which in turn lead to greater pension uptake. Theoretically, this shows that achieving pension fund growth will lead to improvements in capital and labour markets and hence fiscal sustainability, which will eventually spur economic growth; however, this is not always the case (Ortiz et al. 2018; Sanusi and Kapingura 2021). Despite this, it is expected that increased social pension coverage will provide assurance of basic support and may positively influence savings, as the risk will be covered not by individuals but by the state.

3. Demographic characteristics of SSA countries

An understanding of the pension systems in SSA needs to take into consideration the demographic characteristics of these countries. Among the issues to consider are population structure and population growth rates. People are living longer and the share and number of older persons is also growing rapidly (United Nations 2020). The population growth rate in SSA is much higher, averaging at 2.7% in 2015–20, almost double the population growth rate in other regions (see Nyang'oro and Njenga 2022: Tables 1–2). The share of the population aged 65 years and above is expected to rise from 9.3% in 2020 to 16.0% in 2050. The number of older persons in SSA is projected to more than triple between 2015 and 2050 (United Nations 2016). Despite the high population growth rates, the old age–dependency ratio[3] in SSA is lower compared with other regions; however, it is experiencing steady growth as age composition shifts and people have fewer children (Dorfman 2015; Amaglobeli et al. 2020). The challenge that SSA countries are likely to face is the low level of pension coverage and access; therefore, even with increased population growth, these countries may not enjoy the benefits of increased pension contributions. In addition, the unemployment rate is high among the young (who form a higher proportion of the population), thus limiting their ability to save for retirement. This, together with the bigger size of the informal sector, complicates matters for SSA countries as far as pension contributions are concerned, hence the need for further improvements to the pension sector.

4. Classification of retirement income provision

The classification of pension funds can follow the World Bank's five-pillar system or the Organisation for Economic Co-operation and Development's (OECD) three-tier system. The World Bank's (2008) conceptual framework provides a multi-pillar system for the provision of old-age pensions: the zero pillar, which is a non-contributory public pension system providing a minimal level of protection to the elderly; the first pillar, which is mandatory and public, and where contributions are linked to earnings and financed on a pay-as-you-go (PAYG) basis; the second pillar, which is a mandatory, private, and fully funded system (i.e. defined contribution (DC) plan); a third pillar, which is a voluntary and fully funded system; and a fourth pillar, which is a non-financial system providing informal support, other formal social programmes, and individual financial and non-financial assets. The OECD's (2017) three-tier system comprises tier 1, which is a universal or targeted pension and can be a basic, social assistance, or minimum pension; tier 2, which is a mandatory savings system, public or private, and can be defined benefits (DBs), DCs, points, or notional accounts; and tier 3, which is a voluntary savings system managed by the private sector and can be DBs or DCs. The World Bank approach provides a basis on which retirement systems can be compared, while the OECD approach provides a basis for understanding the roles of each type of pension (Mercer 2021). However, the two approaches overlap in terms of classification, so it is possible to classify a retirement pension system using either approach.

Pension schemes in most SSA countries are predominantly state-run schemes meant to provide a basic pension for old age. These pensions fall under the zero pillar or tier 1, as per the classifications. However, the pension system has been

[3] The population aged 65 years and above relative to the total number of persons aged 15–64 years.

evolving with the emergence of privately managed, employer-based schemes in the wake of pension reforms since the late 2000s, which has resulted in a shift from DB to DC schemes (Irving 2020). The reforms introduced mandatory contributions that are linked to earnings run by the public or private sector. The motivation was mainly to increase pension coverage and address the challenges of financing non-contributory schemes. It is notable, however, that SSA countries are at different stages in reforming their pension systems. The pension reforms have enabled privately managed pension fund administrators to play a bigger role in pensions administration, leading to improved fund management practices within national pension systems and resulting in an increase in assets under management (Irving 2020).

5. Performance of pension funds

The performance of pension funds can be established by considering the asset base of the funds, investment, membership, and contributions. One challenge to understanding the performance of pension funds in SSA is the dearth of data, with data only available for a few countries and incomplete for some countries. Despite this, analysis is conducted with the available data complemented by the available literature, and then inferences are made on performance of pension funds in SSA.

5.1 Asset base and asset allocation

Pension assets in SSA countries tend to be small, and asset allocation tends to favour equities (Arezki and Sy 2016; RisCura 2020). Heavy investment in equities is mainly done by the Southern African countries of Botswana, Eswatini, Namibia, and South Africa, while asset allocation in Nigeria and East Africa is dominated by fixed-income assets (mainly government bonds), driven by local regulations and the deficiency of alternative investment opportunities (AfDB 2018; Juvonen et al. 2019; RisCura 2020). The asset allocation of pension funds depends on (among other factors) market trends, investment strategies, regulation and governance structures, risk appetites, tax structures, and the availability of assets domestically (Juvonen et al. 2019). Asset allocation may also depend on the type of retirement scheme under consideration—for example, in the case of DB pension funds, asset allocation is dependent on the scheme maturity, the funding ratio, and a time trend (Zhao and Sutcliffe 2021).

The basis of asset allocation reflects familiarity with alternative asset classes, the development of local capital markets, and the availability of investment opportunities, among other factors (RisCura 2020). Some countries have diversified into different asset classes, which has widened the alternative investment opportunities. Countries such as Botswana, Namibia, Nigeria, and South Africa have invested in private equity (RisCura 2020).

A huge asset base of a pension fund is an indicator of its size and a reflection of the better performance and stability of retirement savings plans. Total assets in retirement savings plans are higher in Kenya, Namibia, Nigeria, and South Africa compared with the other countries, with South Africa having almost 10 times more assets in retirement savings plan than Nigeria, which has the second-highest asset base in retirement (see Nyang'oro and Njenga 2022: Table 3). Pension assets in Nigeria have improved over time, and this is attributed to (among other things) regulatory changes that were implemented in 2006 (AfDB 2018).

As a ratio to gross domestic product (GDP), pension assets in developing countries are low, at about 20% in 2019 compared with 92% in OECD countries (United Nations 2021). The proportion varies considerably for different regions and even within regions. The dominance of Southern Africa countries in retirement savings is also evident when total assets in retirement savings plans as a ratio of GDP are considered (Table 4.1). South Africa and Namibia reports over 70%, Botswana over 40%, and Kenya between 11 and 13%. Nigeria, despite having a large value of assets in retirement savings plans, has a small proportion of pension assets to GDP, the highest being 8% recorded in 2020. This shows the small size of retirement savings plans relative to the size of the economy and, hence, an untapped potential compared with the ratios for South Africa. For specific pension funds, the top three pension funds by share of assets to GDP are in South Africa (87%), Namibia (77%), and Botswana (47%) (AfDB 2018).

Thus, Southern African countries perform much better than the rest of SSA when performance of pension funds is considered by asset base. Only Namibia and South Africa have pension asset ratios that are comparable to those of OECD countries. Substantial investment in pension schemes is necessary for the other countries to increase their asset ratios towards the OECD average.

5.2 Investment returns

Institutional investors in SSA mostly invest in short-term assets such as term and saving deposits instead of long-term investments (AfDB 2021), creating a mismatch between their investments and the long-term savings they hold. In terms of the annual nominal investment rate of return, Malawi outperforms the other countries, with investment returns averaging about 20%, followed by Ghana and Uganda at 17 and 14%, respectively (Table 4.2). Nominal investment returns for South Africa declined from a peak of 16% in 2013 to 0.1% in 2020 before picking up. The nominal investment returns of retirement savings plans are relatively low in general in the selected countries; hence, real returns will tend to be much

Table 4.1 Total assets in retirement savings plans, 2012–22 (% of GDP)

	2012	2013	2014	2015	2016	2017	2018	2019	2020	2021	2022
Southern Africa											
Angola	—	—	1.3	1.7	0.9	0.7	1.0	1.3	1.9	1.3	1.5
Botswana	—	49.0	40.7	50.6	44.0	49.2	46.5	51.9	61.5	57.7	50.1
Lesotho	12.5	—	—	—	—	—	—	—	—	—	6.7
Malawi	—	6.3	6.8	6.8	6.9	8.1	9.6	10.4	11.6	12.8	14.1
Mauritius	1.9	2.1	—	4.1	4.2	4.5	—	10.8	12.6	13.1	10.6
Mozambique	—	—	—	0.5	0.5	0.8	1.1	1.1	1.2	1.4	—
Namibia	80.2	88.2	86.9	—	86.5	90.3	92.7	95.1	101.7	116.3	101.3
South Africa	77.1	83.0	89.0	91.3	87.1	83.9	84.0	82.5	78.2	—	—
Zambia	2.9	3.1	3.0	3.1	3.1	3.2	3.2	3.1	3.3	2.8	2.9
Zimbabwe	—	—	—	—	—	—	—	7.8	8.0	10.0	8.6
West Africa											
Ghana	—	—	1.6	2.5	3.1	4.2	4.2	4.9	5.6	6.1	5.6
Nigeria	4.3	5.0	5.1	5.6	6.0	6.5	6.7	7.0	8.0	7.6	7.4
East Africa											
Kenya	11.5	13.1	12.6	11.8	12.9	12.7	12.5	12.7	13.1	12.8	11.5
Tanzania	—	6.5	8.1	9.4	8.3	8.3	—	—	—	—	—
Uganda	—	—	5.6	6.6	7.2	7.9	9.0	9.3	10.7	12.7	—

Source: authors' compilation based on data from NBFIRA (2014–16) and OECD (2023).

Table 4.2 Annual nominal investment rates of return of retirement savings plans, 2012–22 (%)

	2012	2013	2014	2015	2016	2017	2018	2019	2020	2021	2022
Southern Africa											
Angola	—	—	—	—	—	—	5.1	5.5	5.0	8.0	9.0
Botswana	—	—	—	—	—	12.0	3.1	8.0	0.8	15.1	5.5
Malawi	—	36.0	24.2	15.2	14.2	26.1	20.7	13.0	13.1	19.0	19.6
Namibia	14.4	16.5	9.6	—	2.5	8.4	—	—	6.8	16.9	−0.8
South Africa	11.1	15.6	14.7	9.0	6.0	5.8	4.4	5.2	0.1	16.0	—
Zambia	9.3	15.8	14.6	20.0	8.0	17.0	13.0	10.0	13.4	16.3	12.7
Zimbabwe	—	—	—	—	—	—	—	—	—	29.8	54.5
West Africa											
Ghana	—	—	21.0	24.0	20.0	—	—	—	—	1.6	17.7
Nigeria	11.9	12.8	8.0	9.1	11.8	15.4	9.3	11.4	18.3	6.2	8.2
East Africa											
Kenya	17.5	−9.9	—	17.6	13.1	—	7.3	10.0	—	—	—
Uganda	—	—	16.0	18.2	11.6	14.6	18.4	8.9	13.0	14.3	—

Source: authors' compilation based on data from OECD (2023).

lower. Given that retirement savings plans are long term in nature, the value of savings upon retirement will have been eroded by inflation, making the amount of pension benefit to be small in real terms.

Relatively low levels of return on retirement savings plans have implications for pension incomes upon retirement, especially in contributory schemes where pension incomes depend on contributions made over a working life and the interest earned on contributions. In the case of non-contributory schemes, the benefit level will depend on the statutory prescribed amount rather than on contributions and interest. The annual real return on retirement savings are very low or even negative in some countries due to high inflation rates, meaning a loss to the pensioner. This may affect individuals' decisions regarding whether to join a retirement savings plan at all, especially where retirement savings are contributory.

The way out is to ensure higher annual nominal returns on retirement savings, hence the deliberate choice in the portfolio of assets in which pension funds invest. In most jurisdictions, there are regulations that define the distribution of pension schemes' asset holdings to protect retirement savings against exposure by holding classes that may be risky in a single (or few) asset(s). This is mainly aimed at securing the funds against investment in risky assets. This, coupled with the challenge of having a diversity of attractive assets for investment, also poses a challenge to retirement schemes.

5.3 Membership and contributions

The performance of pension schemes can also be evaluated based on membership and pension contributions, especially in contributory schemes. Membership of pension schemes shows the extent to which the working-age population is participating in the pension process. In countries that have a universal social pension system, all of the working-age population is covered due to its non-contributory nature. In this situation, a basic minimum living standard is ensured in old age. Contributory pension schemes, either private or public, can also coexist with a universal pension system, and individuals with high earnings can join such schemes to guarantee a high level of pension income upon retirement.

In a country where membership encompasses a higher proportion of the working-age population and contributions are growing or are substantial enough, pension schemes can be said to be performing better. With information about contributions, it is possible to project the expected savings made and thus the availability of funds that can be put into infrastructure development as the pension schemes invest and earn returns to members.

Membership of contributory schemes may reflect the extent to which the working-age population wants to maintain a given standard of living in future and may also indirectly reflect the inadequacy of pension benefits withdrawn in old age under the universal pension scheme. Contributions to retirement as a percentage of GDP are low overall for SSA countries (see Nyang'oro and Njenga 2022: Table 7). The highest contribution rates are in South Africa at about 5%, followed by Namibia at 4% and Tanzania at 2%. Some countries have developed innovative pension arrangements, which are DC schemes that include informal-sector workers in the pension system. For example, Kenya started the Mbao Pension Plan in 2009, targeting informal-sector workers, but opened the plan to all citizens in 2011, while Rwanda established Ejo Heza, a government-sponsored voluntary DC long-term savings scheme, in 2017, which is open to all citizens (see Nyang'oro and Njenga 2022).

6. Pension coverage and programmes

The need to improve pensions is clearly evident when coverage and pension programmes that are available to the population are considered. SSA has the lowest ratio of the population above statutory pensionable age that is receiving pensions compared with other regions, with a pension coverage of about 20% in 2020, a decline from 23% in 2016 (Table 4.3). Apart from North Africa, which had a coverage rate of 44% in 2020, the other regions recorded proportions of over 50%, with all people of pensionable age receiving a pension in North America. Within SSA regions, Southern African countries have the highest coverage, with 92% of those above pensionable age receiving a pension; in other regions, this figure was below 19% in 2016. The same pattern was replicated in 2020 but with an across-the-board

Table 4.3 Population above statutory pensionable age receiving a pension (%)

Geographical area	2016	2020
Asia	55.9	—
Europe	96.4	96.7
Latin America and the Caribbean	70.8	75.4
North Africa	47.0	43.8
North America	100	100
Oceania	74.1	94.8
SSA	22.7	19.8
East Africa	14.5	11.4
Central Africa	17.9	14.9
Southern Africa	92.4	83.0
West Africa	12.8	11.3

Source: authors' compilation based on data from ILOSTAT (2022) and United Nations (2022).

decline in the number of people above pensionable age receiving pensions within SSA. In Southern Africa, the proportion of those receiving a pension dropped to 83% in 2020.

Despite the low levels of pension coverage in SSA regions, pension coverage varies widely across specific countries. Data from the 2017–19 World Social Protection Report (ILO 2017) shows that coverage was highest in Botswana, Mauritius, and Seychelles, where 100% of old-age pension beneficiaries were covered (Table 4.4). Other countries with a coverage of over 80% were Cabo Verde at 86%, Eswatini at 86%, Lesotho at 94%, Namibia at 98%, and South Africa at 93%. Most SSA countries had very low coverage of pension beneficiaries, with Serra Leone having the lowest at 1%.

Most countries in SSA have contributory pension schemes, except Botswana, Eswatini, Lesotho, Mauritius, and Namibia, which have non-contributory pension schemes, while Mozambique, Seychelles, and Uganda have both contributory and non-contributory schemes. For countries running both schemes, non-contributory schemes serve a higher number of beneficiaries, except in Uganda. The adoption of contributory schemes points to the low coverage rates in SSA. SSA countries are characterized by low income levels, high levels of unemployment, high levels of informality, and intergenerational households, which limit people's enrolment in contributory pension schemes—hence the low coverage levels. As is evident from Table 4.4, SSA countries with non-contributory schemes have higher levels of coverage owing to the fact that pensions are financed mainly by the state. This shows that if SSA countries wish to record a substantial increase in pensions coverage, their pension policy should be geared towards a public pension which is non-contributory. Although financing non-contributory schemes can be a challenge, such schemes can be structured with some targeting (e.g. income- or means-testing) to ensure that they provide a basic minimum benefit to the worst-off elderly population, alongside contributory schemes that are mainly targeted at the employed.

The statutory pensionable age also varies across countries, although for most countries, the age is 60 years and above, while some have different statutory pensionable ages for men and women. In Burundi and Democratic Republic of the Congo, the pensionable ages for men and women are 65+ years and 60+ years, respectively, while in Mozambique, they are 60+ years and 55+ years, respectively. The gender dimension is a prominent feature of pension coverage, which is a major concern for SSA countries. Women tend to be less represented in the formal labour market, are mainly in less skilled jobs, receive less pay, are mostly in part-time or temporary jobs compared with men, and tend to have discontinuous careers (Sarfati and Ghellab 2012). Elderly women, therefore, tend to have low pension benefits, and some will have no pension at all in situations where contributory schemes are encouraged. Public pension schemes address such gender and income inequalities and provide solidarity across generations (Ortiz et al. 2018).

Table 4.4 Old-age effective coverage: Old-age pension beneficiaries

Country/territory	Proportion by type of programme (%)				Statutory pensionable age (basis for reference population)
	Total	Contributory	Non-contributory	Year	
Southern Africa					
Angola	14.5	14.5	—	2012	60+
Botswana	100.0	—	100.0	2015	65+
Lesotho	94.0	—	94.0	2015	70+
Madagascar	4.6	4.6	—	2011	60+
Malawi	2.3	2.3	—	2016	—
Mauritania	9.3	9.3	—	2002	60+
Mauritius	100.0	—	100.0	2010	63+
Mozambique	17.3	1.7	15.6	2011	60+ men|55+ women
Namibia	98.4	—	98.4	2011	60+
South Africa	92.6	—	—	2015	60+
Swaziland (Eswatini)	86.0	—	86.0	2011	60+
Zambia	8.8	—	—	2015	55+
Zimbabwe	6.2	6.2	—	2006	60+
West Africa					
Benin	9.7	9.7	—	2009	60+
Burkina Faso	2.7	2.7	—	2015	56–63+
Cabo Verde	85.8	—	—	2015	60+
Côte d’Ivoire	7.7	7.7	—	2010	60+
Gambia	17.0	17.0	—	2015	60+
Ghana	33.3	33.3	—	2015	60+
Guinea	8.8	8.8	—	2008	55–65+
Guinea-Bissau	6.2	6.2	—	2008	60+

Mali	2.7	2.7	—	2015	58+
Niger	5.8	5.8	—	2015	60+
Nigeria	7.8	7.8	—	2015	50+
Sao Tome and Principe	52.5	52.5	—	2015	60 +
Senegal	23.5	23.5	—	2010	55+
Sierra Leone	0.9	0.9	—	2007	60+
Togo	10.9	10.9	—	2009	60+
East Africa					
Burundi	4.0	4.0	—	2015	65+ men|60+ women
Djibouti	12.0	12.0	—	2002	60+
Ethiopia	15.3	15.3	—	2015	60+
Kenya	24.8	—	—	2015	60+
Rwanda	4.7	4.7	—	2004	60+
Seychelles	100.0	11.4	88.6	2011	63+
Tanzania	3.2	3.2	—	2008	60+
Uganda	6.6	4.5	2.1	2012	55+
Central Africa					
Cameroon	13.0	13.0	—	2015	60+
Chad	1.6	1.6	—	2008	60+
Congo	22.1	22.1	—	2011	57–65+
Democratic Republic of the Congo	15.0	15.0	—	2009	65+ men|60+ women
Gabon	38.8	38.8	—	2010	55+

Source: adapted from Table B.12 in ILO (2017: 261), with permission.

A number of SSA countries have non-contributory elderly assistance arrangements in place to complement the contributory programmes; however, their coverage is limited in most countries. The non-contributory schemes are governed by varying legal requirements and benefit levels, depending on the objectives of each scheme (see Nyang'oro and Njenga 2022: Table 10). The schemes are characterized by age-based eligibility, which, in some cases, is at variance with the statutory pensionable age. For example, Kenya has the Older Persons Cash Transfer and the Hunger Safety Net Programme, with eligible ages of 65 years and 55 years, respectively, while the retirement age is 60 years.

Among the non-contributory schemes, Seychelles' Old-Age Pension pays the highest monthly benefit of US$222, followed by Mauritius's Basic Retirement Pension with a benefit of US$141. Most of the schemes have monthly benefit levels that are below US$50, which can only cover the basic needs of the old given that most of them are unlikely to have an alternative source of income. The high disparity in non-contributory pension benefits may be due to a number of factors, such as the need to have a larger proportion of the qualifying population benefit from the funds and challenges in financing these schemes. The proportion of benefit to GDP per capita, ranging above 10% in most of the schemes, is somewhat high, but this is due to the smaller sizes of these economies in per capita terms. Non-contributory programmes that are based on universal targeting cover much higher proportions of the population aged 60 years and above compared with means- or pensions-tested programmes. The non-contributory schemes in Mauritius and Namibia fully cover the targeted population. Most of these schemes are recent, with some still at the pilot stage. The oldest schemes are in Mauritius, Namibia, Seychelles, and South Africa. The features and types of mandatory old-age income security programmes are presented in Table 4.5. Most countries in SSA have contributory schemes that are earnings-related; most of the schemes are national social security schemes and peg contributions to the incomes of members. The schemes are for the employed, mainly in the formal sector, leaving out those in the informal sector. Only Madagascar and Namibia have contributory schemes that are flat rate; however, they combine them with an earnings-related contributory scheme and non-contributory schemes, respectively. Some countries, such as Namibia, have both contributory and non-contributory schemes, while countries such as Malawi and Nigeria have individual accounts schemes. Eswatini, Gambia, Kenya, and Uganda have provident funds. Among these countries, Eswatini and Kenya also have universal non-contributory schemes, while Gambia has an earnings-related contributory scheme.

The analysis shows that SSA countries have very low pension coverage, thus raising the question of whether contributory schemes are the best for these countries. If these countries are to increase their pension coverage, then the type of scheme adopted should be reconsidered. Given the high levels of informality in the labour market, with a predominance of part-time/temporary jobs and low

Table 4.5 Mandatory old-age income security programmes

Country	Contributory		Non-contributory		Provident funds	Occupational persons	Individual accounts
	Flat rate	Earnings-related	Means-tested	Universal			
Southern Africa							
Angola		x					
Botswana				x			
Lesotho		x					
Madagascar	x	x					
Malawi							x
Mauritius		x					
Mozambique		x	x				
Namibia	x		x	x			
South Africa			x				
Swaziland (Eswatini)				x	x		
Zambia		x					
Zimbabwe		x					
West Africa							
Benin		x					
Burkina Faso		x					
Cabo Verde		x	x				
Côte d'Ivoire		x					
Gambia		x			x		
Ghana		x				x	
Guinea		x					
Guinea-Bissau		x					
Liberia		x					
Mali		x					
Niger		x					
Nigeria							x

Continued

Table 4.5 *Continued*

Country	Contributory		Non-contributory		Provident funds	Occupational persons	Individual accounts
	Flat rate	Earnings-related	Means-tested	Universal			
Sao Tome and Principe		x					
Senegal		x					
Sierra Leone		x					
Togo		x					
East Africa							
Burundi		x					
Ethiopia		x					
Kenya				x	x		x
Rwanda		x					
Seychelles		x		x			
Sudan		x					
Tanzania		x					
Uganda					x		
Central Africa							
Cameroon		x					
Central African Republic		x					
Chad		x					
Democratic Republic of the Congo		x					
Congo		x					
Equatorial Guinea		x					
Gabon		x					

Source: based on SSA and ISSA (2019).

earnings, contributory schemes do not seem to address the pension needs of SSA countries, as large proportions of the population are left outside such a pension system. SSA should consider putting in place non-contributory schemes, which should be universal, where possible, or means-tested due to the challenge of financing non-contributory schemes. This will address the issue of pension coverage and help to provide social assistance to the elderly. Non-contributory schemes, in this case, will complement existing contributory schemes rather than replacing them.

A number of SSA countries have both national schemes and civil servant schemes. Civil servant schemes are dedicated to employees in the public sector. In terms of total public spending, the proportion of pension spending to GDP is minimal irrespective of the type of scheme considered (see Nyang'oro and Njenga 2022: Table 12). Expenditure on contributory schemes as a percentage of GDP is low, with the highest proportions of about 2% recorded only in Namibia and South Africa in the civil servant scheme. All national schemes record expenditures of less than 1% of GDP. For social pensions, the highest expenditure ratio is 3.8% in Mauritius. Overall, total pension spending is less than 4% of GDP. The highest total pension spending as a proportion of GDP are Mauritius at 3.8%, South Africa at 3.4%, and Namibia at 3.1%. The low levels of spending on pension schemes may be due to the low levels of income in these economies and the prominence given to old-age support. The problem is that low expenditure levels are reflected in low levels of benefit, which then means that even for the few who benefit from pension schemes, the benefits may do little to cover their basic needs, and hence their living standards are not very different from those who are not covered by the schemes.

Available data on public social protection expenditure on pensions for persons above statutory pensionable age shows a variance across countries (Figure 4.2).

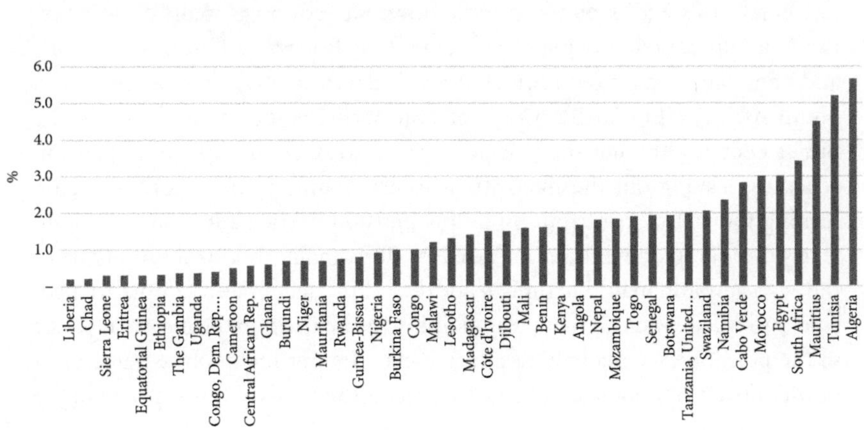

Figure 4.2 Public social protection expenditure on pensions and other benefits, excluding health, for persons above statutory pensionable age (% of GDP)

Source: authors' illustration based on data from ILO (2017).

Higher proportions of expenditure on pensions are evident in the northern Africa countries of Algeria and Tunisia. SSA countries still fare very poorly, with most of them recording social protection expenditures below 2% of GDP.

7. Challenges to pension fund development in SSA

The pension systems in SSA have evolved over time, albeit at a much slower rate compared with other regions. The progress in the pension sector has not had any tangible effect on most economies in SSA, pointing to the need to introduce reforms to enhance growth in the pension sector. While early reforms in the pension sector focused on a move from a universal pension system to a contributory system through individual retirement savings instruments, this structure of reform is not beneficial for SSA countries. A social protection system should meet certain conditions to be considered as strengthened: it should have universal coverage, adequate benefit levels, a comprehensive range of benefits, be sustainably financed, and have inclusive provisions (ILO 2021). What is evident is that pension penetration and coverage rates are very low in most SSA countries, and pension benefits are low for those who are covered, thus calling for measures to strengthen the pension systems. These observations point to the issues facing the pension systems in SSA countries, which, if addressed, can propel growth of the pension systems. A number of challenges that emerge and should be considered for the growth and development of pension systems in SSA are as follows:

- *Pension participation rates in SSA countries are generally low, coupled with high levels of informality.* Only a small fraction of SSA countries have almost universal coverage. Countries with universal coverage mainly have tax-funded, non-contributory social schemes (e.g. Botswana, Lesotho, Namibia, and Zanzibar) or have both contributory and non-contributory schemes (e.g. South Africa) (ILO 2018). Most pension participants are employed in the public sector, although the private sector also offers occupational pension schemes, leaving out the majority, who are mainly in the informal sector. Among the factors contributing to low pension participation rates are high levels of unemployment and informality. Informality is a structural issue of the economy and may take time to address; thus, deliberate attempts are necessary to ensure inclusion of the unemployed and those in the informal sector in the pension system. This can be achieved by putting in place a universal non-contributory pension scheme that meets the needs of this segment of the population.
- *Contribution rates among pension participants tend to be very low, especially in situations of mandatory pensions.* Low contributions are mainly due to low earnings, which limits the amount contributed as a proportion of earnings, but they can also be due to a lack of proper information about the benefit of

making adequate contributions for future pension withdrawals. This limits overall savings and benefit levels upon retirement, which may not guarantee income security in old age. Low contributions, together with low participation rates, imply that the pension systems in SSA countries are not able to mobilize considerable savings that could be used to support economic activities. One way of increasing contributions is by having incentives such as a matching contribution or some guaranteed insurance cover.

- *Pension coverage tends to be very low in SSA countries, with a pension coverage of 19.8% against a world average of 77.5%* (ILO 2021). The number of old-age pension beneficiaries is very low, especially in countries where there is no universal pension coverage. This can be attributed to low pension participation rates and low returns from pension assets. Low real returns imply low benefit levels. Given the high levels of informality in SSA countries, coverage can only be increased by the adoption of universal non-contributory pension schemes.
- *The regulatory environment of the pension sector in SSA is very restrictive.* Despite the pension reforms that have been initiated in a number of SSA countries, the regulatory environment in most countries is not very supportive of pension-sector development. Most pension policies do not guarantee universal pension systems, and hence most people are left out of the pension system. The regulations also specify asset classes and the proportions of investment in those asset classes, thus limiting investment diversification and the returns that pension funds generate. In some SSA countries, the regulations do not allow pension funds to invest in infrastructure projects or foreign countries (AfDB 2018). One major reason for restricting investment to specific assets is to limit the exposure of pension funds to risk in certain investments. However, these risks can be diversified by raising limits on the foreign investment of pension funds (AfDB 2021). With a well-structured legal and regulatory framework, management of pensions will be streamlined and costs of administration minimized, especially for private pensions.
- *Most SSA countries have a problem meeting the financing requirements for pensions, especially if non-contributory schemes are adopted.* With low participation rates and coverage, a universal pension system is more appropriate in SSA countries, although financing is a challenge. Most public pensions are financed by revenues and thus cause fiscal constraints, since revenues generated in SSA are not enough to cover budgetary needs. This has been addressed by the introduction of contributory pension schemes, but this has not encouraged pensions uptake due to low income levels and high informality. Universal schemes can be implemented gradually and targeted. It is also possible to target a higher age of eligibility in the initial period, then gradually reduce the eligible age towards the national retirement age over time, as a way to address financial shortages while ensuring that the needs of most elderly people are met.

8. Lessons from case studies on pension funds

A better understanding of the dynamics in the pension systems and the reform process is inferred from the pension system developments in Chile, South Africa, and the Netherlands. Chile was among the first countries to introduce a social insurance scheme and among the very first to reform its pension system. South Africa has an advanced pension system compared with most countries in the SSA region and has initiated a number of reforms to expand its pension system to cover most of the elderly population. The Netherlands is among the countries with the best-performing pension systems in the world and has made several reforms to its pension sector. Experiences of the three countries provide lessons for best practice and challenges in the process of reforming a pension system, from which inferences are drawn to improve pension systems in SSA (see Nyang'oro and Njenga 2022 for the case studies).

It is evident that pension reform is a continuous process, and though well intentioned, some reforms may result in unexpected negative impacts, such as widening the income gap between rich and poor and increasing fiscal constraints, hence making them unsustainable. Lessons learnt from the case studies with regard to reforming pension funds in SSA countries are as follows:

- Having in place a mix of universal non-contributory social pension schemes that cover everyone together with a contributory scheme for the employed is important for pension development. The non-contributory scheme will address the income needs and livelihoods of the poor, while the contributory scheme should be for those who aim to enhance their pension benefits in future. The non-contributory scheme can be means-tested and financed by tax contributions for those who do not meet a given income threshold as set by regulations.
- Pension funds can be made attractive by enhancing the benefits through bundling of other products with pensions to encourage participation and long-term savings. Contributory pension schemes that are designed to include additional group insurance cover for life, disability, and operating costs can lead to increased flows of long-term savings into pension funds.
- Pension benefits should mainly be based on annuity rather than lump sum withdrawals, to ensure the sustainability of the funds and also to guarantee a given minimum income to the beneficiaries. Pension benefits should be indexed to prices to protect against the erosion of purchasing power.
- Contributions could be increased and pension funds grown by providing incentives for pension fund contributions through provision of favourable tax considerations, especially for employer contributions and in accessing benefits. While incentives in this sense seem to benefit people with an income

during their working life—mostly those in the formal sector—it will enhance the growth of contributions and assets under management, and thus the overall growth of the pension sector.

References

AfDB (African Development Bank Group) (2018). 'African Economic Outlook 2018'. Abidjan: AfDB. Available at: https://www.afdb.org/fileadmin/uploads/afdb/Documents/Publications/African_Economic_Outlook_2018_-_EN.pdf (accessed 16 August 2022).

AfDB (2021). 'Africa Long-Term Finance Initiative: Annual Report 2020'. Abidjan: AfDB. Available at: https://altf.afdb.org/sites/default/files/2021-11/Africa%20Long-Term%20Finance%20Initiative%20-%202020%20Annual%20Report.pdf (accessed 2 August 2022).

Alfers, L., F. Galvani, E. Grapsa, F. Juergens, and A. Sevilla (2021). 'Older Informal Workers in the COVID-19 Crisis'. Policy Insights 5, May. Manchester: Women in Informal Employment: Globalizing and Organizing (WIEGO). Available at: https://www.wiego.org/sites/default/files/resources/file/PolicyInsights5.pdf (accessed 2 August 2022).

Alonso, J., A. Arellano, and D. Tuesta (2016). 'Factors That Impact on Pension Fund Investments in Infrastructure Under the Current Global Financial Regulation'. Working Paper 16/19. Madrid: BBVA Research. Available at: https://www.bbvaresearch.com/wp-content/uploads/2016/11/WP_16-19.pdf (accessed 16 August 2022).

Amaglobeli, D., E. Dabla-Norris, and V. Gaspar (2020). 'Getting Older But Not Poorer: As Societies Age Worldwide, Pensions and Public Policies Must Adapt'. *Finance & Development* (March): 31–34.

Arezki, R., and A. Sy (2016). 'Financing Africa's Infrastructure Deficit: From Development Banking to Long-Term Investing'. Global Views 2. Washington, DC: Brookings Institution.

Baker McKenzie (2021). 'New Dynamics: Shifting Patterns in Africa's Infrastructure Funding'. Available at: https://www.bakermckenzie.com/-/media/files/insight/publications/2021/04/new-dynamics_africa_report_update.pdf?la=en (accessed 2 August 2022).

Bank of Zambia (2020). *FinScope Zambia 2020 Survey Report*. Lusaka: Bank of Zambia.

Bloom, D. E., and R. McKinnon (2013). 'The Design and Implementation of Public Pension Systems in Developing Countries: Issues and Options'. Policy Paper 59. Bonn: Institute of Labour Economics.

Casey, B. H., and R. McKinnon (2009). 'Social Pensions and Policy Learning: The Case of Southern Africa'. *International Social Security Review*, 62(4): 81–102. https://doi.org/10.1111/j.1468-246X.2009.01347.x.

Commonwealth Secretariat (2014). *Pension Funds and Private Equity: Unlocking Africa's Potential*. London: Commonwealth Secretariat.

Dorfman, M. (2015). 'Pension Patterns in Sub-Saharan Africa'. Social Protection and Labor Discussion Paper 1503. Washington, DC: World Bank.

Durán-Valverde, F., J. F. Pacheco-Jiménez, T. Muzaffar, and H. Elizondo-Barboza (2019). 'Measuring Financing Gaps in Social Protection for Achieving SDG Target 1.3: Global Estimates and Strategies for Developing Countries'. Extension of Social Security Working Paper 73. Geneva: International Labour Organization (ILO).

Enache, C., L. R. Miloş, and M. C. Miloş (2015). 'Pension Reform and Capital Market Development in Central and Eastern European Countries'. *Economic Research/Ekonomska Istraživanja*, 28(1): 75–84. https://doi.org/10.1080/1331677X.2015.1022388.

Ezeh, A. C., G. Chepngeno, A. Z. Kasiira, and Z. Woubalem (2006). 'The Situation of Older People in Poor Urban Settings: The Case of Nairobi, Kenya'. In National Research Council (ed.), *Aging in Sub-Saharan Africa: Recommendations for Furthering Research*. Washington, DC: National Academies Press. Available at: https://www.nap.edu/catalog/11708.html (accessed 2 August 2022).

FinAccess (2021). *2021 FinAccess Household Survey*. Nairobi: Central Bank of Kenya, Kenya National Bureau of Statistics, and FSD Kenya.

Gill, I. S., T. Packard, and J. Yermo (2004). *Keeping the Promise of Social Security in Latin America*. Stanford, CA: Stanford University Press.

Guven, M. (2019). 'Extending Pension Coverage to the Informal Sector in Africa'. Social Protection and Jobs Discussion Paper 1933. Washington, DC: World Bank.

ICA (Infrastructure Consortium for Africa) (2018). *Infrastructure Financing Trends in Africa 2017*. Abidjan: AfDB.

ILO (International Labour Organization) (2010a). *World Social Security Report 2010–11: Providing Coverage in Times of Crisis and Beyond*. Geneva: ILO.

ILO (2010b). 'Yaounde Tripartite Declaration on the Implementation of the Social Protection Floor'. Second African Decent Work Programme 2010: Building a Social Protection Floor with the Global Jobs Pact, 6–8 October 2010, Palais des Congrès, Yaounde, Cameroon. Geneva: ILO. Available at: https://www.ilo.org/wcmsp5/groups/public/---africa/---ro-abidjan/documents/publication/wcms_181374.pdf (accessed 16 August 2022).

ILO (2017). *World Social Protection Report 2017–19: Universal Social Protection to Achieve the Sustainable Development Goals*. Geneva: ILO.

ILO (2018). 'Social Protection for Older Persons: Policy Trends and Statistics 2017–19'. Social Protection Policy Paper 17. Geneva: ILO.

ILO (2021). *World Social Protection Report 2020–22: Social Protection at the Crossroads—in Pursuit of a Better Future*. Geneva: ILO.

ILOSTAT (2022). 'Data: Free and Open Access to Labour Statistics'. Available at: https://ilostat.ilo.org/data (accessed 18 August 2022).

Irving, J. (2020). 'How the COVID-19 Crisis Is Impacting African Pension Fund Approaches to Portfolio Management'. Washington, DC: World Bank Group. Available at: http://documents.worldbank.org/curated/en/676561613717583893/How-the-COVID-19-Crisis-is-Impacting-African-Pension-Fund-Approaches-to-Portfolio-Management (accessed 16 August 2022).

Juergens, F., and F. Galvani (2020). *Why Social Pensions? Achieving Income Security for All in Older Age*. London: HelpAge International.

Juvonen, K., A. Kumar, B. H. Ayed, and A. O. Marin (2019). 'Unleashing the Potential of Institutional Investors in Africa'. Working Paper 325. Abidjan: AfDB.

Kakwani, N., and K. Subbarao (2005). 'Ageing and Poverty in Africa and the Role of Social Pensions'. International Poverty Centre Working Paper 8. New York: United Nations Development Programme.

Mercer (2021). 'Mercer CFA Institute Global Pensions Index 2020', 15 October. Melbourne: Mercer. Available at: https://www.mercer.com/globalpensionindex (accessed 16 August 2022).

NBFIRA (Non-Bank Financial Institutions Regulatory Authority) (2014–16). 'Annual Statistical Bulletins'. Available at: https://www.nbfira.org.bw/document-category/statistical-bulletin (accessed 23 August 2022).

Nyang'oro, O., and G. Njenga (2022). 'Pension Funds in Sub-Saharan Africa'. WIDER Working Paper 2022/95. Helsinki: United Nations University-World Institute for Public Policy Research and Analysis (UNU-WIDER).

OECD (Organisation for Economic Co-operation and Development) (2017). 'Pensions at a Glance 2017: OECD and G20 Indicators'. Paris: OECD. http://dx.doi.org/10.1787/pension_glance-2017-en.

OECD (2023). 'Pension Markets in Focus 2023'. Paris: OECD. Available at: https://doi.org/10.1787/28970baf-en (accessed 24 April 2024).

Ortiz, I., F. Durán-Valverde, S. Urban, V. Wodsak, and Z. Yu (2018). 'Reversing Pension Privatizations: Rebuilding Public Pension Systems in Eastern Europe and Latin America'. In I. Ortiz, F. Durán-Valverde, S. Urban, and V. Wodsak (eds), *Reversing Pension Privatizations: Rebuilding Public Pension Systems in Eastern Europe and Latin America*. Geneva: ILO.

RisCura (2020). 'BrightAfrica Report 2019'. Available at: https://www.riscura.com/wp-content/uploads/2021/03/Bright_Africa_Report_2019.pdf (accessed 2 August 2022).

Sanusi, K. A., and F. M. Kapingura (2021). 'Pension Funds as Fuel for Overall Investment Level and Economic Growth: An Empirical Insight from South African Economy'. *Cogent Business & Management*, 8(1): 1935661. https://doi.org/10.1080/23311975.2021.1935661.

Sarfati, H., and Y. Ghellab (2012). 'The Political Economy of Pension Reforms in Times of Global Crisis: State Unilateralism or Social Dialogue?' Working Paper 37. Geneva: ILO.

SSA (Social Security Administration) and ISSA (International Social Security Association) (2019). 'Social Security Programs throughout the World: Africa 2019'. SSA Publication 13-11803, September. Baltimore, MD: SSA. Available at: https://www.ssa.gov/policy/docs/progdesc/ssptw/2018-2019/africa/index.html (accessed 16 August 2022).

Stewart, F., and J. Yermo (2009). 'Pensions in Africa'. Working Paper on Insurance and Private Pensions 30. Paris: OECD. https://doi.org/10.1787/227444006716.

Suzuki, T., K. Miyaki, and J. T. Pace (2016). 'Infrastructure Financing Trends: What Are the Current Trends in Emerging Market Infrastructure Spending?' EMCompass 5. Washington, DC: World Bank Group. Available at: http://documents.worldbank.org/curated/en/193791468197952709/Infrastructure-financing-trends-what-are-the-current-trends-in-emerging-market-infrastructure-spending (accessed 18 August 2022).

Sy, A. N. R. (2017). *Leveraging African Pension Funds for Financing Infrastructure Development*. Washington, DC: Brookings Institution.

United Nations (2016). 'Sub-Saharan Africa's Growing Population of Older Persons'. Population Facts 2016/1. New York: United Nations, Population Division.

United Nations (2019). 'Financing for Sustainable Development Report 2019'. New York: United Nations, Inter-agency Task Force on Financing for Development. Available at: https://inff.org/assets/resource/financing-for-sustainable-development-2019.pdf (accessed 2 August 2022).

United Nations (2020). *World Population Aging 2020 Highlights: Living Arrangements of Older Persons*. New York: United Nations, Population Division.

United Nations (2021). 'Financing for Sustainable Development Report 2021'. New York: United Nations, Inter-agency Task Force on Financing for Development.

Available at: https://www.un.org/sustainabledevelopment/wp-content/uploads/2022/03/2021-Report.pdf (accessed 2 August 2022).

United Nations (2022). 'SDG Indicators Database'. Available at: https://unstats.un.org/sdgs/dataportal (accessed 18 August 2022).

URBRA (Uganda Retirement Benefits Regulatory Authority) (2021). 'Retirement Benefits Sector Report 2020'. Kampala: URBRA. Available at: http://urbra.go.ug/download/retirement-benefits-sector-report-2020-full-version/?wpdmdl=1916&refresh=61eec31b6d7e71643037467 (accessed 2 August 2022).

World Bank (2008). 'The World Bank Pension Conceptual Framework'. World Bank Pension Reform Primer Series, September. Washington, DC: World Bank. Available at: https://openknowledge.worldbank.org/handle/10986/11139 (accessed 2 August 2022).

World Bank (2018). *The State of Social Safety Nets 2018*. Washington, DC: World Bank.

World Bank (2019b). 'World Development Report 2019: The Changing Nature of Work'. Washington, DC: World Bank. https://doi.org/10.1596/978-1-4648-1328-3.

Zhao, Z., and C. Sutcliffe (2021). 'What Determines the Asset Allocation of Defined Benefit Pension Funds?' *Applied Economics*, 53(36): 4178–91. https://doi.org/10.1080/00036846.2021.1897512.

5

Sovereign wealth funds in Africa

*Tony Addison and Amir Lebdioui**

1. Introduction

There are now more than 100 sovereign wealth funds (SWFs) worldwide. Collectively, they hold US$8 trillion in assets, making them truly global financial players.[1] They grew following the commodity booms of the 2000s, and Africa's SWFs largely originate in public savings from the revenues of oil and gas, including Libya's (the region's largest) and mining (notably Botswana's Pula fund). However, Africa's 19 SWFs (with a capitalization of US$72.9 billion) represent less than 1% of the global total, and many have shrunk in recent years.

SWFs can have many objectives. Three are of most relevance to African policymaking and are the focus of section 2: stabilization (to smooth public spending in the face of shocks), intergenerational savings (to transfer wealth across generations), and domestic development (to fund infrastructure and domestic companies with growth-potential).[2] There is, nevertheless, ambiguity in the terminology around SWFs resulting from the evolution of the funds themselves as well as shifting government objectives.[3]

* We thank participants in the Kenya Institute for Public Policy Research (KIPPRA)-United Nations University (UNU)-World Institute for Public Policy Research and Analysis (WIDER) 'Domestic Savings Workshop', 16–17 March 2022, for their comments, and especially Abrams Tagem, our discussant. Kunal Sen, Alan Roe, Finn Tarp, and an anonymous referee also provided very helpful comments on an earlier draft. Addison and Lebdioui (2022) provide a fuller discussion of the issues.

[1] See the Sovereign Wealth Fund Institute home page, available at: https://www.swfinstitute.org (accessed 18 December 2024).

[2] A sample of the literature on SWFs includes Truman (2008), Belaicha et al. (2009), Dixon and Monk (2011), Triki and Faye (2011), Cieslik (2014), Megginson and Fotak (2015), and Diallo et al. (2016).

[3] Sovereign wealth funds are sometimes referred to simply as 'sovereign funds' in the policy debate. We add the description 'intergenerational' to savings funds as all three main types of SWFs are constituted out of public savings, but their asset portfolios differ depending on the fund's objective. Note also that before public saving takes place, public money is spent via the budget on infrastructure, as well as on education and health etc., which build human capital—all of these constitute investments. Accordingly, we avoid describing public spending as 'consumption' (the policy debate sometimes frames the choice as one of 'consuming' versus 'saving' the government's revenue from a resource windfall, but this is misleading). An SWF focused on infrastructure and enterprise investments, which we label a 'development SWF' is sometimes called a 'strategic SWF' (see https://globalswf.com, accessed 18 December 2024) and sometimes a 'strategic investment fund' (OECD 2020).

Tony Addison and Amir Lebdioui, *Sovereign wealth funds in Africa*. In: *The Domestic Savings Shortfall in Sub-Saharan Africa*. Edited by: Rose Ngugi and Kunal Sen, Oxford University Press. © UNU-WIDER (2025).
DOI: 10.1093/oso/9780198932482.003.0005

Our chapter discusses what we know about Africa's SWFs with the proviso that, for many countries, the statistical picture is opaque. Building on this, we then assess whether SWFs are fulfilling national development objectives and how they could be improved. We first consider a stabilization SWF in the context of adverse shocks and compare it to paying down the national debt instead. Next, we analyse the use of public savings to capitalize a sovereign development fund (SDF) or a national development bank (NDB), which can then also leverage private savings via domestic and foreign capital markets. We also discuss a SWF whose main purpose is intergenerational savings, and we compare this to the alternatives, notably human capital investment as a means for intergenerational wealth transfer.

The chapter concludes that the case for intergenerational SWFs in Africa is weak, except for countries with exceptionally large revenues relative to gross domestic product (GDP). The returns on investment in human capital and critical infrastructure far exceed those on financial investments and so offer superior intergenerational wealth transfer—in addition to benefiting the current generation (many of whom are extremely poor). There is a stronger case for an SDF and/or an NDB *if* they have clear mandates and are protected from disruptive elite interference by strong governance and legislative oversight. However, Africa's low- and lower-middle-income countries (LICs and LMICs) have limited managerial and regulatory capacity. It is therefore better to have one truly effective institution rather than two weaker ones, and an NDB offers the greater potential. Stabilization funds are necessary for 'self-insurance' but are often inadequate, given the scale of shocks (especially from pandemics, climate, and conflict), and a better system of multilateral financial assistance is necessary.

2. Public savings and sovereign wealth funds

2.1 Fund types and asset allocations

When current public revenues exceed current expenditures, then the surplus can be used to reduce public debt or saved. The resulting funds then accumulate over time as additional principal is added and as the returns are reinvested (Al-Hassan et al. 2013).

We focus on *three* objectives for SWFs, namely (i) fiscal stabilization, (ii) intergenerational wealth transfer, and (iii) development via investment in infrastructure and companies with growth potential (see Table 5.1).[4]

[4] An SWF may also be used to earn a higher return on foreign exchange reserves than just holding them in 'cash': these are typically used when reserves are very large (China and Singapore are examples).

Table 5.1 Summary of the different objectives of SWFs, with African examples

Type of SWF	Stabilization funds	Intergenerational savings funds	Development funds
Objectives	Provide a fiscal 'buffer' in the event of negative shocks, enabling the government to sustain spending (if the fund is large enough and the shock is temporary) without increasing debt or, if the fund is small relative to the size of the fiscal shock, to at least cushion the impact and allow a more gradual and less painful adjustment to spending (with less urgency to borrow as well). The fund will also indirectly dampen currency volatility arising from shocks as it provides some reassurance to investors regarding the trajectory of government finances.	Transfer current resource wealth to future generations. The fund may aim to meet specific future liabilities (e.g. pensions), but the future use of the funds is often left undefined. Once the fund has reached its target size, regular withdrawals (ideally subject to legislative approval) can contribute to financing spending. Exceptionally large withdrawals to meet unexpected shocks imply a stabilization role as well.	Encourage national development by investing in the equity and debt of local companies with growth potential. Invest in infrastructure, often entities that can provide a steady and secure income such as utilities. Governments may transfer state assets for eventual privatization to SDFs as well, the SDF retaining an equity stake after privatization (as in Egypt or Malaysia). Their foreign investment portfolio will include the equity of companies that can partner with domestic companies on joint ventures and to transfer technologies and skills.
Types of assets	Mostly liquid (and therefore low yielding), such as sovereign bonds with an investment grade rating (typically US Treasuries).	Mostly illiquid assets such as investment-grade bonds of long duration, corporate debt, private equity, and commercial property overseas.	Relatively illiquid domestic assets, such as equity positions in unlisted 'start-ups' and newly privatized companies.
Examples	Algeria's Fond de Regulation des Recettes Botswana's Pula Fund Ghana's Stabilization Fund Sao Tome and Principe's National Oil Account	Ghana's Heritage Fund Nigeria's Future Generations Fund Equatorial Guinea's Fonds de Réserves pour Générations Futures	Gabon's Strategic Investment Fund Ghana Infrastructure Investment Fund Senegal's FONSIS

Source: authors' construction using information provided by national sources on the funds.

A fiscal stabilization fund aims to smooth public spending in the event of shocks, especially the market volatility characterizing commodity exports. A portion of the annual revenue is saved, sometimes according to a fiscal rule set in law. If the fund becomes especially large, then an annual amount (subject to a rule) may be withdrawn (as in Botswana, Chile, and Norway). Without a stabilization fund, expenditures, non-resource taxation, and/or debt will take the burden of any fiscal adjustment when shocks strike. An additional rule may allow larger withdrawals during extreme events such as natural disasters or pandemics. An *intergenerational SWF* shares resource wealth with future generations by retaining a portion of revenue for investment in financial assets. Once the fund has reached a target size, then a future government can make regular withdrawals of income to fund spending. A *sovereign development fund* provides finance for infrastructure investment and companies with strong growth potential that private capital markets find unappealing. In effect, public savings take on the role of private savings when the domestic financial system fails to efficiently intermediate the latter (e.g. by lending to promising small and medium-sized enterprises, SMEs). It therefore offers the potential to correct for market failures, which are especially pervasive in LICs.

In addition to these specific fund goals, there is often an overarching aim: to prevent the 'resource curse' and, more specifically 'Dutch Disease'. Thus, the Bank of Mozambique's report on the country's SWF states upfront that 'In addition to helping to minimize the undesirable macroeconomic impacts of an excessive inflow of revenue into the economy, the creation of an SWF helps to discipline the use of revenue and create conditions for its sustainable management' (Bank of Mozambique 2020: 1). We return to the resource curse later.

Governments can establish more than one fund, each with its own objective and a matching asset portfolio. For example, the Ghana Stabilization Fund is intended to cushion public spending during periods of unanticipated petroleum revenue shortfall, the Ghana Heritage Fund is an intergenerational investment fund, and the Ghana Infrastructure Investment Fund is an SDF.[5] Nigeria's Sovereign Investment Authority (NSIA) likewise has three funds: stabilization, infrastructure, and a 'future generations' fund. However, SWFs with more than one objective for a single fund are also quite common: Botswana's Pula Fund and Mozambique's prospective SWF have both stabilization and intergenerational savings objectives (Bank of Mozambique (2020: 2). Running several funds entails additional administration but has the merit of only one objective against which to match assets. If a single fund has several objectives, then its portfolio should reflect the relative *weight* of each objective to policymakers. When the purpose of the fund is unclear, its governance becomes harder.

[5] See https://nsia.com.ng/stabilization-fund/. Bawumia and Halland (2018) discuss Ghana's oil revenues.

The assets selected by the different types of SWF should match the fund's objectives:

- The assets of a stabilization fund are mostly liquid (and therefore low yielding) to permit sales at short notice to support the current budget. Stabilization funds favour sovereign bonds with an investment grade rating and of the shortest duration (US Treasury bonds most often).
- To maximize its returns, an intergenerational SWF holds a high proportion of relatively illiquid assets such as investment-grade bonds of long duration and corporate debt, together with listed equities, private equity funds, and commercial property.
- An SDF holds a much higher proportion of its assets in domestic investments, often relatively illiquid such as equity positions in unlisted 'start-up' companies or shares in newly privatized companies, whereas stabilization and intergenerational funds hold mostly foreign assets.

These distinctions are not watertight, and a fund set up for one purpose may eventually take on another if policy towards public savings changes. The investment portfolio will then shift towards assets aligned with the new objective.

Fiscal crises often turn intergenerational SWFs into *de facto* stabilization funds as assets are sold to shore up the budget. Sellers may find ready buyers if global asset markets are buoyant but risk losses otherwise. If the shock originates in major financial markets—for example, the global financial crisis (GFC) of 2007–09—then buyers will be scarce and the markets illiquid.

SWFs that started out with an entirely foreign asset portfolio may eventually invest domestically as well, as the risk-adjusted returns of domestic assets start to match those of foreign assets. More troubling, governments may use them to prop up failing enterprises or to benefit the businesses of politically connected elites.

Timing an SWF's commencement is an important consideration. Policymakers wishing to dampen the ambitious spending plans of over-eager politicians may push for an early announcement, including the underlying fiscal rule as well. The revenues are held in a treasury account until sufficient to capitalize the fund and start investing.

2.2 Preventing the resource curse

A new resource discovery gives rise to expectations about future revenues. Yet, there is also much uncertainty due to (i) completing the project appraisal, including environmental and social assessments; (ii) negotiating and agreeing the fiscal terms that govern the apportionment of revenues between the producing companies and the state; (iii) the timescale for constructing the oil and gas or mining infrastructure; and (iv) the trajectory of prices and market conditions.[6] Much can change before the first revenues arrive, and these are often limited in the first years when the state has granted companies tax allowances permitting them to recoup their investment expenditures.

Grandiose spending is all too common after resource discoveries, with projects—often financed by debt accumulation—being implemented many years before the revenues arrive. This is the 'pre-resource curse' (Bauer and Mihalyi 2018; Roe 2020; Mihalyi and Scurfield (2020). The resource curse itself includes Dutch Disease whereby a large demand injection—if the revenues are fully spent—distorts the real economy and undermines growth in agriculture and manufacturing (Addison and Roe 2018; Henstridge and Roe 2018: 161–78; Lahn and Stevens 2018: 93–113; Van der Ploeg and Venables 2018). Angola, Equatorial Guinea, and Nigeria in their oil-boom years typify Dutch Disease.

Public savings reduce the risk of such macroeconomic instability. A small LIC economy with multiple supply constraints and a large resource windfall should, in principle, save more than a middle-income country (MIC) with greater supply elasticity. Using some of the savings to capitalize an SDF or an NDB can, together with investments from the capital budget, reduce supply constraints—if prospective projects are carefully evaluated and then well executed. This includes human capital investments as skills are usually in short supply.[7] We return to this issue later in the chapter.

We now turn to what is known about the size of Africa's SWFs and their modus operandi, before proceeding to an evaluation.

3. Sovereign wealth funds in Africa

This section considers the investment profiles and objectives of SWFs, makes comparisons within Africa and between Africa and other regions, and sets SWFs in the context of Africa's development financing needs.

3.1 A profile of Africa's sovereign wealth funds

The data is fragmentary, but Africa had 19 SWFs amounting to US$72.9 billion in 2020 (well below US$174 billion in 2013).[8] The fall in capitalization resulted from the end of the 2000–14 commodities super-cycle, which had generated most

[6] Uganda illustrates the lengthy time lags (Kayizzi-Mugerwa 2020).

[7] Another supply-side constraint is weakness in the domestic construction sector: see Cruz et al. (2020) and Page and Tarp (2020).

[8] This calculation is based on our assessment of national sources.

of the public savings (many of Africa's SWFs were created during that time: see Figure 5.1). Subsequent shocks, notably the COVID-19 pandemic, led to public *dis*-saving as governments sought to maintain current spending. The prospects for Africa's SWFs very much depend on the pace of the 'net zero' transition, which is a positive for producers of critical minerals (for electric vehicles and renewable energy infrastructure) and an eventual negative for oil and gas producers (see Lebdioui 2024; Addison and Roe 2024).

Fiscal stabilization and intergenerational wealth transfer are the main objectives of Africa's SWFs, and domestic investment is low down in their list of priorities (exceptions are Ghana and Nigeria and, perhaps, Angola and Senegal) as shown in Figure 5.1. This contrasts with, for example, Malaysia's Khazanah Nasional Berhad (Khazanah Nasional 2023).[9] Most African SWFs are small stabilization funds. Some also aim to save for future generations (e.g. Equatorial Guinea and Mozambique). In 2013, Africa's largest SWFs were those of Algeria and Libya (both over US$50 billion in assets). Libya has the only large fund left (US$60 billion),

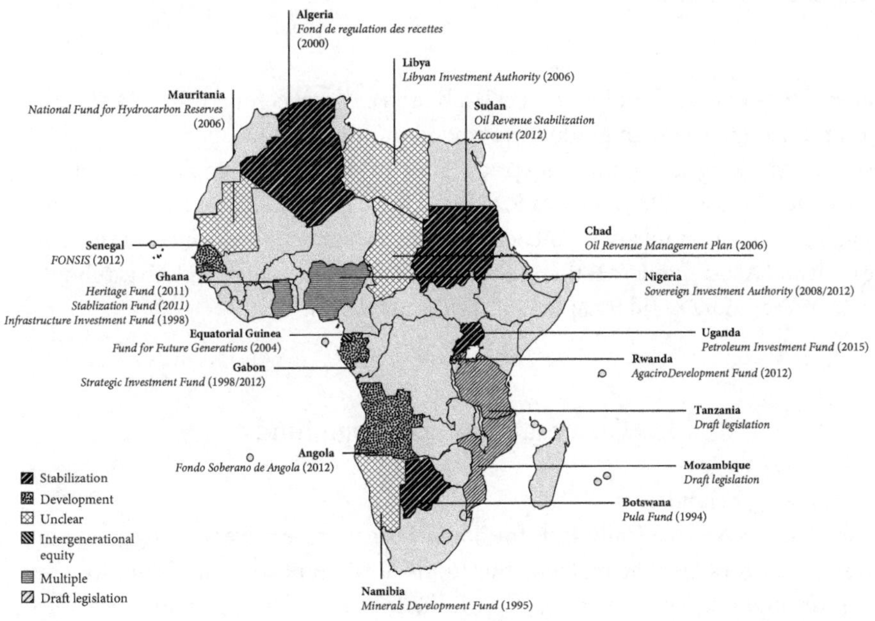

Figure 5.1 Mapping the objectives of SWFs in Africa

Source: author's illustration using mapchart.net (coloured countries and legend) and Microsoft PowerPoint (text and lines). MapChart's work is under the Creative Commons license CC BY-SA 4.0.

[9] Lebdioui (2020) discusses Malaysia.

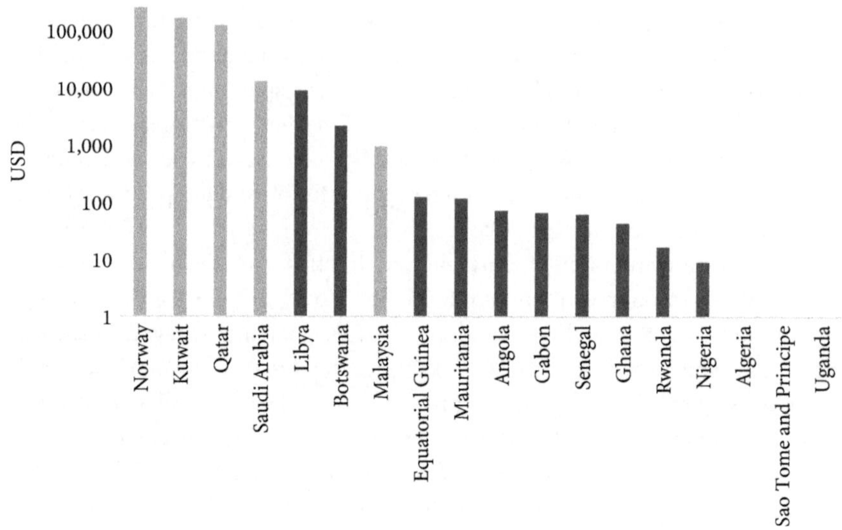

Figure 5.2 Capitalization of SWFs on a per capita basis by country (log scale)
Source: authors' construction.

followed by Botswana's Pula fund (US$5 billion). Algeria's fund was US$77.2 billion in 2013 but was then gradually emptied out to maintain spending as public revenues fell alongside commodity prices after 2014 and was completely empty by 2017 (Hadj Moussa 2021). Figure 5.2 shows the capitalization of SWFs on a per capita basis for a sample of countries. The biggest global SWFs, such as those in the Gulf and Asia regions, are themselves large foreign investors, and Africa should aim to attract more of their capital (as we discuss later).

3.2 Governance of sovereign funds

Two challenges stand out:

First, new SWFs typically lack the financial expertise necessary to create an investment portfolio that matches the funds' goals (and that also conforms to the government's risk tolerance). With limited local expertise, small SWFs outsource their fund management to international fund managers (which can inflate expected returns in their pitch to prospective SWF clients). Libya's SWF illustrates the potential losses that can then occur (see Addison and Lebdioui 2022: 10). This danger has been compounded by the financial globalization of the past 30 years, resulting in a myriad of complex and risky financial instruments (derivatives especially) that promise high returns. SWFs must hire a cadre of national expertise capable of selecting and monitoring external fund managers.

Second, SWFs are vulnerable to mismanagement and corruption. Red flags include fund managers appointed behind closed doors and non-disclosure of basic financial information. Transparency in the composition of the fund's investments, its management structure, and disclosure of any investments or decisions linked to politically exposed persons (PEPs) are vital.[10] SWFs can exhibit what Pritchett (2013) terms 'isomorphic mimicry': they look like functioning institutions operating in the public interest but in reality they serve private purposes (see Addison and Lebdioui 2022).

4. An assessment: Are SWFs a good use of public savings?

Are SWFs good for Africa? We first discuss stabilization funds and, relatedly, paying off public debt. We then discuss intergenerational SWFs, before turning to development finance institutions, such as SDFs, and relatedly NDBs, for which there is a much stronger case. Each option has its pros and cons; these vary across countries and depend on specific contextual factors (see Figure 5.3).

4.1 Fiscal stabilization funds

Stabilization funds aim to deal with *unanticipated* fiscal shocks, but this raises the question of what can be reasonably anticipated—and built into the programming of public expenditures—and what cannot. The collapse in oil demand and in the revenues of producers such as Angola and Nigeria in 2020 as the COVID-19 pandemic took hold was unanticipated, placed immense pressure on maintaining essential services, and illustrates the point (Addison and Lebdioui (2022: 14–15). No LIC or LMIC is likely to accumulate a fund sufficient to protect completely against such shocks. Only those countries with the very largest revenues can come close to 'self-insurance'.[11]

An international monetary system that provides comprehensive and fast help is needed to reduce the necessity for self-insurance and free up fiscal space for education, health, and infrastructure. Progress on reform has, however, been disappointing. In its absence, most countries must increase the size of their stabilization funds and contain their borrowing.

[10] A scorecard of transparency across SWFs has been available since 2007, developed by Edwin Truman of the Peterson Institute for International Economics (Truman 2008). The first scorecard influenced the creation of the 2008 Santiago Principles for the governance, accountability, and transparency of SWFs by an international working group of SWFs and the creation of the International Forum of Sovereign Wealth Funds (IFSWF) (see IWG 2008; Das et al. 2010: 137–50; Stone and Truman 2016; Maire et al. 2021).

[11] Nigeria's resource rents per capita are about 40 times lower than Norway's (Lebdioui 2021).

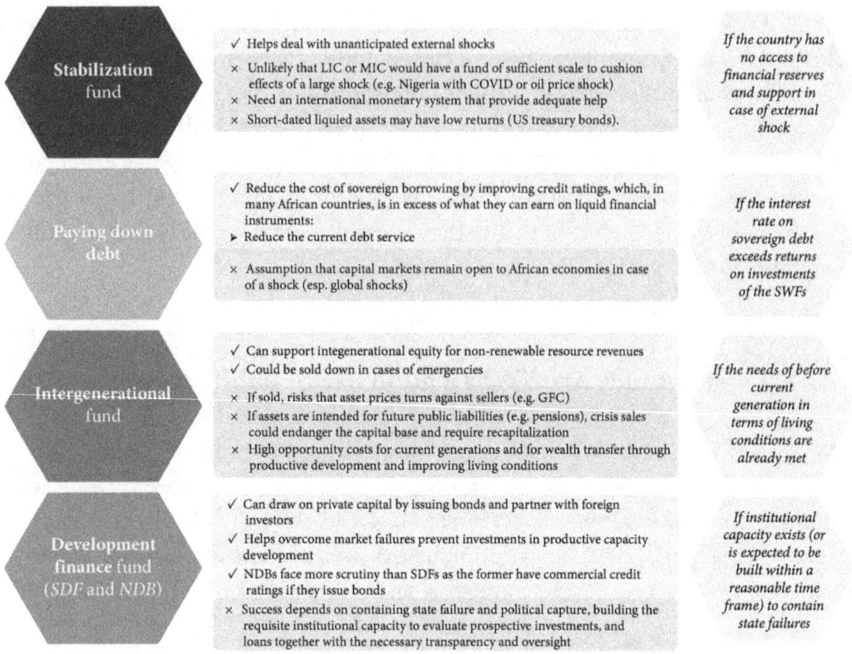

Figure 5.3 Pros and cons of different resource revenue management options
Source: authors' construction.

4.2 Reducing sovereign debt

Although a fiscal stabilization fund is desirable, the fund must keep the bulk of its assets in short-dated and liquid financial instruments such as US Treasury bills. These have low returns, certainly well below the rates at which African countries can borrow commercially. An intergenerational fund invests in less-liquid assets with longer duration: these have higher expected returns but are unlikely to exceed the cost of sovereign commercial borrowing when African Eurobonds have yields over 10%.[12]

If public savings are large—consequent upon a resource boom, for instance—then one option is to reduce the stock of outstanding sovereign debt rather than build sovereign funds.[13] This will (i) reduce the claim of current debt service on the budget, releasing funds for spending; (ii) improve the country's credit rating, allowing future borrowing on more favourable terms; and (iii) provide more scope

[12] To close the gap, an African SWF would need yields exceeding those of Norway's SWF (the best in class, with an annual return of 4.6% (after costs) over 1998–2021) (see Norges Bank Investment Management, available at: https://www.nbim.no/en/the-fund/returns, accessed 18 December 2024).

[13] Van der Ploeg and Venables (2018: 179–99) discuss this choice.

to borrow in the event of a shock given a lower initial debt stock. It also signals policy credibility to private investors, which encourages private capital inflow.

This argument does, however, assume that capital markets remain open to borrowers when a shock strikes. A global or regional shock can lead to a sudden cessation in lending, irrespective of the borrower's fundamentals, as 'contagion' takes hold. Risk-averse policymakers will therefore want to save, even if the country's borrowing costs exceeds the yields on its SWFs. And countries with very large resource booms (relative to GDP) must save to avoid the Dutch Disease effects of absorbing all the earnings immediately into the economy.

If policymakers do decide to pay down debt, then by how much should they do so? One rule of thumb is to repay debt after the requirements of any fiscal rule are fulfilled. This was the Chilean strategy in the lead up to the GFC. Earnings from copper (Chile's main export) were accumulated in its SWFs, and public debt was substantially reduced, leaving Chile well placed to withstand the shock to copper prices as the GFC took hold.[14]

4.3 Intergenerational wealth transfer

Two questions arise regarding intergenerational SWFs. First, why would the present generation want to transfer wealth to the future? And second, if this is the aim, what is the best means?

Regarding the first question, citizens may want to transfer wealth to their future selves to fund a comfortable old age or to future generations to ensure their financial security. Altruism towards the not yet born may reflect an expectation that they will face worse economic circumstances and be poorer than today's generation (if it is hard to diversify the economy from depleting non-renewable resources or if climate change threatens future prosperity). SWFs are then a vehicle to build assets to cover pension liabilities or other forms of intergenerational wealth transfer (e.g. Australia's Future Fund or Ghana's Heritage Fund).

When it comes to the needs of the elderly, in SSA only 11.6% of those aged 60 and above are in a contributory pension scheme, mostly in the MICs (the figure is less than 5% in Africa's LICs) (Guven 2019: 1). Most young Africans enter informal employment—accounting for 80% of SSA's total employment—with negligible pension prospects and therefore face poverty in old age (Danquah et al. 2019). That said, non-contributory pensions do mitigate old-age poverty, and the benefit is shared within extended families (Barrientos 2004). An intergenerational SWF to top up the funding of a general public pension, or more targeted assistance to the elderly poor, could be popular among citizens.

[14] Solimano and Calderón Guajardo (2018: 200–19) discuss Chile.

Nevertheless, there is a robust case against an intergenerational SWF. We highlight three issues.

First, citizens with unmet basic needs may well prefer more spending on child nutrition, basic health care, education, and conditional cash transfers (or a basic income entitlement) of benefit to everyone. A large cohort of Africans never reach adulthood, let alone old age. The infant mortality rate (IMR) for Africa is shocking; one out of every 13 children in SSA dies before their fifth birthday, and Africa accounts for 19 of the world's 20 countries with the highest IMR (including Angola, Chad, and Equatorial Guinea, with oil-funded SWFs and others, such as the Democratic Republic of the Congo (DRC), Guinea, and Sierra Leone, abundant in metals and gemstones) (UNICEF 2024). Figure 5.4 shows a selection of countries with SWFs and their IMRs: Nigeria stands out as a nation rich in resource revenues and poor in child survival. Children who survive their early years and go on to a well-nourished and well-educated childhood followed by a productive adulthood constitute society's most important intergenerational transfer of wealth.

While investing a portion of non-renewable resource wealth in *financial assets* acts as a mechanism for transferring wealth across the generations, future generations can instead be made richer by today's investments in *real assets*: human capital together with physical capital and infrastructure. Both financial and real assets add to future wealth at a compounding rate. However, real assets also

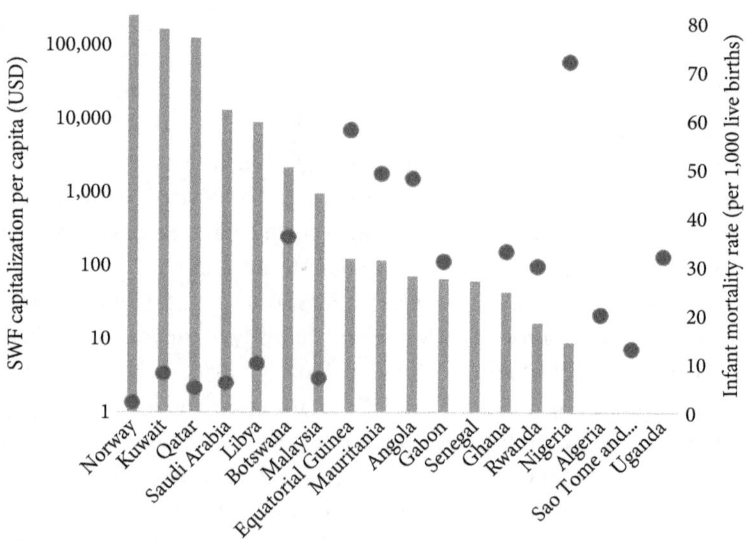

Figure 5.4 Infant mortality rate in relation to SWFs capitalization per capita

Source: authors' construction using their own calculations and data from the World Development Indicators.

benefit today's citizens through education and health care that builds human capital and enables better livelihoods. Maternal health care during pregnancy, childbirth, and postnatal care, together with under-five health care and nutrition all increase child survival as well as overall life expectancy (and quality of life). These benefits compound as healthy, well-educated and better-off parents invest more in their children, thereby reducing the intergenerational transmission of poverty.[15]

Returns are highest when asset stocks are low: the case for human capital investment in poorer counties. The social return to secondary and higher education is, for instance, above 10% in developing countries (Psacharopoulos and Patrinos 2018: 13). And education's private and social returns are higher for women than men. Africa has the highest returns as it has the world's lowest average rates of schooling (Africa's labour force averages half the years of schooling of labour in advanced economies) (Barouni and Broecke 2014; Psacharopoulos and Patrinos 2018: 13). For Africa, the returns to basic education range from 7–10% and 25–30% for upper-secondary and tertiary education (per year of education) (Barouni and Broecke 2014: 1593). The returns to education are greatest in economies undergoing structural transformation as rates of unemployment are lower, skills are in demand, and job creation occurs in more productive and better-paid sectors.

The financial return on African SWFs is far less than the returns on investing in good-quality education. Norway's sovereign fund—which arguably offers an institutional model for Africa—returns 4.6% (after costs).[16] Even if an African SWF did match that—which is unlikely given the sheer size of Norway's fund together with its low management costs—education's returns would still be far greater.

Second, it is far easier for citizens, civil society, the media, and legislatures to monitor investments in human capital than in complex financial instruments. Many tools are now available to track expenditures through the education and health systems and to monitor local service delivery and its quality. Citizens can more easily assess whether their children are getting a good education than whether their country's SWF is yielding the best risk-adjusted return.

Third, the prospects for all intergenerational SWFs must be evaluated in the context of climate change which, if it runs out of control, will reduce future global prosperity. All financial assets are at risk if global temperatures go beyond 1.5°C above pre-industrial levels, with accelerating damage at 2.0°C+ scenarios.

[15] See the Chronic Poverty Advisory Network home page, available at: https://www.chronicpovertynetwork.org (accessed 18 December 2024).

[16] See Norges Bank Investment Management, available at: https://www.nbim.no/en/the-fund/returns (accessed 18 December 2024).

Estimates are inevitably speculative, but using the concept of expected climate value at risk (VaR), Dietz et al. (2016: 3) calculate the loss at US$2.5 trillion (of a global value of non-bank financial assets of US$143.3 trillion in 2013).[17] As the polar ice sheets melt away, financial assets will sink along with the world economy. If the 1.5°C Paris climate agreement goal[18] is met, then financial markets can perhaps remain functional. Yet, it is a paradox that oil economies might save more to mitigate the damage to their agriculture and natural capital from a world that continues to burn fossil fuels.

4.4 Sovereign development funds and national development banks

4.4.1 The rationale: Fixing market failures and promoting structural transformation

While an intergenerational SWF may find some opportunities in domestic assets, many will not have high enough risk-adjusted returns to meet the fund's mandate. It is better to fund development finance institutions (DFIs) with a mandate to invest in domestic private-sector projects with good prospects (Marbuah et al. (2022). DFIs are useful for fixing market failures, incubating markets, and promoting structural transformation—as East Asia illustrates (Chang 1994; Lebdioui 2020; Anzolin and Lebdioui 2021).

Credit market failures are pervasive (Stiglitz (1989). LICs have limited *formal* provision of equity and debt finance, despite the existence of investment opportunities with potentially good returns. Instead, narrow commercial banking and informal lending dominates their financial landscape. Their stock markets are thin and illiquid with few institutional investors (e.g. domestic private pension funds). International investors are wary of currency risk, largely ignore the smaller LICs, and favour the much larger and better-regulated markets of the MICs. Yet, MICs also exhibit market failures notably in long-term SME funding.

Additionally, some investments have *social* returns well in excess of their private returns.[19] Social returns include positive externalities for enterprise development as whole (e.g. the production of a vital input such as improved seeds), the provision of social goods (e.g. affordable housing), and the provision of health inputs (e.g. vaccines). Positive environmental externalities include carbon offsetting; carbon

[17] For the emissions path at the time of the estimates undertaken by Dietz et al. (2016). Note that this is an *expected* loss, and the loss in the ninety-ninth tail of the distribution is US$24.2 trillion (17% of the global stock of financial assets in 2013).

[18] On the Paris Agreement, see: https://unfccc.int/process-and-meetings/the-paris-agreement.

[19] We distinguish between private and social rates of return, as from the perspective of the public funds the calculation of costs and benefits must include environmental and social impacts, both positive and negative.

capture, usage, and storage (CCUS), emissions reduction technologies, and clean energy and storage. Left to their own devices, private financial markets will undersupply finance to such enterprises, not least because they have large upfront capital costs (e.g. in research and development as well as production facilities) before any income is generated. Infrastructure finance is especially deficient, with a financing gap of around 50–60% of Africa's annual investment needs (AfDB 2018: 82). Such investments are critical to raising Africa's low private-sector investment rates and to overcoming the region's lack of economic diversification. Indeed, Africa is home to 8 of the world's 15 least economically diversified countries (Usman and Landry 2021). Undiversified economies are especially vulnerable to sudden external shocks, which weaken their long-term economic progress (Collier et al. 2010; Chang and Lebdioui 2020).

In summary, market failures leave many projects (with high expected returns) on the shelf. The policy challenge is to identify the very best of them by rigorous project and financial analysis. This requires significant institutional capacity development.

SDFs and NDBs will help address these market failures. They have broadly similar objectives, namely to invest in domestic enterprises with growth potential as well as in those building and running domestic infrastructure. Both can be capitalized using public savings and then leveraged through borrowing in domestic and international capital markets. In principle, an SDF makes *equity* investments in companies, while NDBs provide *loans*. In practice, some SDFs also make loans and some NDBs take equity positions.[20] Both SDFs and NDBs can be established if there is enough managerial and regulatory capacity, but for a small LIC this is a stretch. It is better to start with one effective and well-regulated institution instead of two weak ones.

In addition to public savings, NDBs and SDFs can attract private capital by issuing bonds (which deepens domestic financial markets) and partnering with foreign investors. Attracting foreign capital is the primary motive for creating an SDF when a country runs persistent current account deficits (rather than the surpluses that characterize the wealthiest oil economies).[21] Rwanda and Senegal are examples. SDFs are then a way to use public savings to leverage foreign savings, including investment from large global SWFs such as China's Investment Corporation (CIC), Saudi Arabia's Public Investment Fund (PIF) and Singapore's Temasek. Africa today receives only around 9% of SWF investments globally (see Figure 5.5). Attracting such capital should be a priority.

[20] For this reason, some discussions classify NDBs as a form of sovereign fund. The Bangladesh Infrastructure Development Fund (BIDF) is labelled an SWF in policy discussions but makes only loans.

[21] India's National Investment and Infrastructure Fund (NIIF) and the Turkey Wealth Fund (TWF) are examples.

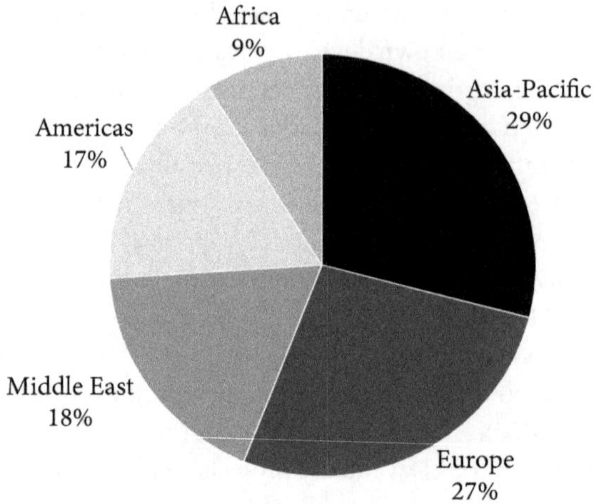

Figure 5.5 World sovereign wealth fund investments by target regions
Source: elaboration based on Diallo et al. (2016) and Monitor—FEEM SWF data.

SDFs also facilitate privatization when the government's shares in state companies are placed into the fund, with the aim of attracting private investment. They are then in effect state-holding companies. Egypt's SDF is used in this way.[22]

NDBs and SDFs can be used as counter-cyclical instruments. NDBs can expand lending to enterprises during downturns and ease back during upswings (if policy-makers fear overheating). Latin America's NDBs have done this successfully (Brei and Schclarek 2018).[23] NDBs can also introduce special and innovative credit lines to speed up loan decisions and disbursements during recessions. This is useful during financial crises when distressed private banks cut their lending. Notably, NDBs lent more than private lenders in the 2008–09 GFC: de Luna-Martínez and Vicente (2012: 8) found that, globally, the increase in NDB lending was more than three times that of private lenders. An SDF can also take an equity stake in distressed enterprises to facilitate their restructuring and recovery.

Historically, NDBs provided long-term financing for industrialization, agricultural upgrading, and structural transformation (Di John 2020; Lebdioui 2024). Given their role in mobilizing public and private investment for structural transformation and export diversification, there is a strong case for using public savings to add capital to Africa's NDBs (Santiso 2008; Gelb et al. 2014; Zalk 2021). There are 80 members of the Association of African Development Finance Institutions

[22] See the International Forum of Sovereign Wealth Funds (IFSWF) home page, available at: https://www.ifswf.org/members/sovereign-fund-egypt (accessed 18 December 2024).

[23] NDBs have grown to be the principal long-term lenders and loan guarantors and the principal source of financial services in housing, infrastructure, and agriculture in MICs (de Luna-Martínez and Vicente 2012). Latin America has been especially successful in its use of NDBs (Griffith-Jones and Ocampo 2018).

and upwards of 100 DFIs on the continent, depending on the definition used, varying from the biggest—the African Development Bank (AfDB) and African Export and Import Bank (Afreximbank), which have regional mandates and report to many governments—to national banks (mostly focused on infrastructure) in Algeria, Egypt, Morocco, Nigeria, and South Africa and sector-focused banks such as Ghana's Agricultural Development Bank.[24] A handful dominate the region's capital assets and Africa's NDBs collectively account for only 1% of development bank assets worldwide and are much smaller relative to national economies than their peers elsewhere (Fitch Ratings 2022: 4).

The evidence base on Africa's NDBs is smaller than that for Asia and Latin America. Ndikumana, Naidoo, and Perez (2021) find that, on average, African NDBs do undertake more medium- and long-term financing than private banks; they also have lower non-performing loan ratios and a higher return on assets. However, there are many underperformers, especially among the small and undercapitalized ones. Attridge, Chen, and Mbate (2021) find that while two-thirds of development banks in their sample are profitable—and compare favourably to European development finance institutions—one-third are not, and half the sample have high non-performing loan ratios. Ethiopia, Rwanda, and Uganda are reforming their development banks and injecting capital and expertise, but others remain stagnant.

In summary, NDBs have had a renaissance since 2010. Yet, their potential has not been fully exploited.

4.4.2 Containing state failure and building institutional capacity

The case for DFIs rests on the presence of *market failures*. But their success depends on containing *state failure*. NDBs and SDFs are vulnerable to political capture, resulting in unsound investments or simply theft. The scandal of Malaysia's 1MDB, an SDF from which US$4.5 billion of public money was stolen, offers a salutatory warning for Africa.

Legislatures must exercise strong oversight of both NDBs and SDFs, given the fiscal risks arising from insolvency, and full transparency facilitates monitoring by civil society and independent media. NDBs face more scrutiny than SDFs as the former have commercial credit ratings if they issue bonds (Quist 2022). Fundamentally, transparency and oversight improve the ability of NDBs and SDFs to leverage additional funds from capital markets and to encourage multilateral lenders to co-finance projects. It is also necessary to build the requisite institutional capacity to evaluate prospective investments and loans together with the necessary transparency and oversight to achieve effective DFI governance. Valuable efforts to improve project evaluation capacity exist at the

[24] See the Association of African Development Finance Institutions (AADFI) home page, available at: https://adfi-ci.org (accessed 18 December 2024); Attridge et al. (2021) count 107.

national and regional level, such as the African Association of Development Finance Institutions (AADFI) standards.

5. Conclusions

SWFs are often seen by politicians as a symbol of national success and a signal to the world that the country will manage its resource revenues responsibly. But do SWFs contribute to national development goals? What has been Africa's experience to date? These are the questions addressed in our chapter, and we conclude with five observations.

The first is that fiscal stabilization funds are necessary but rarely of sufficient size and, more fundamentally, it is vital to diversify economies to reduce the impact of sector-specific shocks on the public revenues, especially those from commodity price volatility. This is well illustrated by the COVID-19 pandemic, when governments came under intense fiscal pressure. Many (perhaps all) African governments ceased public saving and drew down their funds to try and finance essential services. Larger fiscal buffers would have eased the adjustment pain but today most of Africa's fiscal stabilization funds have shrunk (and some are empty).

Second, the revenues, and therefore the public savings of oil and gas exporters, face headwinds from the net zero transition, which will eventually strand fossil fuels. Their non-resource revenues—from value-added tax (VAT), income taxes, and property taxes—need to grow further. Africa's tax administration has, on average, improved over the past decade. Yet, many of Africa's oil-rich countries are lagging—their tax–GDP ratios are below the regional average—and it would be better to spend a good portion of their revenues on improving tax institutions before considering an intergenerational SWF.

Third, our view is that an intergenerational SWF is only one of the many ways that a society can invest in its future generations and should only be considered after a stabilization fund has been replenished and debt reduced (when too high). And these decisions must be integrated with public spending decisions on education, health care, social protection, and development infrastructure in the annual budget and five-year plan. It is hard to prioritize intergenerational saving if the government is not budgeting enough for vital sector ministries. Service delivery in education and health has improved after intensive effort, with donor support, over the past three decades, and many now have the institutional capacities to absorb more funding and channel them effectively into frontline services with high social returns for both current and future generations.

Fourth, there is merit in starting (or recapitalizing existing) development funds—either SDFs or NDBs. And SDFs and NDBs need full transparency, strong governance, and the necessary analytical capacity to ensure that their investments do contribute to structural transformation. At its heart, successful economic and social development is a process of *relaxing constraints*. In project evaluation, a constraint is the availability and skill of economists, sector planners, and engineers in the public and private sectors. Above all, there is the need to build an institutional framework of planning not only for DFIs but also for local and central government administrations whose task is to bring the private and public sector together to deliver on priority objectives.

Fifth, it is hard for governments to pursue a consistent strategy regarding public savings. Political expediency can too often win out, especially around election time, when the temptations of spending beckon most acutely. But there is also the vulnerability of African economies to economic shocks—the result of undiversified commodity-dependent economies—to be considered. Fiscal rules are invariably introduced with the best of intentions, but they have a very high rate of failure when revenues take a sharp downturn. SWFs that began as intergenerational funds turn into de facto stabilization funds when hard-pressed governments need to maintain spending, but the asset composition of the former is not suitable for the task of the latter. And it is hard to build a stabilization fund of sufficient size when the opportunity cost in terms of development spending foregone is so high. Developing countries need much greater concessional and grant funding to deal with economic shocks, not least those from climate change.

So, in summary, to what extent do African SWFs serve development? In some ways, the answer depends on how we define development. By creating sovereign stabilization funds, many African nations have followed the standard policy rule when it comes to managing resource revenues and have managed to (partially) smooth public spending. This contributes to macroeconomic stability, which encourages investment and growth. But if we understand economic development as the process of structural transformation to diversify economies away from 'low-quality activities', characterized by diminishing returns, price volatility, flat learning, low productivity and wages, towards 'high-quality activities' that are characterized by economies of scale, technological upgrading, high productivity and wages, then we can argue that most African SWFs have not fully delivered on development in this broader sense. It is therefore time to reconsider sovereign wealth management and to better align it with the continent's needs and ambitions.

References

Addison, T., and A. Lebdioui (2022). 'Public Savings in Africa: Do Sovereign Wealth Funds Serve Development?' World Institute for Public Policy Research and Analysis (WIDER) Working Paper 159/2022. Helsinki: United Nations University (UNU)-WIDER.

Addison, T., and A. Roe (eds) (2018). *Extractive Industries: The Management of Resources as a Driver of Sustainable Development.* Oxford: Oxford University Press for UNU-WIDER.

Addison, T. and A. Roe (2024). *Resources Matter: Ending Poverty While Protecting Nature.* Oxford: Oxford University Press for UNU-WIDER. DOI: https://doi.org/10.1093/oso/9780192872197.001.0001

AfDB (African Development Bank Group) (2018). *Africa Economic Outlook 2018.* Abidjan: African Development Bank.

Al-Hassan, A., M. Papaioannou, M. Skancke, and C. C. Sung (2013). 'Sovereign Wealth Funds: Aspects of Governance Structures and Investment Management'. International Monetary Fund (IMF) Working Paper 13/231. Washington, DC: IMF.

Anzolin, G., and A. Lebdioui (2021). 'Three Dimensions of Green Industrial Policy in the Context of Climate Change and Sustainable Development'. *European Journal of Development Research*, 33(2): 371–405.

Attridge, S., Y. Chen, and M. Mbate (2021). *Financial Performance and Corporate Governance: Evidence from National Development Banks in Africa. ODI Report.* London: Overseas Development Institute.

Bank of Mozambique (2020). 'Proposal of Sovereign Wealth Fund Model for Mozambique'. Report. Maputo: Bank of Mozambique.

Barouni, M., and S. Broecke (2014). 'The Returns to Education in Africa: Some New Estimates'. *Journal of Development Studies*, 50(12): 1593–613.

Barrientos, A. (2004). 'Cash Transfers for Older People Reduce Poverty and Inequality'. Background Paper for WDR 2006: Equity and Development. Washington, DC: World Bank.

Bauer, A., and D. Mihalyi (2018). 'Premature Funds: How Overenthusiasm and Bad Advice Can Leave Countries Poorer'. Briefing. New York: Natural Resource Governance Institute.

Bawumia, M., and H. Halland (2018). 'Oil Discovery and Macroeconomic Management: The Recent Ghanaian Experience'. In T. Addison and A. Roe (eds), *Extractive Industries: The Management of Resources as a Driver of Sustainable Development*, 220–42. Oxford: Oxford University Press for UNU-WIDER. DOI: https://doi.org/10.1093/oso/9780198817369.003.0011.

Belaicha, A., A. Bouzidim, and D. Labaronne (2009). 'Un fonds d'Investissement d'État pour l'Algérie: Approche Institutionnelle et Confrontation au Modèle Traditionnels des Fonds Souverains'. Working paper, faculté des sciences économies, des sciences de gestion et des sciences commerciales, Université Abderrahmane Mira de Bejaia (Algérie).

Brei, M., and A. Schclarek (2018). 'The Countercyclical Behaviour of National Development Banks in Latin America and the Caribbean'. In S. Griffith-Jones and J. A. Ocampo (eds), *The Future of National Development Banks*, 278–301. Oxford: Oxford University Press for the Initiative for Policy Dialogue (IPD). DOI: https://doi.org/10.1093/oso/9780198827948.003.0011.

Chang, H. J. (1994). *The Political Economy of Industrial Policy.* London: Macmillan.

Chang, H. J., and A. Lebdioui (2020). 'From Fiscal Stabilization to Economic Diversification: a Developmental Approach to Managing Resource Revenues'. WIDER Working Paper 2021/108. Helsinki: UNU-WIDER.

Cieślik, E. (2014). 'African Sovereign Wealth Funds: Facts and Figures'. *Polish Journal of Economics/Gospodarka Narodowa*, 274(6): 103–22.

Collier, P., R. Van Der Ploeg, M. Spence, and A. J. Venables (2010). 'Managing Resource Revenues in Developing Economies'. *IMF Staff Papers*, 57(1): 84–118.

Cruz, A. S., F. Fernandes, F. J. Mafambissa, and F. Pereira (2020). 'The Construction Sector in Mozambique'. In J. Page and F. Tarp (eds), *Mining for Change: Natural Resources and*

Industry in Africa, 183–208. Oxford: Oxford University Press for UNU-WIDER. DOI: https://doi.org/10.1093/oso/9780198851172.003.0009.

Danquah, M., S. Schotte, and K. Sen (2019). 'Informal Work in Sub-Saharan Africa; Dead End or Steppingstone?' WIDER Working Paper, 2019/107. Helsinki: UNU-WIDER.

Das, U. S., A. Mazarei, and A. Stuart (2010). 'Sovereign Wealth Funds and the Santiago Principles'. In U. S. Das, A. Mazarei, and H. van der Hoon (eds), *Economics of Sovereign Wealth Funds, Issues for Policy-makers*, 59–74. Washington, DC: IMF.

de Luna-Martínez, J., and C. Vicente (2012). 'Global Survey of Development Banks'. Policy Research Working Paper 5969. Washington, DC: World Bank.

Diallo, B., F. T. Tchana, and A. Zeufack (2016). 'Sovereign Wealth Funds and Long-Term Investments in Sub-Saharan Africa'. Policy Research Working Paper 7903. Washington, DC: World Bank.

Dietz, S., A. Bowen, C. Dixon, and P. Gladwell (2016). '"Climate Value at Risk" of Global Financial Assets'. *Nature Climate Change*, 6: 676–79.

Di John, J. (2020). 'The Political Economy of Development Banking'. In A. Oqubay, C. Cramer, H-J. Chang, and R. Kozul-Wright (eds), *Oxford Handbook of Industrial Policy*, 337–68. Oxford: Oxford University Press. DOI: https://doi.org/10.1093/oxfordhb/9780198862420.013.13.

Dixon, A. D., and A. H. B. Monk (2011). 'What Role for Sovereign Wealth Funds in Africa's Development?', Oil-to-Cash Initiative Background Paper. Washington, DC: Center for Global Development.

Fitch Ratings (2022). 'The Revival of African National Development Banks'. Press release. New York: Fitch Ratings.

Gelb, A., S. Tordo, H. Halland, N. Arfaa, and G. Smith (2014). 'Sovereign Wealth Funds and Long-Term Development Finance: Risks and Opportunities'. Policy Research Working Paper 6776. Washington, DC: World Bank.

Griffith-Jones, S., and J. A. Ocampo (eds) (2018). *The Future of National Development Banks*. Oxford: Oxford University Press for the IPD.

Guven, M. (2019). 'Extending Pension Coverage to the Informal Sector in Africa'. Social Protection and Jobs Working Paper 1933. Washington, DC: World Bank.

Hadj Moussa, N. (2021). 'Fonds de régulation des recettes algérienne entre nécessité et gaspillage des ressources rares de l'État (2000–2020)'. *Revue Internationale de la Performance Economique*, 4(3): 19–35.

Henstridge, M., and A. Roe (2018). 'The Macroeconomic Management of Natural Resources'. In T. Addison and A. Roe (eds), *Extractive Industries: The Management of Resources as a Driver of Sustainable Development*, 161–78. Oxford: Oxford University Press for UNU-WIDER. DOI: https://doi.org/10.1093/oso/9780198817369.003.0008.

IWG (International Workplace Group plc) (2008). *Sovereign Wealth Funds: Generally Accepted Principles and Practices: 'Santiago Principles'*. Washington, DC: International Working Group of Sovereign Wealth Funds.

Kayizzi-Mugerwa, S. (2020). 'Uganda's Nascent Oil Sector: Revenue Generation, Investor–Stakeholder Alignment, and Public Policy'. WIDER Working Paper, 2020/175. Helsinki: UNU-WIDER.

Khazanah Nasional (2021). 'Strengthening Resilience, Advancing Malaysia: Khazanah Report 2023'. Available at: https://www.khazanah.com.my (accessed 18 December 2024).

Lahn, G., and P. Stevens (2018). 'The Curse of the One-Size-Fits-All: Re-evaluating What We Know about Extractives and Economic Development'. In T. Addison and A. Roe (eds), *Extractive Industries: The Management of Resources as a Driver of Sustainable*

Development, 93–113. Oxford: Oxford University Press for UNU-WIDER. DOI: https://doi.org/10.1093/oso/9780198817369.003.0005.

Lebdioui, A. (2020). 'The Political Economy of Moving Up in Global Value Chains: How Malaysia Added Value to Its Natural Resources through Industrial Policy'. *Review of International Political Economy*, 29(3): 870–903.

Lebdioui, A. (2021). 'The Multidimensional Indicator of Extractives-Based Development (MINDEX): A New Approach to Measuring Resource Wealth and Dependence'. *World Development*, 147: 105633. DOI: https://doi.org/10.1016/j.worlddev.2021.105633.

Lebdioui, A. (2024). *Survival of the Greenest: Economic Transformation in a Climate-Conscious World*. Cambridge: Cambridge University Press for UNU-WIDER.

Maire, J., A. Mazarei, and E. M. Truman (2021). 'Sovereign Wealth Funds Are Growing More Slowly, and Governance Issues Remain'. Policy Brief 21-03. Washington, DC: Peterson Institute for International Economics.

Marbuah, G., D. W. te Velde, S. Attridge, A. Lemma, and J. Keane (2022). *Understanding the Role of Development Finance Institutions in Promoting Development: An Assessment of Three African Countries*. Stockholm: Stockholm Environment Institute (SEI).

Megginson, W. L., and V. Fotak (2015). 'Rise of the Fiduciary State: A Survey of Sovereign Wealth Fund Research'. *Journal of Economic Surveys*, 29(4): 733–88.

Mihalyi, D., and T. Scurfield (2020). 'How Did Africa's Prospective Petroleum Producers Fall Victim to the Presource Curse?' Policy Research Working Paper 9384. Washington, DC: World Bank.

Ndikumana, L., K. Naidoo, and F. Perez (2021). 'Is There a Case for National Development Banks in Africa? Conceptual Rationale and Empirical Evidence'. PERI Working Paper 542. Amherst, MA: Political Economy Research Institute, University of Massachusetts.

OECD (Organisation for Economic Co-operation and Development) (2020). *The Role of Sovereign and Strategic Investment Funds in the Low-Carbon Transition*. Paris: OECD Development Centre.

Page, J., and F. Tarp (eds) (2020). *Mining for Change: Natural Resources and Industry in Africa*. Oxford: Oxford University Press for UNU-WIDER.

Pritchett, L. (2013). 'Folk and the Formula: Fact and Fiction in Development'. WIDER Annual Lecture 16. Helsinki: UNU-WIDER.

Psacharopoulos, G., and H. Patrinos (2018). 'Returns to Investment in Education: A Decennial Review of the Global Literature'. Policy Research Working Paper 8402. Washington, DC: World Bank.

Quist, G. (2022). 'A Financial Straitjacket? Côte d'Ivoire's National Development Banks'. *Cambridge Journal of Economics*, 46(5): 1087–108.

Roe, A. (2020). 'Mozambique: Bust before Boom: Reflections on Investment Surges and New Gas'. In J. Page and F. Tarp (eds), *Mining for Change: Natural Resources and Industry in Africa*161–82. Oxford: Oxford University Press for UNU-WIDER. DOI: https://doi.org/10.1093/oso/9780198851172.003.0008.

Santiso, J. (2008). 'Sovereign Development Funds: Key Financial Actors of the Shifting Wealth of Nations'. EmNet Working Paper. Paris: OECD Development Centre.

Solimano, A., and D. Calderón Guajardo (2018). 'The Copper Sector, Fiscal Rules, and Stabilization Funds in Chile: Scope and Limits'. In T. Addison and A. Roe (eds), *Extractive Industries: The Management of Resources as a Driver of Sustainable Development*, 200–219. Oxford: Oxford University Press for UNU-WIDER. DOI: https://doi.org/10.1093/oso/9780198817369.003.0010.

Stiglitz, J. (1989). 'Markets, Market Failures, and Development'. *American Economic Review*, 79(2): 197–202.

Stone, S. E. and E. M. Truman (2016). 'Uneven Progress on Sovereign Wealth Fund Transparency and Accountability'. Policy Brief 2016/18. Washington, DC: Peterson Institute for International Economics.

Triki, T., and I. Faye (2011). 'Africa's Quest for Development: Can Sovereign Wealth Funds Help?' In N. Boubakri and J.-C. Cosset (eds), *Institutional Investors in Global Capital Markets (International Finance Review, Vol. 12)*, 263–90. Leeds: Emerald Group Publishing Limited, Leeds. https://doi.org/10.1108/S1569-3767(2011)0000012013.

Truman, E.M. (2008). 'A Blueprint for Sovereign Wealth Funds Best Practices'. PIIE Policy Brief 2008/3. Washington DC: Peterson Institute for International Economics.

UNICEF (United Nations Children's Fund) (2024). 'Under-Five Mortality', March. Available at: https://data.unicef.org/topic/child-survival/under-five-mortality (accessed 18 December 2024).

Usman, Z., and D. Landry (2021). 'Economic Diversification in Africa: How and Why It Matters'. Working Paper. Washington, DC: Carnegie Endowment for International Peace.

Van der Ploeg, R., and A. J. Venables (2018). 'Extractive Revenues and Government Spending: Short- versus Long-Term Considerations'. In T. Addison and A. Roe (eds), *Extractive Industries: The Management of Resources as a Driver of Sustainable Development*, 179–99. Oxford: Oxford University Press for UNU-WIDER. DOI: https://doi.org/10.1093/oso/9780198817369.003.0009.

Zalk, N. (2021). 'Africa's Development Banks: The Urgent Need for Scale'. *LSE Blogs*, 17 November. https://blogs.lse.ac.uk/businessreview/2021/11/17/africas-development-banks-the-urgent-need-for-scale/.

6

Public debt challenges in sub-Saharan Africa

*Maureen Were**

1. Introduction

Sub-Saharan Africa (SSA)'s rising public debt burden amid limited fiscal space and multiple shocks remains a key challenge to development. Public debt in SSA has increased steadily over the past two decades. Unlike the debt crisis of the 1980s, which was mainly due to debt owed to multilateral institutions, the current debt burden is mainly linked to the rapid accumulation of commercial and bilateral debt following increased access to international financial markets and China's emergence as a significant creditor. Additionally, the COVID-19 pandemic, which emerged in March 2020, had an adverse impact on the economies, thereby exacerbating public debt challenges as COVID-related spending increased while revenues and economic growth plummeted. Consequently, SSA's public debt as a ratio of gross domestic product (GDP) increased notably from an average of about 50% in 2019 before the pandemic to 57.1% (63.3%, excluding Nigeria and South Africa) in 2020 (IMF 2023b).

On average, SSA economies contracted by 1.7% in 2020, compared with a 3.1% growth recorded in 2019. Before the economies could fully recover, the Russian–Ukraine war kicked in in early 2022, leading to a disruption of supply chains and a surge in international oil and food prices. Meanwhile, global inflation rose from historically low levels of less than 2% before 2020 to 8.7% in 2022, leading to aggressive monetary policy tightening in advanced economies. The latter led to higher interest rates, tightening of financing conditions in the global markets, and depreciation of domestic currencies, thus further increasing debt vulnerabilities and the cost of borrowing. After a lengthy period of low interest rates and low inflation, the global economy entered a new phase characterized by elevated inflation, a rise in interest rates, high debt levels, and subdued growth.

*The author is grateful for the insightful comments received from colleagues and the book editors: Kunal Sen, the current Director of UNU-WIDER, and Rose Ngugi, previously Executive Director of KIPPRA. The views expressed in this chapter are the author's and should not be misconstrued to represent those of the institution she is affiliated to.

Maureen Were, *Public debt challenges in sub-Saharan Africa*. In: *The Domestic Savings Shortfall in Sub-Saharan Africa*. Edited by: Rose Ngugi and Kunal Sen, Oxford University Press. © UNU-WIDER (2025).
DOI: 10.1093/oso/9780198932482.003.0006

The multiple shocks have not only complicated SSA's economic recovery efforts but also heightened macroeconomic vulnerabilities and made sustainable management of public debt difficult, amid limited finances and other pressing challenges such as climate change and food insecurity.[1] From the last quarter of 2020 to early 2023, the horn of Africa experienced one of the worst droughts in over 40 years, placing millions of people at the risk of starvation. It is estimated that about 132 million people were acutely food insecure in 2022, at a time when half of the countries in the region reported double-digit inflation, thus contributing to the high cost of living (IMF 2023a). By the end of 2022, nearly one-third of the SSA economies had debt levels above 70% of GDP.[2] One-half of the low-income countries in SSA are either in debt distress or at high risk of distress. Moreover, even if countries do not default, the heightened public debt distress or risk of default drive market sentiments and credit ratings negatively. Following the lower credit ratings and interest rate hikes in advanced countries, SSA's sovereign spreads increased by three times the emerging markets average since the global tightening cycle that started around the first quarter of 2022[3] (IMF 2023a). This, coupled with the depreciation pressures of domestic currencies and the high cost of borrowing in the global and domestic financial markets, could lead to a vicious cycle of debt.

In light of the above, the rising public debt burden is not only a threat to debt sustainability and macroeconomic stability but also a key constraint to sustainable development in SSA. The opportunity costs associated with the high costs of debt servicing are huge, given the high rates of unemployment, widespread poverty, and limited access to basic public utilities such as water and electricity. Ndulu and O'Connell (2021) note that development assets, including major public infrastructure projects that were nearing fruition and improvements in human capital formation, are at stake. While domestic savings have a role to play in providing the necessary resources needed for promoting financial independence and sustainable development, saving rates in SSA have remained generally low. To supplement the low levels of savings and limited tax revenues, governments mainly rely on domestic and external borrowing to finance public spending, including public investment. Thus, given the increased debt burden, lack of fiscal space, and multiple challenges in the context of a global environment that has become more uncertain, the achievement of Sustainable Development Goals (SDGs) is in jeopardy. Against this background, this chapter provides an assessment of the SSA's public debt, drivers, and the implications for debt sustainability, mainly focusing on external debt.

[1] The drought conditions that started in the last quarter of 2020 and lasted until around March 2023 adversely affected agricultural activity in the most affected countries such as Kenya and Ethiopia.

[2] Based on public debt-to-GDP data availed in IMF (2023b).

[3] The European Central Bank started its policy rate hike in July 2022, while the Fed started in March 2022.

The rest of the chapter is organized as follows. Trends and composition of public debt is given in section 2, while drivers of public debt accumulation are discussed in section 3. Section 4 provides an overview of the different approaches to debt sustainability assessment. Implications of public debt accumulation on debt sustainability are discussed in section 5, while section 6 provides an overview of international debt-related initiatives. Policy insights are summarized and a conclusion given in section 7.

2. Trends and composition of public debt

Public debt has generally been on the rise not only in developing economies but also globally, especially after the 2009 global financial crisis (GFC). However, public debt-to-GDP ratios in developing economies, including SSA, edged up sharply in 2020 following the increased spending and fiscal interventions occasioned by the impact of the COVID-19 pandemic (Figure 6.1). On average, SSA's public debt-to-GDP ratio has increased steadily over the past two or so decades. It nearly doubled from 27% in 2010 to about 52% in 2019, before increasing notably to 57.1% in 2020, following the adverse socio-economic impact of the COVID-19 pandemic. SSA's public debt-to-GDP ratio averaged 56.2% (60% excluding Nigeria and South Africa) in 2021 and 57.2% in 2022. However, the ratios were much higher for middle-income countries (excluding South Africa and Nigeria) at 74.1%, 68.4%,

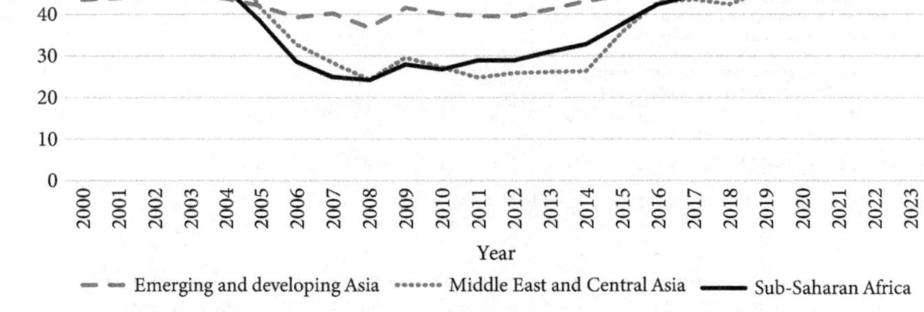

Figure 6.1 Trends in public debt-to-GDP ratios in developing economies

Source: author's illustration based on World Economic Outlook database (IMF 2024a).

and 67.3% in 2020, 2021, and 2022, respectively (IMF 2023b).[4] Moreover, SSA's public debt-to-GDP ratio increased further in 2023 to about 60.1%.[5]

The public debt accumulation was preceded by a period of decline in the debt-to-GDP ratios from about 66% to 24% between 2000 and 2008. This was largely on account of the debt relief programmes, that is the Heavily Indebted Poor Countries (HIPCs) debt relief initiative of 1996 that was later complemented by the Multilateral Debt Relief Initiative (MDRI) in 2005.

Following increased debt accumulation, over three-quarters (76%) of SSA countries had a public debt-to-GDP ratio of above 50% in 2021 (Figure 6.2). One-third had debt levels of above 70% of GDP. These included Eritrea (176.2%), Cabo Verde (142.3%), Zambia (119.1%), Mozambique (106.4%), Congo Republic (103.6%), Mauritius (93.5%), Angola (86.4%), Gambia (83.8%), and Ghana (82.1%) (IMF 2022). Of these, Mozambique and the Congo Republic were in debt distress as of 2019, while Zambia and Ghana slid into debt distress in 2020 and 2023, respectively.

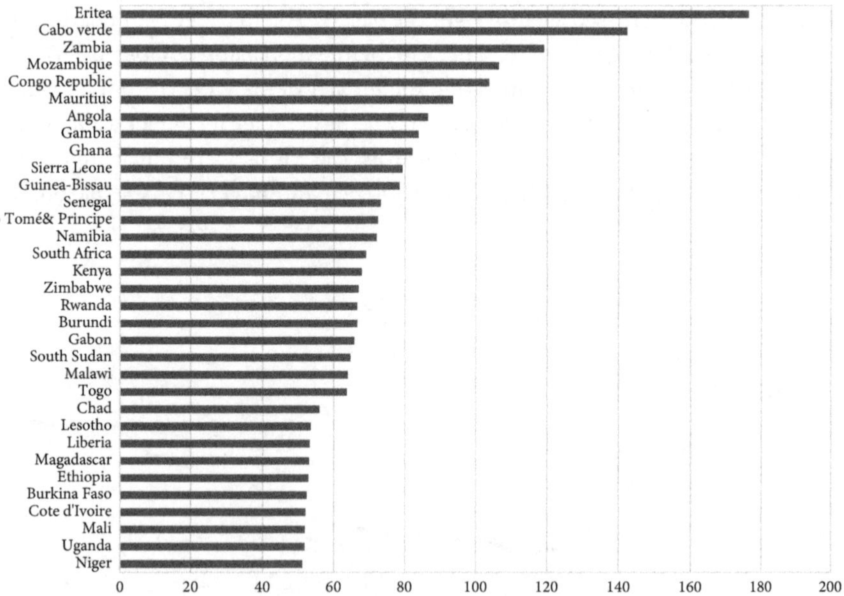

Figure 6.2 SSA countries with public debt-to-GDP ratio > 50% in 2021

Source: author's illustration based data from IMF (2022).

[4] Based on the IMF–World Bank classification, middle-income countries are those whose per capita gross national income averaged US$1085 or more over the period 2019–2021. These are Angola, Benin, Botswana, Cabo Verde, Cameroon, Comoros, Republic of Congo, Cote d'Ivoire, Equatorial Guinea, Eswatini, Gabon, Ghana, Kenya, Lesotho, Mauritius, Namibia, Nigeria, São Tomė and Principe, Senegal, Seychelles, South Africa, and Zambia.

[5] Based on IMF (2024b).

The composition of public debt is varied. For example, South Africa, Tanzania, Angola, Ghana, and Zambia's public debt is largely comprised of external debt, which account for over 60% on average (see Were 2024: Figure 3). As of December 2020, Tanzania's external debt as a percentage of total public debt was 72% compared to Kenya's at 52%. As of 2021, about 40% of SSA's debt was external (IMF 2023a). The risks associated with the domestic and external debt are not necessarily the same. Whereas increased appetite for domestic borrowing can put pressure on local interest rates in economies with thin or underdeveloped financial markets, it is arguably easier to deal with in terms of rollover, and there is less exposure to interest rate and exchange rate volatility given borrowing is in local currency. Domestic borrowing is considered as a form of transfer of resources within the country. Nonetheless, it accounts for a significant amount of interest payments.

In general, the share of multilateral debt has declined for most countries, including the HIPCs such as Tanzania and Ethiopia that traditionally had a significant share of multilateral debt. For most countries, the share is below 40%. This is mainly due to change in creditor composition, as exemplified by the rise in bilateral and private debt (which includes commercial debt and bonds). In particular, there has been a steady increase in private debt since 2006. Public and publicly guaranteed debt from private creditors for SSA excluding high-income countries increased by more than six times from US$33,258 million to US$220,376 million between 2006 and 2021 (Figure 6.3). Consequently, the share of public and publicly guaranteed debt from private creditors for SSA excluding high-income

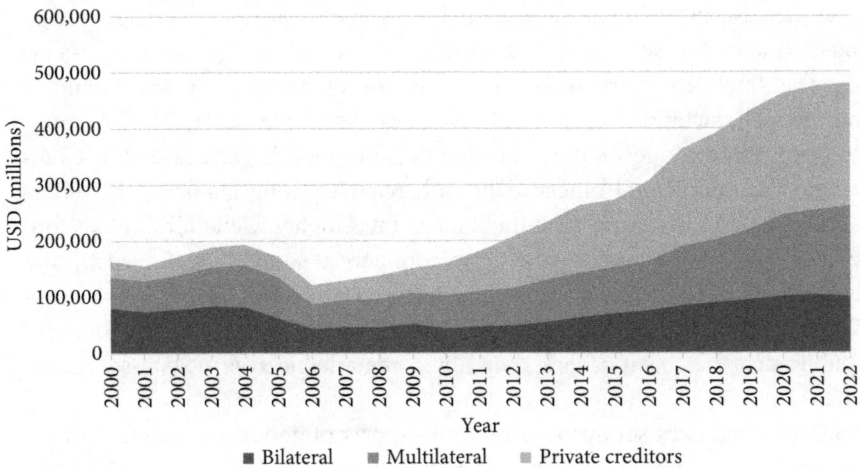

Figure 6.3 External debt stock by creditor: SSA excluding high-income countries (US$ millions)

Source: author's illustration based on data from International Debt Statistics.

countries increased substantially from 27.4% in 2006 to 46.4% in 2021, with a slight decline to 45.4% in 2022 (Figure 6.3). The decline largely reflects the impact of tight global financial market conditions experienced in 2022. On the other hand, the share of multilateral debt declined from 35.7 to 31.7% between 2006 and 2021, with a slight increase to 33.5% in 2022.

In terms of bilateral lending, China has emerged as the largest bilateral lender to African governments through its network of state-owned banks. Over the period 2000–20, the top 10 recipients of loans from China were Angola, Ethiopia, Zambia, Kenya, Egypt, Nigeria, Cameroon, South Africa, Republic of Congo, and Ghana. According to Global China Initiative researchers at Boston University Global Development Policy Center (BUGDPC), these countries accounted for 71% of all commitments between 2000 and 2020, with loans to Angola constituting 27% (Hwang et al. 2022). Over the same period, loan commitments estimated at US$160 billion were signed with 49 African governments, their state-owned enterprises, and five regional multilateral organizations (Hwang et al. 2022). The lending has largely been geared towards infrastructure projects in the transport, energy, and mining sectors.

The surge in Chinese loans has not been without criticism, especially with regard to the terms and conditions, leading to calls for more transparency, particularly by international financial organizations and the West. However, after a rapid growth that peaked in 2016 (2013 excluding Angola), China's lending to Africa has generally declined. The decline was more drastic in 2020, with a reduction in new loan commitments to US$1.9 billion, down from US$8.2 billion recorded in 2019, possibly due to COVID-19 pandemic challenges (Hwang et al. 2022).

The increase in the share of private debt is mainly attributable to sovereign bonds.[6] Since 2006, several SSA countries have issued foreign currency bonds in international debt markets following a period of favourable global financing conditions characterized by low interest rates. As of July 2021, 21 SSA countries were holding one or more outstanding Eurobonds (Icyeza 2021). Compared to the multilateral official debt with relatively long maturity, the tenors for bonds tend to be shorter and the interest rates higher. Generally, unlike concessional multilateral lending, debt from commercial sources is more costly and subject to interest rate fluctuations, and hence gives higher exposure to vulnerabilities in financing conditions. It is, therefore, not surprising that the increase in public debt has been accompanied by a remarkable rise in debt-servicing burden.

SSA's external debt service as a ratio of exports of goods and services shows an upward trend and had already risen sharply by 2019 before the COVID-19

[6] Debt from private creditors include bonds and commercial bank loans from private banks and other private financial institutions.

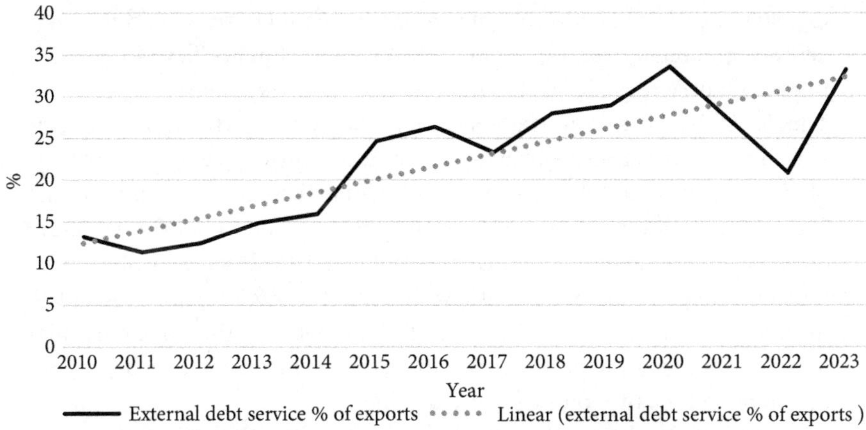

Figure 6.4 External debt service as a share of exports of goods and services (%)
Source: author's illustration based on World Economic Outlook database (IMF 2024a).

pandemic (Figure 6.4). The slight decline in 2021 partly reflects the temporary suspension of debt service during the COVID period. On average, the ratio nearly tripled from 11.3% in 2011 to 33.2% in 2023 (Figure 6.4). SSA governments are grappling with the high costs of debt servicing. Most are spending over 30% of domestic revenue on debt servicing, some as high as 50% or more. For example, Kenya's total debt service as a percentage of ordinary revenue increased to 58.8% in the fiscal year ending 2023 from 47.9% in the fiscal year ending 2022 (Republic of Kenya 2023).

3. Drivers of public debt accumulation

The rapid accumulation of public debt is attributable to various factors. These include pursuit of development objectives, especially infrastructure development, costly financing sources, negative shocks, interest rate and exchange rate volatilities, and maturity and currency mismatches, among others. The key drivers are briefly discussed below.

1. Increased investment demand for infrastructure development to fill the huge infrastructure gap has led to large-scale financing of development projects, mainly through loans from China. Investment in infrastructure and public utilities is deemed to promote growth and job creation by enhancing productivity and competitiveness. However, the former has led to widening of fiscal deficits and increased borrowing, especially in the absence of long-term infrastructure finance. Melina et al. (2016) note that

frontloading of public investment through increased borrowing can induce debt sustainability risks, especially with lower investment efficiency or when future resource revenues turn out to be lower than expected.

2. The risk of debt distress is heightened by maturity and currency mismatches, as well as coordination challenges in debt restructuring, particularly in view of the plurality of creditors (Ndulu and O'Connell 2021). In relation to what is discussed under (1) above, the relatively short loan maturity structure does not match the life of some of development infrastructure projects with much longer gestation periods of investment returns (Coulibaly et al. 2019). Additionally, as noted by Moreira (2023), the deteriorating debt dynamics in many countries are partly driven by currency-mismatch exposure given the increased reliance on external financing.
3. The multiple shocks, particularly the outbreak of the COVID-19 pandemic in March 2020, had an adverse impact on economic activities and domestic revenues. Although public debt was already rising, debt vulnerabilities became more elevated as borrowing to fund COVID-related expenditures increased, leading to a sharp increase in SSA's debt-to-GDP ratio to about 57.1% in 2020, the highest in nearly 20 years. The negative impact of subsequent shocks, including the Russia–Ukraine war, prolonged drought in the horn of Africa, and other climate-related shocks on the economies have also exacerbated debt vulnerabilities.
4. A general improvement in macroeconomic management, the fiscal space availed by the debt relief under the HIPCs initiative, and the fairly strong economic performance driven by the commodity boom during the period 2000–14 expanded the borrowing ability and capacity. Ndulu and O'Connell (2021) observe that the debt sustainability assessments (DSAs) that became integral to the post-2005 lending and surveillance activities of the IMF and World Bank also played a role in 'certifying improvements in borrowing capacity and reducing the cost of screening for private and bilateral official creditors including China' (Ndulu and O'Connell 2021: i59).
5. Whereas the debt crisis of the 1970s and 1980s was mainly characterized by debt owed to multilateral institutions, the current debt burden is largely due to increased bilateral and commercial borrowing. The latter was particularly occasioned by the significant interest rate cuts witnessed in advanced economies in response to the 2008/09 global financial crisis. Following a period of low global interest rates, bond issuances in Africa expanded eight times from an average of US$10 billion annually in the early 2000s, to about US$80 billion annually by 2016–20. While the access to international financial markets increased the financing options, it exposed the economies to increased risks associated with volatility in interest rates and capital flows. The financing conditions tightened drastically following the policy rate hikes by leading central banks in response to elevated inflation in advanced

economies. Consequently, most African countries are facing rollover risks as their sovereign bonds mature. Primary spreads for sovereign bonds for an average SSA issuer are, on average, higher than in other regions (Presbitero et al. 2016). A study by Brauning and Ivashina (2018) found that changes in US bond rates feed through more than point for point to emerging-market sovereign bond rates. Moreover, the heightened debt vulnerabilities have led to poor credit ranking, thus exacerbating the sovereign spreads. The high interest rates have increased the cost of borrowing and debt servicing, thus leading to a vicious cycle.

6. Dependency on commodity exports, which are subject to volatile prices in the global market (e.g. Angola, Nigeria, South Sudan on oil; Ghana on cocoa; and Zambia on copper), has also contributed to the debt challenges. A collapse in international prices as it happened to oil prices during the COVID-19 pandemic implies a drastic loss of revenue. For instance, the sharp decline in the price of copper exacerbated Zambia's financial challenges, which contributed to the country's default in November 2020, the first African country to default on its debt during the COVID-19 period. Zambia is Africa's second largest exporter of copper after the Democratic Republic of Congo.
7. Exchange rate volatility has a large impact: most of the debt is denominated in foreign currency, especially in US dollars, hence making countries vulnerable to exchange rate risks. Emerging market economies such as Zambia, Kenya, Ghana, and Angola experienced immense depreciation pressure on their domestic currencies, especially following the strengthening of the US dollar since 2020, thereby increasing the amount of debt in domestic currency and the cost of servicing dollar-denominated debt. On average, between 2022 and 2023 the domestic currencies of Sierra Leone, Angola, Ghana, Zambia, and Kenya depreciated by 51.7, 48.7, 33.2, 19.3, and 18.6%, respectively, against the US dollar (Figure 6.5).
8. Fragility of some of the economies (i.e. civil strife, political instability, and susceptibility to natural disasters) has aggravated the public debt burden. Thus, it is not surprising that some of the countries in debt stress fall under this category.
9. Fiscal management challenges have an impact: whereas macroeconomic management has generally improved over time, fiscal management, including public spending, is still hampered by inefficiency, wastage, and governance challenges, including misappropriation of funds. The numerous concerns often flagged out in the Auditor General reports in several SSA countries attest to these challenges. Lack of proper planning, cost–benefit analysis, and prioritization has, in some cases, led to poor implementation of projects, some of which end up becoming white elephants. Additionally, though often underestimated or less stated, politically driven

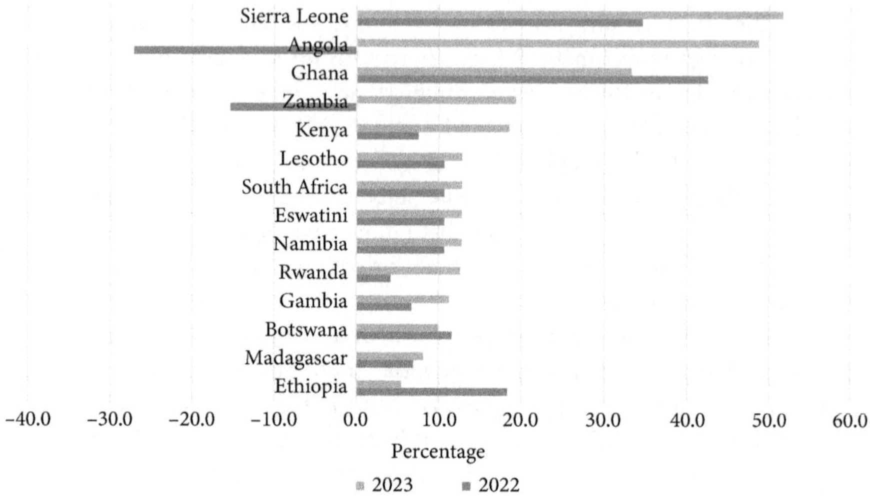

Figure 6.5 Local currency depreciation (%) against US$ (period average)
Source: author's illustration based on IMF International Financial Statistics database.

factors, including the urge to establish political legacies, have also played a role in driving debt accumulation. This is often manifested in multiple development projects hastily initiated without comprehensive planning and assessing of their viability and financing options.

4. Approaches to debt sustainability assessment

There is no universally accepted definition of sustainable debt. Low or high debt levels do not necessarily imply that debt is sustainable or unsustainable. Although various public-to-GDP debt thresholds are often proposed or suggested in the literature, the critical level of debt depends on a variety of factors and is bound to vary across countries. In the literature, perspectives to debt sustainability generally revolve around fiscal sustainability. That notwithstanding, fiscal sustainability is an elusive concept, particularly owing to the key challenge of accurately determining a government's inter-temporal budget constraint, which is the core of fiscal sustainability analysis (Pradhan 2019). The complexity has been worsened by increased integration of financial markets in a global environment that has become highly uncertain. Whereas there are various approaches to fiscal sustainability assessment, the solvency approach is perhaps the most widely adopted. Others include Domar's stability approach, the backward-looking approach, the balance-sheet approach, and the Ricardian equivalence approach (see Pradhan 2019).

A government is considered solvent if net debt obligations over a finite horizon, with a stream of future primary surpluses, can be achieved (Brady and Magazzino 2018). Governments are faced with a present-value borrowing constraint such that they have to intertemporally balance their budgets by setting the current market value of debt equal to the discounted sum of expected future surpluses. A violation of intertemporal budget balance could be taken as indication that the fiscal policy is not sustainable in the long run, as the value of debt could explode over time (Collignon 2012).

An overview of fiscal/debt sustainability approaches in the empirical literature and the commonly used IMF–World Bank debt sustainability framework is summarized below.

4.1 Debt sustainability assessment in the empirical literature

The empirical literature on assessment of public debt sustainability has mainly focused on testing the sustainability of the intertemporal budget constraint using various techniques. In this regard, the most influential and commonly used empirical approach is the model-based approach following Bohn (1998), under which a policy rule (i.e. a fiscal reaction function of primary surplus to increases in public debt) is estimated to ascertain the fiscal sustainability of debt. Based on Bohn (1998), the risk of public debt becoming unsustainable can be averted if the government reacts effectively to changes in public debt through primary balance. Thus, the fiscal reaction function describes a country's fiscal response via primary balance, which is often specified as a function of lagged public debt-to-GDP ratio and business cycle fluctuations (output gap). The lagged primary balance is typically included as part of the explanatory variables to control for possible deficit bias or sluggish budget response. In a nutshell, the relationship captures the link between a fiscal instrument (primary balance) and debt stability as the fiscal goal. The responsibility of ensuring debt sustainability is, thus, placed on the behaviour of fiscal policy such that when the debt rises, a sustainable fiscal policy requires an increase in primary surplus or reduction in fiscal deficit.

The fiscal reaction approach is underpinned by the intuition that to ensure debt sustainability, governments need to take corrective actions by increasing primary balance to take care of increases in debt accumulation.The limitation of this approach is the emphasis placed on the role of fiscal policy in isolation from other factors such as developments in international financial markets and the role of monetary policy (see Leeper 1991).

The empirical literature on fiscal sustainability of debt has been growing and continues to evolve. However, most of the studies have largely focused on advanced and emerging economies, mainly using the fiscal reaction function approach (e.g. Paret 2017; Beqiraj et al. 2018; Joy and Panda 2020; Park and Sung 2020; Small et al. 2020). For instance, focusing on six major emerging economies (Argentina, Brazil, Russia, Turkey, Philippines, and South Africa), Paret (2017) found evidence suggesting the countries' fiscal policies were responsive to debt. However, Joy and Panda (2020) found sustainability of public debt for Brazil, Russia, India, China, and South Africa (BRICS countries) to be weak. Country-level studies include Lankester-Campos et al. (2020), Rathnayake (2020), and Serju-Thomas (2020), who found evidence of unsustainable public debt for Costa Rica, Sri Lanka, and Jamaica, respectively.

Despite the growing literature, studies focusing on SSA are still limited and show mixed results. For example, using 2000–16 panel data for 32 SSA countries, Mupunga and Ngundu (2020) found a positive and significant response of primary balances to increases in debt levels, thus implying fiscal sustainability of public debt. Based on 2008–17 data for 37 SSA countries, Abubakar (2020) found that fiscal tightening led to a decline in public debt while fiscal loosening increased public debt. However, in a relatively more recent study covering 45 countries for the period 2010–20, Olaoye and Olomola (2023) found SSA's public debts to be weakly sustainable. Additionally, a highly procyclical fiscal policy bias was noted, particularly in resource-rich and oil-exporting countries. Focusing on the Economic Community of West Africa States (ECOWAS), Omotor (2021) found the public debt levels to be unsustainable. Based on a case study of Tanzania, Were and Mollel (2020) found sustainability of public debt to be weak.

In summary, the evidence of fiscal sustainability of public debt in SSA based on recent studies is generally weak, if any. This is corroborated by the weak relationship between fiscal balance and public debt-to-GDP ratios (see Were 2024: Appendix Figure 1).

4.2 IMF–World Bank Debt Sustainability Framework

In practice, the joint IMF–World Bank Debt Sustainability Framework (DSF) for Low-Income Countries (LIC–DSF) and Market Access Countries (MAC–DSF) is the most commonly and widely used framework for conducting DSAs. The latter constitute part of the surveillance activities under Article IV consultations by the IMF. Since the introduction of DSF in 2005, the DSAs are often relied upon to inform borrowing and lending decisions, particularly in low-income and emerging market economies. SSA countries' DSAs are mainly analysed using LIC–DSF.

The analysis entails projection of a country's debt burden over the next 10 years and its vulnerability to shocks, based on medium-term macroeconomic projections and assumptions for key variables such as growth and changes in the primary balance, on the basis of which baseline and stress tests are calculated. The assessment of risk of external and overall debt distress is based on various debt burden thresholds and benchmarks.[7]

The debt sustainability thresholds are based on the country's debt-carrying capacity, which is measured by a composite indicator (CI). CI is computed using a measure of quality of institutions and policies (i.e. country policy and institutional assessments, CPIAs) and macroeconomic performance indicators. It is a weighted average of CPIA score, real GDP growth, reserve coverage, remittances, and world growth. Countries are classified on the basis of their debt-carrying capacity according to the CI ranking: strong (CI > 3.05), medium (2.69 ≤ CI ≤ 3.05) or weak (CI < 2.69), underpinned by the assumption that countries with better policies, institutions, and macroeconomic prospects can sustain a higher debt level. The threshold indicators are assessed in terms of GDP, exports, and revenue, with higher thresholds for countries considered to be stronger performers. The computed debt burden indicators are compared to indicative thresholds over the projection period to assess sustainability of debt. The debt-carrying capacity determines the applicable thresholds and benchmarks used in the debt DSAs, with different threshold values for weak, medium, and strong performers.[8] The risk of public debt distress is based on four types of ratings: 'low risk', 'moderate risk', 'high risk', and 'in debt distress'. A country is considered to be in debt distress if it is unable to fulfil its financial obligations and debt restructuring is required (Rakara 2020).

The main advantage of the IMF–World Bank DSF lies in its simplicity, which makes it easier to replicate across countries. This, in turn, facilitates comparison and makes it easier to obtain a bird's eye view of the debt sustainability landscape in SSA or generally across the countries covered. That notwithstanding, the framework has some shortcomings. For instance, concerns have been raised regarding its simplistic assumptions, reliability of medium-term projections including growth and fiscal adjustments, analytical challenges, and the emphasis on present value of debt despite the profusion of multiplicity of creditors with different interest rates (see Bonizzi et al. 2019; Atingi-Ego et al. 2021).

[7] Present value of debt obligations is computed using a 5% discount rate for external debt.
[8] For more details, see IMF (2018).

5. Implications of debt accumulation on debt sustainability

The analysis of SSA's debt sustainability challenges in this chapter is mainly based on the published DSA outcomes. Based on the joint World Bank–IMF DSAs, the risk of debt distress in SSA has generally increased. The combined impact of multiple shocks, tighter financial conditions, and exchange rate pressures on the domestic currencies amid lack of fiscal space and high cost of debt servicing have, among other factors, heightened debt sustainability challenges. Basically, all the SSA economies covered under the LIC–DSF are facing some form of debt sustainability risks, at varying degrees ranging from moderate to high, or in distress.[9] By end of September 2022, one-half of SSA's low-income countries were either already in debt distress or at high risk of distress, while the rest were facing moderate risk of debt distress (Figure 6.6a).[10] The latter include HIPCs—such as Madagascar, Rwanda, Senegal, Tanzania, and Uganda—that had generally been considered to have a low risk of debt distress following the HIPCs debt relief initiative.

Based on the published DSAs as of 30 June 2023, the number of SSA countries in debt distress increased to 7 out of the total 11 countries in debt distress, with Ghana and Malawi being the latest countries to have joined the list. Other countries in debt distress included Zambia, Congo Republic, Mozambique, and Zimbabwe. Malawi quickly transitioned from 'moderate' risk of debt distress

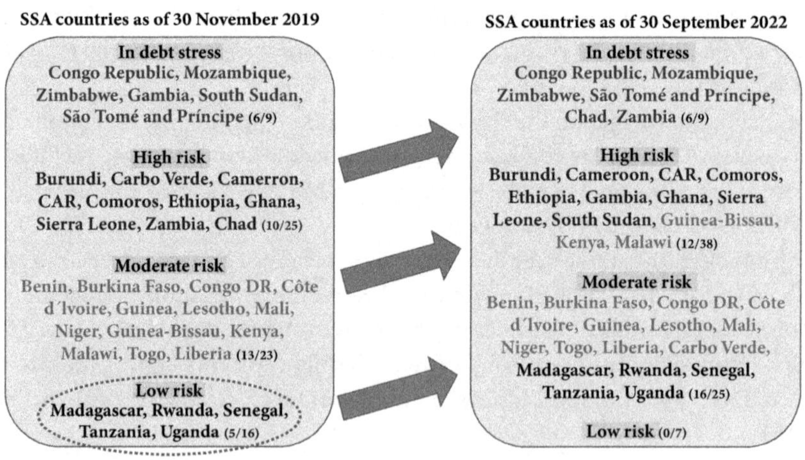

Figure 6.6a Overview of SSA countries' DSAs as of 2019 and 2022
Source: author's illustration based on various published DSAs.

[9] Excluding Eritrea, whose DSA is not publicly available. South Africa, Nigeria, Botswana, Angola, Mauritius, Namibia, Seychelles, and Eswatini are usually excluded.
[10] Excluding Eritrea, whose DSA is not publicly available.

before 2020 to 'high' risk and eventual distress, following multiple shocks, including a cyclone. Ghana was rocked by economic and financial challenges that worsened in 2022, leading to a default on some of its debt in December 2022. That notwithstanding, Ghana's fiscal balance (excluding grants) had deteriorated significantly from an average of −6.6% in the period 2011–19 to −17.4% in 2020—the highest recorded among SSA countries in the COVID year 2020. Public debt-to-GDP ratio increased remarkably from an average of 49.6% to 72.3 and 93.3% in 2020 and 2022, respectively.[11] The country's challenges seem to have been further heightened by the multiple downgrades that were made by credit rating agencies.

As of February 2024, four out of the six SSA countries in debt distress were middle-income countries (Zambia, Ghana, Republic of Congo, and São Tomé and Príncipe) (Figure 6.6b). On a positive note, the latest DSA outcomes show that Chad has since graduated from being 'in debt distress' to 'high risk' of debt distress following a debt-restructuring agreement with its creditors (Figure 6.6b). The same applies to Mozambique, which also reached an agreement on some of its defaulted debt. Meanwhile, several countries are facing high risks of debt distress. These include Ethiopia, Cameroon, Gambia, Sierra Leone, South Sudan, Burundi, Comoros, and Burundi (Figure 6.6a and 6.6b). Kenya and Guinea-Bissau, whose risk of debt risk was classified as moderate before the COVID-19 pandemic, also joined the list of countries at high risk of distress.[12] Kenya's public

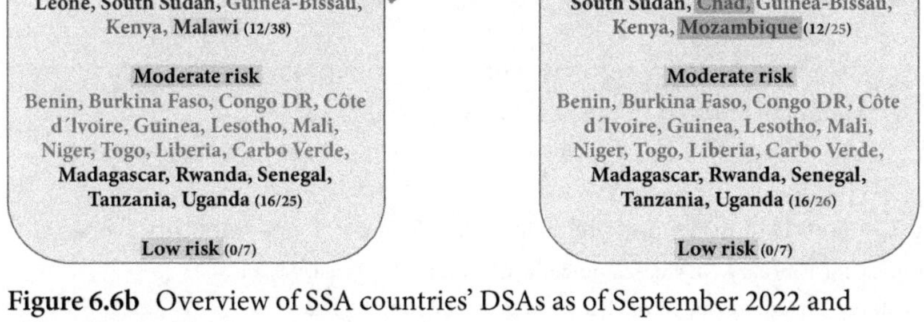

Figure 6.6b Overview of SSA countries' DSAs as of September 2022 and February 2024

Source: author's illustration based on various published DSAs.

[11] Based on data in IMF (2024b).
[12] Both countries are classified as middle-income countries.

debt-to-GDP increased rapidly from 45.8% in 2015 to 68.4% in 2022. As of end of March 2023, total outstanding public debt was KES9.4 trillion against a ceiling of KES10 trillion.[13] Although the economy exhibited resilience in the face of multiple shocks, the country experienced a credit squeeze considering the high costs of debt servicing and constrained fiscal space. This led to increase in taxes in a bid to increase domestic revenue as the government embarked on implementation of fiscal consolidation plan.

It is worth noting that all the low-income SSA countries (Tanzania, Rwanda, Senegal, Uganda, and Madagascar) whose risk of debt distress remained 'low' before the COVID-19 pandemic have since shifted to 'moderate' risk category, which suggests increased vulnerability to debt sustainability challenges. Moreover, even for countries that are not in distress, the cost of debt servicing nearly doubled after the emergence of the pandemic, with an average yield of over 12% on outstanding Eurobonds compared to 7% before the pandemic (IMF 2023b). The average yield on sovereign bonds increased notably in 2022 and 2023, leading to significant rollover risks. Figure 6.7 shows the average monthly yields on 10-year Eurobonds for Kenya, Ethiopia, and Angola; the 11-year bond for Ghana; and the 12-year bold for Zambia.[14] The heightened impact of the COVID-19 pandemic in 2020 and interest rate hikes in advanced economies in 2022, coupled

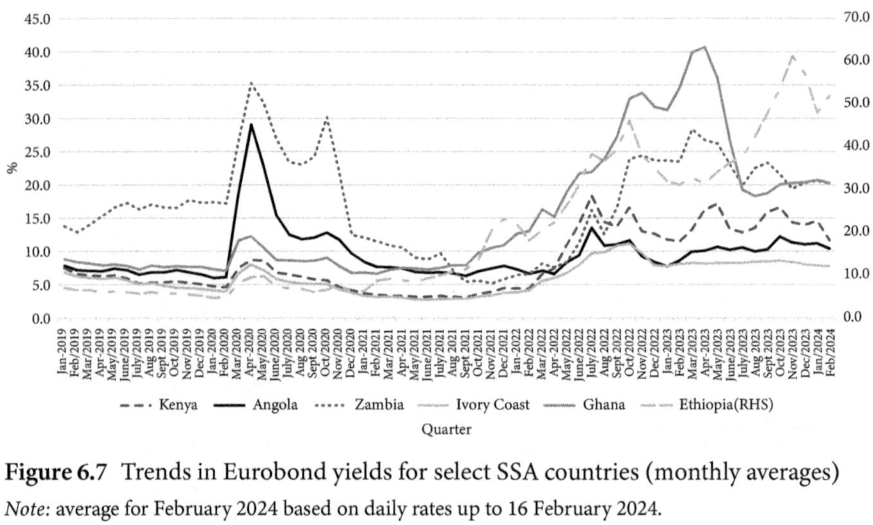

Figure 6.7 Trends in Eurobond yields for select SSA countries (monthly averages)

Note: average for February 2024 based on daily rates up to 16 February 2024.

Source: author's illustration based on Thomas Reuters (Refinitiv) data.

[13] The government has since shifted from specifying the debt ceiling in terms of levels (maximum amount of public debt) to the case where the public debt ceiling is set as a percentage of GDP (i.e. 55%).

[14] Maturity dates for Kenya and Ethiopia are June and December 2024, while maturity dates for Angola, Zambia, and Ghana are May 2025, July 2027, and May 2029, respectively.

with a downgrade in credit ratings, is clearly evident, especially for Ghana, Zambia, and Ethiopia, which slid into debt distress. For instance, the yields for Ghana's sovereign bond had remained relatively low and stable at an average of 7.9% in 2019. While they temporarily increased slightly during the March–May 2020 COVID period (to an average of 11.4%), they remained below 10% on average (8.9% in 2020, and 8.1% in 2021) but increased sharply to an average of 22.4% in 2022. By the time Ghana defaulted on payment of its external debt, the yield on its 11-year outstanding Eurobond had surged to over 30%. Meanwhile, annual average inflation soared to 31.3% and 38.1% in 2022 and 2023, respectively.[15] Similarly, the yields on Ethiopia's 10-year outstanding Eurobond increased substantially from 7% and 11.6% in 2020 and 2021 to an average of 31.1% in 2022 and continued rising in 2023 (Figure 6.7).

Zambia's public debt challenges started biting much earlier following multiple issuances of sovereign bonds and increased reliance on bilateral lending from China. The country issued its first Eurobond in 2012, followed by two subsequent sovereign bonds in 2014 and 2015. Zambia was assessed to be at high risk of debt distress in 2017 as the macroeconomic environment and quality and pricing of Eurobonds continued to deteriorate over time. The country was downgraded several times in 2018 to the grade of CCC, just before the COVID-19 crisis. By 2019, commercial debt accounted for one-half of the external debt. The rapid debt accumulation was accompanied by the prohibitive cost of debt servicing—by 2019, debt service became Zambia's largest spending category, accounting for over 30% of expenditure (Mbewe et al. 2024). Following a period of expansionary fiscal policy and ambitious infrastructural development drive, the stock of public debt doubled from 60.6% of GDP in 2016 to an unsustainable level of 120% in 2019, before increasing further to 140.2% in 2020. Meanwhile, overall fiscal balance (including grants) deteriorated substantially to −13.8% of GDP in 2020. The yields on its sovereign bonds increased substantially; for example, the yields on a 12-year outstanding bond increased from 15.9% in 2019 to 24.2% in 2020 on average, having risen to as high as 35.4% and 30.1% in April and October 2020, respectively (Figure 6.7). It was, therefore, not surprising when Zambia defaulted on its external debt payment in November 2020 during the COVID-19 period. Furthermore, in 2020, the Zambian kwacha depreciated notably against the US dollar, following the fall in copper prices and downgrade of credit scores. This fuelled inflation, which rose to 22% in 2021 from 9.1% in 2019, though it has since declined to 11% in 2022 and 2023. Although the yields declined to 8.4% after Zambia sought debt restructuring, they increased to over 10% beginning the first half of 2022 and remained relatively high.

[15] Figures from World Bank Open Data at https://data.worldbank.org/indicator/FP.CPI.TOTL.ZG?locations=GH (accessed 7 February 2025).

The tighter financing conditions in international financial markets priced out low- and middle-income countries (LMICs). According to the World Bank (2023), total net debt flows to this category turned negative in 2022 for the first time since 2015, reflecting a sharp retrenchment in bond issuance by sovereigns and other public and private borrowers.[16] However, after an absence of Eurobond issuance by SSA countries since April 2022, there seems to be some light at the end of the tunnel following successful Eurobond issuances by Côte d'Ivoire, Benin, and Kenya early in 2024. The trio managed to raise a total of US$4.8 billion. Yields on Côte d'Ivoire's sovereign bonds remained relatively low and stable, a factor that is likely to have facilitated the country in being the first one to resume sovereign bond issuance after a lengthy period of no issuance by SSA countries. Kenya's seven-year bond of US$1.5 billion was slightly higher priced with a coupon rate of 9.75% compared to Côte d'Ivoire's with a slightly longer maturity at 8.5%. Nonetheless, it seems to be what the country needed most to avert the steady decline in the value of its domestic currency, which had depreciated sharply to over 150 against the US dollar by December 2023, partly driven by increased speculation about the risk of defaulting on its 10-year Eurobond of US$2 billion that was due for maturity in June 2024. Following the bond issuance, the government also succeeded in averting a default.

Notwithstanding the positive signal, the public debt burden still remains a major challenge, considering the murky horizon the SSA economies are facing. Although inflation in advanced economies has eased, core inflation has been relatively sticky and, hence, policy rate cuts are unlikely to be drastic. This implies that international financial markets could remain relatively tight or volatile, with high rollover risks for several countries whose sovereign bonds are due to mature in the next few years. Meanwhile, domestic tax revenue mobilization remains a challenge in light of subdued demand, a large informal economy, adverse climate change impact, and the high cost of production as exchange rate pressures continue to persist. The global economic environment remains uncertain given the rising geopolitical tensions, including the Israel–Palestine war. On the upside, a faster-than-expected fall in global inflation could lead to further easing of financial conditions. Nonetheless, long-term solutions to SSA's debt sustainability challenges are needed.

[16] According to World Bank (2023), there was a net outflow of US$127.1 billion from LMICs to bondholders in 2022, compared to an average annual inflow of US$202billion in 2019–21.

6. International initiatives towards public debt challenges

Despite the biting public debt challenges, a comprehensive debt relief initiative akin to the HIPC debt relief package is yet to be seen. There have been some international initiatives, albeit patchy with limited scope, coverage, and impact. The key ones include the G20 Debt Service Suspension Initiative (DSSI) and the Common Framework for Debt Treatment beyond the DSSI.

Launched in May 2020, the DSSI was initiated by the G20 countries with the support of the World Bank and the IMF to assist LICs by providing a temporary suspension (without cancellation) of debt-service payments owed to official bilateral creditors during the challenging COVID-19 period. Although the initiative was extended twice, it lasted for a short period of about one-and-a-half years until December 2021, forcing participating countries to resume debt-service payments thereafter. While the initiative offered some temporary relief, it was short lived and limited in scope. Moreover, only a small fraction of Africa's total bilateral debt was covered. Overall, two-thirds (48 countries) of the 73 eligible debtor countries participated in the DSSI. That notwithstanding, the low-income countries were eventually confronted by the additional burden of having to pay the accumulated principal, interest, and fees incurred under the DSSI, besides paying the steeper interest rates countries are generally paying for their debt (World Bank 2023).

Given the temporary nature of the DSSI and mounting concerns of debt distress, the G20, in conjunction with the Paris Club, launched the Common Framework for Debt Treatment beyond the DSSI in November 2020, with the aim of providing a more structured and comprehensive debt treatment support to LICs with unsustainable debt, on a case-by-case basis. Upon receiving a request for debt treatment from an eligible debtor country, a Creditor Committee is convened, with the IMF and the World Bank providing the necessary support to the negotiations. The debt treatment, which could be anything from short-term debt reprofiling to deep restructuring, should be accompanied by various reforms, including IMF-supported reform programmes to ensure future sustainability of public debt (Cassimon et al. 2023). The debtor is expected to seek 'comparable' (i.e. at least as favourable) debt treatments from all other official bilateral and private creditors. However, participation remains limited and, hence, many eligible countries have not benefitted. The framework has been rocked with coordination challenges and prolonged negotiations for the few countries that have made requests, partly due to the multiplicity of creditors. The latter include the traditional Paris Club creditors and new creditors, particularly China, whose share of public debt in LICs has increased significantly. Chad was the first country to reach a debt restructuring agreement with its official and private creditors under the G20 Common Framework (IFC 2023). Other countries that have sought debt restructuring under the framework are Ethiopia and Zambia in 2021 and Ghana in 2023. Although Zambia applied for debt treatment in early 2021, the negotiations were prolonged. It was not until June 2023 that Zambia eventually finalized a US$6.3 billion debt-restructuring deal, which included China but excluded private creditors.[17]

Besides coordination challenges, the multiplicity of creditors, particularly the participation of private creditors, remains a challenge. Volz et al. (2020) note that the brief time frame set for DSSI liquidity relief by the G20 made private-sector participation less likely, partly because the debtor governments refrained from requesting their involvement. From the debtors' perspective, the limited participation in the G20 debt-relief initiatives can be attributed to concerns about potential implications associated with the negative stigma of taking part. Cassimon et al. (2023) argue that in considering whether to participate or not, the eligible debtor countries only choose to participate when the expected net benefit of doing so exceeds the value of waiting and being able to gather more information about the net benefits. Of particular concern is the negative signal their participation could send about their creditworthiness and thereby lead to a sovereign default and prolonged exclusion from capital markets (Volz et al. 2020). Arguably, countries guard against such repercussions, including being downgraded by credit rating agencies. A missed debt-service payment to a private creditor implies an outright default. Moreover, in the case of distressed debt exchange (DDE), a default does not require a missed payment.[18] The Common Framework for Debt Treatment still lacks a mechanism for meaningful private creditor involvement and fails to address the first-mover problem for participating countries.

In general, the current G20 initiatives, besides being inadequate, have seemingly remained less attractive and fallen short of providing the much-needed restoration of a debt sustainability pathway for the SSA economies in distress or at high risk of debt distress. The G20 framework as currently structured is not up to the debt challenges facing African countries (Moreira 2023). While a timely and orderly debt resolution could help to foster confidence and encourage participation, a comprehensive package including debt relief is vital. Additionally, debt contracts should include clauses that automatically lower or suspend debt service in the event of significant economic shocks or natural catastrophes. Debt restructuring need not wait until a country defaults.

Most SSA economies have had no choice but to turn to the multilateral financial institutions, particularly the Bretton Wood Institutions, for support through their various respective lending facilities. According to the World Bank (2023), the World Bank accounted for 42% of the debt stock owed to multilateral creditors by countries eligible for borrowing from its International Development Association

[17] The country has been working out a deal with its international bondholders.

[18] 'A DDE is a situation in which the issuer offers bondholders a new package of securities that amounts to a diminished financial obligation or where the exchange has the apparent purpose of helping the borrower avoid default (Moody's 2002)' (Volz et al. 2020: 41).

(IDA) in 2022. As of March 2023, the IMF had 21 lending arrangements with countries in the SSA region, with additional programmes under request or discussion. Since March 2020, the IMF stepped up its lending, including emergency financing, following the immense challenges caused by the COVID-19 pandemic. The IMF financial assistance to LICs increased markedly from an average of US$2 billion a year before the pandemic to about US$12 billion in 2020, largely through emergency financing instruments (IMF 2021). More than one-half of the countries that received that financial support were in SSA.[19] Additionally, in 2021, the IMF Board approved a general allocation of special drawing rights (SDRs) of about 456 billion (equivalent to US$650 billion) to boost global liquidity. However, since the allocations are traditionally based on existing quotas and not on a need basis, Africa's share was meagre—US$27billion, which is equivalent to 4.2% of total allocation.

While the IMF's balance-of-payment financial support has been handy, the programme loans often come with several stringent conditionalities. These currently include fiscal consolidation attained through increased taxation, removal of subsidies, and expenditure cuts. Whereas aggressive fiscal consolidation could be one of the key strategies of managing public debt, it is coming at a time when the African governments and economies are writhing from tough economic challenges, ranging from depleted fiscal buffers following the aftermaths of the COVID-19 pandemic, high cost of living, the impact of the Russia–Ukraine war, subdued demand, and the ravaging climate change impact, among others. In a bid to increase domestic tax revenue, the Kenyan government, for instance, instituted multiple taxes and levies, leading to a public outcry and concern with regard to their efficacy and impact on the economy.[20] Excessive blanket budget cuts, coupled with the high debt-servicing costs, could derail development progress in the region, including investment in infrastructure, social sectors such as health and education, and provision of safety nets to the vulnerable population.

Avenues for long-term concessional sources of finance are needed. The New Development Bank set up by BRICS[21]—a group of emerging economies—has potential to play a more prominent role in supporting Africa's sustainable development agenda, for example through concessional financing. The Bank was set up in 2015 with the aim of mobilizing resources for infrastructure and sustainable development projects in emerging market economies and developing countries. However, so far, its impact on the continent is limited. Meanwhile, calls for reforms to the international financial architecture are increasingly gaining momentum,

[19] In 2021, the Catastrophe Containment and Relief Trust was modified to allow for debt service relief for LICs affected by pandemic.

[20] A contentious finance bill laden with tax measures, including hikes, led to countrywide protests in June 2024, leading to the withdrawal of the bill after the president declined to sign it into law.

[21] Brazil, India, China, and South Africa (BRICS), Saudi Arabia, Iran, Egypt, Ethiopia, and the United Arab Emirates joined recently.

partly driven by the inability of the current architecture to facilitate mobilization of stable and long-term finance, deep-rooted inequities, biases, and inefficiencies of the system. Some of the concerns include higher borrowing costs for developing and low-income countries in financial markets, even after taking into account default risks and market volatility (United Nations 2023).

7. Conclusion and policy insights

SSA's rising public debt burden remains a challenge to sustainable development in the region. This follows a period of increased debt accumulation, largely propelled by access to commercial debt via international financial markets and bilateral lending, particularly from China. The debt accumulation is mainly attributable to large-scale financing of increased investment demand for infrastructure projects in a bid to fill the huge infrastructure gaps, maturity and currency mismatches, and vulnerability to interest rate and exchange rate volatility, among others. The public debt challenges have been heightened by multiple shocks, particularly the adverse impact of the COVID-19 pandemic, the tight global financial conditions following monetary policy tightening in advanced economies, depreciation of domestic currencies, climate change impacts, and the increased cost of servicing debt. Unlike multilateral concessional lending, commercial debt is more costly and subject to interest rate changes. SSA governments are grappling with a high debt-servicing burden amidst multiple development challenges and limited revenues.

The heavy debt burden has led to heightened public debt sustainability challenges. Consequently, the risk of debt distress has increased. One-half of SSA's low-income countries are either already in debt distress or at high risk of it. Basically, all the SSA countries whose debt sustainability is assessed using the joint World Bank–IMF LIC–DSF are facing some form of debt sustainability risk, ranging from 'moderate' to 'distressed'. Based on the published DSAs as of end of February 2024, six out of the nine countries in debt distress are in SSA. Of the six, four are middle-income countries (Congo Republic, São Tomé and Príncipe, Zambia, and Ghana), while two (Zimbabwe and Malawi) are LICs, with Malawi and Ghana being the latest countries to join the group. Additionally, 12 SSA countries are at high risk of debt distress, including countries like Kenya and Guinea-Bissau, whose debt distress risk was moderate before the COVID-19 pandemic. Meanwhile, the debt sustainability risk of the countries that were traditionally known to be at low risk of debt distress before the pandemic has since increased from 'low' to 'moderate'—these include the HIPCs: Tanzania, Rwanda, Senegal, Madagascar, and Uganda.

There are no quick fixes nor a one-size-fits-all solution to SSA's rising public debt burden—particularly considering the multiplicity of creditors and challenges. Sustainable long-term solutions will require a concerted multi-pronged approach.

This calls for critical role of various stakeholders at the domestic and international levels. Despite the pressing public debt challenges, and unlike the debt crisis of the 1980s, a debt relief programme is still largely missing in global public debt-related initiatives and debates. In the short run, and at the very worst, most countries in debt distress require debt restructuring to get breathing space to reorganize. Unfortunately, the G20 Common Framework has been rocked with coordination challenges and protracted negotiations for the very few countries that have sought debt treatment and, hence, not lived up to expectations. More needs to be done to make the framework more effective in addressing SSA's public debt burden. While timely and orderly debt restructuring could help to foster confidence and encourage participation, a comprehensive package, including debt relief and expansion of the framework to debt-burdened countries at high risk of distress, is crucial. More importantly, access to long-term international finance in the form of concessional flows remain a critical source of external financing, particularly for LICs. Hence, there is a need for concerted efforts by the international community to enhance its availability and predictability.

Domestically, fiscal consolidation has become inevitable, particularly for countries on IMF lending programmes. However, fiscal consolidation comes at a cost and at a time when the economies are struggling with multiple challenges, such as climate change impact, high debt-servicing costs, increased cost of living, and widespread unemployment. Huge blanket cuts in government spending are likely to curtail public investment and expenditure towards provision of public utilities, social protection, and human capital development. Hence, there is a need to safeguard these and other key sectors. Domestic resource mobilization through widening of the tax base, digitalization, financial deepening, and capital market development as well as innovative public–private partnership strategies are viable options to be explored. These strategies should be accompanied by enhanced efficiency in public spending, accountability, proper planning, and effective debt management, particularly considering the complexities of multiple creditors. SSA's long-term sustainability of public debt and socio-economic development will require economic transformation, for example export-led growth through increased access to global markets and value chains, leveraging regional trade integration opportunities such as African Continental Free Trade Area, increased value addition, and unlocking domestic supply constraints. Development banks geared towards providing long-term finance could also prove helpful. In this regard, BRICs' New Development Bank should play a more prominent role in supporting Africa's quest for development.

References

Abubakar, A. B. (2020). 'Does Fiscal Tightening (Loosening) Reduce Public Debt?' *African Development Review*, 32(4): 528–39. https://doi.org/10.1111/1467-8268.12458.

Atingi-Ego, M., S. Timuno, and T. Makuve (2021). 'Public Debt Accumulation in Africa: A Looming Debt Crisis'. *Journal of African Economies*, 30(AERC Supplement 1): i103–i139. https://doi.org/10.1093/jae/ejab023.

Beqiraj, E., S. Fedeli, and F. Forte (2018). 'Public Debt Sustainability: An Empirical Study on OECD Countries'. *Journal of Macroeconomics*, 58: 238–48. https://doi.org/10.1016/j.jmacro.2018.10.002.

Brady, G., and C. Magazzino (2018). 'Government Debt in EMU Countries'. *Journal of Economic Asymmetries*, 18: e00096. https://doi.org/10.1016/j.jeca.2018.e00096.

Brauning F., and V. Ivashina (2018) 'U.S. Monetary Policy and Emerging Market Credit Cycles'. National Bureau of Economic Research (NBER) Working Paper 25185, October. https://doi.org/10.3386/w25185.

Bonizzi, B., C. Laskaridis, and J. Toporowski. (2019). 'Global Liquidity, the Private Sector and Debt Sustainability in Sub-Saharan Africa'. *Development and Change*, 50(5): 1430–54. https://doi.org/10.1111/dech.12507.

Bohn, H. (1998). 'The Behavior of US Public Debt and Deficits'. *Quarterly Journal of Economics*, 113(3): 949–63. https://doi.org/10.1162/003355398555793.

Cassimon, D., D. Essers, and A. F. Presbitero (2023). 'Why Are Debtor Countries Hesitant to Participate in Debt Relief Initiatives?' SUERF Policy Brief 756, December. Wien: The European Money and Finance Forum (SUERF).

Collignon, S. (2012). 'Fiscal Policy Rules and the Sustainability of Public Debt in Europe'. *International Economic Review*, 53(2): 539–67. https://doi.org/10.1111/j.1468-2354.2012.00691.x.

Coulibaly, B., D. Gandhi, and L. Senbet (2019). 'Is Sub-Saharan Africa Facing Another Systemic Sovereign Debt Crisis?' Africa Growth Initiative, April, 1–16. Available at: https://www.brookings.edu/wp-content/uploads/2019/04/africa_sovereign_debt_sustainability.pdf (accessed 18 December 2024).

Hwang, J., O. Moses, L. Engel, and S. Shadbar (2022). 'Chinese Loans to Africa during the COVID-19 Pandemic'. Global China Initiative Policy Brief 012. Boston: Global Development Policy Center.

Icyeza, P. (2021). 'Summer in the Field: Bond, Eurobond: Tracking African Eurobonds Issued between 2006–2021'. Blog. Boston University Global Development Policy Center. Available at: https://www.bu.edu/gdp/2021/10/22/bond-eurobond-tracking-african-eurobonds-issued-between-2006-2021 (accessed 18 December 2024).

IFC (International Finance Corporation) (2023). *Country Private Sector Diagnostic: Mobilizing Private Investment for Inclusive: Growth Creating Markets in Chad.* Washington, DC: IFC.

IMF (International Monetary Fund) (2018). 'Guidance Note on the Bank-Fund Debt Sustainability Framework for Low Income Countries', 14 February. Available at: https://www.imf.org/en/Publications/Policy-Papers/Issues/2018/02/14/pp122617guidance-note-on-lic-dsf (accessed 18 December 2024).

IMF (2021). *International Monetary Fund Annual Report 2021*. Washington, DC: IMF. https://doi.org/10.5089/9781513568812.011.

IMF (2022). *Regional Economic Outlook: Sub-Saharan Africa—Living on the Edge*. Washington, DC: IMF.

IMF (2023a). *Regional Economic Outlook: Sub-Saharan Africa, April 2023*. Washington, DC: IMF. https://doi.org/10.5089/9798400235641.086.

IMF (2023b). *Regional Economic Outlook: Sub-Saharan Africa, October 2023*. Washington, DC: IMF. https://doi.org/10.5089/9798400253508.086.

IMF (2024a). *World Economic Outlook, April 2024*. Washington, DC: IMF. https://doi.org/10.5089/9798400255892.081.

IMF (2024b). *Regional Economic Outlook: Sub-Saharan Africa, April 2024*. Washington, DC: IMF. https://doi.org/10.5089/9798400267895.086.

Joy, J., and P. K. Panda (2020). 'An Empirical Analysis of Sustainability of Public Debt among BRICS Nations'. *Journal of Public Affairs*, 21(2): e2170. https://doi.org/10.1002/pa.2170.

Lankester-Campos, V., K. Loaiza-Marín, and C. Monge-Badilla (2020). 'Assessing Public Debt Sustainability for Costa Rica Using the Fiscal Reaction Function'. *Latin American Journal of Central Banking*, 1(1–4): 100014. https://doi.org/10.1016/j.latcb.2020.100014.

Leeper, E. M. (1991). 'Equilibria under "Active" and "Passive" Monetary and Fiscal Policies'. *Journal of Monetary Economics*, 27(1): 129–47. https://doi.org/10.1016/0304-3932(91)90007-B.

Mbewe, M., I. Masilokwa, T. Humann, M. Kalikeka, M. Kessler, and S. Mwamba (2024). 'The Road to Zambia's 2020 Sovereign Debt Default'. Zambia Institute for Policy Analysis and Research (ZIPAR) and Finance for Development Lab, January. Available at: https://findevlab.org/wp-content/uploads/2023/12/The-Road-to-Zambias-2020-Sovereign-Debt-Default-vf.pdf (accessed 18 December 2024).

Melina, G., S. S. Yang, and L. Zanna (2016). 'Debt Sustainability, Public Investment, and Natural Resources in Developing Countries: The DIGNAR Model'. *Economic Modelling*, 52: 630–49. https://doi.org/10.1016/j.econmod.2015.10.007.

Moreira, E. M. (2023). 'Debt Dynamics and Financial Stability in Africa'. Policy Brief 25/23. Rabat: Policy Center for the New South. https://www.policycenter.ma/sites/default/files/2023-06/PB_25-23_Emmanuel%20Pinto%20Moreira%20VF.pdf (accessed August 2024).

Mupunga, N., and T. Ngundu (2020). 'Escalating Public Debt Levels and Fiscal Responses in Sub-Saharan African Countries'. Research Paper 385. African Economic Research Consortium (AERC).

Ndulu, B. J., and S. A. O'Connell (2021). 'Africa's Development Debts'. *Journal of African Economies*, 30(Issue Supplement_1): i33–i73. https://doi.org/10.1093/jae/ejab021.

Olaoye, O. O., and P. A. Olomola (2023). 'Sub-Saharan Africa's Rising Public Debt Stock: Is There a Cause for Concern?' *South African Journal of Economics*, 91(1): 85–115. https://doi.org/10.1111/saje.12334.

Omotor, D. (2021). 'External Debt Sustainability in West African Countries'. *Review of Economics and Political Science* (ahead-of-print), 6(2): 118–41. https://doi.org/10.1108/reps-11-2019-0144.

Paret, A. C. (2017). 'Debt Sustainability in Emerging Market Countries: Some Policy Guidelines from a Fan-Chart Approach'. *Economic Modelling*, 63: 26–45. https://doi.org/10.1016/j.econmod.2017.01.010

Park, D., and T. Sung (2020). 'Foreign debt, global liquidity, and fiscal sustainability'. *Japan and the World Economy*, 54(March), 101008. https://doi.org/10.1016/j.japwor.2020.101008.

Pradhan, K. (2019). 'Analytical Framework for Fiscal Sustainability: A Review'. *Review of Development and Change*, 24(1): 100–122. https://doi.org/10.1177/0972266119845951.

Presbitero, A. F., D. Ghura, O. S. Adedeji, and L. Njie (2016). 'Sovereign Bonds in Developing Countries: Drivers of Issuance and Spreads'. *Review of Development Finance*, 6(1): 1–15. https://doi.org/10.1016/j.rdf.2016.05.002.

Rakara, D. (2020). 'Back to Basics: What Is Debt Sustainability?' Finance and Development Magazine. Available at: https://www.imf.org/en/Publications/fandd/issues/2020/09/what-is-debt-sustainability-basics (accessed 18 December 2024).

Rathnayake, A. S. K. (2020). 'Sustainability of the Fiscal Imbalance and Public Debt under Fiscal Policy Asymmetries in Sri Lanka'. *Journal of Asian Economics*, 66: 101161. https://doi.org/10.1016/j.asieco.2019.101161.

Republic of Kenya (2023). *Annual Public Debt Management Report for Financial Year 2022/2023*. Nairobi: National Treasury and Planning.

Serju-Thomas, P. (2020). 'Fiscal Sustainability: The Case for Jamaica'. *Latin American Journal of Central Banking*, 1(1–4): 100018. https://doi.org/10.1016/j.latcb.2020.100018.

Small, O., L. Brown, and G. Canavire-Bacarreza (2020). 'The Fiscal Policy Response to Public Debt in Developing Countries'. *Contemporary Economic Policy*, 38(1): 155–65. https://doi.org/10.1111/coep.12432.

United Nations (2023). 'Reforms to the International Financial Architecture'. Our Common Agenda Policy Brief 6. Available at: https://sdgs.un.org/sites/default/files/2023-08/our-common-agenda-policy-brief-international-finance-architecture-en.pdf (accessed August 2024).

Volz, U., S. Akhtar, K. P. Gallagher, S. Griffith-Jones, J. Haas, and M. Kraemer (2020). *Debt Relief for a Green and Inclusive Recovery: A Proposal*. Berlin, London, and Boston, MA: Heinrich-Böll-Stiftung, SOAS University of London, and Boston University.

Were, M. (2024). 'Emerging Public Debt Challenges in Sub-Saharan Africa'. World Institute for Public Policy Research and Analysis (WIDER) Working Paper 2024/36. Helsinki: UNU-WIDER. https://doi.org/10.35188/UNU-WIDER/2024/494-6.

Were, M., and L. Mollel (2020). 'Public Debt Sustainability and Debt Dynamics: The Case of Tanzania'. World Institute for Public Policy Research and Analysis (WIDER) Working Paper 2020/112. Helsinki: United Nations University (UNU)-WIDER. https://doi.org/10.35188/UNU-WIDER/2020/869-6.

World Bank (2023). *International Debt Report 2023*. Washington, DC: World Bank.

7

The effects of financial liberalization on private savings in sub-Saharan Africa

*Elizabeth Asiedu, Fafanyo Asiseh, Theresa Mannah-Blankson, and Jones Arkoh Paintsil**

1. Introduction

The private savings rate for Sub-Saharan Africa (SSA) is much lower than the rate for developing countries outside SSA. For example, the average of the ratio of private savings to gross personal disposable income (GPDI), from 1981 to 2012, is about 13% for SSA (see Table 7.4 in section 4). This compares with a savings rate of about 20% for developing countries outside SSA. An important question that arises is what accounts for the difference in savings rate between SSA countries and non-SSA developing countries? Answering this question is important because if the determinants of savings in SSA differ significantly from the determinants of savings in non-SSA developing countries, then policies that have been successful in other regions may not be (equally) successful in SSA. This chapter focuses on one specific policy—domestic financial reform. From the late 1980s to the early 2000s, many developing countries, including countries in SSA, liberalized their financial sector. A relevant question is whether financial liberalization was successful in boosting savings in developing (SSA and non-SSA) countries and whether the effect of financial liberalization on private savings is similar for SSA and non-SSA developing countries. We also determine whether, all else being equal, there are variations in the levels of the private savings rates and differences in the effect of financial liberalization on private savings for SSA countries in a monetary union versus SSA countries outside a monetary union.

Several papers have examined the effect of financial liberalization on private savings. Schmidt-Hebbel and Servén (2002) conduct an extensive review of the literature on financial liberalization and private savings. They conclude, 'If a general consensus could be derived from the existing literature, it would be summarized as follows: while financial development appears to be a relevant determinant of growth, its effect on saving is unclear, although some evidence suggests that it

*This chapter is based on an earlier working paper: Asiedu et al. (2022a).

Elizabeth Asiedu et al., *The effects of financial liberalization on private savings in sub-Saharan Africa*. In: *The Domestic Savings Shortfall in Sub-Saharan Africa*. Edited by: Rose Ngugi and Kunal Sen, Oxford University Press.
 DOI: 10.1093/oso/9780198932482.003.0007

is negative' (Schmidt-Hebbel and Servén 2002: 13). We note that the papers surveyed by Schmidt-Hebbel and Servén (2002) do not include papers that focus on SSA. We reviewed the literature on the determinants of private savings in SSA and came to a similar conclusion—that the effect of liberalization on private savings is inconclusive. Furthermore, we found only four papers that employed panel data (Seck and El Nil 1993; Mwega 1997; Elbadawi and Mwega 2000; Kelley and Mavrotas 2008). There are two notable points: all these papers used data from before 2001, and the sample sizes are small, with most SSA countries being excluded from the analyses. Another important point is that several studies have found that private savings are persistent (Loayza et al. 2000; Schmidt-Hebbel and Servén 2002), suggesting that current levels of private savings are correlated with past levels. This suggests that the lagged private savings should be included as an explanatory variable in the estimations. However, none of the papers include the lagged private savings as an explanatory variable in their regressions. Another concern is simultaneity and reverse causality between the explanatory variables and private savings. For example, causality may run from gross domestic product (GDP) per capita growth to private savings, resulting in endogeneity. However, none of the papers address this potential endogeneity problem. Finally, none of the papers examine whether the effect of liberalization on private savings in SSA differs significantly for countries that are not members of a monetary union.

This chapter contributes to the literature by answering the following questions. (i) What are the determinants of private savings in developing countries? (ii) Are the determinants of private savings similar for SSA countries and for developing countries outside SSA? (iii) Is the effect of financial liberalization on savings similar for SSA and non-SSA developing countries? (iv) What accounts for the variation in private savings rates among countries in SSA? (v) Does financial liberalization have a significant impact on private savings in SSA? (vi) Is the effect of financial liberalization on private savings different for SSA countries that belong to a monetary union?

To answer these questions, we draw on the most comprehensive, current, and readily available data on private savings, constructed by Grigoli et al. (2018).[1] Our chapter makes at least three important contributions to the literature. First, our data set is large and more recent. Specifically, our data covers 103 developing countries (42 SSA and 61 non-SSA) over the period 1981–2012. Second, we use the system generalized method of moments (GMM) proposed by Blundell and Bond (1998) for our estimations, and we thereby address the endogeneity and dynamic issues not addressed in previous studies. Finally, to the best of our knowledge, this is the first study to examine whether the determinants of private savings to SSA are different from that of other regions. The exceptionality of SSA has been examined in many studies. For example, Asiedu (2002) finds that the factors that drive

[1] See Loayza et al. (2000) and Grigoli et al. (2018) and for a detailed description of the data.

foreign direct investment (FDI) to SSA countries are different from those for other developing countries. Indeed, examining the 'Africa effect' on private savings is one of the innovations of our study.

Our main results are as follows. (i) Financial liberalization has no significant effect on private savings in both country groups (SSA and non-SSA). (ii) The private savings rate for SSA is similar to the rate for non-SSA developing countries, after controlling for relevant determinants of private savings. (iii) Private savings are persistent; however, the degree of persistence is lower in SSA countries. (iv) Public savings crowd out private savings; however, the crowding out is more severe in SSA countries. (v) The growth rate of income per capita has a significant and positive effect on personal savings in both country groups. (vi) The effect of financial liberalization on private savings is similar for SSA countries in a monetary union and SSA countries outside a monetary union.

The remainder of the chapter is organized as follows. Section 2 describes liberalization policies employed by SSA countries and compares them with non-SSA countries. Section 3 provides information about trends of private savings in the countries in the sample and compares these with non-SSA countries. Section 4 presents the empirical analysis, and section 5 concludes.

2. Financial liberalization

We start with an overview of the financial liberalization process in SSA and then provide a detailed analysis of financial reforms in selected SSA countries. Finally, we compare financial reforms in the following regions: emerging Asia, SSA, Latin America and the Caribbean (LAC), and the Middle East and North Africa (MENA).

2.1 An overview of financial liberalization in sub-Saharan Africa

Prior to the early 1990s, the financial system in most African countries was extremely repressive. Most economies in the region were characterized by restrictions on interest rates, credit rationing, lack of bank supervision, and high reserve requirements. In addition, several countries set up their own banks and used them as a means to provide credit to their preferred industries, finance their budget deficits, and fund state-owned enterprises (Briffaut et al. 1998). Moreover, between the 1980s and the early 1990s, many countries in the region experienced high inflation and stagnant growth. The growth rate of real gross domestic product (GDP) per capita over the period 1981 to 1993 was about −2.6% for SSA (World Bank 2022). This compares with growth rates of 9.8%, 2.5%, −0.58%, and −0.54% for developing countries in East Asia and the Pacific (EAP), South Asia, LAC, and MENA, respectively. To turn their economies around, many countries in the region joined the International Monetary Fund (IMF)/World Bank's structural adjustment programme (SAP). One of the conditions for a country to participate in the SAP was that the country had to agree to restructure its economy, including reforming its financial sector. Financial-sector reforms included the privatization of banks, the removal of credit controls, and the deregulation of interest rates such that prevailing interest rates were market-determined.

Table 7.1 shows the years when 46 countries in the region initiated major financial reforms, and it also indicates whether the country in question was part of the SAP. Thirty-two of the 46 countries initiated reforms as part of the SAP, suggesting that for about 70% of the countries in SSA, financial liberalization was 'forced' by the IMF/World Bank. One peculiarity of financial reform in SSA is that some of the countries are in a monetary union that shares a common currency and interest rate structure, and therefore the central bank associated with the monetary union makes the decisions about monetary policy. This implies that financial reforms relating to credit controls, reserve requirements, and interest rate deregulation for countries in a monetary union are a shared or common experience. There are two monetary unions that share a common currency: the West African Economic and Monetary Union (WAEMU) and the Central African Economic and Monetary Community Union (CAEMU). The Banque Centrale des États de l'Afrique de l'Ouest (BCEAO) is the central bank of the WAEMU, and the Banque des États de l'Afrique Centrale (BEAC) is the central bank of the CAEMU.[2] There is also Southern Africa's Common Monetary Area (CMA); however, the CMA is different in that member countries have their own central banks that oversee monetary policies. Table 7.1 shows a list of the countries in the three monetary zones. The WAEMU comprises eight countries, the CAEMU has six countries, and there are four countries in the CMA. It is interesting to note that all the WAEMU countries

Table 7.1 Overview of financial liberalization in 46 countries in SSA

Country	Start date of major liberalization	Monetary union status	IMF programme at start of liberalization
Angola	1990	No	No
Benin	1989	WAEMU	Yes
Botswana	1986	No	No
Burkina Faso	1989	WAEMU	Yes
Burundi	1986	No	Yes
Cameroon	1990	CAEMC	Yes

[2] The currencies of the WAEMU and CAEMU countries were pegged to the French franc until 1999 and have been pegged to the euro since then.

Country	Start date of major liberalization	Monetary union status	IMF programme at start of liberalization
Cape Verde	1990	No	No
Central African Republic	1990	CAEMC	Yes
Chad	1990	CAEMC	Yes
Comoros	1990	No	No
Congo, DR	1990	No	Yes
Congo, Rep	1990	CAEMC	Yes
Cote D' Ivoire	1989	WAEMU	Yes
Djibouti	1990	No	No
Equatorial Guinea	1990	CAEMC	No
Ethiopia	1990	No	Yes
Gabon	1990	CAEMC	Yes
Gambia, The	1985	No	Yes
Ghana	1987	No	Yes
Guinea-Bissau	1989	WAEMU	Yes
Guinea	1989	No	Yes
Kenya	1985	No	Yes
Lesotho	1980	CMA	No
Liberia	1990	No	No
Madagascar	1985	No	Yes
Malawi	1988	No	Yes
Mali	1989	WAEMU	Yes
Mauritania	1990	No	Yes
Mauritius	1981	No	No
Mozambique	1994	No	Yes
Namibia	1991	CMA	No
Niger	1989	WAEMU	Yes
Nigeria	1985	No	Yes
Rwanda	1990	No	No
Sao Tome & Principe	1990	No	Yes
Senegal	1981	WAEMU	Yes
Seychelles	1990	No	No
Sierra Leone	1992	No	Yes
South Africa	1980	CMA	No
Sudan	1997	No	No
Swaziland	1982	CMA	No
Tanzania	1991	No	Yes
Togo	1989	WAEMU	Yes
Uganda	1992	No	Yes
Zambia	1991	No	Yes
Zimbabwe	1991	No	Yes

Note: CAEMU means Central African Economic and Monetary Community Union, WAEMU means West African Economic and Monetary Union, CMA means South Africa Common Monetary Area.

Source: authors' compilation based on data from MF and World Bank country reports and working papers and, for financial liberalization dates, from Abiad et al. (2010), Fowowe (2008), Reinhart and Tokatlidis (2003).

participated in the SAP. In addition, with the exception of Equatorial Guinea, all the countries in the CAEMU also participated in the SAP. By contrast, none of the CMA countries signed up for the SAP.

We conclude by noting that recent data suggest that interest rate controls (IRCs), often considered a primary tool and measure of financial repression, seem to remain an issue for some SSA countries, particularly countries in the WAEMU. A recent study by Calice et al. (2020) reports the *de jure* IRCs—administered caps or floors on interest rates in lending and deposit markets via explicit regulations. The report is based on a survey of 108 countries, including 17 SSA countries.

Table 7.2 shows the list and interest rate liberalization status of the 17 SSA countries included in the survey as of 2019. Only six countries (Ghana, Kenya, Mauritius, Seychelles, Sudan, and Zambia) reported fully liberalized interest rates. Note that all the eight countries in the WAEMU are included in the list and that restrictions on deposit and lending rates were imposed in 1992. It is important to note that interest rates deregulation in the WAEMU countries was close to achieving full liberalization status in 1989. Specifically, in 1989 the only interest rates that were fixed by the BCEAO were the discount rate and a minimum rate on the

Table 7.2 Interest rate controls (IRCs) as of 2019 in selected countries in SSA

Country	IRCs (2019)	Type of IRC		Year IRC was imposed
		Lending rate	Deposit rate	
		Cap	Floor	
Benin*	Yes	Yes	Yes	1992
Burkina Faso*	Yes	Yes	Yes	1992
Côte d'Ivoire*	Yes	Yes	Yes	1992
Ethiopia	Yes	No	Yes	2017
Guinea-Bissau*	Yes	Yes	Yes	1992
Mali*	Yes	Yes	Yes	1992
Mauritania	Yes	Yes	Yes	2008
Niger*	Yes	Yes	Yes	1992
Senegal*	Yes	Yes	Yes	1992
South Africa	Yes	Yes	No	2005
Togo*	Yes	Yes	Yes	1992
Ghana	No	No	No	NA
Kenya	No	No	No	NA
Mauritius	No	No	No	NA
Seychelles	No	No	No	NA
Sudan	No	No	No	NA
Zambia	No	No	No	NA

Note: * refers to countries that are part of the WAEMU.

Source: authors' compilation based on data from Calice et al. (2020).

passport savings deposit (Briffaut et al. 1998). This suggests that the policy reversal in 1992 was quite drastic. Interest rate restrictions for three non-WAEMU countries were imposed at later dates: for Ethiopia in 2017, for Mauritania in 2008, and for South Africa in 2005. In addition, with the exception of Ethiopia and South Africa, all the countries that imposed interest restrictions had restrictions on both lending and deposit rates. Ethiopia imposed restrictions on deposit rates and not on lending rates; South Africa was the opposite, as it imposed restrictions on lending rates and not deposit rates.

2.2 Financial liberalization in selected countries in SSA

In this section, we employ data from Abiad et al. (2010) to provide a historical account of financial reform in 14 countries from 1973 to 2005. These authors provide information on seven financial liberalization policies: IRCs, credit controls, entry barriers to the banking sector, bank privatization, banking-sector supervision, capital account restrictions, and securities market policy. Each type of liberalization policy can take on four values: zero indicates full repression, one indicates partial repression, two indicates partial liberalization, and three indicates full liberalization. We do not include capital account restrictions and securities market policy in our discussion because the scores are very low and show very little variation across countries or over time. Thus, we focus on the other five liberalization policies. We derive an aggregate financial liberalization index (FLI), which is the sum of the five indices; therefore, the aggregate FLI ranges from zero to 15. Note that the aggregate FLI may be interpreted as a measure of overall financial liberalization. We make two modifications to facilitate the discussion. First, for the aggregate FLI, we define a score from 0 to 3 as fully repressed, from 4 to 9 as partially repressed, from 10 to 14 as partially liberalized, and a score of 15 as fully liberalized. Second, we break the years down into eight periods: 1973–74 (period 1), 1975–79 (period 2), 1980–84 (period 3), 1985–89 (period 4), 1990–94 (period 5), 1995–99 (period 6), 2000–04 (period 7), and 2005 (period 8). For each period, we report the average of the aggregate FLI. In addition, we report the average FLI for each of the five subindices for the SSA country group.

Figure 7.1 illustrates the trend of aggregate financial liberalization (FLI) for SSA countries from 1973 to 2005. There are a few notable points. Figure 7.1 shows that SSA was fully repressed prior to 1988, and the aggregate FLI increased significantly after 1990. Specifically, from period 4 to period 6, the aggregate FLI increased significantly, showing substantial progress in financial liberalization. It is important to note that all the countries in the sample except South Africa were part of the SAP. Thus, the data supports the assertion that in many countries, financial reform was induced by the SAP. We now provide detailed information about the specific types of financial reform policies implemented by the group of SSA countries.

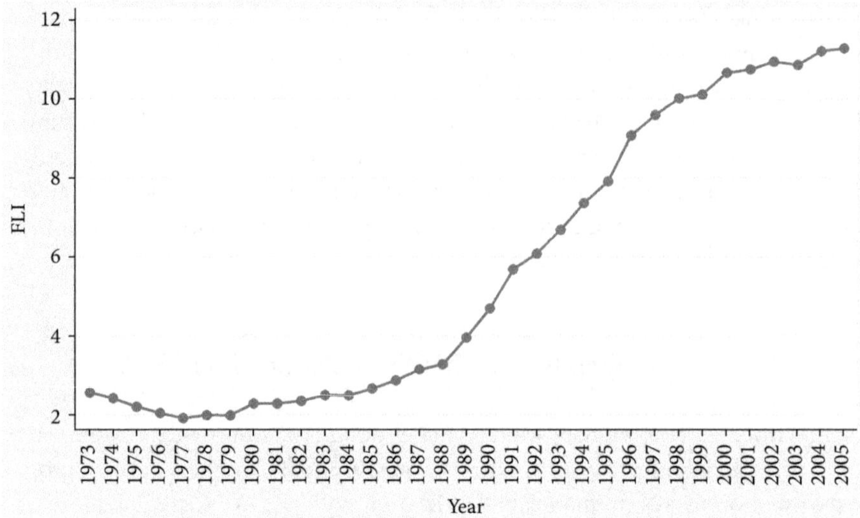

Figure 7.1 Aggregate financial liberalization index (FLI) for 14 countries in SSA, 1973–2005

Note: the aggregate FLI ranges from 0 to 15. A higher number implies more liberalization.*Source:* authors' illustration based on data from Abiad et al. (2010)

Figure 7.2 shows the graph of the FLI for each of the five types of liberalization policy from 1973 to 2005, across the eight periods. The graph shows that SSA has made progress in all areas except for banking-sector supervision. In period 1, SSA was fully repressed in areas such as bank supervision, interest rate controls, credit controls, and privatization. Entry barriers to the banking sector were only partially repressed during this period. However, by period 8, SSA was almost fully liberalized in all the four areas except for banking-sector supervision, where it was partially repressed. Another observation is that there is a variation in the periods when liberalization began for the various policies. The liberalization status of entry barriers to the banking sector changed from fully repressed to partially repressed in period 3, that of credit and IRCs in period 5, bank privatization in period 6, and banking-sector supervision in period 8. This suggests that the sequence of liberalization was as follows: entry barriers to the banking sector, credit and IRCs, bank privatization, and banking-sector supervision.

The above discussion has focused on aggregate indices for all the countries. This masks the variation in the types of financial reform policies enacted by the various countries. We address this issue by reporting the liberalization efforts of each of the 14 countries. Figure 7.3 shows the graph of the aggregate FLI for each of the 14 countries from 1973 to 2005. There are four notable points. First, there was wide cross-country variation in the liberalization status in the initial years; however, by 2005, the status had converged. For example, in the early years (period 1: 1973–74), Ghana, Madagascar, and Tanzania were fully repressed,

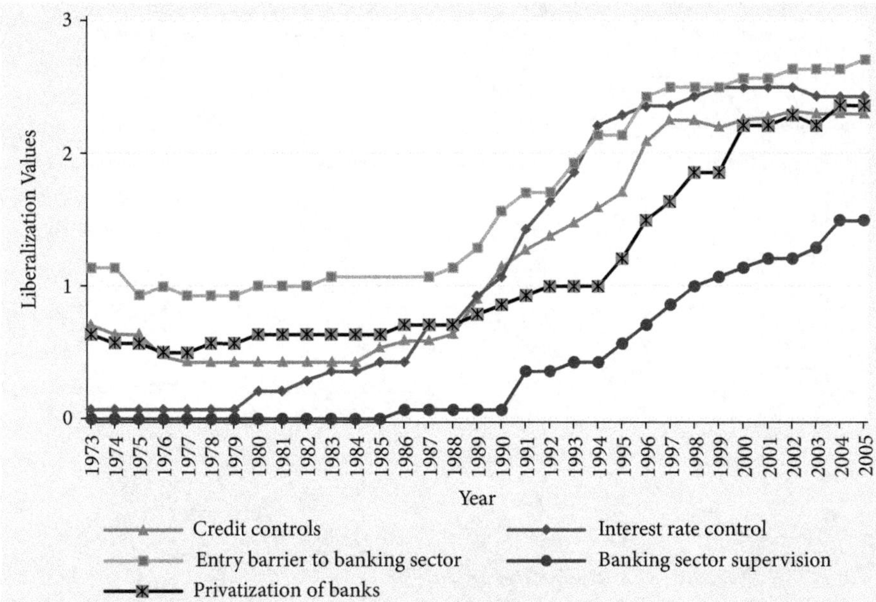

Figure 7.2 Types of financial liberalization policies implemented by 14 countries in SSA, 1973–2021

Note: the data are available from 1973 to 2005. Each measure of liberalization ranges 0–3, where 0 = fully repressed, 1 = partially repressed, 2 = partially liberalized, and 3 = fully liberalized.*Source:* authors' illustration based on data from Abiad et al. (2010).

while Côte d'Ivoire had already achieved a partially repressed status. However, by period 8, 12 out of the 14 countries had attained the partially repressed status. The two exceptions were Ghana, which had progressed to a higher level of partial liberalization, and Ethiopia, which remained less liberalized compared to the others.

The second notable point is that the speed of liberalization varied significantly by country. For example, Tanzania's liberalization status changed from fully repressed to partially repressed in just one period. Specifically, Tanzania began liberalization in period 5. Prior to that, it was fully repressed. However, its liberation status changed to partially repressed in period 6. In contrast, Kenya began liberalization in period 2 and attained partially repressed status in period 7.

Third, the data suggests that overall, the level of liberalization improved with time. However, four countries experienced policy reversals, and the duration of the reversal varied by country. For instance, South Africa experienced a brief policy reversal from period 1 to period 2, while Nigeria's reversal lasted until period 3. Senegal's reversal persisted until period 4, and Ethiopia faced the longest reversal, lasting until period 5. Finally, with the exception of Ethiopia, all the countries made significant progress in financial reform during the 31-year period. Finally, we note that, with the exception of Ethiopia, all countries made significant progress

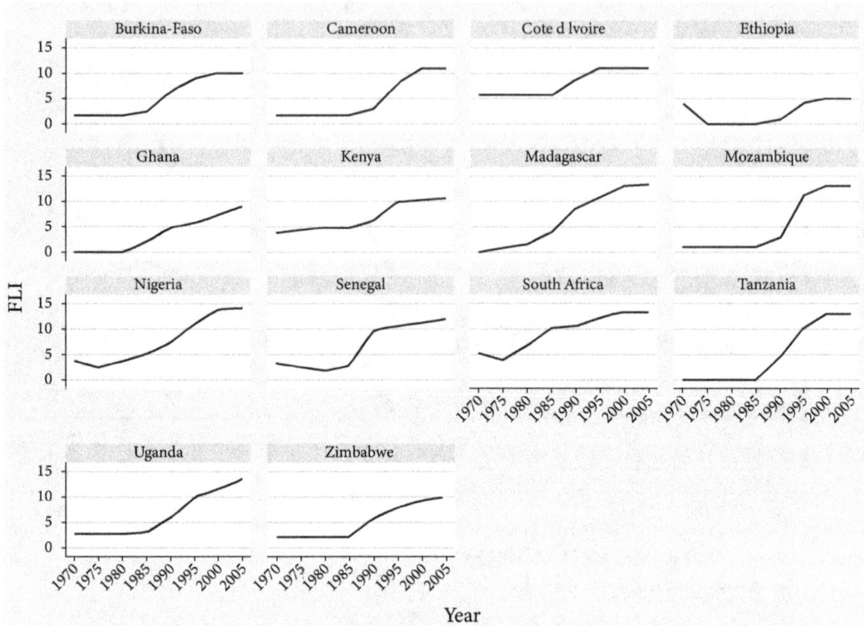

Figure 7.3 Aggregate FLI for 14 SSA countries, 1973–2005

Note: the aggregate FLI ranges from 0 to 15. A higher number implies more liberalization.*Source:* authors' calculations and illustration based on data from Abiad et al. (2010).

in financial reform during the 31-year period. Specifically, the liberalization status of Ethiopia changed from partially repressed in period 1 to fully repressed in periods 2–5, returning to partially repressed status in periods 7 and 8.

2.3 Regional comparison of financial liberalization

We now compare the liberalization efforts of SSA with those of developing countries in Asia, LAC, and MENA.

Figure 7.4 shows the graph of the aggregate FLI for these four regions from 1973 to 2005. The data indicate that all regions were fully repressed in the first period (1973–74), with SSA recording the highest FLI, followed by MENA, emerging Asia, and LAC, suggesting that SSA was the least repressed region at the outset. We also note there was a significant increase in aggregate FLI in all regions between periods 4 and 5. Specifically, between periods 4 and 5, the FLI increased by about 36% in emerging Asia, 114% in LAC, 91% in SSA, and 104% in MENA. This suggests that there was sweeping reform in developing countries during that period. Finally, we note that all the regions were partially repressed in period 8, an indication of convergence.

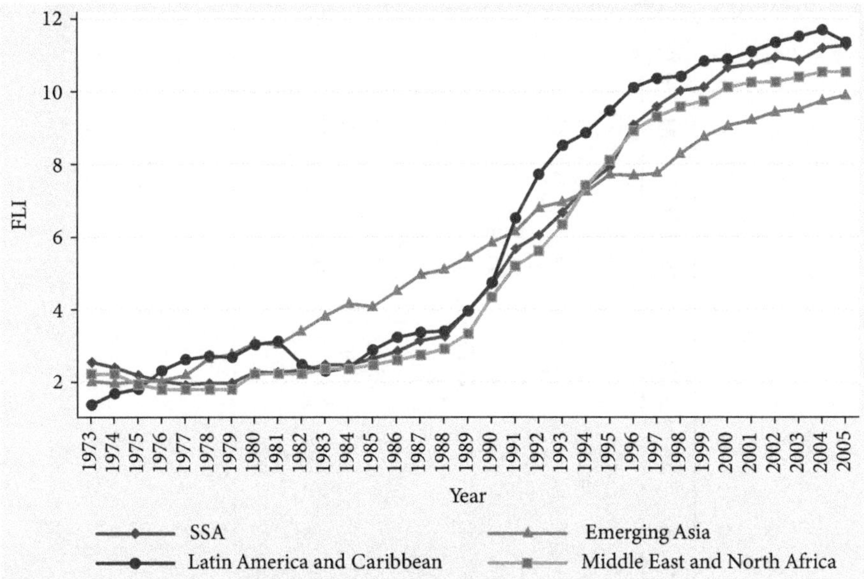

Figure 7.4 Aggregate FLI by region, 1973–2005

Note: the aggregate FLI ranges from 0 to 15. A higher number implies more liberalization. *Source:* authors' illustration based on data from Abiad et al. (2010).

3. Private savings in developing countries

In this section, we use data from Grigoli et al. (2018) to describe the trends in private savings for 103 developing countries from 1981 to 2012 (see the list of countries in Appendix Table A1 of Asiedu et al. 2022a: 26). Table 7.3a reports the annual averages of the ratio of private savings to gross personal disposable income (GPDI) for the full sample and the regional groups. It also reports the private savings rates for the top four high-savings countries in SSA: Angola (ANG), Botswana (BOT), Gabon (GAB), and Namibia (NAM).

The data shows that overall, the private savings rate for SSA is much lower than the rate for non-SSA developing countries and the savings gap widens when the four countries are excluded. For example, the average private savings rate for the period 1980–2012 for SSA was about 13%, and it drops to about 11% when the four countries are excluded. This compares to a savings rate of 20% for countries outside SSA. The regional comparison shows that overall, the savings rate for SSA is lower than the rate for MENA, South Asia, EAP, and Europe and Central Asia; however, the SSA rate is comparable to that of LAC. Specifically, the average savings rate over the period 1981–2012 for South Asia is about 1.6 times that of SSA, while the rate for MENA and the rates for EAP and LAC are 1.3 times and 1.1 times the rate for SSA.

Table 7.3a Annual averages of private savings rate for developing countries, 1981–2012

Region/country	1981–84	1985–89	1990–94	1995–99	2000–04	2005–09	2010–12	1981–2012
Developing countries (LDC)	12.61	13.66	17.20	16.15	18.49	17.19	16.91	16.79
LDCs outside SSA	18.10	17.53	21.49	20.01	20.34	20.14	19.09	19.96
SSA	10.44	11.57	13.23	11.42	15.78	12.88	13.63	13.03
Botswana (BDI)	31.72	46.43	36.67	31.36	28.69	24.33	22.54	32.27
Gabon (GAB)	—	—	32.82	39.57	42.30	43.56	45.14	40.63
Namibia (NAM)	—	—	24.19	29.90	28.11	26.82	20.52	26.59
Angola (ANG)	—	—	—	—	—	51.67	48.74	50.57
SSA excluding ANG, BDI, GAB, and NAM	9.34	9.86	11.11	9.14	14.28	10.26	11.21	10.98
South Asia	18.96	15.59	20.02	21.37	24.17	22.00	21.31	21.19
Middle East and North Africa	24.68	25.68	29.47	25.31	25.99	28.07	27.42	26.90
Latin America and Caribbean	10.94	12.99	15.14	14.96	15.03	15.12	14.57	14.77
East Asia and Pacific	24.68	25.07	28.81	26.76	28.14	29.50	25.59	27.57
Europe and Central Asia	—	18.93	16.43	—	17.85	16.59	16.65	16.99

Source: authors' calculations based on data from Grigoli et al. (2018).

Table 7.3b Private savings rate for SSA countries, average 1981–2012

Country	Mean	SD	Minimum	Maximum
Angola	50.57	12.58	25.21	70.13
Benin	7.32	5.51	−8.65	14.64
Botswana	32.27	9.93	8.51	56.98
Burkina Faso	6.49	6.08	−9.54	17.31
Burundi	6.69	14.78	−41.41	22.37
Cameroon	12.53	9.68	−37.04	20.40
Cape Verde	18.10	6.68	4.23	31.39
Central African	−1.18	6.67	−23.49	11.44
Chad	4.01	18.59	−45.53	29.76
Comoros	2.96	4.39	−3.14	12.59
Congo, Democratic Republic	9.77	3.47	4.47	15.10
Congo, Republic	17.35	31.43	−54.21	63.70
Cote d'Ivoire	12.07	6.25	3.70	30.68
Eritrea	24.11	9.48	12.12	37.13
Ethiopia	10.02	5.35	1.95	19.88
Gabon	40.63	5.88	26.93	52.78
Gambia, The	12.07	5.01	4.97	24.36
Ghana	11.48	6.45	−1.43	27.69
Guinea	12.44	7.33	−1.96	25.61
Guinea-Bissau	8.93	4.74	2.76	19.39
Kenya	15.22	4.08	7.74	25.14
Lesotho	15.74	7.45	2.84	29.69
Madagascar	10.21	5.43	3.37	20.95
Malawi	17.78	6.99	6.97	32.18
Mali	18.11	6.33	5.42	32.50
Mauritania	7.96	11.57	−8.38	23.52
Mauritius	21.10	5.32	13.08	31.92
Mozambique	0.62	6.94	−7.66	14.96
Namibia	26.59	4.66	18.41	35.81
Niger	7.04	6.08	−1.84	22.31
Nigeria	19.28	15.34	−17.93	49.06
Rwanda	8.36	3.88	0.02	15.29
Senegal	6.73	4.81	−3.24	14.53
Seychelles	18.11	20.14	−13.69	53.59
Sierra Leone	3.04	6.12	−12.23	12.67
South Africa	20.12	3.68	12.19	26.70
Sudan	14.25	3.55	5.63	19.70
Swaziland	7.31	10.20	−23.02	23.58
Sao Tome and Principe	1.08	16.60	−27.27	21.30
Tanzania	8.92	5.75	−6.06	17.10
Togo	1.88	8.74	−18.50	12.22
Uganda	11.25	3.15	5.97	16.22
Total	13.03	13.32	−54.21	70.13

Note: the data are available from 1981 to 2012.
Source: authors' calculations based on data from Grigoli et al. (2018).

We now provide a sense of the trend in private savings in the SSA countries over the sample period. Table 7.3b presents the average savings rate for the 42 SSA countries in our sample. The data shows a wide cross-country variation in private savings, with a private rate as low as −1.18% for the Central African Republic, 0.62% for Mozambique, and 2.18% for Sierra Leone, up to highs of about 50.57% and 42.9% for Angola and Gabon, respectively. An important observation is that three of the top four countries with high private savings rates are oil-exporting countries.

4. Empirical analysis

The discussion in section 2 shows that the financial repressive policies implemented by most developing countries included interest rate regulation and the imposition of credit controls. Hence, the measures of financial liberalization typically employed in the literature are real interest rates and a measure of private-sector credit. Some studies also use a dummy variable that reflects the year a country initiated major financial reforms. Clearly, all three measures have significant limitations.[3] For example, financial liberalization can move real interest rates upwards and downwards. Furthermore, movement in the real interest rate may happen due to other macroeconomic factors, and hence the marginal effect may not necessarily represent the effect of financial liberalization. The dummy variable—the financial reform indicator—neither reflects the intensity of reform nor captures situations of policy reversal. This is problematic because, as noted in section 2, the intensity of reform varies by country. Furthermore, countries in the WAEMU removed IRCs in 1989 but reimposed controls in 1992. Clearly, the liberalization measures described in section 2 are more appropriate for our empirical analysis; however, the data are available for only 14 African countries. Furthermore, data for the year of financial reform is available for only SSA countries (see Table 7.1).

Despite the limitations identified in the measures used in previous studies, the absence of appropriate variables to capture financial liberalization leads us to employ the same set of variables for our empirical analysis. Specifically, we use the real deposit rate, the flow of private-sector credit to GPDI, and a financial liberalization dummy. The regressions for the full sample employ real deposit rates and credit flows as measures of liberalization, and the regressions for SSA employ all three measures. Using three different measures of liberalization serves as a robustness check and also increases the credibility of our results. We note that theoretically, the effect of the real interest rate on private savings is ambiguous. The real interest rate may increase personal savings through the substitution effect;

[3] See Abiad et al. (2010) for a description of the various measures of financial liberalization.

however, it may decrease personal savings if the wealth and income effect dominates over the substitution effect (Fowowe 2013). Similarly, the theoretical effect of domestic borrowing constraint on private savings is unclear. Current credit constraints, if binding, may force households to save for future purchases, and therefore a relaxation of the constraints may lead to a decrease in precautionary savings. The ambiguous theoretical effect of these variables on private savings is reflected in empirical studies. Specifically, Grigoli et al. (2018) conduct a literature review regarding the determinants of private savings and find that out of 13 papers that included real interest rates as explanatory variables, the estimated coefficient of the real interest rate was not significant in 7 papers, was negative and significant in 2 papers, and was positive and significant in 4 papers. For domestic credit borrowing constraints, they reviewed nine papers and found that domestic credit borrowing constraints were positive and significant in four studies and negative and significant in five. Our empirical analysis utilize an unbalanced panel data for 103 developing countries from 1981 to 2012.[4] Following Grigoli et al. (2018), we employ the two-step system GMM estimator with collapsed instrument matrix and perform the Windmeijer (2005) correction to estimate the model:[5]

$$y_{it} = \gamma y_{it-1} + \beta X_{it} + \delta Z_{it} + c_i + \tau_t + u_{it} \qquad (1)$$

where y_{it} is the ratio of private savings to GPDI, X_{it} includes the endogenous (and predetermined) covariates for country i at time t, Z_{it} includes strictly exogenous variables premised, c_i and τ_t are country-fixed effects and time-fixed effects, respectively, and u_{it} is the error term. The explanatory variables are as follows: real per capita GPDI (purchasing power parity, PPP); real growth rate of per capita GPDI (PPP); real deposit rate; terms of trade; inflation; flow of private-sector credit/GPDI; public saving/GPDI; old age–dependency ratio; and share of urban population. Furthermore, the log of real per capita GPDI (PPP), real growth rate of per capita GPDI (PPP), real deposit rate, terms of trade, inflation, and flow of private-sector credit/GPDI are treated as endogenous, and the old age–dependency ratio and share of urban population are treated as exogenous.[6] To facilitate the discussion, we consider equation (1) as our benchmark model, where only the variables listed above are included as explanatory variables in the regressions.

We perform two separate analyses. We start by answering the first three questions posed in the introduction: (i) What are the determinants of private savings in developing countries? (ii) Are the determinants of private savings similar for SSA countries and for developing countries outside SSA? (iii) Is the effect of financial

[4] For the list of countries included in the regressions, see Appendix Table A1 in Asiedu et al. (2022b: 26).

[5] We thank Grigoli et al. (2018) for sharing their data and DO file.

[6] See Loayza et al. (1998) and Grigoli et al. (2018) and for a detailed data description.

liberalization on savings similar for SSA and non-SSA developing countries? The second set of regressions focuses on SSA, and we answer the following questions: (iv) What accounts for the variation in private savings rates among countries in SSA? (v) Does financial liberalization have a significant impact on private savings in SSA? (vi) Is the effect of financial liberalization on private savings different for SSA countries that belong to a monetary union?

Table 7.4 shows the summary statistics of the variables included in the regressions. There are a few notable points. The private savings rate, real deposit rate, and private credit ratios are much lower in SSA. Specifically, the private savings rate for non-SSA countries is about 1.6 times the rate for SSA countries. The real interest rate for non-SSA countries is about 3.6 times the rate for SSA countries, and the private credit ratio for non-SSA countries is about double that of SSA countries. This suggests that overall, countries in SSA are more financially repressed than countries in other regions. An important question is whether the difference in private savings rates between SSA and other regions will hold after we control for other important determinants of private savings. Another relevant question is whether the relationship between private-sector credit ratio and private savings, as well as other determinants of private savings, is similar for SSA and non-SSA countries.

We start by estimating the benchmark model. The results reported in column (1) of Table 7.5 show that the estimated coefficients of real deposit rate and private-sector ratio are not significantly different from zero, suggesting that, other things being equal, financial liberalization does not have a significant effect on private savings in the developing countries in our sample. Loayza et al. (2000) also find that the estimated coefficient of real interest rate is not significant for their developing country sample; however, the estimated coefficient of the private credit ratio is significant, negative, and quite large—about 0.51.[7] The authors note that 'the relaxation of credit constraints leads to a decrease in the private saving rate' (Loayza et al. 2000: 174), and they add that 'the direct effects of financial liberalization are largely detrimental to private saving rates' (Loayza et al. 2000: 180). Edwards (1996: 21) also finds that the real interest rate does not have a significant effect on private savings and suggests that 'the financial liberalization hypothesis should be interpreted broadly going well beyond the effect of higher interest rates on savings'.

We now turn our attention to the other determinants of private savings. The estimated coefficient of the lagged private savings rate is positive and significant

[7] In Loayza et al. (2000), the estimated coefficient of the real interest rate is not significant for the developing country sample; however, it is negative and significant for the full sample. Furthermore, the estimated coefficient of the private credit ratio is significant and negative for both the full sample and the developing country sample. For their full sample, Grigoli et al. (2018) find that the estimated coefficient of the real interest rate is not significant; however, the private credit ratio is negative and significant.

Table 7.4 Summary statistics

Variable	SSA				Non-SSA			
	Mean	SD	Minimum	Maximum	Mean	SD	Minimum	Maximum
Private saving/GPDI	13.03	13.32	−54.21	70.13	19.96	11.42	−41.27	58.94
Ln real per capita GPDI in (PPP)	717.07	85.53	546.26	972.07	825.44	64.2	638.02	1058.29
Real growth rate of per capita GPDI	2.07	12.58	−47.72	127.8	3.54	7.74	−38.4	75.04
Ln terms of trade	465.83	34.53	349.06	623.48	460.09	23.77	324.7	576.44
Public saving/GPDI	6	13.25	−29.58	108.18	4.46	7.55	−20.02	73.93
Real deposit rate	0.26	6.44	−27.5	21.34	1.21	5.52	−26.01	26.53
Flow of private-sector credit/GPDI	2.85	4.62	−13.46	43.14	5.81	7.1	−26.96	56.73
Inflation (bounded)	6.97	6.69	−15.01	32.89	6.91	5.89	−9.32	32.94
Old age–dependency ratio	6.2	1.54	3.5	12.66	9.67	4.44	4.25	28.01
Share of urban population	34.23	16.01	4.69	86.46	51.56	19.38	12.43	93.7
Observation	951				1,129			

Note: the data are available from 1981 to 2012.

Source: authors' calculations based on data from Grigoli et al. (2018).

Table 7.5 Determinants of private savings in developing countries

Variables	(1)	(2)	(3)
Lag private saving/GPDI	0.5161***	0.5101***	0.9122***
	(0.0634)	(0.0607)	(0.0833)
Ln real per capita GPDI (PPP)	0.1526***	0.1602**	0.1117
	(0.0548)	(0.0644)	(0.0714)
Real growth rate of per capita GPDI(PPP)	0.2061***	0.2150***	0.3593***
	(0.0379)	(0.0414)	(0.1077)
Ln terms of trade	0.0485**	0.0386**	0.0287
	(0.0192)	(0.0180)	(0.0255)
Public saving/GPDI	−0.3575***	−0.3749***	−0.0358
	(0.1038)	(0.1112)	(0.1488)
Real deposit rate	0.1254	0.1159	0.2255
	(0.1579)	(0.1635)	(0.2417)
Flow of private-sector credit/GPDI	−0.1133	−0.1203	−0.2206*
	(0.1159)	(0.1215)	(0.1272)
Inflation	0.2977*	0.2950	0.3713
	(0.1789)	(0.1878)	(0.2617)
Old age–dependency ratio	−1.2581***	−1.1409***	−0.5648
	(0.4537)	(0.4011)	(0.3690)
Share of urban population	−0.2952*	−0.2642	−0.2152
	(0.1669)	(0.1663)	(0.1589)
SSA		5.0102	29.9122
		(4.2882)	(47.6467)
SSA* Ln real per capita GPDI (PPP)			−0.0198
			(0.0744)
SSA* Real growth rate of per capita GPDI(PPP)			−0.2188*
			(0.1206)
SSA*Ln terms of trade			−0.0111
			(0.0284)
SSA* Public saving/GPDI			−0.3899**
			(0.1695)
SSA*Real deposit rate			−0.0465
			(0.2877)
SSA*Flow of private sector credit/GPDI			0.3546
			(0.2496)
SSA* Inflation			−0.1203
			(0.3243)
SSA*Old age–dependency ratio			−0.2942
			(0.8149)

Variables	(1)	(2)	(3)
SSA* Share of urban population			0.1638 (0.2078)
SSA* Lag private saving/GPDI			−0.5363*** (0.1031)
Constant	−111.9063*** (34.1027)	−117.7920*** (42.1826)	−89.6532* (46.9202)
Lags/instruments	1/48	1/49	1/66
AR (1) *p*-value	0.002	0.003	0.000
AR (2) *p*-value	0.634	0.608	0.669
Hansen J-test *p*-value	0.736	0.652	0.737
Observations	2,080	2,080	2,080
Number of countries	103	103	103

Note: standard errors in parentheses are corrected for heteroscedasticity and autocorrelation of the error term. We use the two-step systems GMM estimations with collapsed instrument matrix and perform the Windmeijer (2005) correction of the covariance matrix. The null hypothesis for the Hansen J-test is that the full set of instruments is valid. Standard errors in parentheses. *** $p < 0.01$, ** $p < 0.05$, * $p < 0.1$.
Source: authors' calculations based on data from Grigoli et al. (2018).

at the 1% level, suggesting that private savings are persistent. A point estimate of 0.502 implies that, other things being equal, the effect of a change in the other determinants of private savings in the long run is equal to about double the effect in the first year. The level and growth rate of per capita GPDI and the terms of trade have a positive and significant effect on private savings. Other things being equal, a one percentage point increase in the growth rate of real per capita GPDI will raise the private savings rate by about 0.21 percentage points, and a 10% improvement in the terms of trade increases the private savings rate by 0.49 percentage points in the short run. The estimated coefficient of public savings is negative and significant at the 1% level; however, the point estimate is less than one, suggesting that, other things being equal, public savings *partially* crowd out private savings. Thus, the result does not support the Ricardian equivalence hypothesis. Our finding is consistent with several studies, including Edwards (1996), Loayza et al. (2000), and Grigoli et al. (2018). An important implication of this result is that an increase in public savings raises national savings. The estimated coefficient of inflation is positive; however, it is significant only at the 10% level. With regard to the demographic variables, we find that the estimated coefficient of the old age–dependency ratio is negative and significant at the 5%t level. Other things being equal, a one percentage point increase in the old age–dependency ratio decreases the private savings ratio by about 1.3 percentage points. This result is consistent with the standard life-cycle models of consumption. The estimated coefficient of the urbanization ratio is negative but significant only at the 10% level. To the extent that urbanization increases (precautionary) private savings, this result (coupled with that for inflation) suggests that the precautionary motive for private savings in developing countries is not very strong.

We next examine whether the difference in private savings rates across the regions reported in Table 7.4 holds after we control for relevant determinants of private savings. Here, we include a dummy variable that takes on the value of one for countries in SSA and zero otherwise. The results in column (2) show that the estimated coefficient of the SSA dummy variable is not significantly different from zero, suggesting that after controls for the relevant determinants of private savings, the private savings rate for SSA countries is comparable to that of non-SSA countries. This is interesting because, as pointed out earlier, the average private savings rate for SSA is much lower than the savings rate for the other regions when we do not control for the relevant determinants of private savings. Edwards (1996) arrives at a similar conclusion for countries in Latin America.

We next examine whether the determinants of private savings for SSA differ significantly from those for developing countries outside SSA. Here, we interact the SSA dummy variable with all the explanatory variables. Note that our variables of interest are those for which the estimated coefficients of the interaction terms are significantly different from zero. The results reported in column (3) show that the estimated coefficients of all the interaction terms are not significantly different from zero, except the estimated coefficients of public savings and lagged private savings. The estimated coefficient of SSA public savings is negative and significant—other things being equal, a one percentage point increase in the public savings rate reduces the private savings rate by 0.39 percentage points more in SSA countries than in non-SSA developing countries. This implies that the crowding-out effect of public savings is more pronounced in SSA countries than in non-SSA countries. The estimated coefficient of the interaction term of the lagged private savings ratio and SSA is negative and significant, suggesting that private savings are less persistent in SSA (0.38) than in other regions (0.91). This implies that for countries outside SSA, the long-run effect of a permanent change in the other determinants of the private savings rate is about 11 times the respective effect in the short run. This compares with a long-run effect of only 1.6 times for SSA. This result has important implications because it suggests that in the long run, similar (permanent and positive) changes in the determinants of private savings provide more dividends to non-SSA countries than SSA countries.

The next analysis focuses exclusively on SSA countries. Specifically, we limit the analysis to 42 countries in SSA. Furthermore, unlike the previous set of regressions, our regressions do not include time-fixed effects—including time-fixed effects raises the number of instruments to 48, which exceeds the number of countries and therefore makes the results unreliable (Roodman 2009). The results in Table 7.6 employ the real deposit rate and private credit ratio as measures of liberalization. We report our robustness results in Table 7.7, where we use the reform dummy as a proxy for financial liberalization.

Column (1) of Table 7.6 presents the results for the benchmark model. The estimated coefficients of the real deposit rate and the credit ratio are not significantly different from zero, suggesting that, other things being equal, financial liberalization does not have a significant impact on private savings in SSA. Similarly to the results for the full sample, the estimated coefficient of the lagged private savings and growth rate of real GPDI per capita is positive and significant, and the estimated coefficient of public savings is negative and significant. Other things being equal, a one percentage point increase in the growth rate of real per capita GPDI increases the private savings rate by about 0.14 percentage points in the short run and about 0.22 percentage points in the long run. Public savings partially crowd out private savings: other things being equal, the short-run (adverse) effect of a one percentage point increase in public savings is about 0.38 percentage points, and the long-run effect is about 0.61 percentage points. In column (2) we include two dummy variables to represent the WAEMU and CAEMU to test whether the private savings rate for countries in these monetary unions is different from that for countries outside them. The first dummy variable, WAEMU, takes on the value one for countries in the WAEMU and zero otherwise. The second dummy variable, CAEMU, takes on the value one for countries in the CAEMU and zero otherwise. The estimated coefficients of WAEMU and CAEMU are not significantly different from zero, suggesting that the savings rates for the countries in the sample are comparable after controls for relevant determinants of savings. Finally, we examine whether the effect of financial liberalization on private savings is different for SSA countries that belong to a monetary union. Here, we interact the liberalization variables with the monetary union dummy variables. As shown in column (3) the estimated coefficients of all the interaction terms are not significantly different from zero, suggesting that the effect of financial liberalization on private savings is comparable for all the countries in the sample.

We next report the robustness regression results, where we employ the financial liberalization dummy, ('liberal') as our measure of liberalization. The results reported in Table 7.7 are qualitatively similar to the results in Table 7.6. Specifically, the estimated coefficients of liberal, liberal∗WAEMU, and liberal∗CAEMU are not significantly different from zero. This lends credence to our finding that financial liberalization does not have a significant impact on private savings and that this applies to countries both within and outside the Communauté Financière Africaine (CFA).

Table 7.6 Determinants of private savings in SSA: Benchmark regression

Variables	(1)	(2)	(3)
Lag private saving/GPDI	0.3897***	0.3832***	0.4562***
	(0.0620)	(0.0634)	(0.0578)
Ln real per capita GPDI (PPP)	0.1020***	0.1095***	0.0798*
	(0.0332)	(0.0401)	(0.0483)
Real growth rate of per capita GPDI(PPP)	0.1397***	0.1453***	0.2021***
	(0.0399)	(0.0435)	(0.0463)
Ln terms of trade	0.0084	−0.0014	0.0019
	(0.0123)	(0.0141)	(0.0170)
Public saving/GPDI	−0.3770***	−0.3769***	−0.4326***
	(0.1241)	(0.1381)	(0.1136)
Real deposit rate	0.0115	0.0295	0.1765
	(0.1688)	(0.1517)	(0.2331)
Flow of private-sector credit/GPDI	0.0972	0.0987	0.0575
	(0.1941)	(0.2261)	(0.3038)
Inflation	0.0936	0.1237	0.3164
	(0.2055)	(0.1972)	(0.2459)
Old age–dependency ratio	−0.8202	−1.1567	−0.8640
	(0.7209)	(0.9077)	(1.1001)
Share of urban population	−0.1203	−0.1393	−0.0558
	(0.1218)	(0.1176)	(0.1536)
West African Economic and Monetary Union (WAEMU)		2.8119	2.8914
		(2.5946)	(2.9474)
Central African Economic and Monetary Union (CAEMU)		5.9010	9.0511*
		(4.2714)	(4.6340)
WAEMU*Flow of private-sector credit/GPDI			0.3107
			(0.5563)
CAEMU*Flow of private-sector credit/GPDI			−0.1250
			(0.6431)
WAEMU* Real deposit rate			−0.0379
			(0.2300)
CAEMU Real deposit rate			−0.3109
			(0.2526)
Constant	−59.6796***	−59.0217***	−45.7464**
	(16.8331)	(18.5776)	(22.4458)
Lags/instruments	1/18	1/20	1/30
AR (1) *p*-value	0.007	0.009	0.010
AR (2) *p*-value	0.591	0.579	0.498
Hansen J-test *p*-value	0.805	0.705	0.349
Observations	951	951	951
Number of countries	42	42	42

Note: standard errors in parentheses *** $p < 0.01$, ** $p < 0.05$, * $p < 0.1$.

Source: authors' calculations based on data from Grigoli et al. (2018).

Table 7.7 Determinants of private savings in SSA: Robustness regression

Variables	(1)	(2)	(3)
Lag private saving/GPDI	0.3888***	0.3928***	0.3974***
	(0.0578)	(0.0602)	(0.0699)
Ln real per capita GPDI (PPP)	0.0363	0.0404	0.0780
	(0.0529)	(0.0595)	(0.1363)
Real growth rate of per capita GPDI(PPP)	0.1802***	0.1874***	0.2004***
	(0.0493)	(0.0469)	(0.0668)
Ln terms of trade	0.0022	−0.0000	−0.0038
	(0.0186)	(0.0240)	(0.0349)
Public saving/GPDI	−0.4988***	−0.4886***	−0.4013***
	(0.0720)	(0.0837)	(0.1358)
Inflation	0.2447**	0.2184**	0.2707***
	(0.1005)	(0.0984)	(0.1004)
Old age–dependency ratio	0.8069	0.2656	−1.5341
	(1.3878)	(1.4900)	(3.3504)
Share of urban population	0.0724	0.0719	−0.0180
	(0.2067)	(0.2340)	(0.3935)
Financial liberalization dummy, liberal	1.4426	0.4341	−3.3968
	(4.4160)	(7.4875)	(12.9635)
WAEMU		0.5543	−6.1839
		(3.7664)	(10.1565)
CAEMU		1.8662	30.3649
		(6.2642)	(27.9214)
Liberal* WAEMU			11.5784
			(15.1709)
Liberal* CAEMU			−28.2112
			(21.7298)
Constant	−27.1603	−25.2375	−35.4229
	(30.6056)	(29.8524)	(49.3792)
Lags/instruments	1/16	1/16	1/20
AR (1) *p*-value	0.008	0.008	0.009
AR (2) *p*-value	0.266	0.273	0.274
Hansen J-test *p*-value	0.330	0.201	0.318
Observations	835	835	835
Number of countries	31	31	31

Note: the financial liberalization dummy takes on the value zero (0) for years preceding the year of financial reforms and one (1) for years after the financial reform. Standard errors in parentheses *** $p < 0.01$, ** $p < 0.05$, * $p < 0.1$.

Source: authors' calculations based on data from Grigoli et al. (2018).

5. Conclusion

Relative to other developing regions, low savings rates characterize the SSA region. To boost domestic investment and facilitate higher growth in the SSA region, the domestic savings rate—a key determinant of economic growth—must increase. An important question is what accounts for the difference in savings rates between SSA countries and non-SSA developing countries. This chapter has analysed the determinants of private savings in developing countries, focusing on the effect of financial liberalization on private savings. The chapter has also analysed whether the determinants of private savings in SSA countries differ significantly from the determinants of private savings in non-SSA developing countries. Further, we have examined whether there are variations in the levels of private savings rates and the effects of financial liberalization on private savings for countries in SSA that are part of a monetary union compared with their counterparts outside a monetary union.

We conclude by making four policy recommendations that governments in SSA might implement to boost private savings. First, our study shows that the factors that drive private savings in the SSA region are similar to those in other developing regions. An important implication of this finding is that countries in the SSA region can learn from countries with high private savings, such as the four Asian tigers—Hong Kong, Singapore, South Korea, and Taiwan (Hamilton and Clemens 1999). However, we also find that due to the persistent nature of private savings, the long-run effect of a permanent change in the other determinants of the private savings rate is about 11 times its respective effect in the short run for countries outside SSA. This compares with a long-run effect of only 1.6 times for SSA. This result has important implications because it suggests that in the long run, similar (permanent and positive) changes in the determinants of private savings provide more dividends to non-SSA countries than to SSA countries. This means that SSA countries need to implement more aggressive policies than other developing countries in order to realize similar positive effects to non-SSA developing countries.

Second, we find that financial liberalization does not have a significant impact on private savings. Section 2 showed that many countries reformed their financial sector. These reforms are still important, since financial deepening is relevant for long term-growth (King and Levine 1993; Rioja and Valev 2004; Levine 2005). However, our study shows that several countries, particularly countries in the WAEMU, have reversed their policies and reimposed interest rate controls. This development is clearly concerning because the reimposition of IRCs may have a broader adverse effect, such as growth reduction, even if it does not reduce private savings.

Third, we find that the growth rate of per capita income has a positive and significant impact on private savings in both the short and long run. This suggests that implementing policies that raise long-term growth will boost private savings.

Such policies would include promoting good institutions and investing in human capital, physical capital, and technology. More importantly, Rodrik et al. (2004) conclude that when it comes to the determinants of growth, the quality of institutions trumps everything else. It is important to note that overall, countries in SSA have weaker institutions—thanks to factors such as high levels of corruption, weak property rights, and a lack of enforcement of contracts—than non-SSA developing countries (Sobrinho and Thakoor 2019). Hence, improving institutional quality in the SSA region may facilitate higher growth and thereby promote private savings.

Finally, our results also show that, other things being equal, a one percentage point increase in public savings reduces private savings by 0.38 percentage points in the short run, which translates into a 0.62 percentage point increase in national savings. This suggests that a decrease in government deficit will lead to an increase in national savings, which in turn will raise investment and thereby increase growth. We note that the fiscal deficit for SSA is higher than in other regions. For example, the average fiscal deficit as a share of GDP for SSA in 2021 was about 5.3%. This compares with 4.5% for LAC and 3.2% for the Middle East and Central Asia (IMF 2022). In policy terms, this suggests that it would be beneficial for SSA governments to reduce their high fiscal deficits. Our results show that the determinants of savings are similar for countries within and outside the monetary unions in SSA. Therefore, countries in the region may need to engage in the harmonization of their macroeconomic policies in order to promote higher private savings rates in the region. Similarly to the European Union's Maastricht convergence criteria, which bind member countries to a budget deficit less than or equal to 3% of national GDP, the 15 members of the Economic Community of West African States (ECOWAS)[8] have adopted rationalized convergence criteria[9] in preparation for the launch of the community's single currency. Under these criteria, members are also required to reduce their budget deficit to less than 3% of national GDP. Reducing fiscal deficits can potentially increase national savings, boost investment and growth, and create a virtuous circle.

References

Abiad, A., E. Detragiache, and T. Tressel (2010). 'A New Database of Financial Reforms'. *IMF Staff Papers*, 57(2): 281–302. https://doi.org/10.1057/imfsp.2009.23.

Asiedu, E. (2002). 'On the Determinants of Foreign Direct Investment to Developing Countries: Is Africa Different?' *World Development*, 30(1): 107–19. https://doi.org/10.1016/S0305-750X(01)00100-0.

[8] The 15 ECOWAS economies include Benin, Burkina Faso, Cabo Verde, Cote d'Ivoire, the Gambia, Ghana, Guinea, Guinea-Bissau, Liberia, Mali, Niger, Nigeria, Senegal, Sierra Leone, and Togo.

[9] The rationalized macroeconomic convergence criteria were adopted by the Authority of ECOWAS Heads of State and Governments in 2015. See the West African Monetary Agency, available at: https://amao-wama.org/publicationtype/statusofconvergence (accessed 18 December 2024).

Asiedu, E., F. Asiseh, T. Mannah-Blankson, and J. A. Paintsil (2022a). 'Financial Liberalization and Its Implications for Private Savings in Sub-Saharan Africa'. World Institute for Public Policy Research and Analysis (WIDER) Working Paper 2022/79. Helsinki: United Nations University (UNU)-WIDER. https://doi.org/10.35188/UNU-WIDER/2022/210-2.

Asiedu, E., N. B. Gaekwad, M. Nanivazo, M. Nkusu, and Y. Jin (2022b). 'On the Impact of Income per Capita on Health Outcomes: Is Africa Different?' Working paper.

Blundell, R., and S. Bond (1998). 'Initial Conditions and Moment Restrictions in Dynamic Panel Data Models'. *Journal of Econometrics*, 87(1): 115–43. https://doi.org/10.1016/S0304-4076(98)00009-8.

Briffaut, J.-P., M. G. Iden, M. P. C. Hayward, M. T. Lybek, M. H. Mehran, M. P. Ugolini, and M. S. Swaray (1998). *Financial Sector Development in Sub-Saharan African Countries*. Washington, DC: International Monetary Fund (IMF). https://doi.org/10.5089/9781557757586.084.

Calice, P., F. Diaz Kalan, and O. Masetti (2020). 'Interest Rate Repression around the World'. Working Paper, 15 October. Washington, DC: World Bank. Available at: http://hdl.handle.net/10986/34672 (accessed 28 June 2022).

Edwards, S. (1996). 'Why Are Latin America's Savings Rates So Low? An International Comparative Analysis'. *Journal of Development Economics*, 51(1): 5–44. https://doi.org/10.1016/S0304-3878(96)00424-5.

Elbadawi, I., and F. M. Mwega (2000). 'Can Africa's Saving Collapse Be Reversed?' *World Bank Economic Review*, 14(3): 415–30. https://doi.org/10.1093/wber/14.3.415.

Fowowe, B. (2008). 'Financial Liberalization Policies and Economic Growth: Panel Data Evidence from Sub-Saharan Africa'. *African Development Review*, 20(3): 549–74. https://doi.org/10.1111/j.1467-8268.2008.00198.x.

Fowowe, B. (2013). 'Financial Liberalization in Sub-Saharan Africa: What Do We Know?' *Journal of Economic Surveys*, 27(1): 1–37. https://doi.org/10.1111/j.1467-6419.2011.00689.x.

Grigoli, F., A. Herman, and K. Schmidt-Hebbel (2018). 'Saving in the World'. *World Development*, 104: 257–70. https://doi.org/10.1016/j.worlddev.2017.11.022.

Hamilton, K., and M. Clemens (1999). 'Genuine Savings Rates in Developing Countries'. *World Bank Economic Review*, 13(2): 333–56. https://doi.org/10.1093/wber/13.2.333.

IMF (International Monetary Fund) (2022). 'World Economic Outlook Database'. Available at: https://www.imf.org/external/pubs/ft/weo/disclaim.htm (accessed 15 April 2021).

Kelly, R., and G. Mavrotas (2008). 'Savings and Financial Sector Development: Panel Cointegration Evidence from Africa'. *European Journal of Finance*, 14(7): 563–81. https://doi.org/10.1080/13518470801890602.

King, R. G., and R. Levine (1993). 'Finance and Growth: Schumpeter Might Be Right'. *Quarterly Journal of Economics*, 108(3): 717–37. https://doi.org/10.2307/2118406.

Levine, R. (2005). 'Finance and Growth: Theory and Evidence'. National Bureau of Economic Research (NBER) Working Paper 10766. Cambridge, MA: NBER. Available at: https://www.nber.org/papers/w10766 (accessed 28 June 2022).

Loayza, N., H. Lopez, K. Schmidt-Hebbel, and L. Serven (1998). 'The World Saving Data Base'. Unpublished paper.

Loayza, N., K. Schmidt-Hebbel, and L. Servén (2000). 'What Drives Private Saving around the World?' *Review of Economics and Statistics*, 82(2): 165–81.

Mwega, F. M. (1997). 'Saving in Sub-Saharan Africa: A Comparative Analysis'. *Journal of African Economies*, 82(2): 199–228.

Reinhart, C. M., and I. Tokatlidis (2003). 'Financial Liberalisation: The African Experience'. *Journal of African Economies*, 12(supp. 2): 53–88.

Rioja, F., and N. Valev (2004). 'Does One Size Fit All? A Re-examination of the Finance and Growth Relationship'. *Journal of Development Economics*, 74(2): 429–47. https://doi.org/10.1016/j.jdeveco.2003.06.006.

Rodrik, D., A. Subramanian, and F. Trebbi (2004). 'Institutions Rule: The Primacy of Institutions Over Geography and Integration in Economic Development'. *Journal of Economic Growth*, 9(2): 131–65. https://doi.org/10.1023/B:Joeg.0000031425.72248.85.

Roodman, D. (2009). 'A Note on the Theme of Too Many Instruments'. *Oxford Bulletin of Economics and Statistics*, 71(1): 135–58. https://doi.org/10.1111/j.1468-0084.2008.00542.x.

Schmidt-Hebbel, K., and L. Servén (2002). 'Financial Liberalization, Saving and Growth'. Conference paper, 'Macroeconomic Stability, Financial Markets, and Economic Development'. Banco de México, 12–13 November 2002. Available at: https://www.researchgate.net/publication/254821223_Financial_liberalization_Saving_and_Growth (accessed 28 June 2022).

Seck, D., and Y. H. El Nil (1993). 'Financial Liberalization in Africa'. *World Development*, 21(11): 1867–81. https://doi.org/10.1016/0305-750X(93)90088-Q.

Sobrinho, N., and V. V. Thakoor (2019). 'More Sand Than Oil: Sub-Saharan Africa Stands to Gain More from Reducing Corruption Than Any Other Region'. *Finance & Development*, 56(3):35–7. https://doi.org/10.5089/9781498316040.022.

Windmeijer, F. (2005). 'A Finite Sample Correction for the Variance of Linear Efficient Two-Step GMM Estimators'. *Journal of Econometrics*, 126(1): 25–51.

World Bank (2022). 'World Development Indicators'. Available at: https://databank.worldbank.org/source/world-development-indicators (accessed 15 April 2021).

8

Economic growth and savings transition in Asia

Unity in diversity

Prema-chandra Athukorala and Wanissa Suanin

1. Introduction

The literature on national saving in the process of economic development and structural change has evolved around two separate but interrelated issues: what is the relationship between the saving rate and growth, and why do saving rates differ across countries and over time in a given country? The debate on the first issue has been virtually settled, even though there has been some controversy about why a given saving rate is associated with different growth rates and in what way the causality runs. In the formative stage of development thinking during the early post-war years, the Harrod–Domar model, which held sway as the workhorse of development policy, linked growth directly and almost exclusively to the saving rate (Meier 1984). Given the perceived structural constraints on domestic saving mobilization in developing countries, foreign saving (foreign capital inflows) was considered a key prerequisite for economic take-off. The supremacy of saving (and hence investment) in the growth process was, however, questioned by the neoclassical growth model (Solow 1956) that received increased attention in the policy debate from the late 1960s. It postulated that an increase in saving rates generates higher growth only in the transition between steady states, and long-term growth depends solely on technological progress. From about the late 1980s, the new endogenous growth models have, however, provided theoretical support for the view that investment results in a permanent increase in growth rates. New multi-country empirical growth studies spawned by these theoretical advances have supported the notion that the rate of investment is the single most robust correlate of long-run growth (Levine and Renelt 1992; Sala-i-Martin 1997; Bond et al. 2010).

In contrast to the emerging consensus on the savings–growth nexus, the issue of why some countries save more than others remains an unresolved issue. What is the process by which a community that was previously saving a low percentage of national income dramatically increases its saving? Do countries need to start with

Prema-chandra Athukorala and Wanissa Suanin, *Economic growth and savings transition in Asia*. In: *The Domestic Savings Shortfall in Sub-Saharan Africa*. Edited by: Rose Ngugi and Kunal Sen, Oxford University Press.
 DOI: 10.1093/oso/9780198932482.003.0008

specific saving proportion policies to initiate the growth process or by harnessing foreign capital inflows? Alternatively, would initiation of the growth process through economy-wide, market-orientated reforms generate a 'virtuous cycle' of growth-induced saving, resulting in a further increase in saving to generate even higher saving and growth? The purpose of this chapter is to contribute to this debate through a comparative analysis of saving behaviour in countries in developing Asia from a historical perspective. The focus on Asia is motivated by two reasons. First, the experiences of these countries as 'model savers' figure prominently in the contemporary policy debate on the role of domestic saving in economic development and how to bridge the domestic investment–saving gap that constrains the growth process in most developing countries (Ranis 1995; Stiglitz 1996). Second, notwithstanding the 'model saver' image, which is based mainly on the experience of high-performing East Asian economies, there are considerable differences in the saving behaviour among countries and over time within individual countries in the region. Therefore, the region provides an ideal laboratory to study the determinants of saving in the process of economic growth and structural transformation.

The chapter aims to add to the existing knowledge of the saving behaviour of countries in developing Asia in several ways. First, for the first time in the study of comparative saving behaviour in the region,[1] the analysis distinguishes between private and the government saving rates, with specific emphasis on the former. The specific focus on private saving is important from the policy point of view because public saving is mostly driven by unobservable political factors. Second, export orientation in the development process is explicitly included in the saving function as a conditioning variable in examining the relationship between the saving rate and per capita income growth. Third, benefitting from recent improvement in the national data reporting systems, we use an annual balance panel data set for the period 1980–2019, encompassing countries in Northeast Asia, Southeast Asia, and South Asia. Finally, we use improved econometric techniques in estimating the saving function to allow for unobserved heterogeneity among countries, a common problem in estimation with cross-sectional data, while addressing endogeneity bias in the savings–growth nexus.

Section 2 presents a comparative analytical narrative of saving performance in Asia in the global context, with emphasis on policy regime shifts. This is followed by an econometric analysis of the determinants of the saving rate. The key findings are summarized in the concluding section.

[1] The previous comparative studies of aggregate national saving in Asia are Collins (1991), World Bank (1993), ADB (1997), and Horioka and Terada-Hagiwara (2012).

2. Saving behaviour in developing Asia: A historical perspective

2.1 Overall patterns

The saving rates in Asian countries were not unusually large in the early post-war years. Rosenstein-Rodan (1961), in a pioneering study undertaken to inform the policy debate on international development aid, estimated the average gross saving rate of Asian countries at 7.0% compared to 9.4% in Latin America and only one percentage higher than that in Africa (5.9%). Interestingly, at the individual country level, Burma (Myanmar) and India had a higher similar saving rate of 8.5% compared to Taiwan (8.0%) and South Korea (6.5%) (Rosenstein-Rodan 1961: Table 3A).

The patterns began to change from about the late 1960s. By the early 1970s, the average Asian saving rate exceeded that of Latin America and was more than double the average rate recorded in Sub-Saharan Africa. During the ensuing years, the gap between the Asian rate and those of the other major regions and the overall world saving rate has widened. Overall, the Asian saving rates have also been much more stable (Figure 8.1 and Table 8.1).

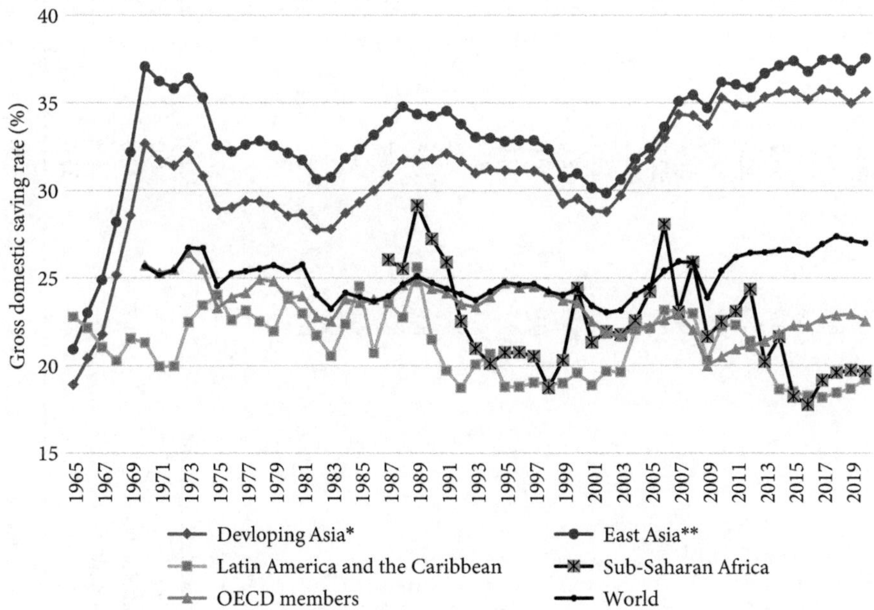

Figure 8.1 World's gross domestic saving rates by major regions, 1965–2019 (%)

Note: *member countries of the Asian Development Bank (ADB); **countries of Northeast Asia and Southeast Asia.

Source: authors' illustration based on World Bank, world development indicators database.

Table 8.1 Gross domestic saving rate (%)

Country/region	1960–69	1970–79	1980–89	1990–99	2000–09	2010–19	2020
Developing Asia,[1,2]	16.5	30.5	29.5	31.1	31.5	35.3	35.6
East Asia,[1,3]	18.1	34.4	32.6	33.0	32.5	36.8	37.5
Northeast Asia[1]	21.6	31.9	33.1	37.1	40.0	41.4	39.2
China	30.7	36.7	35.0	39.6	44.2	47.1	45.2
Hong Kong SAR, China	24.0	30.8	33.6	32.0	31.6	24.5	20.8
Korea, Rep.	8.7	22.5	33.0	37.7	33.9	35.4	35.5
Taiwan	20.3	31.2	33.2	27.4	29.8	26.2	25.3
Southeast Asia[1]	12.9	22.9	28.6	31.7	30.9	33.1	30.0
Cambodia	12.4	—	—	−0.3	12.4	17.8	24.9
Indonesia	5.1	19.9	26.7	28.4	28.3	33.8	31.7
Malaysia	21.4	28.0	33.3	40.6	43.0	34.0	26.2
Philippines	0.0	0.0	23.1	18.2	17.2	16.9	9.6
Singapore	9.7	28.8	43.0	49.0	48.0	53.8	54.6
Thailand	25.7	21.4	26.0	35.7	31.5	32.3	29.4
Vietnam	—	—	—	16.2	27.5	26.9	25.4
South Asia[1]	8.6	11.4	14.6	21.8	26.9	28.1	26.2
Bangladesh	8.4	1.9	12.3	15.4	20.6	22.7	23.8
India	8.2	12.5	15.7	23.9	29.9	31.3	28.9
Pakistan	10.8	10.2	9.7	15.3	14.0	7.9	7.9
Nepal	0.0	6.0	11.0	12.0	10.6	10.0	6.3
Sri Lanka	11.8	15.2	17.8	18.0	16.9	23.1	18.9
Memo items							
Japan	—	37.0	33.3	32.9	27.2	24.1	25.5
Latin America and the Caribbean	21.3	22.1	22.9	19.5	21.1	19.7	19.2
Sub-Saharan Africa	—	0.0	32.4	21.8	23.5	20.6	19.7
Middle East and North Africa	25.7	32.8	24.9	24.9	33.9	28.5	15.6
OECD member countries	—	24.9	23.7	24.1	22.2	21.9	22.5
World	—	25.6	24.4	24.3	24.4	26.5	26.98

Note: [1] GDP-share weighted average; [2] East Asia and South Asia; [3] Northeast Asia, Southeast Asia, Pacific Island small economies, and Central Asia.

Source: authors' compilation using data from the World Bank, World Development Indicators database.

At the formative stage of the emergence of development economics as a separate discipline, Sir Arthur Lewis (1954) made the following highly cited observation on the role of the saving transition in the process of economic development:

> The central problem in the theory of economic development is to understand the process by which a community which was previously saving and investing 4 or 5 per cent of its national income or less, converts itself into an economy where voluntary saving is running at about 12 to 15 per cent of national income or more. This is the central problem because the central fact of economic development is rapid capital accumulation (including knowledge and skills with 'capital'). We cannot explain any 'industrial' revolution (as the economic historians pretend to do) until we can explain why saving increased relatively to national income.
> (Lewis 1954: 155).

When assume a capital consumption allowance of 10%, the saving threshold Lewis considers for lifting a country on to a sustainable growth path is a national saving rate of 22–25% (Srinivasan 1994).

The countries in Northeast Asia and Singapore[2] had already passed the 'Lewisian threshold' by the early 1980s, all major Southeast Asian countries other than Indonesia and the Philippines by the early 1990s, and India in the early 2000s. Nepal, Pakistan, Sri Lanka, and Philippines remain short of reaching the threshold throughout the periods under study (Table 8.1).

2.2 Private and government saving

The data on gross national saving disaggregated by private and public (government) saving are summarized in Table 8.2 for 13 Asian countries for which data are available at least for the past three decades. It is important to note that these data are not strictly comparable with those reported in Table 8.1. The gross national saving rate additionally captures remittances by migrant workers. The saving rates reported here are, therefore, larger for countries that receive a significant inflow of migrant worker remittances (in particular in Sri Lanka and the Philippines). Nonetheless, overall, the general picture presented is comparable.

Overall, both intercountry differences in national saving behaviour and intertemporal patterns within countries are dominated by private saving. The rate of public (government) saving is not as high as observed in some comparative studies. For instance, Edwards (1996) wrote that government saving accounted for between 30 and 40% of total national saving in East Asian countries. However,

[2] From about the early 1980s, Singapore has recorded the highest saving rate in the region (and perhaps in the world). This is partly the result of a unique government policy that required all workers to make an annual contribution to a pension fund.

Table 8.2 Gross national saving (% of GNP), 1980–2019

	Total national saving				Government saving				Private saving			
	1980–89	1990–99	2000–09	2010–19	1980–89	1990–99	2000–09	2010–19	1980–89	1990–99	2000–09	2010–19
Northeast Asia	32.5	34.2	40.7	44.8	5.0	−0.6	1.7	5.2	27.5	34.8	39.0	39.6
China	34.4	37.3	44.7	46.9	6.9	−2.6	1.5	5.2	27.5	39.8	43.1	41.7
Korea	27.3	33.5	33.5	35.4	−0.4	−0.4	1.2	6.4	27.7	34.0	32.3	29.0
Taiwan	33.3	27.4	29.8	29.6	6.2	4.0	2.5	2.2	27.1	23.4	27.3	27.5
Southeast Asia	28.1	32.8	31.4	32.7	6.6	9.7	6.9	5.0	21.6	23.1	24.5	27.6
Indonesia	28.9	28.7	26.1	32.7	8.3	10.3	10.0	6.5	20.6	18.4	16.1	26.1
Malaysia	29.2	37.5	37.5	30.2	10.5	12.0	9.4	4.3	18.7	25.5	28.0	25.9
Philippines	20.8	18.5	23.7	25.2	4.7	6.5	3.9	3.1	16.1	12.0	19.8	22.1
Singapore	33.1	48.3	46.0	48.3	1.8	15.2	5.7	8.1	31.2	33.0	40.3	40.2
Thailand	25.8	34.0	30.2	31.0	3.4	7.6	5.2	5.1	22.5	26.4	25.0	25.9
Vietnam	—	9.5	31.1	28.5	—	5.9	−0.9	−3.0	—	10.2	31.9	31.5
South Asia	16.6	23.0	30.4	31.2	0.1	0.0	0.8	−0.4	16.5	23.0	29.6	31.6
Bangladesh	3.6	17.6	22.5	27.4	−2.7	5.3	6.0	5.9	6.4	12.3	16.4	21.6
India	17.8	23.9	32.4	32.9	−0.3	−1.4	−0.3	−1.5	18.1	25.3	32.7	34.3
Pakistan	16.2	21.3	21.9	20.3	4.2	4.8	4.5	3.1	12.0	16.5	17.4	17.2
Sri Lanka	10.0	19.2	22.0	29.0	8.4	7.1	2.1	4.5	1.6	12.1	20.0	24.5
Asia	26.7	31.7	37.3	41.0	3.9	1.8	2.5	4.3	22.8	29.9	34.9	36.7
Asia excluding China	23.8	29.5	31.5	32.7	2.7	3.5	2.9	3.1	21.0	26.0	28.6	29.6
Memo item												
China's share (in total value) (%)	35.1	34.5	54.5	67.8	48.6	53.7	43.3	70.1	32.8	39.1	55.4	67.5

Source: authors' compilation from Asian Development Bank Key Indicators for Asia and Pacific database.

during the period 1980–2009, on average, government saving in Asia as a percentage of gross national income (GNI) amounted to 4% compared to a private saving rate of 26%.

Government saving in the East Asian countries are notably higher than in South Asia. During the period 1980–2019, the combined government saving rates in Northeast Asia and Southeast Asia were 2.8 and 4.2%, respectively, compared to just 1.5% in South Asia. The government saving rates are notably high in Singapore and Indonesia, averaging to around 9–11% of gross national income in both countries. The high government saving rate in Indonesia, notwithstanding its relatively lower raking in overall saving performance in East Asia, seems to reflect the country's longstanding strict fiscal discipline, enforced by a rule that prohibits the government from borrowing domestically to finance expenditures (ADB 1997; Blöndal et al. 2009.

2.3 Corporate savings

In analysing behaviour of private saving, it is important to examine how corporate saving has behaved compared to household and government saving. Unfortunately, disaggregated data are not available for a sufficient number of countries in the regional sector for a comparative analysis. The available data for China, Taiwan, Korea, the Philippines, and India are plotted in Figure 2 in Athukorala and Suanin (2022) In Korea and Taiwan, corporate saving has been the prime mover of national saving over the past two decades or so, with the gap between household and corporate saving widening over the years. In China, corporate and household saving have contributed almost equally to the increase in national saving during the entire period of 1992–2019, without any notable change in their relative contribution. Corporate saving in India has begun to show a modest increase following the first wave of liberalization reforms in the mid-1980s and gained impetus from the second-wave reforms initiated in the early 1990s.

2.4 Domestic savings: Investment gap and capital mobility

By definition, domestic investment is the sum of domestic saving and foreign saving (net foreign capital inflow). To what extent have the Asian countries relied on foreign saving to finance investment? This question is directly relevant for the ensuing analysis of the savings–growth nexus because the Asian economies have become increasingly opened through not only current account transaction but also capital account transactions during the period under study. In this context, the degree of dependence on foreign saving investment could weaken the postulated link between the national saving and growth.

There are notable intercountry differences in terms of the capital-importing ('deficit' saving) and capital-exporting ('excess' saving) status (Athukorala and Suanin 2022: Table 3). In Northeast Asia, Taiwan has been a net capital exporter throughout this period, with capital exports relative to domestic national income increasing over the past three decades. China and Korea have become net capital exporters in the 2000s, following drawing on foreign saving to meet the investment–saving gap in the 1980s and 1990s. Countries in Southeast Asia exhibit a mixed picture. Malaysia, Thailand, and Singapore have become capital exporters over time, with Singapore becoming by far the largest capital exporter relative to national income in the Asian region. The four South Asian countries have continued to rely on foreign saving to fill the domestic investment–savings gap. However, even in these countries, domestic savings has accounted for over 90% of total domestic investment, after allowing for the exceptional cases of Bangladesh and Sri Lanka in the 1980s. Interesting, unlike in Latin America, net capital flows in all countries during most of the period under study have generally dominated by foreign direct investment (FDI), rather than portfolio capital, which are more volatile and susceptible to external shocks (Athukorala and Rajapatirana 2003).

3. Saving rate determination: Empirical analysis

The section undertakes an econometric analysis of the determinants of saving using a panel data set for 12 Asian countries[3] for which data are available for the entire period 1980–2019. We focus specifically on private saving because preliminary analysis suggested that public saving is mostly driven by unobservable political factors. Data are not available for disaggregating private saving into household saving and corporate saving (retained earnings). Apart from this data constraint, the focus on aggregate private saving is justified by the 'consideration that corporate saving, just like personal (or household) saving, will tend to result, at least in the long run, in an increase in private net worth by way of its net effect on the market value of corporate equity' (Modigliani 1966). Provided the shareholders look through the *corporate veil* and take into account corporate saving (retained earnings) in their lifetime saving/consumption decisions, no separate treatment of household and corporate saving is needed to understand the saving behaviour of the economy. This view is no doubt an approximation (Gersovitz 1988; Poterba 1991). Shareholders may be myopic and fail to devote the necessary resources to monitor corporate performance. Various factors impacting on business operations, such as liquidity constraints, tax policies, and other kinds of capital market imperfections, could limit shareholders' ability to pierce the

[3] Bangladesh, China, India, Indonesia, South Korea, Malaysia, Pakistan, Philippines, Singapore, Sri Lanka, Taiwan, and Thailand.

corporate veil. Perhaps these factors would have become increasingly important for explaining the dichotomy between personal saving and corporate saving in recent years, given the shrinking of labour share in in private income as an integral facet of the ongoing process of economic globalization (Redeker 2022).[4]

3.1 The model

The saving function is formulated based on the life-cycle model (LCM). The attractiveness of the LCM for our analysis lies in both its elegant formulation of the impact of income growth and demographic dynamics, which are central to understanding the saving transition in the process of growth and structural change (Deaton 2005).

The LCM originated in Modigliani and Brumberg (1954), which worked out a theory of spending based on the postulate that working-age people make provision for their retirement by tailoring consumption patterns to income at different ages over the lifetime, independently of the income at each age.[5] Modigliani and co-researchers subsequently extended the theory into an analytical framework applicable to the economy as a whole that led to the important prediction that national saving depends on the rate of national income growth, not its level, and demographic profile of the economy (see Modigliani 1986 and works cited therein). In an economy in which national income is growing so that each generation is better off than their parents, the young will be saving on a larger scale than the old are dis-saving so that the faster the growth, the higher the saving rate: Saving is therefore the consequence of growth, not a wellspring of growth. At the same time, an increase in the population growth rate increases the working-age population (savers) relative to the number of retirees (dis-savers). Thus, even if all the individuals in two given economies have the same saving profile over their life cycles, the aggregate saving rate can be different depending on population dynamics. A sizeable body of literature over the past five decades has further expanded and enriched the core model to deal with a wide range of variables that have the potential to impact the saving rate by conditioning the impact of economic growth and population dynamics.

The core model postulates that the savings rate is related to the growth of per capita income, *not* the current level of per capita income as postulated by the standard Keynesian absolute income hypothesis. This postulate stems from the assumption that individuals are forward-looking and, therefore, base their savings decisions on lifetime income rather than current income. This assumption holds

[4] The findings of Horioka (1991) for Japan, Ha et al. (2010) for South Korea, and Aron and Muellbauer (2000) for South Africa support the hypothesis of households piercing of the corporate veil. Poterba (1991) has come up with mixed results for the United States, United Kingdom, and Canada.

[5] For a succinct formal presentation of the basic model, see Gersovitz (1988: section 2.1).

fairly well for developed countries where a significantly large core of households are able to carry over resources to provide for the old age. However, in developing countries, the portion of the population in the bottom rungs of the income distribution may find it impossible or too burdensome to set aside resources now in order to provide for later consumption. For these reasons, 'conceivably for a sufficiently low value of per capita income,... the saving-income ratio for given growth would... tend to rise with [the level of] income' (Modigliani 1993: 276).

There is a sizeable body of empirical evidence that the degree of export orientation of the development strategy plays an important role in explaining inter-country differences in growth and the savings rate (Maizels 1971; Weisskopf 1972; Balassa 1989). Export orientation leads to better growth performance than policies favouring import substitution by facilitating resource allocation according to comparative advantage, allowing for greater capacity utilization and scale economies and greater technological improvement in response to competition from abroad, and contributing to employment growth. To the extent that the propensity to save associated with marginal rates of growth exceeds that associated with the average rates, the rates of savings would be higher under export orientation. Moreover, in a labour surplus economy, growth through greater export orientation has the potential to tilt income distribution in valour of the entrepreneurs whose propensity to save might be higher (Lewis 1954). We therefore include export orientation on its own (to capture the direct effect of export orientation on the savings rate) as well as interactive with economic growth (to capture the growth-enhancing effect of export orientation on the saving rate) as explanatory variables in the model.

The hypothesized link between income growth and the savings rate is based on the assumption of perfect capital markets that enable households to borrow freely against future income in order to smooth consumption over their lifetime. If the households are liquidity constrained—they are unable to borrow freely against future income—the consumption behaviour might be linked to current income rather than to lifetime income. Thus, the borrowing constraint, in addition to forcing households to maintain consumption at current income levels, can in fact convert a negative saver into a positive saver by forcing them to save more at present in order to undertake lumpy (indivisible) expenditure plans in the future (Gersovitz 1988).

The LCM also assumes certainty of future income streams in the mind of the individual. However, if income prospects are uncertain, saving is about not only accumulation for future consumption but also consumption smoothing in the face of volatile incomes. In other words, a precautionary motive rooted in economic uncertainty can be an important driver of savings behaviour (consideration behind saving). We therefore include the rate of inflation to capture precautionary savings effects of macroeconomic uncertainty. Inflation can have a positive effect on saving, as uncertainty about future real incomes in an inflationary environment may encourage saving for maintaining future consumption levels. However, it can also have negative effects on saving by increasing the uncertainty about future value of accumulated savings (Deaton 1989; Corbo and Schmidt-Hebbel 1991; Loayza et al. 2000).

Social security payments could have a negative impact on personal savings as individuals substitute these expected government transfers for personal savings accumulated for retirement (Modigliani and Sterling 1983; Modigliani and Cao 2004). As in the case of social security payments, the existence of bequests (inherited wealth) has the potential to weaken the postulated impact of income growth on the national saving rate. However, the available evidence suggests that the bequest motive affects the saving/consumption behaviour of rather small number of households mostly belonging to the highest income brackets and therefore it is possible to go a long way in analysing national saving behaviour without dealing with wealth inheritance (Modigliani 1986; Deaton 2005).

The real interest rate has two countervailing effects on savings depending on whether the person is a net borrower or a net lender. In the former case, a higher interest rate increases the present price of consumption relative to the future price and thus provides an incentive to increase savings (the substitution effect). By contrast, in the latter case, an increase in the interest rate raises lifetime income and thus tends to increase consumption and decrease savings (the income effect).

The impact of foreign resource inflows ('foreign savings') on domestic savings remains a debatable issue (Papanek 1972; Weisskopf 1972; Reinhart and Talvi 1998; Obstfeld 1999). Foreign savings can act as a substitute for domestic savings if the agents draw on foreign savings to smooth current expenditure over time. However, there is room for developed-orientated governments to harness foreign resources to meet the gap between domestic investment and domestic savings without an adverse effect on domestic savings. Also, foreign resource inflows are not a homogenous phenomenon. Foreign direct investment, which directly contributes to the domestic production capacity of the economy, unlike concessionary foreign aid and other forms of capital inflows, has the potential to help promote domestic savings.

The fiscal policy can affect private savings behaviour through two possible channels with opposing effects. First, the Ricardian equivalence proposition (Barro 1974) postulates that government dis-saving (budget deficit) results in an equal increase in private savings because the private sector savers anticipate a future increase in taxes to service the deficit. Second, government savings behaviour can be indicative of the soundness of macroeconomic management, including a lower rate of inflation, prudential exchange rate policies, and capable monetary management. Stable economies, in turn, lower the risk for investors and therefore lower the cost of capital for long-term investment and encourage savings (and investment) by the private sector.

The final consideration relates to the role of financial deepening (increasing provision of financial services) in the economy (*FND*) in promoting saving.

Financial deepening has the potential to increase the private saving rate through encouraging financial saving, by improving the accessibility to banking facilities (Athukorala and Sen 2004).

Informed by this literature, and tailored to data availability, we specify the saving function in a panel data setting as follows:

$$PSR_{it} = \beta_0 + \beta_1 GY_{it} + \beta_2 YD_{it} + \beta_3 YDEP_{it} + \beta_4 ADEP_{it}, + \beta_5 EOR_{it} + \beta_6 EOR * GY_{it} + \beta_7 CRP_{it} + \beta_8 RID_{ti} + \beta_9 INF_{ti} + \beta_{10} SSP_{it} + \beta_{11} FND_{it} + \beta_{12} FS + \beta_{13} BBL_{it} + \gamma_i + \eta_t + \epsilon_{i,t} \quad (1)$$

where *PSR* is a private saving rate; γ_i and η_t are country- and time-specific effects; β'_{ik}.

The explanatory variables are defined below with the expected signs of β'_{ik} given in brackets:

GY (+)	The rate of growth of per capita private income
YD (+)	Per capita real private income
YDEP (–)	Young dependency measured as the ratio of the population aged 15 and under to the working-age population (aged 16–64)
ADEP (–)	Aged dependency measured as the ratio of the population aged 65 and older to the working-age population (aged 16–64)
EOR (+)	Export orientation measured as exports relative to gross domestic product (GDP)
RID (?)	The real interest rate on bank deposits
INF (?)	Inflation rate
CRP (–)	Institutional lending to the private sector as a ratio of private income
SSP (–)	Social security payments as a ratio of private income
FND (–)	Financial deepening of the economy
FS (?)	Foreign capital inflow as a percentage of gross national income
BBL (?)	Government budget balance as a percentage of gross national income

3.2 Data source, variable measurement

The estimation of the saving function is undertaken using an annual unbalanced panel data set of 12 Asian countries, covering the period 1980–2019. Data on the saving rate for all countries other than Taiwan are compiled from the *Key Indicators of Asia and the Pacific* (KIAP) database of the Asian Development Bank, which is based on the official records of individual Asian Development Bank (ADB) member countries. In the national accounts of these countries, the data on national saving are estimated indirectly, subtracting net resource inflows ('foreign saving') (after allowing for changes in the holding of foreign exchange reserves) from aggregated domestic investment. Data on national saving disaggregated into private saving and public saving are available from the national data systems only for India and South Korea. For the other countries, we derived private saving by deducting government saving from total national saving. Government saving is derived as the difference between government revenue and government recurrent expenditure. Any data series that is derived as a 'residual' from two other national account aggregates naturally incorporates possible estimation errors of the latter two magnitudes. Therefore, the use of the saving date used in the econometric analysis is based on the assumption that the estimation errors remain consistent over the period under study (Srinivasan 1994).

The data on the other variables are collected or compiled from several sources. The deposit interest rate of India is compiled from the reserve bank of India. The data on deposit interest rates of other countries and money stocks are retrieved from the International Monetary Fund. All other data series (except for Taiwan) are extracted from the World Bank World Development Indicator database. All data series for Taiwan are compiled from various issues of the *Taiwan Statistical Data Book* (Taiwan (Republic of China), Council for Economic Planning and Development, Taipei).

Nominal private income is converted into real terms using the consumer price index (CPI = 2010). The results are remarkably resilient to the use of the GDP deflator as an alternative price deflator The young age–dependency ratio (*YDEP*) is the percentage of the population aged 15 and under relative to the working population aged 15–64. Similarly, the old age–dependency ratio (*ADEP*) is constructed by dividing the population aged 65 and older by the working population aged 15–64. The results are remarkably resilient to the use of the GDP deflator as an alternative price deflator. Financial deepening is proxied by broad money supply (M3) as a percentage of GNI. Social security payments are measured by the government transfer payment, including subsidies, grants, and other social benefits. The real interest rate (*RID*) is measured as $ln[(1 + NID)/(1 + INF)]$, where *NID* is the average time deposit rate in commercial banks and *INF* is the current rate of inflation calculated from the CPI. All variables (except all dummy variables) are used in percentage form.

3.3 Econometric procedure

We began the estimation process by examining the time-series properties of the panel data using the Im-Persara-Shin (CIPS) test (Pesaran 2007). The results indicated that the private saving series, *PSR*, and all other explanatory variables except

GY, *RID*, and *FS* are non-stationary (I(1)). Based on this result, we conducted tests to examine the existence of a long-run relationship among the variables (Pedroni 2004). The results indicated that two of the four test statistics relating to cointegration of the 'within dimension' of the data panel and one of the three relating to cointegration of the 'between dimension' of the data panel are statistically significant. These results (Athukorala and Suanin 2022: Tables 4 and 5) provide sufficient grounds to use the panel-data autoregressive distribution lag (ARDL) estimator to estimate the saving function.

Equation (1) can be rewritten in ARDL form as follows:

$$PSR_{i,t} = \sum_{k=1}^{p} \phi_i PSR_{i,t-k} + \sum_{k=0}^{q} \beta_{ik}' X_{i,t-k} + \gamma_i + \eta_t + \epsilon_{i,t} \qquad (2)$$

where $X_{i,t}$ is a vector of explanatory variables; and ϕ_i is the coefficient of the lagged dependent variable.

When equation (2) is reparametrized in error correction form,

$$\Delta PSR_{i,t} = \rho_i \left[PSR_{i,t-1} - \lambda_i' X_{i,t-1} \right] + \sum_{k=1}^{p-1} \zeta_{ik} \Delta PSR_{i,t-k} + \sum_{k=0}^{q-1} \beta_{ik}' \Delta X_{i,t-k} + \gamma_i + \eta_t + \epsilon_{i,t} \qquad (3)$$

where $\rho_i = -(1 - \phi_i)$ is the speed of adjustment coefficient (expected that $\rho_i < 0$), representing the speed of adjustment of imports to a shock to move back to the long-run equilibrium; λ_i' is the vector of long-run coefficients; $ECT = \left[SR_{i,t-1} - \lambda_i' X_{i,t-1} \right]$ is the error correction term that captures speed of convergence to equilibrium; and ζ_{ik} and β_{ik}' are the short-run coefficients.

Equation (3) permits us to examine short- and long-run dynamics and the speed of adjustment of the model to equilibrium. This formulation is 'robust to integration and cointegration properties of the regressors and, for sufficient lag-orders, could be immune to the endogeneity problem, at least as far as the long-run properties of model are concerned' (Pesaran 2015: 726). Since we work with an annual panel data set of sufficient time coverage (39 years) that permits systematically testing lag orders, possible endogeneity bias could be asymptotically negligible due to the super consistency property resulting from the parametrization of the model in levels and divergences.

The Akaike information criterion (AIC) is used to decide the appropriate lag length.[6] Two alternative estimators are used to explore the potential heterogeneity of parameters among the countries within the data panel: the dynamic fixed effects (DFE) estimator and the mean group (MG) estimator (Pesaran 2015). The DFE estimator allows the intercepts to differ freely across groups, while all other coefficients and error variances are constrained to be the same. The

[6] The results are robust to the use of the Schwarz Bayesian criterions (SBCs).

MG estimator allows coefficients to differ freely across groups by first estimating one equation per group (a country in our case) and taking the average across groups (countries). The Hausman test is used to identify the appropriate estimator (Hausman 1978).

3.4 Results

The saving function was estimated for the 12 countries, and the countries other than China. In both cases, the DFE was the appropriate estimator in terms of the Hausman test. The results are reported in Table 8.3. A comparison of the two equations helps understand the possible sensitivity of the results to China's dominance in the overall saving performance in Asia.

Per capita real private income (*YD*) was dropped by the ARDL estimator because of its high collinearity with the growth rate of *GY*. In alternative estimates that excluded *GY*, the coefficient of *YD* was not statistically significant even though it had the expected positive sign. Dropping *YD* for the final estimates was supported by the standard variable deletion *F* test. The social security payment (SSP) is dropped from the reported equations because data were not available for three countries (China, Indonesia, and India) and data for some years are missing for other countries. In the equation estimated for the other nine countries, the coefficient had the expected negative sign but was not statically significant, and its inclusion had no notable impact on the estimated coefficients of the other variables.[7]

Given our focus on saving transition in the growth process, we are interested mainly in the long-run estimates. In both equations, the coefficient of the error correction model (ECM) term is highly statistically significant with the expected negative sign, suggesting a moderate (about 1.4 years) speed of convergence of *PSR* to equilibrium.

In the equation for all countries (Equation (1)), the coefficient of *GY* is statistically significant at the 1% level. The results suggest that a one percentage point increase in the growth rate of per capita private income is a 1.27 percentage point increase in the long run. The results are remarkably resilient to the exclusion of China from the country coverage (Equation (2)).

Relating to the interpretation of this result, an important issue is the possible endogeneity of *GY* in the model (Deaton 2005). However, as noted, the panel ARDL estimator has the advantage of minimizing possible endogeneity of the right-hand variables by reparametrizing the model in levels and differences. As a further test, we performed the Granger causality test and impulse response function (IRF) analysis using the panel-data vector auto regression procedure developed by Abrigo and Love (2016). The rest results are reported in Table 8.4

[7] The alternative estimates are available on request.

Table 8.3 Determinants of private saving (PSR)[1]

	All 12 countries	Excluding China
Long-run estimates		
GY [Growth rate of GNI (%)]	1.268*** (0.124)	1.448*** (0.241)
YDEP [Young dependency (%)]	−0.169*** (0.054)	−0.169*** (0.044)
ADEP [Aged dependency (%)]	0.286 (0.417)	0.371 (0.403)
EOR [Export/GNI (%)]	0.032*** (0.005)	0.030*** (0.007)
GY*EOR	0.085*** (0.020)	0.048** (0.023)
RID [Real interest rate (%)]	0.387* (0.226)	0.419* (0.225)
BBL [Budget balance/GNI (%)]	0.347 (0.291)	0.290 (0.308)
INF [Inflation rate (%)]	−0.018 (0.485)	0.020 (0.555)
FS [Foreign capital inflow/GNI (%)]	0.300*** (0.043)	0.279*** (0.020)
CRP [Bank lending/GNI (%)]	−0.159** (0.065)	−0.159** (0.071)
FND [Financial deepening; M3/GNI (%)]	0.026 (0.138)	0.022 (0.155)
ECT	−0.154*** (0.016)	−0.156*** (0.013)
Short-run estimates		
$\Delta\ GY_t$	0.252*** (0.050)	0.256*** (0.056)
$\Delta\ RID_t$	−0.061** (0.030)	−0.063* (0.035)
$\Delta\ BBL_t$	−0.101** (0.044)	−0.115*** (0.040)
AFC	0.004** (0.002)	0.004*** (0.002)
GFC	0.005*** (0.000)	0.005*** (0.000)
Constant	0.109*** (0.033)	0.108*** (0.032)
ARDL	(1,1,0,0,0,0,1,1,0,0,0,0)	(1,1,0,0,0,0,1,1,0,0,0,0)
Hausman test (MG, DFE)	0.01	0.01
Estimator	DFE	DFE
Adjust-R square	0.317	0.360
Number of observations	444	407
Number of countries	12	11

Note: [1] heteroscedasticity corrected standard errors are in parentheses; ***, **, and * denote statistically significant at 0.01, 0.05, and 0.1 levels, respectively; ARDL indicates the appropriate lag length of each variable determined in the estimation process.

Source: authors' estimates based on data sources described in section 3.2.

Table 8.4 Panel VAR–Granger causality Wald test

Null hypothesis (Ho)	**Chi-square (χ2) Stats**	**Prob > Chi2**
GY does not Granger-cause PSR	21.43	0.000
PSR does not Granger-cause GY	0.85	0.655

Note: the test is based on the panel VAR model with two lags.
Source: authors' estimates based on data sources described in section 3.2.

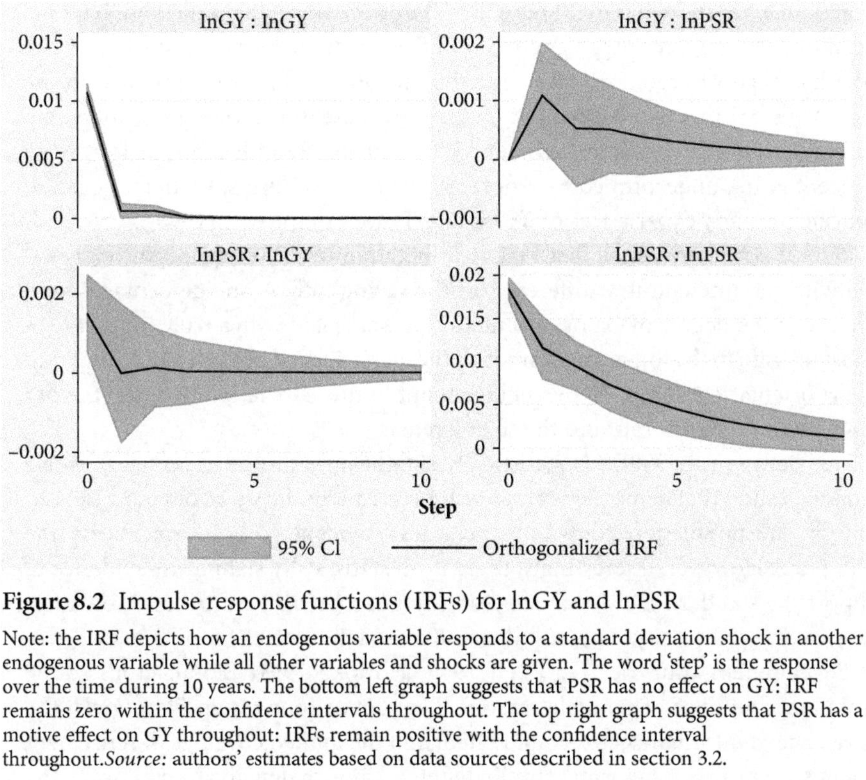

Figure 8.2 Impulse response functions (IRFs) for lnGY and lnPSR

Note: the IRF depicts how an endogenous variable responds to a standard deviation shock in another endogenous variable while all other variables and shocks are given. The word 'step' is the response over the time during 10 years. The bottom left graph suggests that PSR has no effect on GY: IRF remains zero within the confidence intervals throughout. The top right graph suggests that PSR has a motive effect on GY throughout: IRFs remain positive with the confidence interval throughout.*Source:* authors' estimates based on data sources described in section 3.2.

and Figure 8.2. According to the Granger causality test, the null hypothesis that *GY* does not cause *PSR* is rejected; but the hypothesis that *PSR* does not Granger-cause GY is not rejected, at the 0.05 significant level. The impulse response functions (IRFs) confirm this finding (compare the bottom-left and the top-right graphs in Figure 8.2). Thus, there is strong evidence that growth drives saving rather than the reverse.

This inference receives further empirical support when we place the time profile of saving patterns among and within the Asian countries (as surveyed in section 2) within the contest of the extensively documented reform process and growth trajectories of these countries.[8] In particular, we can see a clear relationship between the timing and nature of market-orientated policy reforms and saving transitions. Korea, Taiwan, and Singapore were the earliest reformers in the region in the late 1960s. These countries had decisively passed the Lewisian saving threshold by the early or mid-1980s. Malaysia and Thailand followed Singapore about a decade later. A comparison of the saving rates of these countries for the past three decades with those during 1965–79 points to the impact of policy regime shifts on saving. In Indonesia, the domestic saving rate has recorded a notable increase following reforms that began earlier in that decade. The dramatic saving transition in China began following the country's gradual shift from 'plan to market' in the late 1970s. India has begun to catch up following the liberalization reforms initiated in the early 1990s. Sri Lanka recorded a significant increase in the saving rate following the liberalization reforms in the later 1970s, but the trend has begun to reverse in recent years, underpinned by a notable reversal of reforms. Vietnam began to replicate the early experiences of Korea and Taiwan in the early 1990s.

There is strong evidence that export orientation (*EOR*) is significantly associated with the intercountry difference in the saving rate. A one percentage point increase in the degree of export orientation is associated with a 0.03% increase in the saving rate in the long run. Moreover, the coefficient of $EOR*GY$ indicates that export orientation adds 0.09 percentage point to the association between the per capita income growth rate and the saving rate.

The coefficient of *YDEP* is statistically significant with the expected negative sign, suggesting that a one percentage point increase in the share of young dependents in the population contributes to a 0.17 percentage point decline in the saving rate. However, interestingly, there is no statistically significant evidence to support the standard LCM that aged dependency (*ADEP*) contributes to dampening saving propensity. This result is not consistent with the available evidence for development countries (e.g. Leff 1969; Horioka 1991; Bloom et al. 2007). There are a number of possible reasons that support our result. First, given the prevalence of informal-sector employment and the limited coverage of retirement benefit schemes even in formal employment, the line of demarcation between the working age and formal retirement remains blurred in the Asian context. Second, the rise in life expectancy as an integral facet of economic growth could have a significant effect on saving behaviour in old age, particularly in the East Asian high-performing countries, where mortality transition has been very rapid (Kinugasa and Mason 2007). Third, households in developing countries generally tend to be larger than in advanced countries, and resources are shared between members actively engaged in the labour force and dependents (Gersovitz 1988; Deaton 1989).

[8] See World Bank (1993), Perkins (2013), and Athukorala (2021) for surveys.

There is strong evidence that foreign capital inflows (*FS*) are complementary to private saving. This finding is consistent with the evidence that foreign capital inflows to Asian countries, by and large, have mostly taken the form of direct foreign investment (which directly contributes to the production capacity of the countries) rather than foreign aid (which mostly takes the form of budgetary supports and/or investment in public sector projects) (Reinhart and Talvi 1998; Athukorala and Rajapatirana 2003).

The bank credit variable (*CRP*) has a significant negative effect on private saving, as expected. This result is consistent with the hypothesis that, in the presence of easy access to bank credit, there is no compelling reason for people to save more at present in order to undertake lumpy (indivisible) expenditure plans in the future. The coefficient of financial deepening (*FND*) has the expected positive sign but is not statistically significant.

The coefficient of the real interest rate variable (*RID*) is not statistically significant, and its magnitude is barely different from zero. It seems that the income effect of the real interest rate counterbalances its substitution effect in the Asian context. The coefficient of the budget balance to GNI ratio (*BBL*) does not support for the Ricardian equivalence hypothesis. This result is consistent with the LCM proposition that private saving, being controlled by life cycle considerations, should be nearly independent of the government budget stance (Modigliani 1986).

We estimated the saving equation for the total national saving rate (*NSR*) for comparison (Athukorala and Suanin 2022: Table 8). T Both the long-run and short-run coefficients of *GY* are highly significant as in the private saving equations, but their magnitudes are slightly smaller. The coefficients of the other variables except *EOR&GY* are broadly similar in terms of the signs and statistical significance, but their magnitudes are notably different. The negative and statistically significant coefficient of *EOR**GY* perhaps captures the fiscal costs (tax incentives and other expenditures) involved, which counterbalance the direct positive effect of export orientation on national saving under the export-orientated development strategy. In summary, this comparison alerts the risk of making inferences about the saving behaviour using aggregate national saving data because of the impact of exogenous political factors on government saving.

To comment on the short-run results, the coefficient of *GY* is statistically significant at the 1% level, with a much smaller coefficient (0.25) compared to the long-run coefficient of 1.26 (Equation (1)). This different is consistent with the standard life-cycle postulate that accumulation of saving is an intertemporal process within the working age. Interesting, the coefficients of the two crisis dummies (*AFC* and *GFC*) are statistically significant with the perverse (positive) sign. Presumably, the crisis-propelled economic uncertainly may have induced private saving (Kim 2001). Moreover, as already noted, there was also no massive disruption in export-orientated production in the East Asian economies because of the remarkable resilience of *FDI* to the crises. The result for *RID* suggests modest negative effect of real interest rate (*RID*) on the private saving rate. Presumably, increase in *RID* raises expected lifetime income of net savers and thus tends to increase consumption and decrease saving in the short run before moving towards the steady state based on life-cycle considerations. The coefficient of *BBL* is statically significant, with the negative sign suggesting that the Ricardian equivalence proposition holds in the short run. However, this result is not inconsistent with the long-run results reported earlier given the LCM proposition that the private saving rate in eventually determined by life-cycle considerations.

How do our multi-country results for Asia compare with the findings of the previous individual country studies of private saving in the region (Sun and Liang 1982; Athukorala and Tsai 2003; Athukorala and Sen 2004; Modigliani and Cao 2004; Park and Rhee 2005; Jongwanich 2010; Ang and Sen 2011; Curtis et al. 2015; Ge et al. 2018)? The only explanatory variable commonly used in all studies is the per capita income growth rate. The results for this variable support a positive association between income growth and private saving rates, with the magnitude of the office varying in the range of 0.3–1.7%. Only Athukorala and Tsai (2003) for Taiwan and Jongwanich (2010) for Thailand have included young and aged dependency ratios separately for testing the impact of the demographic transition on the private saving rate. The results in both studies suggest that both young and aged dependency have a negative impact on the private saving rate, and the impact of the former is greater in magnitude compared to that of the latter. However, household survey-based studies of Park and Rhee (2005) for South Korea and Curtis et al. (2015) for China failed to detect a significant impact of population aging on the saving rate. These mixed results seem consistent with the failure of our saving function estimates to detect a negative relationship between population ageing and the saving rate. Consistent with our results, Ang and Sen (2011) for Malaysia and India, and Jongwanich (2010) for Thailand find that access to bank credit is negatively associated with the saving rate.

4. Concluding remarks

The national gross saving rates in Asia were broadly comparable to those in the rest of the developing world in the early post-war years. The patterns began to change from around the late 1960s. During the ensuing years, the difference between the average Asian saving rate and those of the other major regions and the overall world saving rate has widened. By the late 2010s, the average Asian saving rate was about 37% compared to the global average of about 28%.

The regional average hides substantial subregional and individual country differences in saving behaviour in Asia. Countries in Northeast Asia top the saving rate ranking followed by Southeast Asia. Saving rates in countries in South Asia, though much lower compared to Southeast Asia, are higher compared to the other regions. Within Northeast Asia, the high saving rates of Taiwan and South Korea began to decline around the late 1990s, but the spectacular increase in saving in China has more than counterbalanced this decline. China now accounts for over two-thirds of total national saving (in value) in the region. Within Southeast Asia, the saving rate of Singapore has continued to increase in contrast to the recent decline in the saving rates of Korea and Taiwan. In Southeast Asia, a comparison of the saving rates for the past three decades with those during 1965–79 points to the impact of policy regime shifts on saving. Notwithstanding these differences, a unifying theme of overall saving behaviour in Asia is that policy regime shifts in favour of an outward-orientated development strategy have underpinned the time patterns of saving behaviour. The trends and patterns of saving in Asia have been predominantly driven by the private sector: the governments directly accounted for only about 15% of total national saving in the region.

The findings of the econometric analysis are consistent with the LCM hypothesis that growth is the wellspring of saving, not the consequence of prior saving accumulation. There is no evidence to suggest that the prior phase of promoting saving through a specific policy initiative to promote domestic saving or filling the investment–saving gap is needed to initiate the process of growth and structural transformation. There is strong evidence that export orientation contributes to higher private saving both by its direct contribution and by compounding the impact of the rate of income growth on the saving rate. Foreign capital inflows are complementary to domestic saving.

As regards the nexus of demographic transition and domestic saving, only the change in the young–dependency ratio seems to have significant impact on national saving behaviour. The pattern of the aged–dependency ratio dampening national saving in developed countries is not revealed by the data in Asia, presumably because, given the prevalence of informal-sector employment and the limited coverage of retirement benefit schemes even in formal employment, the line of demarcation between working age and formal retirement remains blurred in these countries.

Finally, it is important to emphasize that the econometric evidence reported in the chapter simply reflects the *average* macroeconomic pattern of the saving behaviour of the 12 countries covered in the analysis. Obviously, there can be notable exceptions to the depicted average pattern. Also, the results are subject to the well-known limitations of saving data derived as a residual from the related macroeconomic variables (the 'tyranny of residual'). Presumably, the magnitude of the measurement error varies among countries and even over time in given countries. Because of these reasons, the inferences made in this chapter need to be treated only as *a point of departure* for informing the policy debate in individual countries. Multi-country studies, regardless of methodological issues, are not a substitute for systematic case studies of individual countries undertaken by taking into account socio-economic and structural peculiarities and paying due attention to data quality and consistency.

References

Abrigo, M., and L. Love (2016). 'Estimation of Panel Vector Autoregression in Stata'. *The Stata Journal*, 16(3): 778–804.

ADB (Asian Development Bank) (1997). *Emerging Asia: Changes and Challenges*. Manila: ADB.

Ang, J. B., and K. Sen (2011). 'Private Saving in India and Malaysia Compared: The Roles of Financial Liberalization and Expected Pension Benefits'. *Empirical Economics*, 41(2): 247–67.

Aron, J., and J. Muellbauer (2000). 'Personal and Corporate Saving in South Africa'. *World Bank Economic Review*, 14(3): 509–44.

Athukorala, P. (2021). 'Introduction to Asian Economic Development'. In P.-C. Athukorala (ed.), *Asian Economic Development*, Vol. 1, pp. xxii–xxix. Cheltenham: Edward Elgar.

Athukorala, P., and S. Rajapatirana (2003). 'Capital Inflows and the Real Exchange Rate: A Comparative Study of Asia and Latin America'. *World Economy*, 26(4): 613–37.

Athukorala, P., and K. Sen (2004). 'The Determinants of Private Saving in India'. *World Development*, 32(3): 491–503.

Athukorala, P., and W. Suanin (2022). ' Saving Transition in Asia: Unity in Diversity'. WIDER Working Paper 2022/172. Helsinki: United Nations University (UNU)-World Institute for Public Policy Research and Analysis (WIDER).

Athukorala, P., and P.-L. Tsai (2003). 'Determinants of Household Saving in Taiwan: Growth, Demography and Public Policy'. *Journal of Development Studies*, 39(5): 65–88.

Balassa, B. (1989). 'Outward Orientation.' In H. Chenery and T.N. Srinivasan (eds), *Handbook of Development Economics*, Vol. 2, pp. 1645–89. New York: North Holland.

Barro, R. J. (1974). 'Are Government Bonds Net Worth?' *Journal of Political Economy*, 82(6): 1095–117.

Blöndal, J. R., I. Hawkesworth, and D. Choi (2009). 'Budgeting in Indonesia'. *OECD Journal on Budgeting*, 9(2): 1–31.

Bloom, D. E., D. Canning, R. K. Mansfield, and M. Moore (2007). 'Demographic Change, Social Security Systems, and Savings'. *Journal of Monetary Economics*, 54(1): 92–114.

Bond, S., A. Leblebicioğlu, and F. Schiantarelli (2010). 'Capital Accumulation and Growth: A New Look at the Empirical Evidence'. *Journal of Applied Econometrics*, 25(7): 1073–99.

Collins, S. M. (1991). 'Saving Behaviour in Ten Developing Countries'. In B. D. Bernham and J. B. Shoven (eds), *National Saving and Economic Performance*, pp. 349–76. Chicago, IL: University of Chicago Press.

Corbo, V., and K. Schmidt-Hebbel (1991). 'Public Policies and Saving in Developing Countries'. *Journal of Development Economics*, 36(1): 89–115.

Curtis, C. C., S. Lugauer, and N. C. Mark (2015). 'Demographic Patterns and Household Saving in China'. *American Economic Journal: Macroeconomics*, 7(2): 58–94.

Deaton, A. (1989). 'Saving in Developing Countries: Theory and Review'. *World Bank Economic Review*, 3(supp.1): 61–96.

Deaton, A. (2005). 'Franco Modigliani and the Life-Cycle Theory of Consumption'. *Banca Nazionale del Lavoro Quarterly Review*, 58 (233/234): 91–107.

Edwards, S. (1996). 'Why are Latin America's Savings Rates So Low? An International Comparative Analysis'. *Journal of Development Economics*, 51(1): 5–44.

Ge, S., D. T. Yang, and J. Zhang (2018). 'Population Policies, Demographic Structural Changes, and the Chinese Household Saving Puzzle'. *European Economic Review*, 101(2): 181–209.

Gersovitz, M. (1988). 'Saving and Development'. In H. Chenery and T. N. Srinivasan (eds), *Handbook of Development Economics*, Vol. 1, pp. 381–424. New York: North Holland.

Ha, J., J.-W. Lee, and L. Sumulong (2010). ' Rebalancing Growth in the Republic of Korea'. ADBI Working Paper. Tokyo: Asian Development Bank Institute.

Hausman, J. (1978). 'Specification Tests in Econometrics'. *Econometrica*, 46(6): 1251–71.

Horioka, C. Y. (1991). 'The Determinants of Japan's Saving Rate: The Impact of the Age Structure of the Population and Other Factors'. *Economic Studies Quarterly*, 42(3): 237–53.

Horioka, C. Y., and A. Terada-Hagiwara (2012). 'The Determinants and Long-Term Projections of Saving Rates in Developing Asia'. *Japan and the World Economy*, 24(2): 128–37.

Jongwanich, J. (2010). 'The Determinants of Household and Private Savings in Thailand'. *Applied Economics*, 42(8): 965–76.

Kim, Y. H. (2001). 'The Asian Crisis, Private Sector Saving, and Policy Implications'. *Journal of Asian Economics*, 12(3): 331–351.

Kinugasa, T., and A. Mason (2007). 'Why Countries Become Wealthy: The Effects of Adult Longevity on Saving'. *World Development*, 35(1): 1–23.

Leff, N. H. (1969). 'Dependency Rates and Saving Rates'. *American Economic Review*, 59(5): 886–96.

Levine, R., and D. Renelt (1992). 'A Sensitivity Analysis of Cross-Country Growth Regressions'. *American Economic Review*, 82: 942–63.

Lewis, W. A. (1954). 'Economic Development with Unlimited Supplies of Labour'. *Manchester School of Economics and Social Studies*, 25(1): 1–94.

Loayza, N., K. Schmidt-Hebbel, and L. Servén (2000). 'Saving in Developing Countries: An Overview'. *World Bank Economic Review*, 14(3): 393–414.

Maizels, A. (1971). *Exports and Economic Growth in Developing Countries*. Cambridge: Cambridge University Press.

Meier, G. M. (1984). 'The Formative Period'. In G. M. Meier and D. Seers (eds), *Pioneers in Development*, pp. 3–16. New York: Oxford University Press.

Modigliani, F. (1966). 'The Life Cycle Hypothesis of Saving, the Demand for Wealth and the Supply of Capital'. *Social Research* 33(2): 160–217.

Modigliani, F. (1986). 'Life Cycle, Individual Thrift, and the Wealth of Nations'. *American Economic Review*, 76(2): 297–313.

Modigliani, F. (1993). 'Recent Declines in the Savings Rate: A Life Cycle Perspective'. In M. Baldassarri, L. Paganetto, and E. S. Phelps (eds), *World Sowing, Prosperity and Growth*, pp. 249–86. London: Macmillan.

Modigliani, F., and R. H. Brumberg (1954). 'Utility Analysis and the Consumption Function: An Interpretation of Cross-Section Data.' In K.K. Kurihara (ed.), *Post-Keynesian Economics*, pp. 388–436. New Brunswick, NJ: Rutgers University Press.

Modigliani, F., and S. L. Cao (2004), 'The Chinese Saving Puzzle and the Life-Cycle Hypothesis'. *Journal of Economic Literature*, 42(1): 145–70.

Modigliani F., and A. Sterling (1983). 'Determinants of Private Saving with Special Reference to the Role of Social Security: Cross Country Tests'. In F. Modigliani and

R. Hemming (eds), *The Determinants of National Saving and Wealth*, pp. 24–55. London: Macmillan.

Obstfeld, M. (1999). 'Foreign Resource Inflows, Saving, and Growth'. In K. Schmidt-Hebbel and L. Serven (eds), *The Economics of Saving and Growth*, pp. 107–41. Cambridge: Cambridge University Press.

Papanek, G. F. (1972). 'The Effect of Aid and Other Resource Transfers on Savings and Growth in Less Developed Countries'. *Economic Journal*, 82(327): 934–50.

Park, D., and C. Rhee (2005). 'Saving, Growth, and Demographic Change in Korea'. *Journal of the Japanese and International Economies*, 19(3): 394–413.

Pedroni, P. (2004). 'Panel Cointegration: Asymptotic and Finite Sample Properties of Pooled Time Series Tests with an Application to the PPP Hypothesis'. *Econometric Theory*, 20(3): 597–625.

Perkins, D. (2013). *East Asian Development: Foundations and Strategies*. Cambridge, MA: Harvard University Press.

Pesaran, H. (2007). 'A Simple Panel Unit Root Test in the Presence of Cross-Section Dependence'. *Journal of Applied Econometrics*, 22(2): 265–312.

Pesaran, H. (2015). *Time Series and Panel Data Econometrics*. Oxford: Oxford University Press.

Poterba, J. M. (1991). 'Dividends, Capital Gains and the Corporate Veil: Evidence from Britain, Canada and the United States'. In B. D. Douglas and J. B. Shoven (eds), *National Saving and Economic Performance*, pp. 49–71. Chicago, IL: University of Chicago Press.

Ranis, G. (1995). 'Another Look at the East Asian Miracle'. *World Bank Economic Review*, 9(3): 509–34.

Redeker, N. (2022). 'The Politics of Stashing Wealth: The Decline of Labor Power and the Global Rise in Corporate Saving'. *Journal of Politics*, 84(2): 975–991.

Reinhart, C. M., and E. Talvi (1998). 'Capital Flows and Saving in Latin America and Asia: A Reinterpretation'. *Journal of Development Economics*, 57(1): 45–66.

Rosenstein-Rodan, P. N. (1961). 'International Aid for Underdeveloped Countries'. *Review of Economics and Statistics*, 43(2): 107–38.

Sala-i-Martin, X. X. (1997). 'I Just Ran Two Million Regressions'. *American Economic Review*, 87(2): 178–83.

Solow, R. M. (1956). 'A Contribution to the Theory of Economic Growth'. *Quarterly Journal of Economics*, 70(1): 65–94.

Srinivasan, T. N. (1994). 'Data Base for Development Analysis: An Overview'. *Journal of Development Economics*, 44(1): 3–27.

Stiglitz, J. E. (1996). 'Some Lessons from the East Asian Miracle'. *World Bank Research Observer*, 11(2): 151–77.

Sun, C., and M.-y. Liang (1982). 'Savings in Taiwan, 1953–1980'. In K.-t. Li and T.-S. Yu (eds), *Experiences and Lessons of Economic Development in Taiwan*, pp. 295–312. Taipei: Academia Sinica.

Taiwan (Republic of China). *Taiwan Statistical Data Book*. Taipei: Council for Economic Planning and Development (various issues).

Weisskopf, T. E. (1972). 'The Impact of Foreign Capital Inflow on Domestic Savings in Underdeveloped Countries'. *Journal of International Economics*, 2(1): 25–38.

World Bank (1993). *The East Asian Miracle: Economic Growth and Public Policy*. New York: Oxford University Press.

PART III
COUNTRY STUDIES

9

Drivers of domestic saving in Kenya

Rodgers Musamali, Cecilia Mutia, and Rose Ngugi

1. Introduction

High saving rate spurs long-run economic growth (Athukorala and Sen 2004; Aghion et al. 2006) by triggering increased investment (Ang and Sen 2011). Savings are transformed into capital required to improve the prospective capacity of a country and productivity (Sahoo and Dash 2013; Kapingura 2018). Globally, the role of savings mobilization is buttressed by the United Nations' 2015 Addis Ababa Action Agenda on financing for development. Further, the African Union Agenda 2063 prioritizes strengthening of domestic resource mobilization by building continental capital markets and financial institutions.

Sub-Saharan Africa (SSA) is characterized by low domestic savings. In 2000–19, the average saving rate in SSA was lowest at 22%. In the same period, gross domestic product (GDP) per capita growth rate was lowest averaging 1.8%, partly explaining the low saving rate. In addition, the gross capital formation to GDP ratio for SSA was lowest averaging 22%. Overall, the regions that posted impressive saving rates experienced higher GDP per capita and investments.

Kenya prioritizes savings mobilization to adequately finance investment needs. This is anchored in the Kenya Vision 2030 and tracked periodically through the five-year Medium-Term Plans. The Kenya Vision 2030 envisaged growth in gross national savings from 15.6% of GDP in 2006–07 to about 26% by 2012–13 and 29% by 2030. Public savings were expected to rise from 1.6% of GDP in 2006–07 to 3.0% by 2012–13 and 3.8% by 2030. Private savings were targeted to rise from 14% of GDP in 2007–08 to 23% in 2012–13 and 25.5% in 2030.

At micro level, the FinAccess surveys reveal an increase in access to and usage of saving products in Kenya. As of 2019, 69.4% of households had at least one member using some form of saving product, compared with 52% in 2006. The most preferred informal saving channels as analysed from various FinAccess Household Surveys (2006-2009) (CBK et al. various) include chamas, secret hiding places, and groups of friends (Figure 9.1). However, the use of informal channels has declined over time. The uptake of mobile money as a financial technology (fintech) gained traction as an alternative channel for saving, increasing from 10.7% in 2016 to 41.2% in 2019. Fintech interfaces finance with technology (Chang et al. 2020) and

Rodgers Musamali, Cecilia Mutia, and Rose Ngugi, *Drivers of domestic saving in Kenya*. In: *The Domestic Savings Shortfall in Sub-Saharan Africa*. Edited by: Rose Ngugi and Kunal Sen, Oxford University Press. © UNU-WIDER (2025). DOI: 10.1093/oso/9780198932482.003.0009

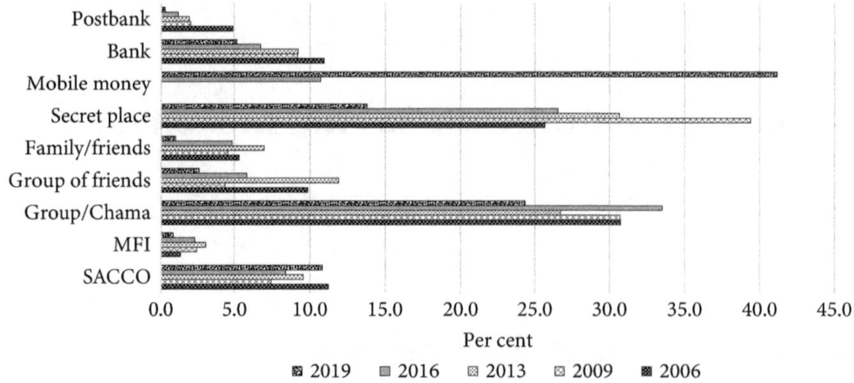

Figure 9.1 Household saving platforms

Note: MFI: microfinance institution. SACCO: savings and credit cooperative.

Source: authors' illustration based on FinAccess data for 2006–19 (CBK et al. various).

incorporates platforms that disrupt traditional financial services, such as mobile payments, money transfers, peer-to-peer lending, and robotic investment advice (Marr 2017).

A decomposition by income shows that those with KES30,000 (US$248.6) and below, the level of saving is lower at 43.4%, compared to those with above KES30,000, with saving at 56.6%. There are indications that the low reported saving rate in Kenya may be a result of unaccounted savings and the use of alternative forms, particularly saving in kind, which may not be monetized in the calculation of total savings (Figure 9.2). FinAccess surveys show that households tend to be targeted savers, saving to purchase livestock or land and to buy or build housing for rent, implying that they convert their financial savings into savings-in-kind.

A few households save for old age. The Kenya Integrated Household Budget Survey (KIHBS) 2015–16 reveals that the incidence of those who receive a pension income is low at 17% and concerns the civil service pension plan (92%). The incidence of private and personal pension plans is small at 6.4 and 0.9%, respectively. Further, the majority (86%) of households receive a monthly pension of less than KES20,000 (US$165.7). While traditionally it is expected that young people take care of the old, implying no motivation to save for old age, the weakening of social ties is changing this. The government is already making cash transfers to the old to enable them to meet their basic needs.

Studies on determinants of saving in Kenya show mixed results. Mwangi (2020) using the life cycle hypothesis (LCH), and permanent income hypothesis (PIH) find that the uptake of formal saving rises with the level of urbanization and formality of employment and declines with family size. Onwuasoeze and Kirori (2016), using Keynes absolute income hypothesis (AIH), found that high per capita income and financial deepening boost saving while high dependency ratio and inflation reduce saving. In addition, Ndirangu and Muturi (2015) using LCH,

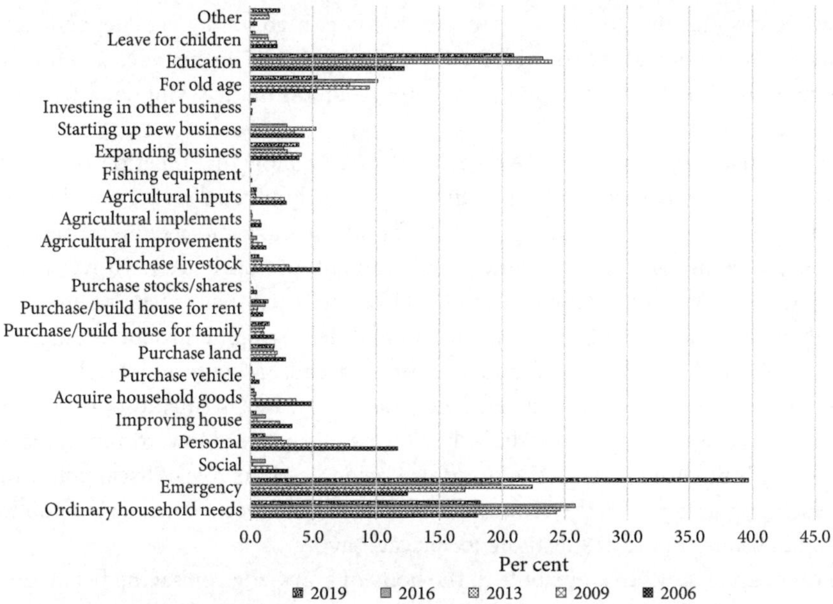

Figure 9.2 Reasons why households save

Source: authors' illustration based on FinAccess data for 2006–19 (CBK et al. various).

PIH, and AIH theories, ascertained positive effects of GDP and inflation on gross domestic savings, while the age–dependency ratio had negative effect. Further, Kibet et al. (2009) found that increased income and interest rates on deposits positively determined household saving, while increased access to credit, dependency ratio, and transport costs to a savings institution had a negative effect.

Other studies focus on financial-sector reforms and financial innovation. For example, Odhiambo's (2002) results support McKinnon's complementarity hypothesis with the coefficients for savings rate (S/Y) in the money demand function and the lagged real money balances (M/P) in the savings function found to be positive and significant. Further, Ngugi and Kabubo (1998) found that the intermediation of financial assets did not yield efficiency due to the widening interest rate spread and non-achievement of positive real interest rates. On the impact of M-Pesa on savings, Mbiti and Weil (2016) found that M-Pesa was overwhelmingly used to transfer funds rather than store value. Further, M-Pesa usage decreased the usage of informal saving platforms and increased the banked proportion of the population.

At regional level, Adewuyi et al. (2010) established that for Economic Community of West African States (ECOWAS) countries, life expectancy positively influenced saving while income per capita, interest rates, financial depth, inflation rates, and terms of trade had negative effects. Further, Elbadawi and Mwega (2000) found that in SSA, private saving rate lagged behind other regions mostly

Asian economies due to lower per capita income, high young age-dependency ratio, and high dependence on aid. Further, Ndung'u (1997) concludes that financial liberalization did not lead to drastic improvements in the saving rates for SSA countries.

From single-country studies, Ahmed et al. (2015) show that inflation rate, real interest rates, and government expenditures negatively affected saving in Pakistan. Similarly, Ogbokor and Samahiya (2014) found inflation and income positively influenced saving in Namibia, while population growth rate had a negative effect. For India and Malaysia, Ang and Sen (2011) established that private saving was significantly determined by income growth and demographic structure. Further, Athukorala and Sen (2004), found real interest rate, growth and level of per capita income, spread of banking facilities, and (mild) rate of inflation influenced domestic saving positively in India, while terms of trade and inward remittances negatively influenced saving. The study also recognized the role of fiscal policy in increasing total saving in the economy, with the private sector considering public saving to be an imperfect substitute for private saving.

This chapter seeks to contribute to the body of knowledge on saving behaviour in Kenya by focusing on the following: (i) the key drivers of domestic saving rates in Kenya, (ii) whether alternative approaches such as fintech might provide new solutions to increase domestic savings, and (iii) lessons that could be drawn from the experience in Kenya so far. The rest of this chapter is organized into four sections. Section 2 provides the policy context for savings mobilization in Kenya. Section 3 discusses patterns and trends in domestic saving. Section 4 provides an analysis of the determinants of domestic saving in Kenya, both discussing econometric methodology and providing results. Section 5 concludes the chapter.

2. The policy context

2.1 Policy evolution in Kenya

Since independence, the government has prioritized mobilizing adequate and appropriate domestic savings. For example, the interest rate policy has evolved from controlled regime to full liberalization with the savings rate experiencing mixed results in the early years of liberalization. That said, the desired saving rate is yet to be achieved.

2.1.1 Government emphasis on savings mobilization

The National Development Plan (1964–70) identified mobilization of domestic savings as critical to adequately finance investment needs. Sessional Paper No. 10 of 1965 recognized the importance of domestic saving in spurring growth and proposed exploiting both voluntary and involuntary saving. In the National Development Plan (1974–78), the government noted that attempts to mobilize savings from low-income people were still far from satisfactory and this contributed to the widening gap between saving and investment. In the National Development Plan (1979–83), the government encouraged saving of a portion of income for use in old age and setting aside something for a rainy day. In Sessional Paper No. 1 of 1986, the government advocated for increased savings mobilization as well as investment for renewed growth while in the eighth development plan cycle (1997–2001) domestic saving was identified as inadequate to spur industrialization. Moreover, the Economic Recovery Strategy (2003–07) prioritized enhancing public saving to ensure that resources were available for domestic capital formation. The Kenya Vision 2030 further sought to promote high levels of saving to finance investment needs.

The savings–investment gap has widened over time. Prior to interest liberalization (1980–91), the gap averaged 4.19%. In the early phase of interest rate liberalization (1992–2002) it averaged 3.36%. Thereafter, it widened during the implementation of both the Economic Recovery Strategy (ERS) (2003–07) and Vision 2030 (2008–19), at 4.43 and 9.44%, respectively. The widening gap during the Vision 2030 period may be attributed to the ambitious investment programmes being implemented to expand the capacity for sustainable inclusive growth.

2.1.2 Channels for savings mobilization

Several channels have been identified over time to mobilize savings. For example, Sessional Paper No. 10 of 1965 noted the need to boost voluntary saving through platforms such as (i) unit trusts and savings bonds tailored to future consumer needs, including education, housing, and medical bills; (ii) development of the money market; (iii) growing interest in stock market participation; and (iv) development of indigenous commercial banks.

The channels identified in the National Development Plan of 1964–70, included establishment of the National Social Security Fund, National Bank of Kenya Limited, Co-operative Bank of Kenya Limited, Post Office Savings Bank, and the Cereals and Sugar Finance Corporation. Further, it removed bottlenecks related to minimum deposits and inconvenient locations for banks (National Development Plan, 1974–78). The government likewise sought to enhance the public confidence to participate in the Nairobi Stock Exchange as an avenue for mobilizing long-term capital (ERS, 2003–07).

All savings institutions (commercial banks, credit societies, building and loan societies, co-operatives, and pension funds) were encouraged to rapidly extend their services into rural areas (National Development Plan, 1979–83). The Post Office Savings Bank was to leverage on its large network of offices across the country to provide opportunities for private saving (National Development Plan, 1984–88). To enhance intermediation, the Capital Markets Authority was expected to foster an orderly capital market, facilitated by an effective stock exchange system (National Development Plan, 1989–93).

The Kenya Vision 2030 promotes deepening the penetration of banking services, particularly in rural areas, and strengthening capital markets for equity and debt (through long-term bonds). Further, there is reorganization of the national social security and pension system, with a view to facilitating higher savings (Medium-Term Plan, 2008–12). Further still, the second Medium-Term Plan (2013–17) emphasized the exploitation of Kenya's established lead in digital finance.

The third Medium-Term Plan (2018–22) envisaged mobilization of savings through the creation of new government debt-based products. This included expansion of the maturity period of Treasury bonds, implementation of the Government Securities Market Makers initiatives, and development of new trading platforms, including Internet banking and an electronic trading platform.

2.1.3 Population growth and savings mobilization

Sessional Paper No. 10 of 1965 emphasized family planning as a key factor to reduce the population growth rate, which was hindering saving for development. Further, the sixth National Development Plan (1989–93) identified the growing and dependent population as a threat to savings mobilization. Moreover, the 2019 Kenya Population and Housing Census demonstrated that most of the population are youth (28.9% of those aged 18–34 years), who are in their most productive years and have the potential to mobilize savings for future use when they start dis-saving.

2.1.4 Fiscal policy and savings mobilization

Sessional Paper No. 1 of 1986 proposed restructuring fiscal policy to increase government saving through reduced expenditure, enhanced public debt management, and budget rationalization. That said, the threat to savings mobilization remained, particularly with the widening budget deficit. Further, the ERS (2003–07) identified removal of maximum allowable tax deductibility of contributions as key to encourage saving through pension schemes. Other tax incentives included making withdrawals at and after retirement tax free. Thanks to further reforms, the first KES600,000 (US$4,971) of pension withdrawal and up to KES25,000 (US$207.1) monthly pension received from such schemes are tax free (Kenya Revenue Authority 2022). Other incentives to save are insurance and mortgage relief and home ownership savings plans.

2.1.5 Evolution of interest rate policy

Sessional Paper No. 10 of 1965, suggested a controlled interest rate regime. As a result, in the 1960s and '70s, the government fixed the minimum savings rates for deposit-taking institutions and lending rates for commercial banks, non-bank financial institutions, and building societies. However, with the oil price shock of the mid-1970s, there was need for a flexible interest rate regime to allow for realization of positive real returns.

Positive interest rates were identified as an incentive for savings mobilization in the National Development Plan (1984–88). Sessional Paper No. 1 of 1986, emphasized a flexible interest rate regime where returns on government securities were market determined, while commercial banks' lending and deposit rates were pegged to returns on government securities. The National Development Plan of 1989–93 sought to encourage domestic saving through real interest rates and improved financial intermediation, and interest rates were fully liberalized in 1991.

The first attempt to reverse the interest rate policy was through amendment of the Central Bank Act in 2000. The second attempt was through an interest rate capping bill in 2015, which received assent in August 2016 and became effective in September 2016. This was revoked in November 2019, when the court ruled interest rate capping unlawful.

The expectation was that liberalization was to encourage effective competition and savings mobilization, which would increase the resources available for investment and reduce the cost of lending. Consequently, the interest rate spreads would narrow after liberalization. The pre-liberalization (1980–91) spread averaged 3.71%, while in 1992–2002 it averaged 12.65%. The spread contracted thereafter, averaging 9.40% (2003–07) and 7.68% (2008–19).

2.1.6 Terms of trade

Theoretically, when terms of trade are worsening, there is more capital outflow than inflow, and this has a negative impact on savings mobilization and vice versa. Some improvements were registered, with terms of trade averaging 100.42 in 1992–2002 compared with 82.01 in 1980–91. This declined to 89.76 in 2003–07 and then improved again to 95.89 in 2008–19. Generally, improved average terms of trade were registered at 95.89 with the implementation of Vision 2030 in 2008–19.

2.2 Patterns and trends in domestic savings

The average saving rate in 1970–79 was 17.76% with a highest rate registered at 24.32% in 1977. The saving rate in the 1980s recorded a high of 24% in 1985 and a low of 15.18% in 1982. The saving rate improved to an average of 18.88% in 1989–91, attributable to the implementation of structural adjustment programmes. Following the full liberalization of interest rates in 1991, the savings rate peaked at 21.62% in 1994. Thereafter, it spiralled downwards, with a low of 8.53% in 2002. The saving rate declined to an average of 13.78% in 1992–2007.

With the new government in 2002, the saving rate rose to a high of 16.66% in 2007. However, this was dampened by the post-election crisis of 2007/08 in Kenya as well as the global financial crisis. In general, saving rates in 1970–79, 1980–91, 1992–2007, and 2008–19 averaged 17.76, 18.88, 13.78, and 11.56%, respectively—below the Vision 2030 target of 29%.

Private saving rate in 1970–79 averaged 17.73%, increasing to 22.89% in 1980–91. During the period 1992–2002, however, the average private saving rate declined to 17.6%. The periods of 2003–07 and 2008–19 saw improved performance, with private saving rates averaging 29.7 and 44.54%, respectively. The increased contribution of private saving, especially in the past two decades, can be attributed to the enhanced policy environment, which focused on enabling the private sector to thrive.

Public saving has remained low. In the periods 1970–79, 1980–91, and 1992–2002, public saving rate posting averages 0.04%, −4.01%, and −3.75%, respectively. Further declines in average public saving were recorded in 2003–07 (−16.1%) and 2008–19 (−32.98%). The average public saving rates in 1970–2007 and 2008–19 were −16.1% and −32.98%, respectively, far below the Vision 2030 target of 3.8%.

2.3 Role of institutions in determining savings

The literature is awash with evidence on the relationship between the quality of institutions and long-term economic growth. The same, however, cannot be said about quality of institutions and formation of savings, an important transmission mechanism to ultimate growth. While there is no theoretical assertion linking institutional quality and savings, existing empirical studies provide mixed evidence.

North (1990) asserts that institutions consist of formal and informal constraints that ensure order, reduce uncertainty and the cost of intermediation between lenders and creditors, and ensure greater feasibility of engaging in economic activities. Institutional frameworks or good governance have become central to economic performances (World Bank, 1998), with well-established institutions increasing the likelihood of promoting economic activities (Acemoglu and Johnson 2005), including savings mobilization.

A comparative view of the quality of institutions shows that Kenya has recorded a poorer aggregate average score on control of corruption (−0.998), political stability and absence of violence/terrorism (−1.169) and rule of law (−0.806) against the rest of SSA (−0.657, −0.577, and −0.736, respectively). Kenya performs favourably on government effectiveness (−0.555), regulatory quality (−0.281), and voice and accountability (−0.365) compared to the rest of SSA (−0.815, −0,746, and −0.6, respectively). The low average scores are an indication of institutional challenges that could impede savings mobilization.

3. Determinants of domestic savings

3.1 Analytical framework

The life-cycle model (LCM) is premised on accumulation of savings for retirement. A consumption or saving behaviour by a representative agent is assumed to maximize the present value of lifetime utility, subject to budget constraint. A key assumption is that consumption during a particular period is dependent on expected lifetime income. It recognizes that income tends to fluctuate over the lifetime of an individual, meaning that saving behaviour is determined by the person's stage in the life cycle. Individuals show smooth consumption over their lifetimes; consequently, they are net savers during their working years and dis-savers during retirement (Modigliani, 1986).

The LCM predicts that an increase in per capita income growth rate (*GY*) increases the aggregate saving rate by increasing the lifetime resources of the younger ones compared to those who are older. Introducing an additional wealth variable (*W*) into the model may lead to unclear findings with respect to the relationship between saving and per capita income growth. Young people have low income in their early life but tend to possess more wealth in the future. As such, they may be forced to borrow now to finance a gap in consumption, which reduces aggregate saving rate among youth compared with the elderly.

Regarding the age structure, the LCM postulates that an increase in the population growth rate (*GPOP*) caused by an increase in age-specific fertility rates, increases the number of savers relative to the number of dis-savers. An economy with faster population growth is expected to show a higher aggregate saving rate. Taking demographic structure into account, Modigliani and Brumberg (1954) introduced the aspect of dependency and argued that a higher age–dependency (*ADR*) in the population tends to reduce the saving rate.

Other variables that influence saving rate include the real interest rate (*DIR*), inflation rate (*INF*), terms of trade (*ToT*), and measures of financial development (*FIN*). Real interest rate applicable to bank deposits has two effects that make relationship with the saving/consumption axis uncertain. First, a higher interest rate causes a substitution effect by increasing the current price of consumption relative to the future price and, hence, is an incentive to increase saving. Second, an income effect can be detected in the model if a household is a net lender. Therefore, an increase in the interest rate in this instance increases lifetime income and consumption and decreases saving. The prevailing interest rate regime becomes critical, including, for example, any attempt to reverse interest rate liberalization by introducing interest rate capping (*IRC*). Further, shocks to the financial sector, such as the global financial crisis (*CRIS*), may have an impact on saving behaviour by creating uncertainty regarding returns.

The effect of inflation on saving is also considered, with indications that if consumers attempt to maintain a target level of wealth or liquid assets relative to income, saving will rise with inflation. Additionally, inflation brings about uncertainty regarding future income streams and can lead to higher saving on precautionary grounds, especially in developing countries, whose income prospects are very uncertain (Athukorala and Sen 2004).

When external terms of trade are considered, the effect on the saving rate can be suggested on several fronts. The first view by Harberger (1950) and Laursen and Metzler (1950) argues that a reduction in the price of domestically produced goods relative to the price of foreign goods reduces real incomes and, in turn, savings. A second view by Obstfeld (1982), Svensson and Razin (1982), and Frankel and Razin (1992) is that a temporary deterioration in terms of trade may lead to a reduction in saving due to increased expenditure measured in terms of domestic goods, as consumers try to offset the decrease in purchasing power of domestic goods to keep real expenditure constant. In contrast, a deterioration in terms of trade that is perceived to be permanent will lead to increased saving in the current period for households to maintain their real standard of living in the future.

The effect of financial development on the promotion of private saving can be proxied by several indicators, including per capita bank density, credit to the private sector, interest rates on deposits, and turnover ratio. An increase in the number of bank branches (per capita bank density) has a two-pronged effect. Lewis (1955) observes that the saving rate is increased if financial institutions are brought nearer to individuals as opposed to when they are some distance away. The shorter the distance to the nearest bank branch, the higher the affinity to save more. Conversely, the degree of substitution between the propensity to save and the household asset allocation portfolio may make the relationship ambiguous (Athukorala and Sen 2004).

Evidence indicates that there is a positive relationship between credit to the private sector and private saving (Onwuasoeze and Kirori 2016). Credit to the private sector (*CPS*) is used to measure financial sector development. Other factors considered include financial innovations such as fintech, which provide alternative savings channels including mobile money (*MM*).

Finally, institutional quality is considered as a key determinant of savings mobilization. Part of the empirical literature around the twin concepts provides varied evidence depending on the institutional quality variable utilized. For instance, Boateng et al. (2019) establish that institutional quality induces savings at aggregate level. At disaggregated level, the absence of voice and accountability, political stability, and the rule of law hinders savings while the control of corruption spurs savings (seen also in us Swaleheen 2008; Abu et al. 2015; Abu and Waldemar Staniewski 2022). Freytag and Voll (2013) provide evidence that property rights and the rule of law influence national and private savings formation.

3.2 Empirical specification

The empirical specification considers private and national saving rates, indicated in equations (1) and (2).

$$SPRV = f[GY, W, INF, SPB, TOT, CPS, DIR, ADR] \tag{1}$$

$$SNAT = f[GY, W, INF, TOT, CPS, DIR, ADR] \tag{2}$$

Equations (1) and (2) form the baseline private and national saving rate models. *SPRV* and *SNAT* are private and gross national saving rates. *SPB* is public saving rate, *GY* is growth of per capita income, *W* is wealth, proxied by M2/GDP, *DIR* is real deposit interest rate, *INF* is inflation rate, *ToT* is terms of trade, and *CPS* is a measure of financial development proxied by credit to the private sector. *ADR* is age–dependency ratio, also proxied by population growth rate, *MM*, *IRC*, and *CRIS* are dummies representing fintech development, interest rate capping, and global financial crisis, respectively. Institutional quality variables include control of corruption (*COR*), government effectiveness (*EFF*), political stability and absence of violence/terrorism (*POL*), regulatory quality (*REG*), rule of law (*RUL*), and voice and accountability (*VAC*) as developed by Kaufmann and Kraay in 1999 (accessed in 2023). Institutional variables were further interacted following Boateng et al. (2019) and Freytag and Voll (2013) intuition. Table 9.A1 in the appendix summarizes the variables and their notations.

The analysis used the autoregressive distributive lag (ARDL) econometric approach proposed by Pesaran et al. (2001). ARDL is preferred where the order of integration of variables is flexible. The generalized ARDL (p, q) model with k explanatory variables are specified as follows:

$$Y_t = \gamma_0 + \beta_1 Y_{t-1} + \ldots + \beta_p Y_{t-p} + \alpha_0 X_t + \alpha_1 X_{t-1} + \ldots + \alpha_q X_{t-q} + \varepsilon_t \tag{3}$$

Y_t is private/national saving rate. X_t is a $(K \times 1)$ independent variable. γ is a constant term, and ε_t is an error term with standard *i.i.d* properties. The dependent variable is explained by lags of itself, as well as current and lagged values of the independent variables. The number of lags for dependent variable is included up to lag order p, and for independent variables up to order q.[1] Instead of using a first difference ordinary least squares (OLS) (by construction), ARDL allows for a mixture of long-run and short-run estimates through an unrestricted error correction model[2] of the form:

[1] The lags are determined by information criteria. The default in Stata is Bayesian information criterion but allows selection of the Akaike information criterion.

[2] For this ARDL to be reparametrized as an error correction model, there must be cointegration (existence of a long-term equilibrium between variables). The cointegration test draws on the ARDL bounds approach of Pesaran et al. (2001).

$$\Delta Y_t = \gamma_0 + \sum_{i=1}^{p} \delta_i \Delta Y_{t-i} + \sum_{i=0}^{q} \delta_i \Delta X_{t-i} + \lambda (Y_t - \theta X_t) + \varepsilon_t \tag{4}$$

$\lambda = \left(1 - \sum_{i=1}^{p} \delta_i\right)$ shows the speed of adjustment in long-run equilibrium after a shock in the short run. If $\lambda = 0$, there is no evidence of a long-run relationship. The parameter is expected to be significantly negative where deviation variables will return to their long-run equilibrium.

3.3 Data sources and descriptive statistics

3.3.1 Data sources

The study uses annual time-series data for the period 1980–2019. Data on national, public, and private saving rates 1980–2000 was sourced and computed from the time-series analytical data compendium of the Kenya Institute for Public Policy Research and Analysis (KIPPRA 2002). Data on national, public, and private saving rates 2001–2019, GDP, per capita income, broad money supply (M2), real interest rates, population, inflation, terms of trade, and credit to the private sector was obtained from the World Development Indicators. Data on institutional quality variables was sourced from the World Governance Indicators (World Bank, 2023) from 2006–2019. Other data on lending and deposit rates was sourced from the Central Bank of Kenya and International Financial Statistics.

The descriptive statistics are reported in the appendix (Table 9.A2). The optimal lags were obtained for each variable using the VAR lag selection criteria and preferred the Akaike information criterion for the exact lags, which ranged from 0 to 4. The augmented Dickey–Fuller (ADF) was used for unit root test and validated through the Phillips–Perron test. Since the variables are either I(0) or I(1), an ARDL model is preferred.

4. Estimation method

4.1 Private saving model estimation results

The private savings estimation results are presented in Table 9.1. From the bounds test, there is a long-run association between the private saving rate and its key determinants, including the per capita income growth rate, inflation rate, age–dependency ratio, public saving rate, and real deposit interest rate. Consistent with LCM predictions, a 1% increase in per capita income growth leads to a 0.01 percentage point increase in the private saving rate in the long run for all the

Table 9.1 Private savings: Long-run and short-run results

Variable	Baseline	Mobile money extension	Mobile money and interest rate capping extension	Mobile money and financial crisis extension
Long-run relationship				
GY	0.010***	0.010***	0.010***	0.009***
	(0.003)	(0.003)	(0.003)	(0.003)
W	−1.391	−1.448	−2.100*	−0.492
	(0.904)	(0.963)	(1.169)	(0.915)
INF	0.011***	0.011***	0.012***	0.011**
	(0.003)	(0.003)	(0.003)	(0.003)
SPB	−0.042***	−0.043***	−0.044***	−0.042***
	(0.003)	(0.004)	(0.004)	(0.004)
LNToT	−0.257	−0.271	−0.196	−0.431
	(0.273)	(0.288)	(0.316)	(0.278)
LNCPS	−0.293	−0.251	−0.305	−0.041
	(0.239)	(0.307)	(0.325)	(0.292)
LNADR	0.867**	0.869**	0.671	1.354***
	(0.404)	(0.415)	(0.476)	(0.431)
DIR	−0.023**	−0.022**	−0.020**	−0.020**
MM	(0.006)	(0.008)	(0.009)	(0.009)
IRC	—	−0.029	0.003	-0.013
CRIS		(0.129)	(0.136)	(0.138)
		—	-0.153	0.123
			(0.121)	(0.098)
Short-run relationship				
ΔINF	−0.008***	−0.008***	−0.009***	−0.010***
	(0.003)	(0.003)	(0.003)	(0.003)
ΔLNCPS	0.566*	0.555*	0.423	—
	(0.302)	(0.311)	(0.296)	
ΔDIR	0.010	0.010	—	—
	(0.008)	(0.008)		
C	1.163	1.091	1.811	−1.071
	(2.459)	(2.525)	(2.614)	(2.602)
ECM (−1)	−0.883***	−0.875***	−0.840***	−0.860***
	(0.059)	(0.070)	(0.071)	(0.071)
Diagnostic checks				
D–W stat	1.854	1.880	2.069	1.982
B–G LM	0.632	0.690	0.785	0.981
W	0.425	0.425	0.425	0.425
J–B	0.867	0.850	0.865	0.980
R^2	0.925	0.925	0.926	0.919
Adj. R^2	0.890	0.886	0.887	0.881
Number of obs	39	39	39	39

Note: estimation coefficients presented; standard errors are in parentheses. *, **, and *** indicate 10%, 5%, and 1% levels of significance, respectively. D–W and B–G denote the Durbin–Watson and Breusch–Godfrey tests for serial correlation, W denotes White's test for homoscedastic errors, J–B denotes the Jarque–Bera test for skewness and kurtosis. D–W statistic presented while Prob > Chi2 is presented for B–G, W, and J–B.

Source: authors' calculations.

four models. Further, a 1% increase in the age–dependency ratio causes a 0.867 (model 1) and 0.869 (model 2) percentage point increase in the private saving rate. Findings in model 4 show that a 1% change in age–dependency ratio is associated with a 1.354 percentage increase in private savings rate.

The inflation rate has a positive effect on the private saving rate, with a 1% increase in inflation rate showing that private saving increases by 0.011 (models 1, 2, and 4) and 0.012 (model 3) percentage points. A 1% increase in the public saving rate is associated with between 0.042 and 0.044 percentage points decline in the private saving rate. A similar negative association is established between wealth and private saving rate in model 3, with a unit change in wealth causing a decline in private saving rate by 2.1 percentage points. The findings for real deposit interest rates indicate a negative association with private saving rate. A 1% change in real deposit rate is associated with between 0.020 to 0.023 percentage points decline in private savings rate. This finding lends credence to the income effect argument about real interest rates.

In the short run, the inflation rate and private-sector credit are important determinants of private savings rate. A 1% change in inflation rate is associated with 0.010 percentage points decline in private savings rate. Contrarily, a 1% increase in the private-sector credit causes a 0.566 (model 1) and 0.555 (model 2) percentage increase in private savings rate. The errors of the previous periods will be corrected in the current period in all the models, with the speed of adjustment ranging between 84 and 88% and highly significant.

4.2 Private saving with inclusion of institutional variables

The results indicate a long-run relationship between private savings and public saving rate, terms of trade, and real deposit interest in some of the estimations (appendix, Table 9.A3). Per capita income growth, wealth, age–dependency ratio, private-sector credit, mobile money, control of corruption, regulatory quality, rule of law, voice and accountability, and political and legal institutions influence private saving in at least one estimation. Consistent with previous results, a 1% increase in public saving rate is associated with a decline in private saving rate of between 0.026 and 0.042 percentage points. Similarly, a 1% increase in the real deposit interest rate significantly causes a decline in private saving rate of between 0.015 and 0.038 percentage points (for models 3, 4, 5, 7, and 9).

Regarding terms of trade, a 1% decline in terms of trade significantly leads to a 1.5 (model 1), 2.8 (model 2), and 0.9 (model 9) percentage points increase in private saving rate. Per capita income growth weakly determines private saving rate in model 4, with a 1% change in per capita income leading to 0.006 percentage points increase in private saving rate. In model 5, a 1% increase in wealth leads to a 5.3 percentage points increase in private saving rate. Other results show that a 1% change in private-sector credit causes a 1.03 percentage points decline in private savings rate (model 5). Similarly, a 1% increase in mobile money causes a 0.48 percentage point decline in private savings rate (model 1). The negative sign shows that the level of private saving is lower with mobile money compared with the period without mobile money. This is perhaps an indicator that mobile money is largely utilized for transactional and credit services.

Introduction of institutional quality variables in the analysis yields mixed results. Control of corruption, rule of law, and voice and accountability impact private saving rate positively while regulatory quality and political and legal institutions have a negative effect on private saving rate. A 1% change in COR, RUL, and VAC increases private saving rate by 3.6, 1.5, and 0.5 percentage points, respectively. Further, a 1% change in REG, POLVAC, and RULREG causes a decline in private saving rate by 0.9, 0.5, and 1 percentage points, respectively.

The short-run results show that per capita income growth, wealth, terms of trade, private-sector credit, age–dependency ratio, real deposit interest rates, political stability, and regulatory quality impact private saving rate. A 1% change in per capita income growth significantly causes a 0.011 percentage points decline in private saving rate. Regarding wealth, a unit change in W leads to 5.2–10.7 percentage points decline in private saving rate. Further, a one unit change in private-sector credit significantly causes 3.7 percentage points decline in private saving rate. Similarly, a unit change in political stability is associated with 0.42 percentage points decline in private saving rate. This is an indication that political instability and/or politically motivated violence, including terrorism, deters saving mobilization.

On a positive note, a unit change in terms of trade causes a 1.1–1.5 percentage points increase in private saving rate. Age–dependency ratio impacts private saving rate with a 1% change in ADR leading to between 22.5 and 40.9 percentage points increase in private saving rate. Likewise, a one-unit change in real deposit interest rates causes 0.015–0.016 percentage points increase in private saving rate. In addition, a unit change in regulatory quality significantly leads to a 0.7 percentage point increase in private saving rate. The speed of adjustment significantly ranges from 47 to 127% across the models.

4.3 National saving model estimation results

The national saving estimations have semblance to private savings analysis. Initially, four models are presented in Table 9.2. The estimations show that there exists a long-run association between national savings rate and its key determinants, namely per capita income growth rate, inflation rate, terms of trade, age–dependency ratio, and real deposit interest rates. Growth in per capita income has a positive effect on the national saving rate, with a 1% increase in per capita income growth showing that national saving increases by 0.016 (models 1 and 2) and 0.017 (model 3) percentage points. Inflation rate has a positive effect on national saving rate, with a 1% increase in inflation rate causing national saving rate to increase by 0.018 (models 1 and 2), 0.019 (model 3), and 0.027 (model 4)

Table 9.2 National savings: Long-run and short-run results

Variable	Baseline model	Mobile money extension	Mobile money and interest rate capping extension	Mobile money and financial crisis extension
Long-run relationship				
GY	0.016*	0.016*	0.017**	0.015
	(0.008)	(0.008)	(0.007)	(0.011)
W	−0.066	−0.024	−2.134	−0.996
	(2.080)	(2.104)	(2.510)	(2.638)
INF	0.018**	0.018**	0.019**	0.027*
	(0.008)	(0.008)	(0.007)	(0.014)
LNToT	−1.085*	−1.016	−0.467	−1.361
	(0.531)	(0.606)	(0.600)	(0.883)
LNCPS	−0.105	−0.187	−0.256	−0.069
	(0.432)	(0.562)	(0.540)	(0.708)
LNADR	1.363*	1.393*	0.821	0.836
	(0.745)	(0.763)	(0.894)	(1.064)
DIR	−0.030**	−0.031*	−0.028*	−0.041*
MM	(0.014)	(0.016)	(0.015)	(0.023)
IRC	—	0.038	0.133	-0.108
CRIS		(0.166)	(0.173)	(0.253)
			−0.221	−0.432
			(0.216)	(0.426)
Short-run relationship				
ΔGY	−0.005	−0.005	−0.004	−0.004
	(0.003)	(0.003)	(0.003)	(0.003)
ΔW	−3.881***	−3.896***	−2.552	−4.317***
	(1.340)	(1.368)	(1.647)	(1.371)
ΔINF	−0.009***	−0.009***	−0.009***	−0.009***
	(0.003)	(0.003)	(0.003)	(0.003)
ΔLNToT	0.327	0.324	—	0.394
	(0.259)	(0.264)		(0.263)
ΔLNCPS	0.493	0.520	0.502	0.607*
ΔCRIS	(0.297)	(0.326)	(0.328)	(0.326)
				0.166
				(0.098)
C	0.829	0.741	1.355	2.242
	(2.481)	(2.560)	(2.825)	(2.825)
ECM (−1)	−0.509***	−0.516***	−0.554***	−0.406**
	(0.137)	(0.143)	(0.153)	(0.158)

Variable	Baseline model	Mobile money extension	Mobile money and interest rate capping extension	Mobile money and financial crisis extension
Diagnostic checks				
D–W stat	1.930	1.961	1.847	2.010
B–G LM	0.782	0.868	0.535	0.948
W	0.425	0.425	0.425	0.425
J–B	0.738	0.676	0.691	0.649
R^2	0.674	0.674	0.667	0.714
Adj. R^2	0.504	0.485	0.473	0.506
Number of obs	39	39	39	39

Note: estimation coefficients presented; standard errors are in parentheses. *, **, and *** indicate 10%, 5%, and 1% levels of significance, respectively. D–W and B–G denote the Durbin–Watson and Breusch–Godfrey tests for serial correlation, W denotes White's test for homoscedastic errors, J–B denotes the Jarque–Bera test for skewness and kurtosis. D–W statistic presented while Prob > Chi2 is presented for B–G, W, and J–B.
Source: authors' calculations.

percentage points. Further, a 1% increase in the age–dependency ratio increases the national saving rate by 1.4 (models 1 and 2) percentage points. The results fail to be important in models 3 and 4.

The terms of trade weakly determine the national saving rate with a 1% decline in terms of trade leading to a 1.1 percentage points increase in the national saving rate. However, this finding is only important in the baseline model. The findings for real deposit interest rates indicate a negative association with national saving rate. A 1% change in real deposit rate is associated with between 0.028 and 0.041 percentage points decline in national savings rate.

In the short run, wealth and inflation rate are determinants of national saving rate. A 1% increase in wealth causes a 3.9 (models 1 and 2) and 4.3 percentage points decline in national saving rate. Similarly, a 1% increase in inflation rate causes a 0.009 percentage point decline in national saving rate across all the models. The speed of adjustment ranges from 41 to 55.4% in all the models.

4.4 National saving with inclusion of institutional variables

Appendix Table 9.A4 presents the national saving model estimations with inclusion of institutional variables. As previously established, there is no cointegration between national saving rate and its key determinants when institutional variables are included in the analysis. The estimation results at level are presented in the appendix (Table 9.A3). As a result, the key determinants of national saving rate include lag of national saving rate, per capita income growth, wealth, inflation, private-sector credit, real deposit interest rates, regulatory quality, and interaction of rule of law and regulatory quality (legal institutions). Therefore, a percentage change in the first lag of national saving rate is significantly associated with an increase in national saving rate by between 0.49 and 0.68 percentage points in the short run. Similarly, a unit change in the first lag of per capita income growth is significantly associated with between 0.008 and 0.016 percentage points increase in national saving rate (models 4, 7, 8, and 9). Private-sector credit stimulates national saving rate with a unit change in credit to the private sector causing between 1.04 and 1.16 percentage points change in national saving rate. In addition, a first lag of credit to the private sector affects national saving rate, albeit negatively. Still on a positive note, a unit change in regulatory quality in model 4 significantly causes an increase in national saving rate by 0.8 percentage points.

The effect of wealth on national saving rate is negative, with a unit change in wealth causing a decline in national saving rate by between 7.6 and 10.9 percentage points. The first lag of wealth, however, has a positive effect on the national saving rate. The study also establishes that inflation rate weakly affects national saving rate in model 3, with a unit change in inflation rate causing a 0.015 percentage point decline in national saving rate at 10% significance level. Regarding real deposit interest rates, a 1% change in real deposit interest rate leads to between 0.022 and 0.023 percentage points decline in national saving rate in the short run. Further, the interaction of rule of law and regulatory quality shows that a unit change in RULREG causes 1.07 percentage point decline in national saving rate.

5. Conclusions and policy implications

5.1 Conclusions

The key findings suggest the following:

- Savings mobilization has retained its policy importance in the development plans since independence to finance the investment needs and economic growth.
- Private saving is primarily influenced by the income growth rate and demographic structure in Kenya, supporting the LCM hypothesis.
- Control of corruption, enforcement of rule of law, upholding of voice and accountability, and strengthening of regulatory quality are key ingredients in spurring savings mobilization in the long run.
- Savings are held in various forms, including bank deposits and informal products.
- While Kenya has made great strides in fintech, particularly through mobile money, the potential to mobilize savings is yet to be exploited.

5.2 Policy implications

Therefore, the following interventions are important to grow savings in Kenya:

- Create decent employment, especially among the youth and securing the real value of savings, including by using fiscal incentives.
- Enhance financial development with a focus on developing savings products that attract small savers.
- Create an enabling environment for the private sector to thrive, which will encourage private savings both at individual and business level.
- Strengthen institutional structures essential for savings formation in the long run—emphasis should be laid on controlling corruption, enforcing rule of law, upholding voice and accountability, and boosting regulatory quality to achieve desired results.
- Promote a policy environment with a clear strategy to create awareness on benefits of saving and closely monitor to yield the desired results.
- Support fiscal consolidation initiatives to boost public saving and in turn overall national saving.
- Account for savings beyond the bank deposits by incorporating savings held in other forms (assets).
- Exploit the potential of mobile money as part of fintech in encouraging savings mobilization.

Appendix

Table 9.A1 Description of variables

Variable	Notation	Derivation
Private saving rate	SPR	Private savings as % GDP
Gross national saving rate	SNAT	Gross national savings as % GDP
Public saving rate	SPB	Public savings as % GDP
Income per capita growth rate	GY	Annual income per capita growth rate (%)
Wealth	W	M2/GDP (%)
Real deposit interest rates	DIR	Nominal deposit interest rate minus inflation (%)
Age–dependency ratio	ADR	Percentage of working-age population
Inflation rate	INF	Inflation for consumer prices (annual %)

Continued

Table 9.A1 *Continued*

Variable	Notation	Derivation
Terms of trade	TOT	Terms of trade index, measured as (price of exports/price of imports) *100
Financial development	CPS	Domestic credit to private sector (% GDP), used as proxy for financial development
Fintech development	MM	Dummy variable coded as 1 (period 2011–19, when mobile money was prevalent) and 0 (period 1980–2010, when mobile money was absent)
Financial crisis	CRIS	Dummy variable coded as 1 (for years 2007 and 2008, during global financial crisis) and 0 (other years)
Interest rate cap	IRC	Dummy variable coded as 1 (for years 2017, 2018, and 2019, when interest rate capping was in place) and 0 (other years)
Control of corruption	COR	Control of corruption captures perceptions of the extent to which public power is exercised for private gain, including both petty and grand forms of corruption, as well as 'capture' of the state by elites and private interests
Government effectiveness	EFF	Government effectiveness captures perceptions of the quality of public services, the quality of the civil service and the degree of its independence from political pressures, the quality of policy formulation and implementation, and the credibility of the government's commitment to such policies
Political stability and absence of violence/terrorism	POL	Political Stability and Absence of Violence/Terrorism measures perceptions of the likelihood of political instability and/or politically motivated violence, including terrorism.
Regulatory quality	REG	Regulatory quality captures perceptions of the ability of the government to formulate and implement sound policies and regulations that permit and promote private sector development
Rule of law	RUL	Rule of law captures perceptions of the extent to which agents have confidence in and abide by the rules of society and, in particular, the quality of contract enforcement, property rights, the police, and the courts, as well as the likelihood of crime and violence

Variable	Notation	Derivation
Voice and accountability	VAC	Voice and accountability captures perceptions of the extent to which a country's citizens are able to participate in selecting their government, as well as freedom of expression, freedom of association, and a free media
Savings and economic institutions	COREFF	Interaction of control of corruption and government effectiveness variables
Savings and political institutions	POLVAC	Interaction of political stability and absence of violence/terrorism and voice and accountability variables
Savings and legal institutions	RULREG	Interaction of rule of law and regulatory quality variables

Source: authors' compilation.

Table 9.A2 Descriptive statistics

Variable	Obs.	Mean	Std dev.	Min.	Max.
SNAT	40	14.64	4.10	7.97	24.00
SPB	40	−14.14	14.87	−44.00	2.52
SPRV	40	28.78	12.77	9.66	53.19
GY	40	11.11	7.20	−1.23	43.63
W	40	36	5	27	43
INF	40	11.80	8.53	1.55	45.98
ToT	40	92.21	10.43	70.15	114.02
CPS	40	25.02	5.81	18.42	40.20
DIR	40	9.72	4.05	2.43	18.40
ADR	40	93.55	13.32	71.28	112.74
COR	24	−1.00	0.10	−1.17	−0.81
EFF	24	−0.56	0.11	−0.76	−0.36
POL	24	−1.17	0.17	−1.43	−0.66
REG	24	−0.28	0.07	−0.39	−0.14
RUL	24	−0.81	0.22	−1.05	−0.41
VAC	24	−0.36	0.25	−0.87	−0.11
COREFF	24	0.55	0.13	0.34	0.76
POLVAC	24	0.40	0.23	0.15	0.87
RULREG	24	0.22	0.07	0.11	0.36

Source: authors' calculations.

Table 9.A3 Private saving with inclusion of institutional variables: Long-run and short-run estimation results

Variable	Baseline model with mobile money extension	Control of corruption extension	Political stability extension	Regulatory quality extension	Rule of law extension	Voice and account-ability extension	Corruption and government effective-ness extension	Political stability and voice and account-ability extension	Rule of law and regulatory quality extension
Long-run relationship									
GY	0.005 (0.004)	−0.000 (0.006)	0.002 (0.005)	0.006* (0.003)	−0.002 (0.006)	−0.001 (0.005)	0.004 (0.004)	−0.002 (0.005)	0.001 (0.004)
W	−0.205 (1.374)	1.570 (2.553)	−0.128 (2.028)	1.817 (1.215)	5.274** (2.077)	−0.888 (1.835)	0.771 (1.511)	−0.673 (1.789)	2.039 (1.398)
SPB	−0.042*** (0.003)	−0.026** (0.008)	−0.041*** (0.004)	−0.033*** (0.003)	−0.040*** (0.004)	−0.035*** (0.004)	−0.035*** (0.004)	−0.034*** (0.004)	−0.038*** (0.003)
INF	−0.009 (0.006)	0.044 (0.026)	−0.012 (0.007)	−0.014 (0.008)	0.001 (0.004)	−0.017 (0.011)	−0.003 (0.005)	−0.011 (0.011)	−0.010 (0.008)
LNToT	−1.535** (0.566)	−2.778* (1.252)	−0.492 (0.504)	−0.038 (0.325)	0.397 (0.420)	−0.378 (0.504)	−0.199 (0.382)	−0.550 (0.488)	−0.946* (0.406)
LNCPS	−0.148 (0.460)	4.020 (2.244)	−0.680 (0.608)	−0.210 (0.222)	−1.028** (0.417)	−0.065 (0.263)	−0.006 (0.263)	−0.071 (0.264)	−0.411 (0.233)
LNADR	−1.406* (0.658)	4.725 (2.514)	−0.632 (0.678)	−0.735 (0.624)	2.054 (1.148)	−0.041 (0.837)	0.103 (0.927)	−0.055 (0.797)	0.245 (0.606)
DIR	−0.000 (0.017)	0.103 (0.061)	−0.038** (0.011)	−0.023*** (0.006)	−0.026** (0.008)	−0.001 (0.011)	−0.024** (0.008)	−0.005 (0.010)	−0.015* (0.007)
MM	−0.481** (0.175)	—	—	—	—	—	—	—	—

COR	—	3.621* (1.615)	—	—	—	—	—	—	—
POL	—	—	0.388 (0.325)	—	—	—	—	—	—
REG	—	—	—	−0.895** (0.378)	—	—	—	—	—
RUL	—	—	—	—	1.622** (0.574)	—	—	—	—
VAC	—	—	—	—	—	0.462* (0.224)	—	—	—
COREFF	—	—	—	—	—	—	−0.360 (0.283)	—	—
POLVAC	—	—	—	—	—	—	—	−0.486* (0.220)	—
RULREG	—	—	—	—	—	—	—	—	−0.975** (0.372)
Short-run relationship									
ΔGY	−0.011** (0.003)	−0.007 (0.003)	−0.004 (0.004)	—	—	—	—	—	−0.011** (0.004)
ΔW	−7.081* (3.389)	−10.683* (4.022)	−6.365 (4.012)	—	−1.243 (1.151)	—	—	—	−5.197* (2.329)
ΔSPB	0.010 (0.010)	−0.008 (0.005)	—	—	−0.006 (0.006)	—	—	—	0.014 (0.009)

Continued

Table 9.A3 *Continued*

Variable	Baseline model with mobile money extension	Control of corruption extension	Political stability extension	Regulatory quality extension	Rule of law extension	Voice and accountability extension	Corruption and government effectiveness extension	Political stability and voice and accountability extension	Rule of law and regulatory quality extension
ΔLNToT	0.958 (0.537)	1.056** (0.274)	0.818 (0.454)	—	—	0.582 (0.451)	—	0.529 (0.465)	1.509* (0.656)
ΔLNCPS	1.456 (0.913)	−3.711** (1.248)	1.634 (1.275)	—	—	—	—	—	—
ΔLNADR		40.917** (9.326)	15.114 (13.132)	28.570*** (6.702)	39.308*** (6.212)	25.188*** (6.959)	22.504*** (5.958)	23.365** (7.519)	30.221** (9.289)
ΔDIR	0.024 (0.012)	−0.018 (0.012)	—	0.015* (0.007)	0.008 (0.006)	0.011 (0.007)	0.016* (0.008)	0.008 (0.008)	0.019 (0.009)
ΔINF	—	—	—	0.006 (0.004)	—	0.008 (0.005)	—	—	0.012 (0.006)
ΔMM	0.420 (0.216)	—	—	—	—	—	—	—	—
ΔCOR	—	0.179 (0.171)	—	—	—	—	—	—	—
ΔPOL	—	—	−0.419* (0.179)	—	—	—	—	—	—

ΔREG	—	—	—	0.678** (0.227)	—	—	—	—	—
ΔRUL	—	—	—	—	−0.215 (0.184)	—	—	—	—
ΔPOLVAC	—	—	—	—	—	—	—	0.129 (0.125)	—
C	20.841* (6.213)	−7.438 (4.113)	10.573* (4.410)	5.962 (3.219)	−3.306 (3.165)	4.914 (3.927)	3.228 (4.196)	5.961 (4.002)	9.065* (3.984)
ECM (−1)	−1.266*** (0.240)	−0.471** (0.150)	−0.971*** (0.089)	−0.917*** (0.063)	−0.700*** (0.153)	−0.843*** (0.080)	−0.924*** (0.077)	−0.905*** (0.094)	−1.274*** (0.220)
Diagnostic checks									
D–W stat	2.419	2.465	2.168	2.799+	2.968+	2.338	1.606	2.631	2.608+
B–G LM	0.05	0.07	0.056	0.009+	0.003+	0.063	0.266	0.051	0.004+
W	0.402	0.402	0.402	0.402	0.402	0.402	0.402	0.402	0.402
J–B	0.069	0.582	0.533	0.95	0.122	0.614	0.269	0.469	0.388
R^2	0.99	0.998	0.991	0.988	0.993	0.985	0.977	0.986	0.99
Adj. R^2	0.956	0.988	0.961	0.968	0.979	0.959	0.95	0.956	0.958
Number of obs	23	23	23	23	23	23	23	23	23

Note: estimation coefficients presented; standard errors are in parentheses. *, **, and *** indicate 10%, 5%, and 1% levels of significance, respectively. D–W and B–G denote the Durbin–Watson and Breusch–Godfrey tests for serial correlation, W denotes White's test for homoscedastic errors, J–B denotes the Jarque–Bera test for skewness and kurtosis. D– W statistic presented while Prob > Chi2 is presented for B–G, W, and J–B. + denotes model suffers from serial correlation.

Source: authors' calculations.

Table 9.A4 National saving with inclusion of institutional variables: Estimation results at level

Variable	Control of corruption extension	Government effectiveness extension	Political stability extension	Regulatory quality extension	Rule of law extension	Voice and accountability extension	Corruption and government effectiveness extension	Political stability and voice and accountability extension	Rule of law and regulatory quality extension
LNSNAT (−1)	0.570** (0.186)	0.612*** (0.165)	0.678** (0.237)	0.451** (0.189)	0.511 (0.300)	0.625*** (0.167)	0.583*** (0.169)	0.466 (0.370)	0.485* (0.172)
GY	0.000 (0.008)	0.001 (0.008)	0.003 (0.007)	−0.006 (0.008)	0.001 (0.008)	0.000 (0.008)	0.001 (0.008)	0.004 (0.010)	−0.005 (0.007)
GY (−1)	0.007 (0.004)	0.007 (0.004)	0.006 (0.004)	0.013** (0.005)	0.008 (0.005)	0.007 (0.004)	0.008* (0.004)	0.016* (0.008)	0.010** (0.004)
W	−8.155** (3.237)	−7.907** (3.063)	−8.776** (3.243)	−10.973** (3.250)	−8.183** (3.445)	−7.573** (2.967)	−8.320** (3.149)	−8.342 (4.770)	−7.982** (2.801)
W (−1)	9.471** (3.633)	9.190** (3.505)	9.722** (3.352)	11.819** (3.524)	8.850** (3.476)	9.289** (3.639)	9.541** (3.536)	12.232* (4.776)	10.437** (3.181)
INF	−0.013 (0.008)	−0.012 (0.007)	−0.015* (0.007)	−0.010 (0.007)	−0.012 (0.007)	−0.012 (0.007)	−0.014 (0.008)	−0.016 (0.011)	−0.003 (0.009)
INF (−1)	—	—	—	—	—	—	—	−0.001 (0.009)	0.008 (0.006)
LNToT	0.289 (0.499)	0.252 (0.499)	0.580 (0.501)	0.116 (0.524)	0.117 (0.625)	0.227 (0.516)	0.266 (0.492)	0.042 (0.668)	−0.165 (0.491)
LNToT (−1)	—	—	—	−0.614 (0.583)	—	—	—	0.106 (0.742)	—
LNCPS	1.043* (0.564)	1.094 (0.602)	1.117* (0.576)	1.158* (0.520)	1.161 (0.733)	0.958 (0.541)	1.151* (0.600)	1.116 (0.771)	0.791 (0.559)

LNCPS (−1)	−1.837** (0.789)	−1.760** (0.737)	−2.239** (0.854)	−1.644* (0.712)	−1.628** (0.720)	−1.663** (0.717)	−1.869** (0.763)	−1.605 (1.193)	−1.529* (0.722)
LNADR	−0.265 (0.834)	−0.242 (0.811)	−14.202 (14.562)	0.095 (0.684)	−0.267 (0.904)	−0.097 (0.728)	−0.372 (0.845)	12.336 (24.220)	0.827 (0.829)
LNADR (−1)	—	—	14.249 (14.589)	—	—	—	—	−13.136 (24.549)	
DIR	−0.016 (0.015)	−0.009 (0.014)	−0.008 (0.013)	−0.009 (0.012)	−0.011 (0.013)	−0.015 (0.015)	−0.011 (0.013)	−0.028 (0.021)	−0.011 (0.012)
DIR (−1)	−0.023* (0.012)	−0.022* (0.012)	−0.029* (0.015)	−0.020 (0.011)	−0.021 (0.012)	−0.023* (0.012)	−0.022* (0.012)	−0.029 (0.020)	−0.018 (0.011)
COR	−0.222 (0.427)	—	—	—	—	—	—	—	—
EFF	—	−0.235 (0.454)	—	—	—	—	—	—	—
POL	—	—	−0.394 (0.244)	—	—	—	—	—	—
REG	—	—	—	0.514 (0.526)	—	—	—	—	—
REG (−1)	—	—	—	0.793* (0.389)	—	—	—	—	—
RUL	—	—	—	—	−0.242 (0.581)	—	—	—	—
VAC	—	—	—	—	—	−0.075 (0.202)	—	—	—
COREFF	—	—	—	—	—	—	0.247 (0.351)	—	—

Continued

Table 9.A4 *Continued*

Variable	Control of corruption extension	Government effectiveness extension	Political stability extension	Regulatory quality extension	Rule of law extension	Voice and accountability extension	Corruption and government effectiveness extension	Political stability and voice and accountability extension	Rule of law and regulatory quality extension
POLVAC	—	—	—	—	—	—	—	0.433 (0.335)	—
POLVAC (−1)	—	—	—	—	—	—	—	0.379 (0.251)	—
RULREG	—	—	—	—	—	—	—	—	−0.589 (0.560)
RULREG (−1)	—	—	—	—	—	—	—	—	−1.069* (0.464)
C	3.148 (4.590)	2.711 (4.216)	0.977 (3.726)	5.080 (4.525)	3.196 (5.006)	2.270 (4.064)	3.512 (4.490)	4.526 (6.354)	0.338 (3.820)
Diagnostic checks									
D–W stat	2.648+	2.541+	2.737+	3.053+	2.568+	2.600+	2.640+	2.787+	3.100+
B–G LM	0.019+	0.028+	0.028+	0.000+	0.041+	0.020+	0.014+	0.000+	0.000+
W	0.402	0.402	0.402	0.402	0.402	0.402	0.402	0.402	0.402
J–B	0.569	0.305	0.943	0.456	0.394	0.396	0.516	0.506	0.300
R^2	0.922	0.922	0.941	0.950	0.921	0.921	0.924	0.948	0.954
Adj. R^2	0.810	0.810	0.838	0.842	0.808	0.807	0.815	0.769	0.857
Number of obs	23	23	23	23	23	23	23	23	23

Note: estimation coefficients presented; standard errors are in parentheses. *, **, and *** indicate 10%, 5%, and 1% levels of significance, respectively. D–W and B–G denote the Durbin–Watson and Breusch–Godfrey tests for serial correlation, W denotes White's test for homoscedastic errors, J–B denotes the Jarque–Bera test for skewness and kurtosis. D–W statistic presented while Prob > Chi2 is presented for B–G, W, and J–B. + denotes model suffers from serial correlation.

Source: authors' calculations.

References

Abu, N., and M. Waldemar Staniewski (2022). 'An Empirical Investigation of the Effect of Corruption on Domestic Savings in Nigeria'. *Economic Research-Ekonomska istraživanja*, 35(1): 4092–112.

Abu, N., M. Z., Abd Karim, and M. I. A. Aziz (2015). 'Low Savings Rates in the Economic Community of West African States (ECOWAS): The Role of Corruption'. *Journal of Economic Cooperation and Development*, 36(2): 3.

Acemoglu, D., and S. Johnson (2005). 'Unbundling Institutions'. *Journal of Political Economy*, 113(5): 949–95.

Adewuyi, A., A. Bankole, and D. Arawomo (2010). 'What Determines Savings in the Economic Community of West African States?' *West African Journal of Monetary and Economic Integration*, 10(2): 71–99.

Aghion, P., D. Comin, and P. Howitt (2006). 'When Does Domestic Saving Matter for Economic Growth?' National Bureau of Economic Research (NBER) Working Paper 12275. Cambridge, MA: NBER. https://doi.org/10.3386/w12275.

Ahmed, S., M. Tariq, and A. Aleemi (2015). 'The Determinants of Saving: Empirical Evidence from Pakistan'. *International Journal of Management Sciences and Business Research*, 4(1): 63–71.

Ang, J. B., and K. Sen (2011). 'Private Saving in India and Malaysia Compared: The Roles of Financial Liberalization and Expected Pension Benefits'. *Empirical Economics*, 41(2): 247–67. https://doi.org/10.1007/s00181-010-0386-3.

Athukorala, P.-C., and K. Sen (2004). 'The Determinants of Private Saving in India'. *World Development*, 32(3): 491–503. https://doi.org/10.1016/j.worlddev.2003.07.008.

Boateng, E., F. W. Agbola, and A. Mahmood (2019). 'Does the Quality of Institutions Enhance Savings? The Case of Sub-Saharan Africa'. *Applied Economics*, 51(58), 6235–63.

Central Bank of Kenya (CBK), Kenya National Bureau of Statistics (KNBS), and Financial Sector Deepening (FSD) (Various). *FinAccess Household Surveys*. Nairobi: CBK/KNBS/FSD.

Chang, V., P. Baudier, H. Zhang, Q. Xu, J. Zhang, and M. Arami (2020). 'How Blockchain Can Impact Financial Services: The Overview, Challenges and Recommendations from Expert Interviewees'. *Technological Forecasting and Social Change*, 158: 120166. https://doi.org/10.1016/j.techfore.2020.120166.

Elbadawi, I. A., and F. M. Mwega (2000). 'Can Africa's Saving Collapse Be Reversed?' *World Bank Economic Review*, 14(3): 415–43. https://doi.org/10.1093/wber/14.3.415.

Frankel, J., and A. Razin (1992). *Fiscal Policies and the World Economy*. Cambridge, MA: MIT Press.

Freytag, A., and S. Voll (2013). 'Institutions and Savings in Developing and Emerging Economies'. *Public Choice*, 157: 475–509.

Harberger, A. (1950). 'Currency Depreciation, Income, and the Balance of Trade'. *Journal of Political Economy*, 58: 47–60. https://doi.org/10.1086/256897.

Kapingura, F. M. (2018). 'Relationship between Foreign Capital Flows, Domestic Investment and Savings in the SADC Region'. *Development Southern Africa*, 35(4): 554–68.

Kaufmann, D., and A. Kraay (2023). 'Worldwide Governance Indicators'. 2023 Update Available at: https://www.govindicators.org (accessed 23 October 2023).

Kenya Revenue Authority (2022). 'Tax Incentives in Retirement Benefit Schemes (RBS)'. Available at: https://www.kra.go.ke/news-center/blog/985-tax-incentives-in-retirement-benefit-schemes-rbs (accessed 8 November 2022).

Kibet, L., B. Mutai, D. Ouma, and S. Ouma (2009). 'Determinants of Household Saving: Case Study of Smallholder Farmers, Entrepreneurs and Teachers in Rural Areas of Kenya'. *Journal of Development and Agricultural Economics*, 1(7): 137–43.

KIPPRA (Kenya Institute for Public Policy Research and Analysis) (2002). 'Policy Timeline and Time Series Data for Kenya: An Analytical Data Compendium'. Special Report 3. Nairobi: KIPPRA.

Laursen, S., and L.A. Metzler (1950). 'Flexible Exchange Rates and the Theory of Employment'. *Review of Economics and Statistics*, 32(4): 281–99. https://doi.org/10.2307/1925577.

Lewis, W. A. (1955). *Theory of Economic Growth*. London: Allen and Unwin.

Marr, B. (2017). 'The Complete Beginner's Guide to FinTech Everyone Can Understand'. Forbes, 10 February. Available at: https://www.forbes.com/sites/bernardmarr/2017/02/10/a-complete-beginners-guide-to-fintech-in-2017 (accessed 28 November 2020).

Mbiti, I., and D. N. Weil (2016). 'Mobile Banking: The Impact of M-Pesa in Kenya'. In S. Edwards, S. Johnson, and D. N. Weil (eds), *African Successes, Volume III: Modernization and Development*. Chicago, IL: University of Chicago Press.

Modigliani, F. (1986). 'Life Cycle, Individual Thrift, and the Wealth of Nations'. *American Economic Review*, 76: 297–313.

Modigliani, F., and R. H. Brumberg (1954). 'Utility Analysis and the Consumption Function: An Interpretation of Cross-Section Data'. In K. K. Kurihara (ed.), *Post-Keynesian Economics*. New Brunswick, NJ: Rutgers University Press.

Mwangi, I. W. (2020). 'Household Saving Behaviour in Kenya: A Discrete Choice'. *Journal of Economics and Sustainable Development*, 11(4): 87–100.

Ndirangu, E., and W. Muturi (2015). 'Determinants of Gross Domestic Savings in Kenya (1970–2013)'. *International Journal of Economics, Commerce and Management*, 3(7): 157–178. Available at: http://ijecm.co.uk/wp-content/uploads/2015/07/3710.pdf (accessed 8 November 2022).

Ndung'u, S. N. (1997). 'The Impact of Financial Sector Liberalization on Savings, Investment, Growth and Financial Development in Anglophone Africa'. *African Development Review*, 9(1): 20–51. https://doi.org/10.1111/j.1467-8268.1997.tb00128.x.

Ngugi, R. W., and J.W. Kabubo (1998). 'Financial Sector Reforms and Interest Rate Liberalization: The Kenya Experience'. AERC Research Paper 72. Nairobi: AERC.

North, D. C. (1990). *Institutions, Institutional Change and Economic Performance*. Cambridge, MA: Cambridge University Press.

Obstfeld, M. (1982). 'Aggregate Spending and the Terms of Trade: Is There a Laursen-Metzler Effect?' *Quarterly Journal of Economics*, 97(2): 251–70. https://doi.org/10.2307/1880757.

Odhiambo, N. (2002). 'Financial Sector Reforms, Savings, and Economic Development in Kenya'. *African Review of Money Finance and Banking*, 2002: 5–22.

Ogbokor, C., and O. Samahiya (2014). 'A Time Series Analysis of the Determinants of Savings in Namibia'. *Journal of Economics and Sustainable Development*, 5(8): 52–63. Available at: https://core.ac.uk/download/pdf/234646352.pdf (accessed 8 November 2022).

Onwuasoeze, M., and G. Kirori (2016). 'Analyzing the Determinants of Private Savings in Kenya over the Period 1993–2013'. *European Journal of Business, Economics, and Accountancy*, 4(2): 67–80.

Pesaran, M. H., Y. Shin, and R. J. Smith (2001). 'Bounds Testing Approaches to the Analysis of Level Relationships'. *Journal of Applied Econometrics*, 16(3): 289–326. https://doi.org/10.1002/jae.616.

Sahoo, P., and R. K. Dash (2013). 'Financial Sector Development and Domestic Savings in South Asia'. *Economic Modelling*, 33: 388–397.

Svensson, L., and A. Razin (1982). 'The Terms of Trade and the Current Account: The Harberger-Laursen-Metzler Effect'. *Journal of Political Economy*, 91(1): 97–125. https://doi.org/10.1086/261130.

us Swaleheen, M. (2008). 'Corruption and Saving in a Panel of Countries'. *Journal of Macroeconomics*, 30(3): 1285–301.

World Bank (1998). 'Assessing Aid: What Works, What Doesn't and Why?' World Bank Policy Research Report. New York: Oxford University Press.

World Bank (2023). 'World Development Indicators'. Available at: https://databank.worldbank.org/reports.aspx?source=world-development-indicators (accessed 18 December 2024)

10
Determinants of domestic savings in Tanzania

*Maureen Were and Cornel Joseph**

1. Introduction

Resource mobilization remains a key challenge to sustainable development in Africa. Domestic savings can play a crucial role in filling the gap and promoting investment and economic growth. Hence, understanding the fundamental drivers of domestic savings is of critical importance to policy formulation and development. Tanzania is one of the few African countries that have witnessed a relatively steady growth of the economy, with the real gross domestic product (GDP) growth rate averaging over 6% over the past decade. Although the national saving rate is still relatively low by global standards, the country has registered a fairly stable growth in domestic savings in recent years, compared with other countries in the region. That notwithstanding, Tanzania is historically known to have been largely dependent on foreign aid. The ratio of domestic tax revenue to GDP is still relatively low, despite the rapid economic growth. That notwithstanding, there are indications of notable improvement following the various tax reform initiatives. These characteristics not only make Tanzania an interesting case study but also raise the question as to what the determinants of domestic savings in Tanzania are, and hence the need for, and focus of, this chapter.

The chapter examines trends and determinants of gross domestic saving in Tanzania using annual time-series data for the period 1990–2020.[1] The autoregressive distributed lag (ARDL) approach is employed to analyse the short-run and long-run relationships among variables. The main source of data is World Development Indicators (WDI), complemented with national data sources.

The rest of the chapter is structured as follows: section 2 presents the policy context, while section 3 examines the role of institutions. Section 4 describes the

*We are grateful to Kunal Sen and Abrams Tagem for their invaluable comments on previous versions of this chapter. Any errors and omissions are ours.

[1] The sample is restricted to this period due to data challenges regarding domestic savings in the preceding period. Additionally, it is during this period that substantive structural reforms were undertaken.

Maureen Were and Cornel Joseph, *Determinants of domestic savings in Tanzania*. In: *The Domestic Savings Shortfall in Sub-Saharan Africa*. Edited by: Rose Ngugi and Kunal Sen, Oxford University Press. © UNU-WIDER (2025).
DOI: 10.1093/oso/9780198932482.003.0010

patterns and trends of domestic savings in Tanzania. Section 5 analyses the theoretical and empirical determinants of domestic savings in Tanzania, while section 6 provides the conclusion and policy implications.

2. The policy context

2.1 Macroeconomic policy

The economic paradigms in Tanzania can be broadly categorized into three phases. The first phase is the pre-Arusha Declaration era, under which Tanzania inherited a market economy from the British colonialists immediately upon gaining independence in 1961. Capitalism was practised for almost six years until 1967. During the period, the country was poor and predominantly characterized by subsistence agricultural economy. The growth rate averaged about 5% per year in the period 1961–66. The economy relied heavily on the agricultural sector, which sustained other minor sectors to produce survival output (Ngowi 2009). This period was followed by the Arusha Declaration in 1967, which marked a paradigm shift. The paradigm shift was characterized by *ujamaa* socialism and an ideology of self-reliance as the grand development paradigm for nearly 20 years, until 1986. Per capita incomes grew by 0.7% per year, and the government had a dominant role in the economy and a monopoly on the marketing of goods and services (Levin 2001).

During the period 1970–85, the economy was characterized by extensive administrative controls, as well as severe internal and external imbalances resulting largely from inappropriate pricing policies, deep-rooted structural problems, and expansionary fiscal policies (Nord et al. 1993). This phase was characterized by an accelerating inflation rate, a decline in growth performance and savings, decreased per capita income and consumption, and general deterioration in social and physical infrastructure. GDP growth was 3% on average per year. It declined to its lowest level of below 1% during the period 1977–84. Inflation was high, averaging over 30% per year. There was a severe shortage of foreign exchange reserves and, as a result, an accumulation of external payment arrears (Mered et al. 1993; Nord et al. 1993; Nord et al. 2009).

The third phase is the liberalization era, which was adopted from the mid-1980s, starting with the infamous structural adjustment programmes (SAPs) of the Bretton Woods institutions—the International Monetary Fund (IMF), and the World Bank. By then, the country was facing multiple challenges: a bloated public sector, low economic growth, and mounting debt service amid low tax revenues and export earnings (Were and Mollel 2020). In reference to the period 1986–90 after the launch of the economic recovery programme in 1986, Agrawal et al. (1993) observe that although the SAPs were accompanied by a substantial increase in foreign aid, the increased aid dependency did not lead to a deterioration in domestic savings. They argue that most of the aid was for investment rather than consumption, though there was little return on investment.

Substantive economic liberalization reforms were undertaken in earnest from the early 1990s, transforming the economy from state control to open market economy. The period from 1996 experienced macroeconomic stabilization whereby, after several years of government dis-saving, government savings turned positive (Naschold and Fozzard 2002). The regime was characterized by restructuring of the financial sector, which included the licensing of numerous foreign banks and providing credit for private investment (Mwase and Ndulu 2008; Nord et al. 2009).

Private domestic and foreign investment fuelled economic growth, which in turn boosted tax revenues. Moreover, a large increase in foreign reserves was experienced. Tanzania also received notable debt relief under the Heavily Indebted Poor Countries (HIPCs) initiative and the Multilateral Debt Relief Initiative (MDRI) in 2001 and 2006, respectively, which substantially relieved the country's debt burden. The total committed debt relief from both initiatives as at the end of August 2018 was over US$6 billion (Were and Mollel 2020). However, debt relief was pegged to commitment to the reform process, which entailed implementing a raft of macroeconomic and structural reforms, including developing a poverty reduction strategy named the National Strategy for Growth and Reduction of Poverty 2006–2010 (NSGRP). Generally, the reforms resulted in a higher GDP growth rate, a lower inflation rate, an increase in international reserves, and (from a financial sector perspective) the creation of an efficient and competitive banking system, coupled with increased credit to the productive sectors of the economy.

The macroeconomic environment has generally remained stable, with steady economic growth. GDP growth averaged 6.8% over the period 2002–16 (Figure 10.1). This placed Tanzania among the fastest-growing African economies. However, in 2020, economic activity slowed down due to the COVID-19 pandemic, leading to a slowdown in economic growth to 4.8% in 2020, from 7% in 2019 (BOT 2021).[2] The slowdown was mainly due to the effect of the pandemic on tourism and external demand. However, since Tanzania did not put in place COVID-19 lockdown measures, it was among the few economies that avoided a negative growth rate.

The fiscal deficit has remained relatively low, which could arguably be attributed to the fairly steady inflow of donor funding. However, the latter has been dwindling, and the country is increasingly facing binding financing constraints, particularly in view of increased public investment demand. The deficit increased slightly

[2] Based on data reported by Tanzania's National Bureau of Statistics. However, the GDP growth for 2020 based on WDI was relatively lower, at 2.1%.

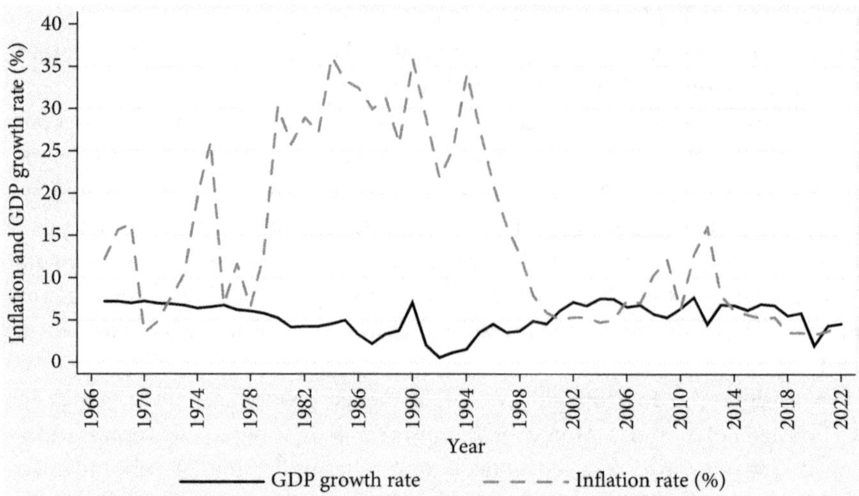

Figure 10.1 Inflation and real GDP growth rates in Tanzania, 1966–2022
Source: authors' illustration based on data from Economic Surveys, various issues.

from 2.0% of GDP in 2019 to 2.3% in 2020. Tax revenue as a percentage of GDP averaged about 11% over the period 2000–17.

Inflation remained stable over the 2001–20 period. In most cases, inflation rates remained below 10%, with the exception of 2008/09 (11.2%), 2011(12.7%), and 2012 (16%). By the end of 2018, the inflation rate had fallen to less than 5%, and it remained in single digits and below the medium-term target of 5.0% in 2020 (Figure 10.1). It fell to 3.3% in 2020 from 3.5% in 2019, following a steady decline in food prices. Foreign exchange rates remained stable, partly due to the interventions of the Bank of Tanzania (BOT) to ensure stability.

2.2 Financial sector reforms and policies

2.2.1 Overview of the financial sector in Tanzania

The financial sector is categorized under five subsectors, namely banking, capital markets, insurance, microfinance, and social security. The banking subsector dominates the financial system and plays a significant role in the economy. It accounts for about 70% of the domestic financial system (BOT 2020). In 2019, banking-sector total assets reached 33 trillion Tanzanian shillings (TZS), a growth of 9% from TZS30 trillion in 2018. The profitability, capital adequacy, liquidity, and asset quality of the banking sector remained generally stable. In 2019/20, the branch network expanded to 960, from 878 in 2018/19.

The banking sector is governed by the Banking and Financial Institutions Act, National Payment System Act of 2015, Financial Leasing Act of 2008, Foreign Exchange Act of 1992, and BOT Act of 2006. These Acts provide powers to BOT to supervise and regulate banking business, payment systems, and foreign exchange business. Financial service providers in the sector comprise commercial banks, community banks, deposit-taking microfinance banks, credit reference bureaus, bureaus de change, financial leasing companies, mortgage finance companies, and development finance institutions.

Bank mergers, closures, and restructuring have taken place in recent times and consequently, the number of banking institutions decreased to 46 in 2020, from 51 reported in 2019. For instance, at the end of 2018, five community banks were closed due to having lower than the amount of capital required by law.[3] The banking institutions comprised 35 commercial banks, 4 microfinance banks, 5 community banks, and 2 development banks in 2020 (see Were and Joseph 2022: Table 1).

Given the potential role of microfinance in poverty reduction and promoting economic growth, BOT has played an instrumental role in the development of microfinance policy and regulations, which are aimed at fostering a viable microfinance industry with wide outreach. The first national microfinance policy (NMP) was adopted in 2000. A review of the policy was undertaken in 2017, leading to the formulation of the NMP 2017 and its implementation strategy for a 10-year period, 2019/20–2029/30. The NMP 2017 is aimed at promoting financial inclusion by creating an enabling environment for an efficient and effective microfinance subsector that serves the needs of low-income individuals, households, and enterprises, thereby contributing to employment creation, poverty reduction, and economic growth.

In addition, the Microfinance Act of 2018 mandates BOT to license, supervise, and regulate microfinance businesses. Under the Act, microfinance service providers are categorized into four tiers: Tier 1 comprises deposit-taking microfinance service institutions, Tier 2 comprises non-deposit-taking microfinance service providers such as individual money lenders, Tier 3 consists of savings and credit co-operatives (SACCOs), and Tier 4 of community microfinance groups. However, in 2020, BOT continued to supervise and license microfinance service providers, while supervision of Tiers 3 and 4 was delegated to the Tanzania Cooperative Development Commission (TCDC) and the President's Office Regional Administration and Local Government (PO—RALG), respectively. As of 2020, SACCOs accounted for the highest proportion of microfinance service providers (see Were and Joseph (2022: Figure 2).

[3] Two financial institutions, namely Twiga Bancorp and Tanzania Women's Bank plc, were merged to form TPB Bank plc, and one commercial bank, Bank M Tanzania plc, was acquired by Azania Bank Limited.

2.2.2 Financial-sector reforms

Following the adoption of the *ujamaa* or African socialist model of development in 1967, all private banks were nationalized, and the BOT was quickly subsumed as an instrument of the state-centred economic policy (BOT 2011). During the 1970s and '80s, Tanzania's financial system was highly repressed and uncompetitive. The period was characterized by price controls (interest and exchange rates), monetary-financed government spending, closely managed credit rationing through selective and direct credit controls, and high operating costs. Commercial banking was highly concentrated in the public sector, state ownership, and restricted entry, leading to rampant inefficiency and a large number of non-performing assets (Epaphra 2014a). Credit was rationed and allocated to specific sectors at preferential interest rates. Moreover, the pursuit of multiple policy objectives and the lack of independence of the central bank curtailed the latter's ability to discharge traditional central banking functions.

By the late 1980s, the financial sector was in crisis owing to multiple challenges, including non-performing loans, the inadequate and inefficient payment system, ineffective instruments of monetary policy, undercapitalization, an inappropriate regulatory system, and the absence of a legal framework for harmonizing the operations of financial institutions (Balele et al. 2018). To complement the economic reforms towards a market-based economy, the government set up a commission of enquiry (the Nyirabu Commission) to address the problems in the financial sector. It was on the basis of the recommendations of this commission that BOT embarked on a series of financial-sector reforms, including the liberalization of the sector in the 1990s (BOT 2011). Various legislations were enacted, leading to the licensing of new banks and financial institutions and market-determined financial resource allocation.

Prior to the adoption of economic reforms in 1986, interest rates had been increased only twice, in 1979 and 1981. Following the commencement of comprehensive financial reforms in 1991, the interest rates increased. The money markets were introduced in 1993/94, during which time the interest rates were completely liberalized. By the early 1990s, various reforms had been undertaken to open up the economy, including the lifting of price controls, the adoption of a floating exchange rate, trade liberalization, and privatization of some state-owned firms.

The financial reforms were implemented in two major phases: first-generation financial-sector reforms (FGFSRs) took place between 1991 and 2003, and second-generation financial-sector reforms (SGFSRs) in 2003. The FGFSRs targeted legal reforms with the aim of creating a competitive environment, modernizing national payment systems, and strengthening BOT's regulatory and supervisory capacity. They were also aimed at the restructuring and privatization of state-owned banks and financial institutions and the establishment of a regulatory and supervisory framework. The SGFSRs focused on the development of financial markets, strengthening the banking sector, providing long-term development finance, creating a credit registry, making land reforms, strengthening micro- and rural finance, and developing a payment system infrastructure to facilitate retail payments.

Reforms in the financial sector were undertaken in tandem with promotion of financial innovations. Innovations in the banking sector include agent banking, which allows the provision of banking services by third parties to customers on behalf of a licensed banking institution. Introduced in 2013, agent banking plays an important role in fostering outreach to the unbanked by addressing the distance barrier to banking services access, combined with cost reduction. Additionally, innovations in digital finance revolutionized the delivery of, and access to, financial services, improved efficiency, created alternative payment instruments, and lowered transaction costs. Digital financial services (DFS), including credit, savings, insurance, transfers, and payments, provided through alternative delivery channels such as debit cards, e-vouchers, biometric readers, and point-of-sale devices, made distribution more efficient. The adoption of DFS, particularly the introduction of mobile money services, has enabled the majority of Tanzanians to access formal financial services.

Following the emergence of the COVID-19 pandemic, the BOT undertook various liquidity-easing policy measures in 2019/20 to cushion the economy from adverse effects. For instance, the statutory minimum reserve (SMR) on private-sector deposit liabilities was lowered from 8 to 7%, while the reserve averaging band was widened from 10 to 20%. Additional measures undertaken in the second half of 2019/20 included an additional cut of the SMR requirement ratio and the discount rate to 6 and 5%, respectively. There was also a reduction of haircuts on government securities pledged by banks for borrowing from the central bank windows. While total credit by the banking system increased modestly by 2.5% in 2019/20 (compared with 17.4% in 2018/19) owing to the decline in government borrowing from the banking system, the increase in credit to the private sector was fairly strong at an average of 8.1%, compared with 6.8% in the preceding year.

Consistent with the accommodative monetary policy measures, there was a slight decline in deposit and lending rates, albeit at varying magnitudes across maturities. On average, the deposit rate declined from 7.58% in 2018/19 to 6.98% in 2019/20, while the overall lending rate averaged 16.82% compared with 17.14% over the same period. Following these developments, the interest rate spread between the one-year lending rate and the deposit rate narrowed to 7.62, from 9.28 percentage points in 2018/19.[4] That notwithstanding, the relatively high interest rate spreads still remain a challenge.

[4] For trends of deposit rate, extended broad money (M3), and domestic credit to the private sector, see Were and Joseph (2022: Figure 3).

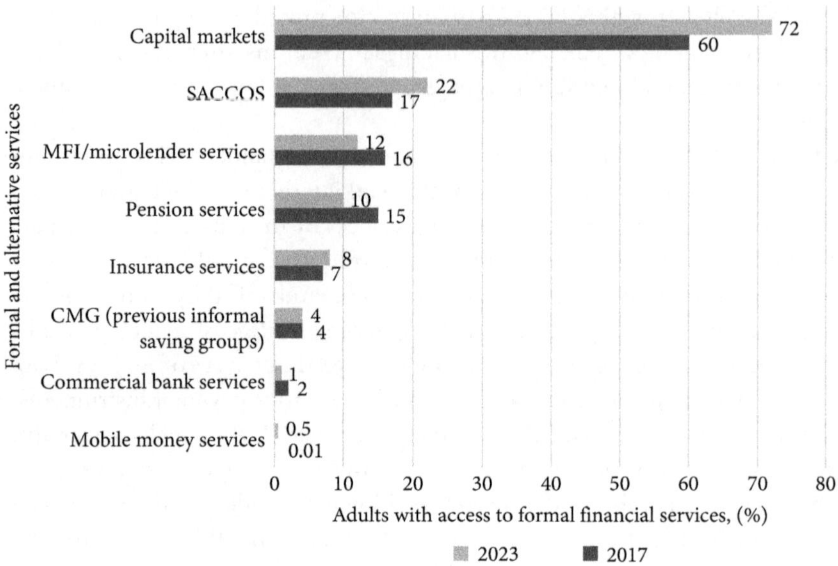

Figure 10.2 Uptake of formal financial services in Tanzania, 2017 and 2023

Source: authors' illustration based on FinScope Tanzania (2023).

2.2.3 The status of financial inclusion in Tanzania

Based on Tanzania's FinScope surveys, access to formal financial services has increased notably from 58% in 2013 to 76% in 2023. The expanded formal financial inclusion is mainly due to increased uptake of formal non-bank financial services, especially mobile money services, which increased from 50% in 2013 to 60 and 72% in 2017 and 2023, respectively (Figure 10.2). Consequently, the proportion of the adult population that rely on informal financial services declined from 16 to 5.7% between 2013 and 2023. These achievements are a result of the rapid adoption and usage of DFS. A partnership between microfinance institutions (MFIs) and mobile money service providers also led an increase in the uptake of financial services via MFIs.

2.3 Traditional savings instruments in Tanzania

Like many other developing African countries, in Tanzania, people save using formal and informal mechanisms (Mori 2019). Notwithstanding the availability of formal saving institutions and semi-formal channels, particularly the notable expansion of mobile financial services, informal means of saving still play a prominent role. However, the majority of people use mobile phones as a formal means of saving. Data from the Tanzania's FinScope Survey 2023 shows that 68% of

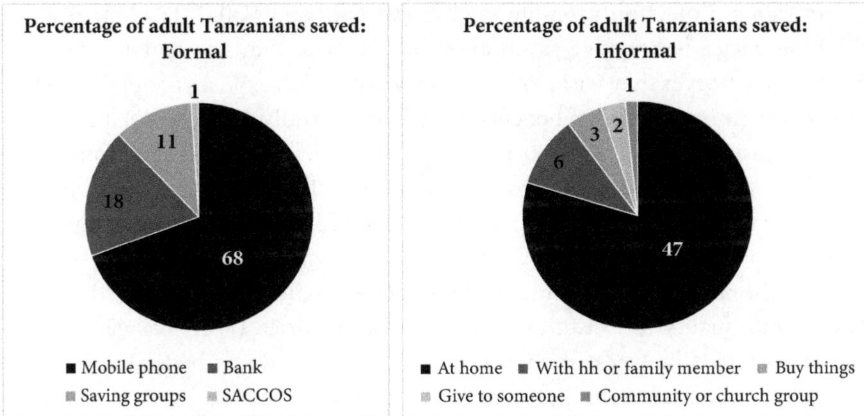

Figure 10.3 Means of saving in Tanzania
Source: author's illustration based on Finscope Tanzania (2023).

adult Tanzanians reported to have saved via mobile phone (Figure 10.3). Only 18% saved through banks, while 11% used savings group as a means for saving. Mobile money accounts are the most convenient due to the high penetration of telecommunication and financial services via mobile phones. Other means of savings, especially in rural areas, include village community banks, savings and credit cooperative societies, and savings groups such as village savings and loan associations (VSLAs), rotating savings and credit associations (ROSCAs), and self-help groups (SHGs).

With regard to informal saving mechanisms, the FinScope Survey 2023 shows that 47% saved in secret hiding places or coin containers at home. Others used family members, other people, or bought goods (Figure 10.3). However, informal savings are susceptible to various risks, such as theft, given the unregulated nature of these mechanisms, particularly for those who save 'under the mattress' (Kasebele and Lopez 2016).

3. Role of institutions

It has been argued that strong institutions generally facilitate efficient resource allocation towards productive activities (Olaniyi and Oladeji 2022). They do so by providing a conducive political and economic environment for savings, sustained growth, and development. On the other hand, weak institutions generate loopholes and gaps in the financial system that facilitate rent-seeking, corrupt practices, and opportunistic behaviour (Olaniyi and Oladeji 2022). Evidence has shown that high levels of corruption and political instability are an impediment to savings, while the quality of market regulations, the rule of law, and well-defined property rights protection promote savings (Freytag and Voll 2013; Abu et al. 2015). From a legal perspective, savers are entitled to what they save and transfer of ownership to whoever they wish. Poor property protection exposes people to high risk of not obtaining maximum benefits from their rightfully acquired wealth, thus acting as a disincentive to long-term savings. Moreover, the uncertainty associated with an unstable political environment adversely affects savings. Additionally, the regulatory environment generated by the rule of law can cause rigid regulations and impediments to bank entry and related activities, thereby leading to an increase in the cost of financial intermediation (Demirgüc-Kunt et al. 2004).

The overall quality of institutions in sub-Saharan Africa (SSA) has generally been considered to be weak, though some countries are doing better than others. Arguably, differences in institutions reflect the disparities in saving rates across countries. Using various institutional indicators available in the Worldwide Governance Indicator database, we broadly examine the quality of Tanzanian institutions in comparison to other select SSA countries (Kenya, Ghana, and Cameroon).[5] Figure 10.4 shows average indicator estimates for government effectiveness, political stability and absence of violence, regulatory quality, rule of law, voice and accountability, and control of corruption for the period 2011–22. Generally, Ghana performs relatively well in all institutional indicators compared to Tanzania, Kenya, and Cameroon. Cameroon performs poorly in virtually all the indicators. With regard to control of corruption and political stability, Tanzania's performance is relatively better compared to Kenya and Cameroon. However, Kenya's performance is relatively better than that of Tanzania and Cameroon in terms of government effectiveness and regulatory quality, though Tanzania has made notable improvement in the former (Figure 10.4).

Moreover, in the indices for the rule of law, voice, and accountability, Tanzania is doing better than Kenya and Cameroon. Likewise, regarding voice and accountability, Tanzania did better than Kenya in the early 2010s. However, Figure 10.4 shows that beyond 2016, the rule of law was good in Kenya compared to Tanzania.

A correlation analysis of Tanzania's domestic savings with the various indicators of institutional quality is undertaken using data for 1996–2022. The analysis shows a strong positive correlation between control of corruption and domestic savings in Tanzania (0.66). Additionally, political stability is positively correlated (albeit weakly) with domestic savings (0.13). However, the correlation of domestic savings with other institutional quality indicators, particularly rule of law and regulatory quality, is strongly negative (−0.74 and −0.56, respectively). While this analysis does not infer causality or control for other factors, the results suggest that control of corruption and political stability play an important role in promoting domestic savings in Tanzania.

[5] The three countries are of interest since they are part of the selected case studies.

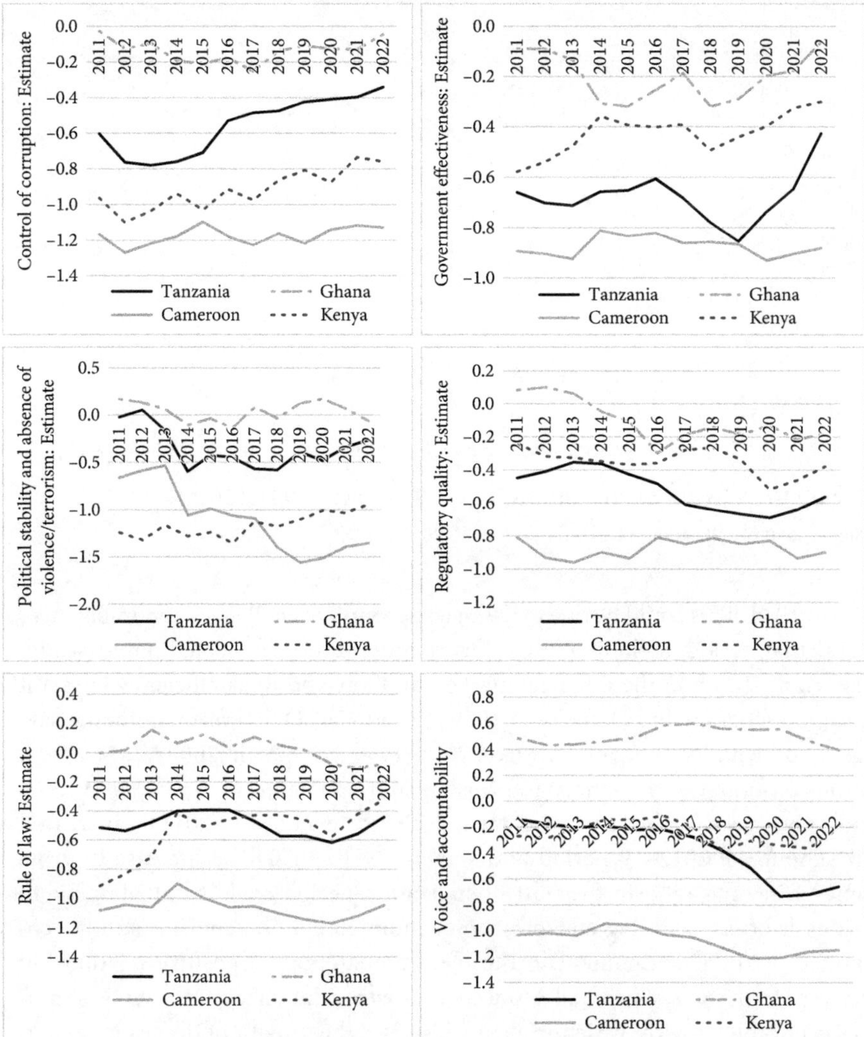

Figure 10.4 Trends in performance of institutional indicators, 2011–22
Source: authors' illustration based on Worldwide Governance Indicator Database (2023).

4. Patterns and trends in domestic savings in Tanzania

There was a fairly steady increase in Tanzania's domestic savings as a percentage of GDP over the period 1990–2019, albeit with considerable fluctuations over time (Figure 10.5). Private savings as a percentage of GDP were computed as gross savings minus public savings, while public savings were obtained as government revenue minus government final consumption. Over the 1990–94 period, gross domestic savings as a percentage of GDP was decreasing, with lowest value being

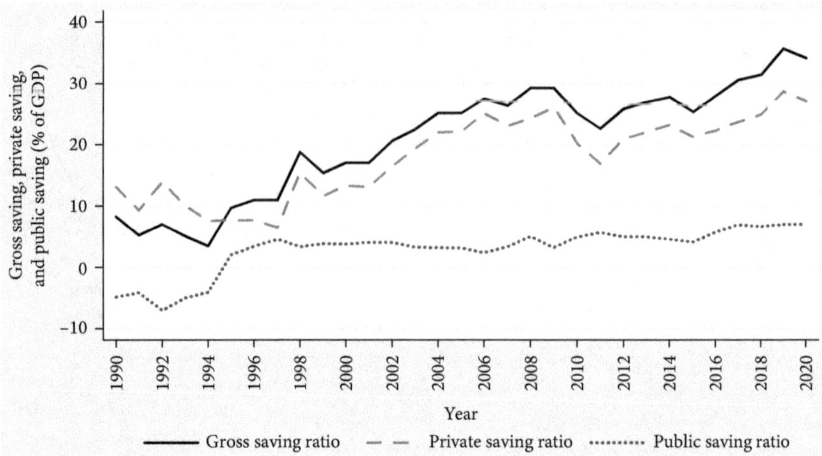

Figure 10.5 Trends in domestic savings in Tanzania, 1990–2020

Source: authors' illustration based on WDI data (2021).

3.4% in 1994. This could be due to the macroeconomic challenges and imbalances during that period, including low resource mobilization, a bloated public sector, weak competition in the financial market, and low and weak efficiency in credit allocation (Bigsten and Danielsson 1999; Kilindo 2001). However, domestic savings ratio increased thereafter, from 9.6% in 1995 to 29.2% in 2009 following the various economic and financial reforms, including liberalization of interest rates. While the gross domestic savings ratio declined to 22.5% in 2011, it increased throughout the 2012–19 period and was 34.1% in 2020. The increase in gross domestic savings ratio in the post-liberalization period could be attributable to various factors, including stable macroeconomic environment and steady economic growth. The argument in the literature supports a positive relationship between domestic savings and economic growth. An increase in savings stimulates economic growth, which in turn stimulates the growth of domestic savings (Alguacil et al. 2004; Singh 2010). Financial-sector developments, including financial innovations aimed at increasing access to financial services, are also envisaged to have played a role in promoting savings in Tanzania.

5. Determinants of domestic savings

5.1 Conceptual framework

The life cycle hypothesis (LCH) developed by Ando and Modigliani (1963) provides the basic conceptual framework. LCH assumes that the prime motive for saving is accumulation for retirement. Since income tends to fluctuate over the course of one's life, the saving behaviour depends on a person's stage in the life cycle. The model assumes an individual's smooth consumption over their lifetime, and hence, they are net savers during working years and dis-savers during retirement (Modigliani 1986). In their late years, individuals spend out of the previously accumulated savings as income decreases (Ando and Modigliani 1963; Nagawa et al. 2020).

Based on the above, the LCH models the consumption/saving behaviour of a representative agent whose aim is to maximize the present value of lifetime utility subject to a budget constraint, where the latter is the current net worth plus the present value of expected labour income. Assuming perfect capital markets and perfect foresight about the income-generating process, the model predicts that consumption in a given period depends on expected lifetime income, as opposed to current income as postulated by the Keynesian model. Consequently, LCH predicts that saving is positively related to income growth, since a higher rate of income growth implies an increase in the income of active workers, which in turn expands their permanent income (Athukorala and Sen 2004).

Extending the model to the national level implies that the key determinants of the saving rate over time in a given country or across countries are the age structure of the population and the rate of growth of per capita income. An increase in the latter leads to a rise in the lifetime resources (and savings) of the younger working population relative to older age groups, which in turn increases the aggregate saving rate. Under the assumption of 'balanced population growth', a rise in the population growth rate brought about by an increase in age-specific fertility rates increases the number of savers relative to dis-savers (Modigliani 1986). Therefore, assuming the saving profile of individual households in two given economies is the same, the economy with the faster population growth is bound to have a higher aggregate saving rate. The question is, does the balanced population growth assumption hold in reality, especially in the context of developing economies? Besides increasing the number of economically active individuals relative to the retired, a rise in population growth rate may lead to an increase in the proportion of the younger population. Given that both the young and the elderly consume more than they can earn, the net effect of population growth on aggregate saving is theoretically ambiguous (Athukorala and Sen 2004). For developing economies with relatively high dependency ratios, the net effect is likely to be negative.

The net impact of an interest rate increase in the LCH model is also ambiguous. On one hand, a higher interest rate increases the current price of consumption relative to the future price (the substitution effect) and therefore provides an incentive to increase savings. However, for net lenders, a higher interest rate also increases lifetime income, which leads to an increase in consumption and a decrease in savings (the income effect). Therefore, the net effect of an interest rate increase on savings is positive only if the substitution effect outweighs the income effect. Arguably, for a typical developing economy with underdeveloped money markets, the substitution effect is stronger (McKinnon 1973; Shaw 1973). In most developing countries, a relatively high proportion of household savings tend to be in the form of cash balances and quasi-monetary assets (mainly bank deposits).

5.1.1 Extensions and modifications

Athukorala and Sen (2004) provide a succinct description of extensions and modifications to the empirical application of the basic LCH based on the following arguments. The first concern is the absence of a link between current savings and current income. The premise that the saving rate is related to the growth of per capita income as opposed to per capita income is underpinned by the assumption that individuals are forward-looking and have a perfect foresight of lifetime income. However, the validity of this premise is highly questionable for low-income countries such as Tanzania.

The second addition relates to the role of key variables or indicators of macroeconomic stability such as inflation. In the basic LCH model, the impact of inflation on savings is captured only implicitly in determining the real interest rate. The model implicitly assumes inflation neutrality (the absence of money illusion) in saving behaviour and the absence of the real balance effect of inflation. However, inflation could influence saving via its impact on real wealth (Nwachukwu and Egwaikhide 2007). To maintain a target level of wealth or liquid assets relative to income, savings have to rise with inflation. Additionally, high inflation can lead to higher savings for precautionary purposes, since it is associated with uncertainty in future income streams (Aberu et al. 2010). This is likely true for households in developing countries, where income prospects are relatively more uncertain than in developed countries (Deaton 1989; Kimball 1990). However, high inflation rates can also deter saving.

The third argument relates to the impact of changes in the external terms of trade (ToT). The Harberger–Laursen–Metzler hypothesis suggests that a deterioration in ToT (a reduction in the price of domestically produced goods relative to that of imported goods) reduces real income and hence savings. Athukorala and Sen (2004) note that when the forward-looking behaviour of private agents who are faced with volatile and unpredictable changes in income is assumed, ToT changes could impact savings through consumption smoothing, over and above the impact operating via the growth or the level of real income. The effect on private savings depends on whether changes in ToT are perceived to be temporary or permanent (Obstfeld 1982). If the deterioration in ToT is perceived to be temporary, it may lead to increased absorption as consumers try to offset the decline in purchasing power of domestic goods so as to keep real expenditure constant. On the other hand, a ToT deterioration that is perceived to be permanent could induce an increase in savings so as to sustain real standards of living in the future.

The fourth consideration is related to the role of financial depth. The range and availability of different financial assets, as well as the improvement in accessibility of banking facilities and other financial services, is likely to motivate individuals to save. Financial depth is often measured by the degree of monetization of the economy as proxied by the ratio of broad money (M3) to GDP (Ozcan et al. 2003). However, credit to the private sector as a ratio of GDP is also used as a proxy for financial development. Evidence in developing countries generally shows that financial depth has a positive impact on saving mobilization.

Fifth is the role of fiscal policy in promoting the national saving rate (Loayza et al. 2000). While the government can choose the level of its own savings directly, a change in this variable need not imply a one-for-one change in household or national saving. This is because private agents may respond in such a way as to offset the government action, at least to some extent. Based on the Ricardian equivalence proposition of Barro (1974), the issuance of bonds to finance government dis-saving results in an equal increase in private savings. This is because individuals save in anticipation of a future increase in taxes to service and repay the debt. However, the proposition is premised on the assumption of perfect capital markets and the absence of uncertainty impacting on saving behaviour. If either or both of these assumptions do not hold, then private and public savings may not be perfect substitutes. Elbadawi and Mwega (1998) note that the impact of public savings on private savings depends on the assumption made—public savings may have some impact (Keynesian assumption) or it may be fully crowded out (Ricardo equivalence). The Keynesian model predicts that public savings may increase private saving when resources are assumed to be idle. Thus, the net impact can be negative or positive.

5.2 Empirical specification

Based on the above conceptual framework, the saving function was specified in two ways as follows: first, by using private savings (*SPV*) as the dependent variable:

$$SPV = f(GY, ADR1, ADR2, RID, W, LY, INF, SPB, TOT, FIN) \tag{1}$$

and second, by using gross national savings (*SNAT*) as the dependent variable expressed as a function of the following:

$$SNAT = f(GY, ADR1, ADR2, RID, W, LY, INF, TOT, FIN) \tag{2}$$

where *SPV* and *SNAT* are the private and gross national savings expressed as a percentage of GDP. *SPB* is the public saving ratio. *GY* and *LY* are GDP growth rate and log of per capita income, *W* is broad money supply (M3)/GDP as a measure of financial deepening, *RID* is the real interest rate (bank deposit rate minus inflation), *ADR*1 is the old age–dependency ratio measured as the ratio of older dependents (people older than 64) to the working-age population, while *ADR*2 is the young age–dependency ratio measured as the ratio of younger dependents (people younger than 15) to the working-age population (*ADR*1 and *ADR*2 are depicted as a proportion of dependents per 100 working-age population). *INF* is the inflation rate, *ToT* is the terms of trade, and *FIN* is a measure of financial development (domestic credit to private sector). *ToT* is calculated as the percentage ratio of the export unit value indexes to the import unit value indexes, measured relative to the base year 2000.

5.3 Estimation strategy and data

The estimation methodology employed is the ARDL approach, following Pesaran and Shin (1995) and Pesaran et al. (2001). ARDL is appealing since the method allows for a mixture of variables with different levels of integration—both I(0) and I(1) variables. For example, the growth rate of per capita income is typically stationary while its level tends to be non-stationary (first-differenced stationary). Additionally, ARDL can be utilized to estimate both the long-run and short-run dynamics of the model simultaneously. Finally, an ARDL model is more efficient for samples with small-to-moderate time-series properties.

The generalized ARDL (*p*,q) model with *k* explanatory variables is specified as follows:

$$SPV_t = \gamma_0 + \beta_1 SPV_{t-1} + \ldots + \beta_p SPV_{t-p} + \alpha_0 X_t + \alpha_1 X_{t-1} + \ldots + \alpha_q X_{t-q} + \mu_t \tag{3}$$

Where SPV_t stands for private savings as a percentage of GDP at time t, X_t is a $(k \times 1)$ matrix of independent variables (see equation (1) above), γ is the constant term, and μ_t is the error term with standard *i.i.d* properties. The dependent variable in equation (3) is explained by lags of itself, as well as current and lagged values of the independent variables. The number of lags of the dependent variable (the autoregressive component) is included up to lag order p, while the number of lags of independent variables is included up to order q. Compressing equation (3) yields:

$$SPV_t = \gamma_0 + \sum_{i=1}^{p} \beta_i SPV_{t-i} + \sum_{i=0}^{q} \alpha_i' X_{t-i} + \mu_t \tag{4}$$

where β and α are coefficients to be estimated. ARDL allows for the possibility of distinguishing between long-run and short-run effects through an unrestricted error correction model (ECM) of the form:

$$\Delta SPV_t = \gamma_0 + \sum_{i=1}^{p} \delta_i \Delta SPV_{t-i} + \sum_{i=0}^{q} \delta_i \Delta X_{t-i} + \lambda (Y_t - \theta X_t) + \mu_t \qquad (5)$$

where $\lambda = (1 - \sum_{i=1}^{p} \delta_i)$ is the speed of adjustment to equilibrium, the expression in brackets is the long-run relationship between variables, and $\theta = \frac{1 - \sum_{i=0}^{q} \pi_i}{1 - \sum_{i=1}^{p} \delta_i}$ is the long-run parameter. If $\lambda = 0$, then there is no evidence of a long-run relationship between private savings and its determinants. The parameter is expected to be significantly negative under the prior assumption that following a deviation, the variables return to their long-run equilibrium (cointegration).

The equations are estimated using time-series data covering the period 1990–2020. Data were sourced from the WDI database, complemented with national data sources, namely the BOT and the National Bureau of Statistics (NBS).

5.4 Empirical results

5.4.1 Descriptive and correlation analysis

Domestic savings as a ratio of GDP was found to be highly and positively correlated with public savings, per capita income, ToT, real deposit rate, and real GDP growth, and negatively correlated with inflation rate and the old age and young age–dependency ratios (for a summary of descriptive statistics and correlation matrix results, see Were and Joseph 2022: Tables A1–A2). The pair-wise correlation between some explanatory variables was quite high, pointing to a high likelihood of multicollinearity. In particular, the age–dependency variables were found to be highly correlated with nearly all the variables and, hence, were dropped from the final estimated equations.

To satisfy the bounds test assumption so that the ARDL model provides consistent and valid standard errors for inference, the variables are supposed to be integrated of the order zero I(0) or one I(1). Augmented Dickey–Fuller (ADF) was used to test for stationarity. The following variables were found to be I(1): private savings, public savings, gross savings, inflation rate, log per capita income, broad money, ToT, old age–dependency ratio, young age–dependency ratio, and domestic credit to private sector. The real deposit rate was found to be I(0).

The selection of appropriate lag length for the variables in the ARDL model is important in ensuring standard normal error terms that do not suffer from autocorrelation and heteroskedasticity (Nkoro and Uko 2016). The Schwarz Bayesian information criterion (SBIC) was used to determine optimal lag length for the respective variables. The SBIC model is more parsimonious and, hence, saves degrees of freedom, particularly in studies with small sample sizes (Pesaran and Smith 1998).

5.4.2 Long-run and short-run analysis

Prior to long-run and short-run analysis, a cointegration test based on the ARDL bounds test approach was conducted. The results confirmed existence of long-run relationships among the variables.[6]

The results of the long-run analyses for the private savings and gross savings equations are reported in Tables 10.1 and 10.2, respectively.[7] The basic diagnostic test statistics are included in both tables. The Durbin–Watson (DW) and Breusch–Godfrey Lagrange multiplier (LM) test statistics suggest absence of autocorrelation and serial correlation, respectively. Furthermore, the test for homoskedasticity using White's test indicates that the data series is homoscedastic. Structural stability tests of the long-run parameters were also performed using the cumulative sum chart (CUSUM) and cumulative sum chart squared (CUSUMSQ) tests to check the stability of the results. The plots of both the CUSUM and the CUSUMSQ are within the boundaries of the 5% significance level, which confirms model stability (see Were and Joseph 2022: Figure A2).

The results show that in the long run, per capita income, public savings, ToT, broad money (M3), and domestic credit to the private sector are robust determinants of private domestic savings in Tanzania (Table 10.1).[8] The coefficient for per capita income is positive and statistically significant, which suggests that the Keynesian 'absolute income hypothesis' holds for saving behaviour in Tanzania. Moreover, in terms of the magnitude, the variable has the biggest impact—a 1% increase in per capita income leads to about a 9.5% increase in private saving (Table 10.1). The results corroborate similar findings by Athukorala and Sen (2004) for India and Larbi (2013) for Ghana, which indicated that savings rose with the level of income. Per capita income seems to play a more prominent role in developing economies like Tanzania, consistent with the Keynesian income hypothesis, compared with the rate of growth of income. Grigoli et al. (2018) found that while private saving rates in advanced economies are relatively more responsive to income growth, the response of private savings to income growth in low-income developing countries was lower. The results are consistent with Tanzania's steady economic growth over the past two decades or so, following the extensive reforms undertaken in the early 1990s, supported by a stable macroeconomic environment and access to external aid inflows. Notwithstanding the

[6] For the results, see Were and Joseph (2022: Table A3).

[7] The error correction terms were found to be negative and statistically significant.

[8] The results are consistent with the positive relationship between the respective variables and private savings as depicted by the scatterplots (see Were and Joseph 2022: Figure A1).

Table 10.1 Results of long-run analysis for private saving

Variables	(1)	(2)	(3)	(4)
Lagged private saving ratio	−1.080***	−0.990***	−1.074***	−0.905***
	(0.228)	(0.228)	(0.203)	(0.165)
Public saving	—	0.566	—	2.300**
		(0.628)		(0.722)
Log of per capita income	9.566**	9.318**	10.202***	—
	(3.316)	(3.656)	(3.193)	
Real deposit rate	0.372	0.493	0.234	1.056*
	(0.466)	(0.454)	(0.331)	(0.478)
M3-to-GDP ratio	0.723**	0.832***	0.814***	—
	(0.292)	(0.217)	(0.190)	—
Terms of trade	− 0.146**	− 0.178**	− 0.149**	− 0.316***
	(0.054)	(0.066)	(0.053)	(0.066)
Real GDP growth	− 0.029	—	—	—
	(0.472)			
Inflation	− 0.132	0.017	− 0.186	0.131
	(0.294)	(0.291)	(0.204)	(0.367)
Domestic credit to private sector	—	—	—	1.807***
				(0.331)
R-squared	0.942	0.943	0.931	0.927
Durbin–Watson statistic	2.46	2.45	2.27	2.71
Breusch–Godfrey LM	2.37	3.32*	1.49	2.41
Breusch–Pagan/Cook–Weisberg test	0.3	0	0	1.29
Number of observations	27	27	27	27

Note: standard errors in parentheses; *** $p < 0.01$, ** $p < 0.05$, * $p < 0.1$.
Source: authors' computations based on data from WDI.

population expansion, GDP per capita increased steadily from about US$174 in 1990 to US$1,076.50 in 2020, ultimately enabling Tanzania's transition from low-income to lower-middle-income country status in 2020.

The coefficient for the public savings ratio is positive and statistically significant. Since public saving is highly correlated with per capita income, the two variables were included in the model separately. A 1% increase in public savings ratio leads to a 2.3% increase in private savings ratio. This finding suggests that public savings crowd in or complement, rather than crowd out, private savings. This could be attributed to the relatively low fiscal deficits witnessed in Tanzania, particularly following the fiscal reforms, and donor funding support, including debt relief, which provided the fiscal space to boost public investments and growth. However, the finding is in contrast with those of other studies, such as Athukorala and Sen (2004), Arok (2014), and Shawa (2016).

Two measures of financial deepening were used interchangeably, namely broad money supply (M3) and domestic credit to the private sector as ratios of GDP. Both have a positive and statistically significant impact as expected; that is, financial deepening promotes private savings in the long run, since financial products such as mobile money and other modalities of saving are readily available. The results suggest that financial deepening has played a role in stimulating domestic resource mobilization in Tanzania. This could be attributed to the various financial reforms, including FGFSR and SGFSR, as well as the promotion of innovations such as agent banking and DFS, leading to increased delivery of financial services and outreach to previously excluded segments of the population. Moreover, the growth of the economy has taken place in tandem with the growth in credit to the private sector. Additionally, the BOT has played an instrumental role in fostering the growth of the financial sector, improving access to financial services and injecting liquidity into the economy through the various policy instruments as deemed appropriate with a view to supporting economic activities. Taken together, these measures appear to have boosted private savings. The results are consistent with the findings of Larbi (2013) in the case of Ghana, Pantaleo and Karamagi (2013) in Tanzania, and Shawa (2016) in SSA countries. As long argued by Mwega (1997), the positive effect of financial deepening on private savings points to the significant potential benefits of reforms geared towards deepening the financial system.

The earlier Keynesian models predicted that an adverse shift in ToT would generate a decline in savings. In line with this prediction, the study finds negative effect of ToT on private savings. Athukorala and Sen (2004) reported similar findings for India. On the other hand, the impact of real rate of return on bank deposits is positive but not statistically significant when included with per capita income in the same model, which is not very surprising given the relatively high correlation between the two variables.

The short-run empirical results show that public savings and real deposit interest rate impacts private savings negatively in the short run, while ToT and inflation rate have a positive effect (see Were and Joseph 2022: Table A4).

The long-run results for the gross savings equation are reported in Table 10.2. Gross domestic saving is positively determined by per capita income, real deposit rate, broad money (M3), and economic growth and negatively impacted by inflation. Similar to the results obtained for private savings, income per capita has a statistically significant and substantive impact on gross domestic saving in Tanzania. Similarly, Epaphra (2014b) finds that national savings in Tanzania are positively influenced by disposable income and real GDP growth rate. Arok (2014)

Table 10.2 Long-run results for gross saving

Variables	(1)	(2)	(3)
Lagged gross saving ratio	– 0.764***	– 0.651**	– 0.499***
	(0.199)	(0.241)	(0.11)
Log of per capita income	5.415***	12.814**	—
	(1.735)	(5.468)	
M3-to-GDP ratio	0.704**		0.313
	(0.242)		(0.287)
Terms of trade		– 0.184	—
		(0.118)	
Real GDP growth	0.158	—	1.568*
	(0.548)		(0.767)
Inflation	– 0.561**	—	—
	(0.227)		
Real deposit rate	– 0.024	1.033**	1.065***
	(0.425)	(0.37)	(0.311)
Domestic credit to private sector		0.574	—
		(0.424)	
R-squared	0.794	0.817	0.607
Durbin–Watson d-statistic	2.65	2.50	2.65
Breusch–Godfrey LM test	10.9***	4.12***	6.72***
Breusch–Pagan/Cook–Weisberg test	0.69	0.61	0.6
Number of observations	28	28	28

Note: standard errors in parentheses; *** $p < 0.01$, ** $p < 0.05$, * $p < 0.1$.
Source: authors' own computations based on data from WDI.

and Keino and Kariuki (2016) report similar findings for Kenya and Uganda, respectively.

As regards the financial sector variables, real deposit rate and broad money (aggregate M3) as a ratio of GDP are significant determinants of gross domestic savings. The latter suggests that the availability of and accessibility to a variety of financial assets acts as a motivation for saving. Girma (2017) and Nagawa et al. (2020) also find a positive effect of broad money on gross savings for Ethiopia and Uganda, respectively. The positive impact of the real deposit interest rate contrasts with the general observation that in most low-income countries, savings do not respond to the real deposit rate (Grigoli et al. 2018). It is, however, consistent with the McKinnon–Shaw proposition that in economies where saving is largely in the form of money and near-money assets, the incentive effect of high real interest rates on savings (income effect) generally outweighs the substitution effect. This implies that for economies characterized by financial repression, liberalization of interest rates is expected to increase savings. This appears to be the case in Tanzania, following liberalization of interest rates in the early 1990s. That notwithstanding, the liberalization period was characterized by high interest rate spreads (low deposit rates vis-à-viz high lending rates) compared with the period before, which according to Epaphra (2014a), is attributable to lack of competition and inefficiency in the financial system. Thus, policies aimed at increasing the deposit rate, besides effectively lowering the interest rate differential and enhancing financial intermediation, have the potential to promote domestic savings. It is sometimes argued that since most people in low-income and developing economies like Tanzania are net borrowers, increases in real deposit rates could increase the cost of borrowing, which may negatively affect access to credit. But this need not necessarily be the case if the financial system works efficiently, since a rise in the rate of return on deposits provides an incentive to mobilize more savings, thus increasing the stock of funds.

The results further show that in the long run, high inflation discourages domestic savings. High inflation increases the opportunity cost of holding money or liquid assets and, thus, negatively affects gross savings. Generally, Tanzania's inflation rate has remained in a single-digit range, at an average rate of about 4.4% over the past decade.

In the short run, with the exception of real deposit interest rate and real GDP growth rate, which have a negative short-run effect on gross national savings, the short-run impact of the other variables is not statistically significant (see Were and Joseph 2022: Table A5). The negative short-run impact of the real deposit rate could be a reflection of the high interest rate spreads as depicted by the relatively low deposit rates that change minimally in the short run.

6. Conclusion and policy implications

This chapter examines the determinants of domestic savings in Tanzania. Using the ARDL approach to examine the long-run and short-run relationships, analysis was conducted separately for private and gross domestic savings. The results show that in the long run, per capita income, public savings, credit to the private sector, and broad money (M3) used as proxies for financial deepening are positive determinants of private domestic savings, while the impact of ToT on private savings is negative. The results for overall gross domestic savings are largely in line with those reported for private savings—income per capita, economic growth, and financial deepening proxied by aggregate money supply as a ratio of GDP have statistically significant positive impact on overall gross domestic savings. Additionally, an increase in the real rate of return on deposits promotes gross domestic savings, while inflation deters savings in the long run. The results suggest that public saving has a complementary effect on private savings, which arguably underscores the role of fiscal policy in promoting domestic savings. However, the short-run impact on private domestic savings of an increase in public savings is negative. Similarly, the impact of real deposit rate on both private and gross domestic savings in the short run was found to be negative. The latter is arguably a reflection of the interest rate structure, which is characterized by relatively higher lending rates and low deposit rates that change minimally in the short run, leading to high interest rate spreads.

The strong evidence regarding the positive impact of per capita income on domestic savings is consistent with the fairly robust economic performance and improved levels of national income witnessed particularly in the past decade or so. The findings are largely in line with the positive role of income in boosting savings, consistent with Keynes's absolute income hypothesis, especially in the context of low-income and developing economies. Tanzania's favourable economic outcomes can be attributed to various factors, including access to foreign aid that largely provided the required fiscal space to enhance public investment, stable macroeconomic environment following the various reforms undertaken in the early 1990s, and political stability. These developments appear to have played a critical role in promoting economic growth as well as domestic savings. In addition, the various reforms, including liberalization of the financial sector, coupled with innovations leading to improved access to financial services seem to have enhanced financial deepening, thereby ultimately boosting domestic savings.

The results suggest that pursuing income-enhancing policies and development strategies has great potential for boosting domestic savings in Tanzania. Additionally, measures aimed at enhancing financial deepening and financial-sector development are also bound to boost the mobilization of domestic savings. Such polices could include expanding access to financial services, particularly in the rural areas, areas and measures aimed at enhancing financial intermediation, such as reducing market fragmentation and interest rate spreads, as well as increased adoption of technology to improve the efficiency of the financial sector. Furthermore, a stable macroeconomic environment, including price stability, is equally crucial for promoting savings and the growth of the economy. Measures to reduce the adverse effects of ToT on domestic savings could also be helpful. These include expanding exports through increased value addition to improve ToT.

References

Aberu, T., T. Ayalew, and T. Tefera (2010). 'Determinants of Inflation Rate in Ethiopia'. MSc thesis. Addis Ababa: Addis Ababa University.

Abu, N., Abd Karim, M. Z., & Aziz, M. I. A. (2015). 'Low Savings Rates in the Economic Community of West African States (ECOWAS): The Role of Corruption'. *Journal of Economic Cooperation & Development*, 36(2): 63–90.

Agrawal, I., Z. U. Ahmed, M. Mered, and R. Nord (1993). 'Structural Adjustment, Economic Performance and Aid Dependency in Tanzania'. IMF Working Paper 1993/066. Washington, DC: International Monetary Fund (IMF). https://doi.org/10.5089/9781451848748.001.

Alguacil, M., A. Cuadros, and V. Orts (2004). 'Does Saving Really Matter for Growth? Mexico (1970–2000)'. *Journal of International Development: The Journal of the Development Studies Association*, 16(2): 281–90. https://doi.org/10.1002/jid.1075.

Ando, A., and F. Modigliani (1963). 'The "Life Cycle" Hypothesis of Saving: Aggregate Implications and Tests'. *American Economic Review*, 53(1): 55–84.

Arok, B. A. (2014). 'Determinants of Gross Domestic Savings in Kenya'. PhD dissertation. Nairobi: University of Nairobi.

Athukorala, P. C., and K. Sen (2004). 'The Determinants of Private Saving in India'. *World Development*, 32(3): 491–503. https://doi.org/10.1016/j.worlddev.2003.07.008.

Balele, N., N. Kessy, Z. Mpemba, F. Aminiel, G. Sije, and E. Mung'ong'o (2018). 'Financial Sector Reforms and Innovations and Their Implications on Monetary Policy Transmission in Tanzania'. Working Paper 13. Dar es Salaam: Bank of Tanzania.

Barro, R. J. (1974). 'Are Government Bonds Net Wealth?' *Journal of Political Economy*, 82(6): 1095–117. https://doi.org/10.1086/260266.

Bigsten, A., and A. Danielsson (1999). *Is Tanzania an Emerging Economy?* Gothenburg and Lund: Organisation for Economic Co-operation and Development (OECD).

BOT (Bank of Tanzania) (2011). *Tanzania Mainland's 50 Years of Independence: A Review of the Role and Functions of the Bank of Tanzania (1961–2011)*. Dar es Salaam: BOT.

BOT (2020). 'Financial Stability Report'. Dar es Salaam: BOT. Available at: https://www.bot.go.tz/Publications/Other/Banking%20Supervision%20Annual%20Reports/en/2021101510115639.pd (accessed 9 September 2021).

BOT. (2021). Bank of Tanzania. Annual Report 2020/21, Bank of Tanzania, December. Dodoma: BOT. Available at: https://www.bot.go.tz/Publications/Regular/Annual%20Report/en/2021122922483700.pdf (accessed 21 April 2022).

Deaton, A. (1989). 'Saving in Developing Countries: Theory and Review'. *World Bank Economic Review*, 3(suppl. 1): 61–96. https://doi.org/10.1093/wber/3.suppl_1.61.

Demirguc-Kunt, A., Laeven, L., & Levine, R. (2004). Regulations, Market Structure, Institutions, and the Cost of Financial Intermediation. *Journal of Money, Credit, and Banking*, 36(3), 593–622.

Elbadawi, I., and F. Mwega (1998). *Can Africa's Savings Collapse Be Averted?* Washington, DC: World Bank.

Epaphra, M. (2014a). 'An Empirical Analysis of Interest Rate Spreads in Tanzania'. *Asian Journal of Research in Banking and Finance*, 4(10): 244–69. https://doi.org/10.5958/2249-7323.2014.01425.4.

Epaphra, M. (2014b). 'Empirical Investigation of the Determinants of Tanzania's National Savings'. *Journal of Economics and Development Studies*, 2(4): 223–41.

Freytag, A., & Voll, S. (2013). Institutions and Savings in Developing and Emerging Economies. *Public Choice*, 157, 475–509.

Girma, G. (2017). 'Trends and Determinants of Gross Domestic Saving in Ethiopia'. *Journal of Economics and Sustainable Development*, 8(5): 72–81.

Grigoli, F., A. Herman, and K. Schmidt-Hebbel (2018). 'Saving in the World'. *World Development*, 104: 257–50. https://doi.org/10.1016/j.worlddev.2017.11.022.

Kasebele, A., and A. O. Lopez (2016). 'Bank for Your Buck: Increasing Savings in Tanzania'. PhD dissertation. Cambridge, MA: Harvard University.

Keino, A., and N. Kariuki (2016) 'Effect of Remittances on Gross Domestic Savings in Uganda'. *International Journal of Management and Business Studies*, 6(4): 343–53.

Kilindo, A. A. (2001). 'Financial Liberalisation and Its Implications for Poverty Reduction in Tanzania'. *Business Management Review*, 7(2): 22–32.

Kimball, M. (1990). 'Precautionary Saving and the Marginal Propensity to Consume'. National Bureau of Economic Research (NBER) Working Paper 3403. Cambridge, MA: NBER. https://doi.org/10.3386/w3403.

Larbi, D. A. (2013). 'The Long Run Determinants of Private Domestic Savings in Ghana: A Cointegration Approach'. *Journal of Economics and Sustainable Development*, 4(4): 125–36.

Levin, J. (2001). 'Taxation in Tanzania'. Discussion Paper 2001/80. Helsinki: United Nations University (UNU)-World Institute for Public Policy Research and Analysis (WIDER).

Loayza, N., K. Schmidt-Hebbel, and L. Servén (2000). 'Saving in Developing Countries: An Overview'. *World Bank Economic Review*, 14(3): 393–414. https://doi.org/10.1093/wber/14.3.393.

McKinnon, R. I. (1973). *Money and Capital in Economic Development*. Washington, DC: Brookings Institute.

Mered, M. M., M. R. Nord, N. Agrawal, and Z. U. Ahmed (1993). *Structural Adjustment, Economic Performance, and Aid Dependency in Tanzania*. Washington, DC: International Monetary Fund (IMF).

Modigliani, F. (1986). 'Life Cycle, Individual Thrift, and the Wealth of Nations'. *Science*, 234(4777): 704–12. https://doi.org/10.1126/science.234.4777.704.

Mori, N. (2019). 'Determinants of Individual Savings among Tanzanians'. *Review of Behavioral Finance*, 11(3), 352–370.

Mwase, N. and Ndulu, B.J. (2008). 'Tanzania: Explaining Four Decades of Episodic Growth'. In B.J. Ndulu, S.A. O'Connell, J.P. Azam, R.H. Bates, A.K. Fosu, J.W. Gunning and D. Njinkeu, eds., *The Political Economic of Growth in Africa 1960–2000: Case Studies*, 426–71. Cambridge, UK: Cambridge University Press.

Mwega, F.M. (1997). 'Saving in Sub-Saharan Africa: A Comparative Analysis'. *Journal of African Economies*, 6(3): 199–228.

Nagawa, V., F. Wasswa, and E. Bbaale (2020). 'Determinants of Gross Domestic Savings in Uganda: An Autoregressive Distributed Lag (ARDL) Approach to Cointegration'. *Journal of Economic Structures*, 9: 1–19. https://doi.org/10.1186/s40008-020-00209-1.

Naschold, F., and A. Fozzard (2002). 'Poverty Reduction Strategy and Public Expenditure in Tanzania'. Overseas Development Institute (ODI) Working Paper 165. London: ODI.

Ngowi, H.P. (2009). 'Economic Development and Change in Tanzania Since Independence: The Political Leadership Factor'. *African Journal of Political Science and International Relations*, 3(5): 259–67.

Nkoro, E., and A. K. Uko (2016). 'Autoregressive Distributed Lag (ARDL) Cointegration Technique: Application and Interpretation'. *Journal of Statistical and Econometric Methods*, 5(4): 63–91.

Nord, N., M. Mered, N. Agrawal, and Z. Ahmed (1993). 'Structural Adjustment, Economic Performance, and Aid Dependency in Tanzania'. Working Paper 1993/066. Washington, DC: IMF. https://doi.org/10.2139/ssrn.883547.

Nord, R., Y. V. Sobolev, D. G. Dunn, A. Hajdenberg, N. A. Hobdari, S. Maziad, and S. Roudet (2009). 'Tanzania: The Story of an African Transition'. Working Paper 09/02. Washington, DC: IMF.

Nwachukwu, T. E., and F. D. Egwaikhide (2007). 'An Error-Correction Model of the Determinants of Saving in Nigeria'. *Ibadad University Journal of Monetary and Economic Integration*, 11(2).

Obstfeld, M. (1982). 'Aggregate Spending and the Terms of Trade: Is There a Laursen–Metzler Effect?' *Quarterly Journal of Economics*, 97(2): 251–70. https://doi.org/10.2307/1880757.

Olaniyi, C. O., and S. I. Oladeji (2022). 'The Interplay between the Financial Sector and the Institutional Framework in Kenya's Economic Growth Process'. *Journal of Public Affairs*, 22(3): e2562.

Ozcan, K. M., A. Gunay, and S. Ertac (2003). 'Determinants of Private Savings Behaviour in Turkey'. *Applied Economics*, 35(12): 1405–16. https://doi.org/10.1080/0003684032000100373.

Pantaleo, I., and I. J. Karamagi (2013). 'Private Saving Behavior and Ricardian Equivalence Theorem: The Case of Tanzania'. *Business Management Review*, 16: 119–39.

Pesaran, H. M., and Y. Shin (1995). 'Autoregressive Distributed Lag Modelling Approach to Cointegration Analysis'. Cambridge Working Papers in Economics 9514. Cambridge: University of Cambridge, Faculty of Economics.

Pesaran, M. H., and R. P. Smith (1998). 'Structural Analysis of Cointegrating VARs'. *Journal of Economic Surveys*, 12(5): 471–505. https://doi.org/10.1111/1467-6419.00065.

Pesaran, M. H., Y. Shin, and R. J. Smith (2001). 'Bounds Testing Approaches to the Analysis of Level Relationships'. *Journal of Applied Econometrics*, 16(3): 289–326. https://doi.org/10.1002/jae.616.

Shaw, E. S. (1973). *Financial Deepening in Economic Development*. Washington, DC: Brookings Institute.

Shawa, K. C. (2016). 'Drivers of Private Saving in Sub-Saharan African Countries'. *Journal of Economic Development*, 41(2): 77–110. https://doi.org/10.35866/caujed.2016.41.2.004.

Singh, T. (2010). 'Does Domestic Saving Cause Economic Growth? A Time-Series Evidence from India'. *Journal of Policy Modeling*, 32(2): 231–53. https://doi.org/10.1016/j.jpolmod.2009.08.008.

Were, M., and L. Mollel (2020). 'Public Debt Sustainability and Debt Dynamics: The Case of Tanzania'. WIDER Working Paper 2020/112). Helsinki: UNU-WIDER. https://doi.org/10.35188/UNU-WIDER/2020/869-6.

11

Understanding domestic savings in sub-Saharan Africa

A case study of Ghana

Charles Godfred Ackah and Monica Lambon-Quayefio

1. Introduction

In the neoclassical economic growth theories, savings is regarded as the main source of capital accumulation and, therefore, an important driver of long-term growth. Predictions from the Harrod–Domar growth model, for instance, encourage developing countries to increase their savings and investments to spur economic growth. However, most countries in sub-Saharan Africa (hereafter SSA), including Ghana, have struggled over the years to mobilize sufficient domestic resources to promote and sustain growth of their economies. According to Elbadawi and Mwega (2000), private savings in the subregion declined consistently from the 1970s to the 1990s, from 11% of disposable income to about 9%. Based on data from the World Development Indicators (WDI) database, for SSA, between 2000 and 2020, the savings ratio (i.e. savings as a percentage of gross domestic product, GDP) declined significantly from 30% to about 20%, although there have been fluctuations in between the period. In Ghana, the story is not any different.

The low levels of savings in Ghana necessitated the heavy reliance on foreign aid and other external sources of finance for economic development in the past. However, the renewed call and resolution towards the 'Ghana beyond Aid' agenda has revived interests in domestic resource mobilization for economic growth and development. In line with this agenda, the Bank of Ghana embarked on an agenda to ensure a resilient financial system required to facilitate economic growth by 'cleaning up' the banking sector between mid-2017 and the end of 2018. The clean-up appeared to have paid off as the total deposits recorded in 2019, according to Bank of Ghana (2020), grew by 22% in 2019 compared with 12% recorded in 2017. A combination of various macroeconomic financial-sector policies as well as population policies may offer an interesting perspective on the relationship between savings and economic growth in Ghana (Gatsi and Appiah 2020). For example, the Financial Sector Adjustment Programmes (FINSAP I

Charles Godfred Ackah and Monica Lambon-Quayefio, *Understanding domestic savings in sub-Saharan Africa*. In: *The Domestic Savings Shortfall in Sub-Saharan Africa*. Edited by: Rose Ngugi and Kunal Sen, Oxford University Press.
 DOI: 10.1093/oso/9780198932482.003.0011

and FINSAP II) implemented between 1988 and 1990 (1990/1991), the Heavily Indebted Poor Country (HIPC) initiative between 2001 and 2006, and the population policy drive geared towards reducing family size during the same period are all noteworthy. The implementation of these policies directly or indirectly affects savings and economic growth in the long run.

Keynes (2018) suggests a positive relationship between consumption and savings, correlated with disposable income. However, the increase in consumption is less than the increase in disposable income, according to Keynes (2018). This suggests that the excess disposable income is used as savings, indicating a positive relationship.

The existing empirical literature on domestic savings suggests a broad range of factors as potential determinants of savings. These include income-related variables (GDP per capita), economic growth rates, and interest rates (Verma and Wilson 2005; Freytag and Voll 2013). Macroeconomic variables often consist of fiscal policy measures such as taxation and government expenditures and monetary policy variables such as the regulation of interest rates, money supply, and inflation. Other important determinants of domestic savings are macroeconomic volatilities and external shocks, especially terms of trade (Chowdhury 2015), financial liberalization (Keho 2011), and the quality and efficiency of the institutional environment within which a country operates (Feng and Yu 2020; Kebede et al. 2021).

External shocks are particularly significant for countries such as Ghana that depend on the production and export of primary commodities, for which changes in international prices affect export receipts. In most cases, the terms of trade fluctuations result in macroeconomic uncertainty (Adler and Magud 2013), and the heavy reliance on primary commodities increases the country's vulnerability to external shocks. This ultimately complicates macroeconomic management, particularly on the fiscal side (Adler and Magud 2013; Céspedes and Velasco 2014). Given the less developed and inefficient domestic credit and capital markets in developing countries, including Ghana, economic agents are often subjected to tight constraints, especially when commodity prices plummet. The adverse shocks ultimately compel them to reduce their savings by a much larger proportion than they would have otherwise had to. Using data on developing countries including Ghana, Chowdhury (2015) established a significant and positive effect of terms of trade on savings.

A growing body of literature documents the role of institutions, legal environments, and regulations on domestic resource mobilization in developing country contexts (e.g. Ntow-Gyamfi et al. 2019; Aluko and Ibrahim 2020; Appiah et al. 2020; Kebede et al. 2021). These studies have described the extent to which the monetary and regulatory environment reposes confidence in the financial system. Haselmann and Wachtel (2010), Troilo et al. (2019), and Gani and Rasul

(2020), and have all emphasized that the strength of legal systems, regulatory quality, and the rule of law have a significant influence on the financial sector and are associated with deeper financial markets in developing countries. Regulatory quality and good governance promote the development of the private sector and reduce the cost of doing business in an economy (Feng and Yu 2020; Sanga and Aziakpono 2022). Weak law enforcement of credit contracts reduces bank credit and increases the cost of intermediation due to prolonged and costly litigation to settle business disputes (Shen et al. 2009; Sanga and Aziakpono 2022). Closely linked to the issue of weak institutions is corruption. Empirical evidence has shown that corruption causes inefficiency, limits access to financial markets, and increases the economic costs and deters entrepreneurs from investing, leading to a negative effect on the development of the financial sector and hence savings (Khwaja and Mian 2011; Robinson and Acemoglu 2012; Sanga and Aziakpono 2022).

In addition, political stability and accountability in democratic regimes allows for financial intermediaries to operate efficiently and ultimately increases financial access and depth (Dutta and Meierrieks 2021). As noted by Ho et al. (2018) and Karikari et al. (2021), political instability and undemocratic regimes have been known to undermine confidence in the financial markets, inhibit bank credit to the private sector, and reduce the confidence of investors and entrepreneurs to increase their investments.

While the literature provides empirical evidence on the various factors that determine domestic savings, most of these studies have largely focused on a group of countries in various regions. However, conclusions drawn from such studies for individual country contexts may mask heterogeneity evident in individual country contexts. Moreover, the existing empirical research has focused more on the determinants of savings in the short run. Nevertheless, understanding the long-run relationship between these variables and savings is critical for effective long-term policymaking regarding the improvement of domestic savings mobilization. This study aims to fill this gap by determining, empirically, the primary long-term determinants of savings in Ghana, using data covering the period from 1980 to 2020. In addition, we aim to establish whether there is a long-term relationship between savings and the variables considered in Ghana's context. The sample period is chosen precisely to capture the effects of the various major policies that have been implemented over the period (see section 2).

The rest of the chapter is organized as follows. Section 2 describes the policy context, discussing the macroeconomic environment, as well as various monetary, fiscal, and financial policies that have shaped savings behaviour in Ghana over the period. In section 3, we describe the data used and the empirical estimations. Section 4 discusses the results from the descriptive analysis and the results from the empirical estimations. Section 5 concludes the chapter.

2. The policy context

2.1 The macroeconomic environment

The Ghanaian economy faced political and macroeconomic instability in the early 1980s, impacting population, banking, and financial-sector confidence. The Economic Recovery Program and Structural Adjustment Programme aimed to stabilize and restore growth, but their impact was short-lived (Aryeetey and Tarp 2000). Inflation reached 23.6% by the mid-1990s, GDP growth averaged 4%, and domestic borrowing increased (Bekoe and Adom 2013). The monetization of foreign debt further pressurized prices, leading to a looming debt crisis and burden on future generations (Aryeetey et al. 2000; Bekoe and Adom 2013).

The government reduced expenditure to achieve fiscal balance, targeting public-sector employment cuts. To increase revenue, taxes were imposed on consumables and wealth (Osei et al. 2020). Although these policies raised revenue, they may have stifled domestic savings, as private savings declined from 12.6% to 7.7% of GDP by 1983.

In the early 2000s, Ghana implemented growth and poverty reduction strategies to create wealth for all citizens. The country's real GDP grew by an average of 4.8% from 2000 to 2008, largely due to good commodity prices and prudent fiscal and monetary policies. Inflation and interest rates also saw significant declines, with average annual cedi-dollar depreciation falling from 49.8 to 0.9% between 2004 and 2008, and inflation rates also declined from about 33% in 2001 to about 12.6% in 2004 and then to 16.5% in 2008. High external debt declined to 28.9% between 2006 and 2008. By 2008, perhaps due to the discovery of oil in commercial quantities, large inflows of foreign direct investments (FDIs) were recorded.

Ghana experienced significant economic growth in the post-2010 era, partly due to oil production. The growth rate increased from 4.8% in 2009 to 7.9% in 2010, reaching a peak of 14% in 2011. However, power crises and the COVID-19 pandemic led to a sharp decline in growth. The significant negative effects of the power crises and the pandemic on economic activities are likely to affect savings due to effects on economic activities. The new administration's ambitious policies, such as the 'Free Senior High School', may have increased private savings, aligning with the Ricardian equivalence hypothesis. Moreover, the core objective of monetary policy in Ghana is to ensure price stability, which has implications for domestic savings and sustained economic growth.

2.2 Monetary and financial-sector reforms

Savings and financial-sector operations are interconnected, with savings contributing to banking-sector liability. Ghana's financial market underwent reforms post-independence, resulting in volatility in financial savings, particularly for the period post-dating 1970 (Aryeetey et al. 1996).

Using a measure of financial deepening (M2/GDP), Aryeetey et al. (1996) observed that Ghana's savings rate declined significantly from 1977 to 1982, causing it to lose its status as one of Africa's deeply financialized countries. Repressive government measures, such as mandatory customer details disclosure, freezing bank deposit accounts, the sudden withdrawal of GHS50 notes, and the recall of bank loans for trading inventory financing eroded public confidence in holding deposits with banks. Banks were also discouraged from actively mobilizing deposits due to unfavourable reserve requirements. In this regard, Leite (1982) recognized that banks occasionally refused to open new accounts for prospective clients (as cited in Brownbridge and Gockel 1996).

Aryeetey et al. (1996) found a steady increase in savings between 1984 and the early 1990s, driven by rising real incomes and economic reforms of the period (particularly the Economic Reform Programme).

In the early 1980s, the central bank implemented banking regulations and policies to counter negative impacts of government programmes and intervention policies. These included establishing a weekly auction in Treasury bills, which was established in 1986, moving away from direct control regimes, and implementing the first Financial Sector Adjustment Programmes (FINSAP I) from 1988 to 1990 aimed to achieve specific objectives, including restructuring of distressed banks, mobilization of savings, efficiency in credit allocation, and development of the money and security markets (Gockel et al. 1997).

FINSAP I and II were amended to strengthen the banking sector in Ghana. In 1989, minimum capital requirements were introduced, eliminating the central bank's discretion to increase ratios. FINSAP II focused on strengthening non-bank financial institutions and divesting state-owned banks between 1990 and 1991. Non-Bank Financial Institutions legislation, the Banking Law, and other legislations were introduced between 2000 and 2001 to liberalize the financial sector. The Banking Bill and Payment Systems Bill were passed in 2003, aiming to improve regulation and payment system efficiency. These regulations improved banking convenience and financial savings. It is important to add that, whereas the liberalization of interest rate controls was intended to shore up savings mobilization, macroeconomic misalignment in high inflation rates eroded most of the nominal gains.

The Bank of Ghana introduced universal banking in 2003, allowing banks to offer commercial, investment, and merchant banking services to customers. The real-time gross settlement system (RTGS) was launched to minimize risks and opportunities associated with running a cash-based economy. Other payment systems, including a paper-based clearing system and the National Switch (E-ZWICH), were introduced in 2006 and 2008. The E-ZWICH, most importantly allowed for the interoperability of all automated teller machines (ATMs) for customers of different banks, according to Bank of Ghana (2007). Since the introduction of the biometric card, it has improved efficiency and interoperability, leading to a 48.9% increase in card holders (Bank of Ghana 2010).

The Foreign Exchange Act (Act 723) in Ghana liberalized the foreign exchange regime, allowing FDI and foreign holdings of equities listed on the Ghana Stock Exchange. Non-residents were also allowed to invest in the money market for at least three years (Bank of Ghana 2007). This led to the creation of a financial market with bonds, equity, foreign exchange, and derivative markets. The reforms attracted foreign banks and investors, increasing competition and forcing banks to adopt best practices (Quartey and Afful-Mensah 2014). The number of commercial banks increased from 3 in the early 1990s to 21 by 2005 (Owusu-Antwi and Southeastern 2011), with about 121 rural and community banks operating in the economy. Innovative products like the Akuafo Bond improving savings habits of farmers in the country. The various reforms that were implemented resulted in a vibrant financial sector compared to other economies within the subregion.

Between mid-2017 and mid-2018, the Bank of Ghana conducted a financial-sector clean-up to sanitize the banking sector and protect depositors' interests. The exercise was prompted by failed regulators' efforts to address compliance lapses, including defiance of minimum capital, risk-taking without risk management, and weak corporate governance systems. The exercise resulted in the revoking of licences for 347 microfinance companies, 39 microcredit companies, and two non-bank institutions. This led to job losses (Mante 2020), loss of entrepreneurs' businesses, and decreased liquidity, affecting customer credit needs. Bank of Ghana data shows positive financial-sector outlook after clean-up, but Affum (2020) suggests that informal-sector workers lost confidence in the sector.

3. Data and empirical estimation

3.1 Data and model specification

Similar to Athukorala and Sen (2004) and Ang and Sen (2011), the empirical specification in this chapter is based on the life-cycle model (hereafter LCM), which provides a framework in which we are able to link the intertemporal decisions about consumption and therefore savings and its implications for investments and capital accumulation for long-term economic growth. Athukorala and Sen (2004) challenge the basic LCM's assumptions in developing countries, highlighting how inflation directly impacts the long-term value of accumulated wealth.

Based on the peculiarity of the Ghanaian context, we also consider other important determinants of savings to include economic growth GDP per capita, the age structure of the country (i.e. dependency ratio), the real interest rate on bank deposits, terms of trade, remittances, and money supply.

Based on the theoretical model discussed above, the empirical specification modelling the determinants of savings in Ghana is represented by the equation below:

$$PSAV = F(GDPG, GDPL, GDPLSQ, INF, RIR, MON, DOMCRE, TOT, DEPRATIO, REM) \quad (1)$$

Private savings (PSAV) is defined as the difference between gross savings and public savings, where public savings refers to the difference between government final consumption from government revenue. Private savings is expressed as a percentage of GDP, similar to its components. PSAV is also influenced by growth of GDP (GDPG) and GDP per capita (GDPL). Including both GDPG and GDPL is important because it captures the capacity of individuals to save, as inferred from the absolute income hypothesis, which directly relates income levels with savings. Both variables give an indication of how the economy is doing and therefore a proxy of household welfare. It is necessary to distinguish between the effect of higher growth on the level of current domestic savings and the effect on the level of GDP per capita on savings. While GDP growth is indicative of how well the economy is faring, GDP per capita captures the capacity of individuals to save. Moreover, the square term of GDPL (GDPLSQ) is included in the analysis to capture the possible non-linear effect of national income on savings.

All things being equal, it is expected that at lower levels of income there is dis-saving, given that consumption expenditure is more than income, which depicts the reality in most Ghanaian households. Many households operate at near-subsistence income levels, which may strengthen the motive for consumption smoothing. As income increases, however, the proportion of saved income should increase given that the proportion of income consumed decreases. This description suggests the inclusion of a square term of the level of income that is represented by GDPSQ. In addition to per capita income and growth, the age structure of the economy influences the capacity of households to save. Households with more dependents are less likely to save. Inward remittances can increase savings, although most are consumed.

While evidence shows that a significant proportion of remittances received by households in Ghana is used for consumption, it may increase the capacity of receiving households to increase their savings. REM in this study is defined as total remittances expressed as a percentage of GDP. As indicated earlier, terms of trade (ToT) serves as a signal for macroeconomic uncertainty in Ghana, which has implications for fiscal policies and hence savings. The ToT variable is computed as the difference between the value of exports and imports and is expressed as a percentage.

Savings are influenced by various financial sector variables, including inflation, real interest rate, money supply, and domestic credit. Inflation measures economic conditions, while real interest rate (RIR) is expressed as the nominal interest rate on deposits adjusted for inflation. Higher RIR leads to increased private savings. Domestic credit to the private sector (DOMCRE) facilitates capital formation. All other things being equal, the higher the credit to the private sector, the higher the savings. Broad money (MON) is a central bank policy tool to control inflation.

It serves as a proxy for the level of financial development in the economy and, therefore, the willingness of households to save. All things being equal, an increase in money supply is a good indication of access to financial assets and instruments, which increases an individual's willingness to save.

3.2 Empirical estimations

In most cases, economic analysis has relied on theoretical models to assume the existence of a long-run relationship between variables. Inherent in such assumptions are further assumptions that the variables in the model have constant means and variances that do not depend on time. Results from estimations that make such assumptions may lead to misleading inferences. To avoid relying on spurious regressions and inferences, recent econometric analysis using time-series data has increasingly relied on cointegration, which has proven to be a robust way of detecting the presence of a steady-state equilibrium between variables. In determining the existence of a true long-run relationship between series that are non-stationary, the bounds test of cointegration by Pesaran and Shin (1999) and Pesaran et al. (2001) has usually been employed.

Generally, the presence of a unit root indicates non-stationarity in a time series, while its absence signifies stationarity. Changes in mean, variance, covariance, and autocorrelation affect long-run relationships, violating ordinary least square (OLS) estimation assumptions.

As mentioned earlier, for any meaningful empirical analysis, the series would have to be purged, often through the process of detrending, which most often is done by undertaking the differencing given that most series are described as following a difference stationary process. In this process, however, the variables lose the relevant information or long-run properties of the equilibrium relationship between the variables under consideration. Cointegration is therefore a way of retaining the relevant long-run information of the relationship between the considered variables that were lost on differencing. Pesaran and Shin (1999) and Pesaran et al. (2001) use the autoregressive distributed lag (ARDL) technique to determine the long-run relationship between series with different orders of integration. The reparametrized results give the short-run dynamics and the long-run relationship of the variables under consideration in the model.

Table 11.1 Unit root test results

Variable	SBIC lag	ADF test		Phillips–Perron	
		t-statistic	Critical value (5%)	t-statistic	Critical value (5%)
SAV	1	−1.955	−2.966	−2.182	−2.964
GDPG	1	−4.604***	−2.966	−3.471**	−2.964
GDQSQ	1	0.446	−2.964	−0.108	−2.964
GDPLevel	1	0.592	−2.966	0.524	−2.966
INFLATION	1	−2.583	−2.966	−6.270***	−2.964
RIR	0	−5.237***	−2.969	−5.237***	−2.966
MON	1	−1.374	−2.966	−1.474	−2.964
ToT	1	−2.889**	−2.966	−3.527**	−2.964
DOMCRED	1	−1.534	−2.966	−1.498	−2.964
DEPRATIO	2	−0.217	−2.972	−1.302	−2.966
REMGDP	3	0.357	−2.972	−1.281	−2.964
EXT_DEBT	1	−4.914	−2.966	−1.569	−2.966

Note: *** $p < 0.01$, ** $p < 0.05$, * $p < 0.10$.
Source: authors' computations from data.

In ensuring that all variables are stationary, we start off with the stationarity test by employing the augmented Dicky–Fuller (ADF) and Phillips–Perron (PP) (Phillips and Perron 1988) tests to ascertain the order of integration of all the variables. The results from the ADF and PP tests are shown in Table 11.3. At levels, the only variables that show stationarity are GDP growth, inflation, real interest rate, and terms of trade for both the ADF and PP tests. However, after first differencing, all the non-stationary variables become stationary[1] (see Table 11.1).

3.3 Test for cointegration

This is a preferred technique because it offers the advantage of not requiring all the variables in the model to be integrated of order one or zero. In addition, the ARDL test can apply a number of lags to the variables separately, unlike the Johansen test, which restricts all variables to a uniform number of lags (Khalil and Dombrecht 2011). In addition, the test has been seen to be efficient with small and finite sample sizes, as seen in the current chapter. Ultimately, the ARDL model produces unbiased estimates of the long-run model (Harris and Sollis 2003).

[1] The dependency ratio was initially included in the model, but this became stationary only at the second difference. This was therefore eliminated from the model to allow for the estimation of the ARDL model in establishing whether or not there is a long-run relationship between the savings and the other variables in the model. The summary statistics for all variables used are shown in the appendix.

Table 11.2 Results of bound test (testing for existence of a level relationship among the variables in the ARDL model)

F-statistic	95% lower bound	95% upper bound	90% lower bound	90% upper bound
1.905	2.06	3.24	1.83	2.94
N = 35				

Source: authors' computations.

The null hypothesis of the bounds test is no long-run relationship or cointegration among the variables, while the alternative hypothesis is a long-run relationship among variables. Results from the bound test are shown in Table 11.2. The estimated *F*-statistic is 1.905. Compared to the lower- and upper-bound values of the Pesaran table of critical values, we accept the null hypothesis of no cointegration.

Based on the results from the bounds test, we conclude that the error correction model would not be appropriate. We therefore implement the ARDL model without the error correction model and show the short-run dynamics of the model. The short-run results from the ARDL model are shown in Table 11.3.

4. Results

4.1 Descriptive analysis of savings in Ghana: Trends

Private savings in Ghana has been remarkably low and characterized by fluctuations over time (Figure 11.1). Between 1980 and 2020 for instance, the country experienced large swings, with rates declining to as low as −13% and increasing to a high rate of about 12%. The significant decline in private savings between the early 1980s and early 1990s is reflective of the high economic instability during this period, which was characterized by en masse migration, loss of monetary control, high inflation, and declining investment (Osei et al. 2020). With the implementation of the Economic Recovery Programme (ERP), private savings began to show a positive response, reflecting stability in the economy, although this was short-lived. Over the following decade, private savings experienced major fluctuations, with the largest decline in private savings coinciding with the 2007/2008 global financial crises, beyond which savings maintained an upward trajectory, largely due to the impact of oil production and its favourable impact on the Ghanaian economy. The onset of Ghana's macroeconomics crises, which began

Table 11.3 Short-run coefficient estimates for the ARDL model

Variables	Coefficients	t-stats
SAV (L1)	0.305	1.01
GDPG	−0.483	−0.86
GDPG (L1)	−0.511	−1.34
GDPLSQ	1.45E-05	2.02*
GDPLSQ (L1)	2.78E-06	0.30
GDPL	−0.05	−1.84*
GDPL (L1)	0.003	0.08
INFLATION	−0.046	−0.47
INFLATION (L1)	−0.046	−1.08
RIR	0.078	0.85
MON	−0.488	−1.12
MON(L1)	1.332	3.02**
DOMCRE	−0.850	−1.51
DOMCRE (L1)	0.408	0.57
ToT	0.043	1.06
ToT (L1)	0.004	0.11
REM_GDP	0.788	1.37
REM_GDP (L1)	−0.139	−0.27
REM_GDP(L2)	0.096	0.13
REM_GDP (L3)	−0.660	−0.98
EXT_DEBT	−0.050	−0.57
EXT_DEBT(L1)	−0.07	−0.56
R-square	0.934	—
Adjusted R-square	0.777	—
Observations	35	—
Diagnostics	Test value	*P*-value
Breusch–Godfrey test for serial autocorrelation	11.108	0.0009
Breush–Pagan test for heteroskedasticity	0.30	0.58

Note: *** $p < 1\%$ significance, ** $p < 5\%$ significance, and * $p < 10\%$ significance.
Source: authors' computations.

in 2022 according to the World Bank,[2] precipitated a sequence of unfavourable outcomes that culminated in high inflation at about 54.3% in 2023. To mitigate the effects of the crises, the government of Ghana implemented the Domestic Debt Exchange Programme (DDEP). This programme negatively impacted households and corporate investors. Overall, the crises have resulted in rising poverty rates and worsening living standards, which is expected to have long-term impacts on private savings, setting in motion a familiar cycle of low private savings.

[2] See the World Bank in Ghana home page, available at: https://www.worldbank.org/en/country/ghana/overview (accessed 19 December 2024).

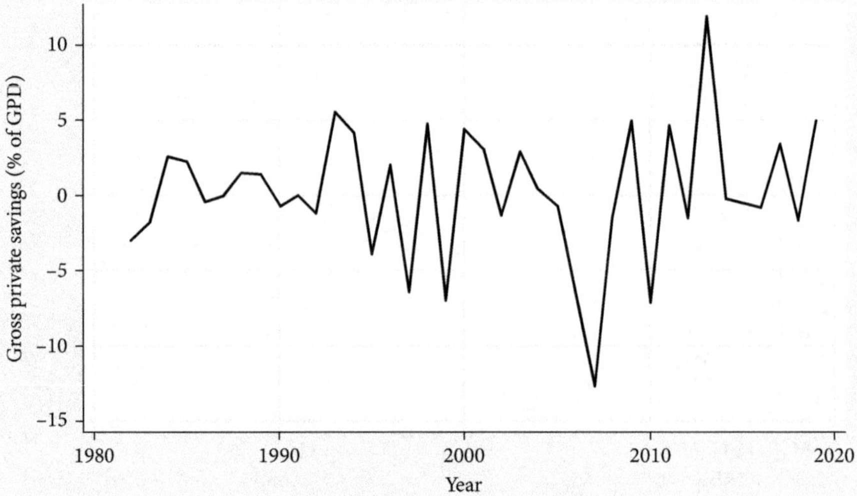

Figure 11.1 Trends in private savings, 1981–2019

Source: authors' calculations based on data from WDIs.

The empirical literature provides several reasons for the low savings rate in Ghana. Issahaku (2011), Osei (2011), Kwakwa (2013), and Larbi (2013) examined the determinants of savings in Ghana. Among other factors, these studies observed that Ghana's domestic savings rate is positively correlated with the level of per capita income. These studies argue that there is a positive relationship between economic wellbeing promotion and savings. They suggest that any policy directed towards the improvement of the welfare of households has the potential to generate increased domestic savings rates. Typically, these studies conclude that Ghana's low savings rate corresponds to low levels of income per capita. The results from these studies are consistent with the theory.

Figure 11.2 shows the trends in economic growth and private savings from 1980 to 2019. From the graph, an interesting patterning is observed. Private savings increase during economic downturns and reduce when the economy is doing better. For example, at the height of the economic crisis in 1981, both economic growth and private savings recorded significant declines. By the mid-1980s when the economy began to stabilize, private savings continued to increase significantly, peaking at 21% between 2003 and 2005 and then declining sharply to 0.6% in 2006. During this same period, economic growth picked up again between 2007 and 2011, during which time private savings had recorded its lowest in the country at −1.6%. Again between 2013 and 2019, economic growth declined steadily while savings continued to increase.

Figure 11.3 highlights the relationship between financial deepening (as measured by the ratio of direct credit to the private sector by banks to GDP) and

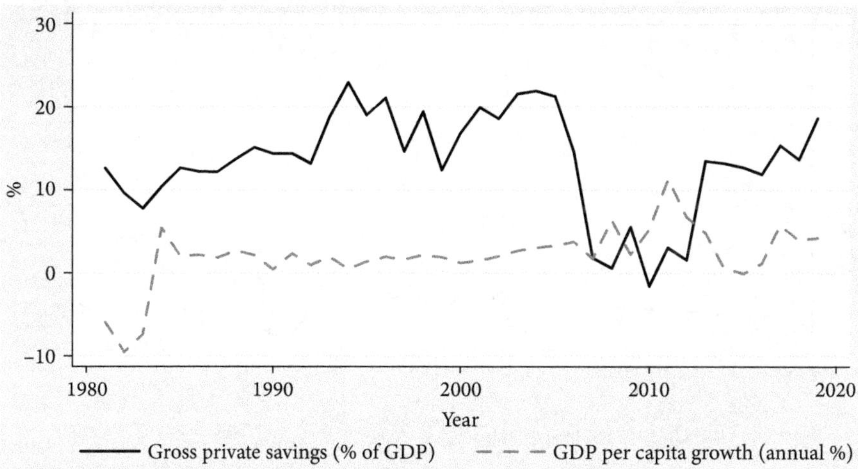

Figure 11.2 Trends in savings and GDP per capita growth, 1981–2019
Source: authors' calculations based on data from WDIs.

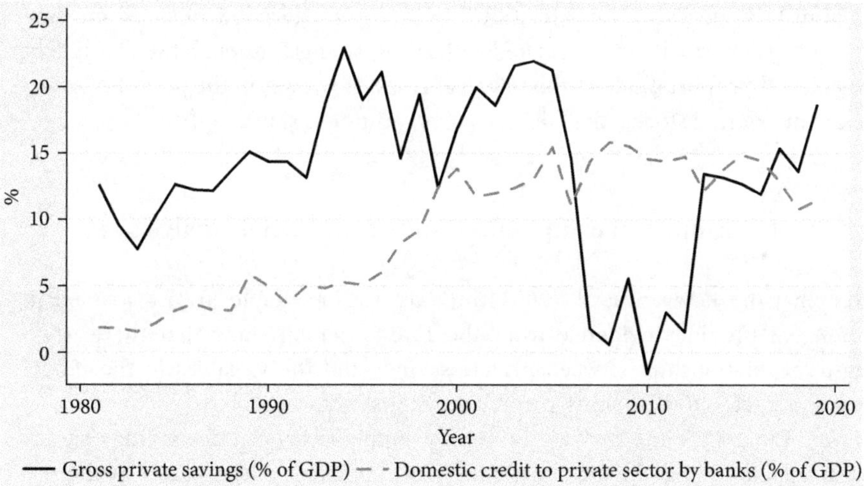

Figure 11.3 Trends in private savings and domestic credit to the private sector by banks, 1981–2019
Source: authors' calculations based on data from WDIs.

private savings. Over a long period, between 1981 and 2006, the data suggest a positive relationship between savings and credit to the private sector. However, from 2007, private savings witnessed a significant decline, while domestic credit remained high. Savings remained below 5% between 2007 and 2013, while domestic credit continued to increase over the same period. In 2014, however, the trend reversed, with domestic credit declining while private savings continued to soar.

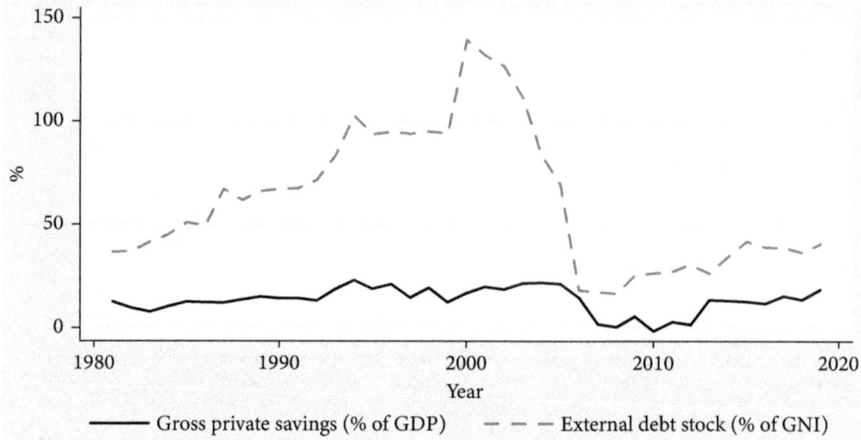

Figure 11.4 Trends in private savings and external debt stock, 1981–2019
Source: authors' calculations based on data from WDIs.

Figure 11.4 suggests a close relationship between external debt stock and savings. Rising debt stocks are associated with rising savings, although the rise in debt stocks is not proportionate to the rise in savings. However, in the period of sharp decline in external stocks, the fall in savings was not as sharp.

4.2 Empirical estimation results from ARDL analysis

Given that the Pesaran et al. (2001) bounds test (see Table 11.2) discussed in section 3.2 provides evidence from the *F*-tests, which show that there is no long-term relationship between private savings and the variables in the model considered, we show the short-run relationships in the model.

From Table 11.3, the first lag of money supply (financial deepening) significantly affects savings in the short run. The coefficient is significant at the 5% level. This finding suggests that the past year's level of money supply significantly impacts current levels of savings. A 1% increase in the previous period money supply increases current savings by about 1.33%, all things being equal. This suggests that economic agents are basing their current savings behaviour on the previous year's money supply. Interestingly, however, current levels of money supply have a negative effect on savings, although this is not statistically significant. We also note that per capita GDP negatively affects savings. This finding is significant at the 10% significance level. All things being equal, the results suggest that a 1% increase in per capita income reduces savings by about 5%. We note that the square term of per capita income is positive and significant at the 10% significance level. Taking these two results together, the results are indicative of the non-linear relationship between per capita income and savings in the Ghanaian context. As indicated earlier, at lower levels of income, there is likely to be dis-saving, given that consumption expenditure is more than income, which is what pertains in most Ghanaian households. Given that most households survive on near-subsistence income levels, all income is used on consumption expenditure. Increases in income at some point will induce some level of savings, as no income will be spent on consumption. This suggests that, beyond some income threshold, the proportion of saved income increases given that the proportion of income consumed decreases. Particularly, an increase in per capita income by US$1,000 beyond a certain threshold results in a 0.15% increase in savings. The Breusch–Godfrey and Breush–Pagan tests indicate evidence of serial correlation but no evidence of heteroscedasticity.

5. Conclusions and policy implications

This study aimed to explore the determinants of savings in Ghana using data from 1980 to 2019 and to establish whether or not there is a long-run relationship between savings and the other variables such as inflation, interest rate, and GDP growth. Overall, the econometric analysis and the bounds test find no compelling evidence that supports a long-run relationship between private savings and the variable in the model. However, estimates from the short-run analysis suggest that per capita income, per capita squared, and money supply significantly increase savings.

Our findings from the short-run dynamics suggest that, in line with the prediction of the absolute income hypothesis, there appears to be a significant relationship between savings and per capita income, although this is negative in the current study context. With a significant effect on the square of per capita income, we conclude that this effect is non-linear. Also, we find that the money supply from the previous period significantly increases savings, suggesting that previous money supply has a lingering effect on savings in the Ghanaian economy.

From the trend analysis, we also note that economic downturns are associated with high savings, indicating the rational expectations of economic agents. The correlation analysis provides evidence to support the importance of monetary and fiscal policies in the savings behaviour of economic agents. We find significant positive correlations between deposit interest rates and broad money and a negative relationship between savings and inflation. Regarding fiscal policies, we note that the external debt stock and budget deficits wield the strongest correlations with savings. While external debt stocks are positively associated with savings, budget deficits negatively correlate with savings.

Based on the findings, we make the following recommendations. First, given that savings become responsive to per capita income after a threshold, there is the need to continuously pursue policies to keep income levels of households high to trigger savings, as continuously rising income beyond a certain point would encourage savings so far as the basic needs of households are catered for. Policies that promote financial deepening should be pursued to improve savings in the country. Steps should be taken to ensure that the population is financially included to effectively increase savings. In view of the significant correlations between monetary and fiscal policies on savings, it is also recommended that sound monetary and fiscal policies be pursued to encourage savings and domestic savings mobilization. The absence of a long-run relationship suggests that the relationship between savings and the variables considered in the model are short-lived. The finding on the effect of the previous year's money supply on current savings is indicative of the importance of previous policies on financial deepening on current savings behaviour. This should guide policymakers given that current policies pursued to promote financial deepening have a significant effect on subsequent savings behaviour.

Appendix

Table 11.A1 presents some summary statistics for the variables considered in the study. The average private savings recorded over the period was about 14% of GDP, with the average GDP per capita of US$860 and growing at a rate of about 3%. Although the money supply was about one-quarter of GDP, the inflation rate also hovered around 25%, pushing the real interest rate below 1%. The high dependency ratio is indicative of the burden on the working population and its implications on savings. Similarly, the high terms of trade recorded may have implications on the average standard of living and, therefore, savings.

The determination of the optimal lag length is a critical component of estimating the ARDL model. The study employs the Schwartz Bayesian information criterion (SBIC) for the selection of optimal lags for the variables in this study for the period 1985–2019. (see Ackah and Lambon-Quayefio 2023: Table A2).

In Figure A1 of Ackah and Lambon-Quayefio (2023: 20), we note a strong correlation (p-value = 0.002) between savings and deposit interest rates. Inflation (p-value = 0.78) and broad money (p-value = 0.83)—even though the correlation coefficients are positive, suggesting a positive association between the variables—are not statistically significant.

Osei (2011) found that inflation negatively impacts domestic savings in Ghana, as it indicates a decline in welfare and increased consumption expenditure. Larbi (2013) found a positive relationship, suggesting individuals increase savings during high prices to protect against economic uncertainty.

Nwachukwu and Egwaikhide (2007) and Abu et al. (2013) found similar results for Nigeria and West Africa, respectively. Therefore, inflation may lead to increases

Table 11.A1 Summary statistics

Variable	Mean	Standard Deviation
Savings (% of GDP) (SAV)	13.6	6.46
GDP growth (%) (GDPG)	2.91	2.25
Square of GDPL (GDPLSQ)	1,263,981	1,693,614
GDP per capita ($USD) (GDPL)	886.749	701.218
Inflation rate (%) (INF)	20.29	12.11
Real interest rate (%) (RIR)	−7.574	15.705
Money supply (% of GDP) (MON)	23.974	6.103
Domestic credit to private sector (% of GDP) (DOMCRE)	9.997	4.578
Terms of trade index (%) (ToT)	96.386	24.388
Remittances (% of GDP) (REM)	1.710	2.481
External debt stock (% of GNI) (EXT_DEBT)	63.383	34.866
Observations	35	

Source: authors' computations.

in precautionary savings or impede savings when the inflation is higher than the returns on savings given that the net effect is not desirable. The correlation coefficients estimated suggests that Ghana's domestic savings rate is inversely related to inflation (see Ackah and Lambon-Quayefio 2023: Figure A1).

Furthermore, correlation analyses suggests that Ghana's domestic savings rate is positively correlated with its external debt accumulation and government spending and negatively correlated with taxes and budget deficit (see Ackah and Lambon-Quayefio 2023: Figure A2). However, the empirical evidence is mixed regarding the direction and magnitude of the impact of government actions on the economy.

Some studies have observed a positive relationship between the government budget deficit and savings (Hondrayiannis 2006; Ang and Sen 2011). Ang and Sen (2011) suggest that when the government runs a budget deficit, the private sector responds by saving more to offset any undesirable effect on future generations. In contrast, Ehikioya and Mohammed (2014) found that the government budget deficit exerts a detrimental effect on domestic savings in Nigeria. They argue that an increase in the budget deficit implies increased government expenditures over revenue. Consequently, public savings decreases. Since public savings constitute a share in domestic savings, a reduction in public savings will lead to a decline in domestic savings.

With regard to external debt, Nwachukwu and Egwaikhide (2007) and Uremadu (2007) found that external debt stock is positively correlated with domestic savings in Nigeria. They suggest that prudent management of government borrowing will have spill-over effects on the economy by increasing domestic savings to promote sustained economic growth. In contrast, other studies found that external debt negatively impacts domestic savings in Nigeria (Aliyu and Usman 2013; Chinaemerem and Anayochukwu 2013). They argue that external debt is a result of external borrowing, and accumulated debt acts as a future tax liability and derails domestic savings in the long run.

In the case of Ghana, the data show a strong correlation (p-value = 0.000 for both) between savings and external debt and government spending. As suggested in the literature, increased government spending and debt stock is a signal for increased liability in the future; hence, households save to hedge against increased taxes in the future. The correlation between budget deficit and savings is negative and statistically significant (p-value = 0.05), which is contrary to Ang and Sen (2011). While the correlation with government revenue is negative, this is not statistically significant (p-value = 0.58).

References

Abu, N., M. Z. Abd Karim, and M. I. A. Aziz (2013). 'Low Savings Rates in the Economic Community of West African States (ECOWAS): The Role of the Political Instability-Income Interaction'. *South-East European Journal of Economics and Business*, 8(2). https://doi.org/10.2478/jeb-2013-0010.

Ackah C. G., and M. Lambon-Quayefio (2023). ' Domestic Savings in Sub-Saharan Africa: The Case of Ghana'. World Institute for Public Policy Research and Analysis (WIDER) Working Paper 2023/38. Helsinki: United Nations University (UNU)-WIDER. https://doi.org/10.35188/UNU-WIDER/2023/346-8.

Adler, G., and M.N.E. Magud (2013). ' Four Decades of Terms-of-Trade Booms: Saving-Investment Patterns and a New Metric of Income Windfall', 9 May. Washington, DC: International Monetary Fund (IMF). https://doi.org/10.2139/ssrn.2276339.

Affum, F. (2020). 'The Unintended Effects of Bank of Ghana's Clean-Up Exercise on Unaffected Financial Institutions: Evidence from Yilo Krobo Municipality, Ghana'. *Asian Journal of Economics, Business and Accounting*, 17(1): 1–12. https://doi.org/10.9734/ajeba/2020/v17i130249.

Aliyu, R. M., and A. Usman (2013). 'An Econometric Study of the Impact of External Debt, Public Debt and Debt Servicing on National Savings in Nigeria: A Cointegration Approach'. *International Journal of Management and Social Sciences Research*, 2(2):73–83.

Aluko, O. A., and M. Ibrahim (2020). 'Institutions and the Financial Development–Economic Growth Nexus in Sub-Saharan Africa'. *Economics Notes*, 49(3): 1–16. https://doi.org/10.1111/ecno.12163.

Ang, J. B., and K. Sen (2011). 'Private Saving in India and Malaysia Compared: The Roles of Financial Liberalization and Expected Pension Benefits'. *Empirical Economics*, 43: 247–67. https://doi.org/10.1007/s00181-010-0386-3.

Appiah, M., F. Li, and D. I. Frowne (2020). 'Financial Development, Institutional Quality and Economic Growth: Evidence from ECOWAS Countries'. *Organizations and Markets in Emerging Economies*, 11(1): 6–17. https://doi.org/10.15388/omee.2020.11.20.

Aryeetey, E., and F. Tarp. (2000). 'Structural Adjustment & After: Which Way Forward?' In E. Aryeetey, J. Harrigan, and M. Nissanke (eds), *Economic Reforms in Ghana, The Miracle and The Mirage*, 344–65. Oxford: James Curry Ltd.

Aryeetey, E., A. Baah-Nuakoh, T. Duggleby, H. Hettige, and W. F. Steel (1996). 'The Formal Financial Sector in Ghana after the Reforms'. London: Overseas Development Institute.

Aryeetey, E., J. T. Harrigan, and M. Nissanke (2000). *Economic Reforms in Ghana: The Miracle and the Mirage*. Trenton, NJ: Africa World Press.

Athukorala, P., and K. Sen (2004). 'The Determinants of Private Saving in India'. *World Development*, 32: 491–503. https://doi.org/10.1016/j.worlddev.2003.07.008.

Bank of Ghana (2007). 'Building a Financial Sector for an Emerging Market Economy: Implications for the Capitalization of Banks and Non-Bank Financial Institutions'. Consultation Paper. Accra: Bank of Ghana.

Bank of Ghana (2010). 'Annual Report'. Accra: Bank of Ghana.

Bank of Ghana (2020). 'Bank of Ghana Banking Sector Report', January. Available at: https://www.bog.gov.gh/wp-content/uploads/2020/03/Banking-Sector-Report-January-2020.pdf (accessed 10 February 2023).

Bekoe, W., and P. K. Adom (2013). 'Macroeconomic Uncertainty and Private Investment in Ghana: An Empirical Investigation'. *International Journal of Economics and Financial Issues*, 3(2): 276–93.

Brownbridge, M., and A. F. Gockel (1996). ' The Impact of Financial Sector Policies on Banking in Ghana'. Institute of Development Studies (IDS) Working Paper 38. Brighton: IDS.

Céspedes, L. F., and A. Velasco (2014). 'Was This Time Different?: Fiscal Policy in Commodity Republics'. *Journal of Development Economics*, 106: 92–106. https://doi.org/10.1016/j.jdeveco.2013.07.012.

Chinaemerem, O. C., and O. B. Anayochukwu (2013). 'Impact of External Debt Financing on Economic Development in Nigeria'. *Research Journal of Finance and Accounting*, 4(4): 92–98.

Chowdhury, A. (2015). 'Terms of Trade Shocks and Private Savings in the Developing Countries'. *Journal of Comparative Economics*, 43(4): 1122–34. https://doi.org/10.1016/j.jce.2015.02.006.

Dutta, N., and D. Meierrieks (2021). 'Financial Development and Entrepreneurship'. *International Review of Economics and Finance*, 73(2021): 114–26. https://doi.org/10.1016/j.iref.2021.01.002.

Ehikioya, I. L., and I. Mohammed (2014). 'An Econometric Analysis of the Determinants of Private Savings in Nigeria (1981–2012)'. *International Journal of Social Science*, 4(5): 12–21.

Elbadawi, I. A., and F. M. Mwega (2000). 'Can Africa's Saving Collapse Be Reversed?' *World Bank Economic Review*, 14(3): 415–43. https://doi.org/10.1093/wber/14.3.415.

Feng, Y., and X. Yu (2020). 'The Impact of Institutions on Financial Development: Evidence from East Asian Countries'. *Australian Economic Papers*, 60: 122–37. https://doi.org/10.1111/1467-8454.12196.

Freytag, A., and S. Voll (2013). 'Institutions and Savings in Developing and Emerging Economies'. *Public Choice*, 157(3–4), 475–509. https://doi.org/10.1007/s11127-013-0121-7.

Gani, A., and T. Rasul, (2020), 'The Institutional Quality Effect on Credits Provided by the Banks'. *International Advances in Economic Research*, 26: 249–58. https://doi.org/10.1007/s11294-020-09794-0.

Gatsi, J. G., and M. Owusu Appiah (2020). 'Population Growth, Income Growth and Savings in Ghana'. *Journal of Economics and Development*, 22(2): 281–96. https://doi.org/10.1108/JED-12-2019-0078.

Gockel, A. F., J. K. Kwakye, and O. Baffour (1997). 'Financial and Monetary Developments: Policies and Options'. In V. K. Nyanteng, (ed.), *Policies and Options for Ghanaian Economic Development*, 2nd edn. Legon: University of Ghana, Institute of Statistical, Social and Economic Research (ISSER).

Harris, R., and R. Sollis (2003). *Applied Time Series Modelling and Forecasting*. New York: Wiley.

Haselmann, R., and P. Wachtel (2010). 'Institutions and Bank Behaviour: Legal Environment, Legal Perception, and the Composition of Bank Lending'. *Journal of Money, Credit and Banking*, 42(5): 965–84. https://doi.org/10.1111/j.1538-4616.2010.00316.x.

Ho, C.-Y., S. Huang, H. Shi, and J. Wu (2018). 'Financial Deepening and Innovation: The Role of Political Institutions'. *World Development*, 109: 1–13. https://doi.org/10.1016/j.worlddev.2018.02.022.

Hondrayiannis, G. (2006). 'Private Saving Determinants in European Countries: A Panel Cointegration Approach'. *Social Science Journal*, 43(4): 553–69. https://doi.org/10.1016/j.soscij.2006.08.004.

Issahaku, H. (2011). 'Determinants of Saving and Investment in Deprived District Capitals in Ghana—A Case Study of Nadowli in the Upper West Region of Ghana'. *Continental Journal of Social Sciences*, 4: 1–11.

Karikari, N. K., K.K. Gyan, M. A. H. Khan, and B. A. Kusi (2021). 'Institutional Quality and Social Cost of Intermediation in Africa: Does the Level of Financial Market Development Matter?' *International Journal of Finance and Economics*, 2021: 1–12. https://doi.org/10.1002/ijfe.2515.

Kebede, J., S. Selvanathan, and A. Naranpanawa (2021). 'Foreign Bank Presence, Institutional Quality, and Financial Inclusion: Evidence from Africa'. *Economic Modelling*, 102(2021): 1–15. https://doi.org/10.1016/j.econmod.2021.105572.

Keho, Y. (2011). 'Long-Run Determinants of Savings Rates in Waemu Countries: An Empirical Assessment from Ardl Bounds Testing Approach'. *South African Journal of Economics*, 79(3): 312–29. https://doi.org/10.1111/j.1813-6982.2011.01282.x.

Keynes, J. M. (2018). *The General Theory of Employment, Interest and Money*. Cham: Springer Nature Switzerland AG. https://doi.org/10.1007/978-3-319-70344-2.

Khalil, S., and M. Dombrecht (2011). ' The Autoregressive Distributed Lag Approach to Co-Integration Testing: Application to OPT Inflation'. Palestine Monetary Authority (PMA) Working Paper 3. Ramallah, Palestine: PMA.

Khwaja, A. I., and A. Mia (2011). 'Rent Seeking and Corruption in Financial Markets'. *Annual Review of Economics*, 3: 579–600. https://doi.org/10.1146/annurev-economics-061109-080310.

Kwakwa, P. A. (2013). 'Determinants of National Savings: A Short and Long Run Investigation in Ghana'. *KCA Journal of Business Management*, 5(1): 1–15.

Larbi, D. A. (2013). 'The Long-Run Determinants of Private Domestic Savings in Ghana: A Cointegration Approach'. *Journal of Economics and Sustainable Development*, 4(4): 125–36.

Leite, S. P. (1982). ' Interest Rate Policies in West Africa'. Staff Papers, 29: 48–76. Washington, DC: IMF. https://doi.org/10.2307/3866944.

Mante, T. (2020). 'Demystifying the Banking Sector Clean-Up', August. Available at: https://www.ghanaweb.com/GhanaHomePage/features/Demystifying-the-banking-sector-clean-up-1022902 (accessed 23 August 2020).

Ntow-Gyamfi, M., G. A. Bokpin, A. Q. Aboagye, and C. G. Ackah (2019). 'Financial Development, Institutional Quality and Inclusive Growth in Africa'. *Global Business Review*, 23(3) :584–607. https://doi.org/10.1177/0972150919875367.

Nwachukwu, T. E., and F. O. Egwaikhide (2007). 'An Error-Correction Model of the Determinants of Private Saving in Nigeria'. Presented at the African Economic Society (AES) Conference, Cape Town, South Africa, July.

Osei, V. (2011). 'Macroeconomic Determinants of Financial Savings in Ghana'. *Journal of Business Research*, 5(1–2): 75–95.

Osei, V., R. Darko, R. Atta-Ankomah, and M. P. Lambon-Quayefio (2020). ' Structural Transformation and Inclusive Growth in Ghana'. WIDER Working Paper 2020/37. Helsinki: UNU-WIDER. https://doi.org/10.35188/UNU-WIDER/2020/794-1.

Owusu-Antwi, G., and N. Southeastern (2011). 'Impact of Financial Reforms on the Banking System in Ghana'. *International Business & Economics Research Journal (IBER)*, 8(3). https://doi.org/10.19030/iber.v8i3.3116.

Pesaran, M., and Y. Shin (1999). 'An Autoregressive Distributed Lag Modeling Approach to Cointegration Analysis'. In S. Strom (ed.), *Econometrics and Economic Theory in the 20th Century: The Ragnar Frisch Centennial Symposium*, 371–413. Cambridge: Cambridge University Press.

Pesaran, M. H., Y. Shin, and R. J. Smith (2001). 'Bounds Testing Approaches to the Analysis of Level Relationship'. *Journal of Applied Economics*, 16: 289–326. https://doi.org/10.1002/jae.616.

Phillips, P. C. B., and P. Perron (1988). 'Testing for a Unit Root in Time Series Regression'. *Biometrika*, 75: 335–46. https://doi.org/10.1093/biomet/75.2.335.

Quartey, P., and G. Afful-Mensah (2014). 'Financial and Monetary Policies in Ghana: A Review of Recent Trends'. *Review of Development Finance*, 4(2): 115–25. https://doi.org/10.1016/j.rdf.2014.07.001.

Sanga, B., and M. Aziakpono (2022). 'The Effect of Institutional Factors on Financial Deepening: Evidence From 50 African Countries'. *Journal of Business and Socio-Economic Development*, 3(2): 150–65. https://doi.org/10.1108/JBSED-12-2021-0175.

Shen, Y., M. Shen, Z. Xu, and Y. Bai (2009). 'Bank Size and Small- and Medium-Sized Enterprise (SME) Lending: Evidence from China'. *World Development*, 37(4): 800–11. https://doi.org/10.1016/j.worlddev.2008.07.014.

Troilo, M., B. Walkup, M. Abe, and S. Lee (2019). 'Legal Systems and the Financing of Working Capital'. *International Review of Economics and Finance*, 64(2019), 641–56. https://doi.org/10.1016/j.iref.2018.01.010.

Uremadu, S. O. (2007). 'Core Determinants of Financial Savings in Nigeria: An Empirical Analysis for National Monetary Policy Formulation.' *International Review of Business Research Papers*, 3(3), 356–67.

Verma, R., and E. J. Wilson (2005). ' Savings, Investment, Foreign Inflows and Economic Growth of the Indian Economy 1950–2001.' Wollongong: University of Wollongong, Department of Economics, July. https://ro.uow.edu.au/commwkpapers/129.

12
The determinants of domestic savings in Cameroon

*Abrams Tagem and Desiree Sama-Lang**

1. Introduction

Domestic savings play a crucial role in the economic development process of countries. By increasing productivity and production in a given country, domestic savings contribute to financial capital accumulation, which is essential for development and increases the availability of capital for investment. Cross-country research has consistently found investment to be a key determinant of economic growth. While there is ambiguity about the direction of causality between domestic savings and growth (see Elbadawi and Mwega 2000 for a brief review), there is an unambiguous relationship between savings and growth (Ang and Sen 2011; Sen 2023). Additionally, high savings rates are associated with high domestic investment rates, as the latter act as a buffer against sudden reversals in international capital flows (e.g. foreign direct investment (FDI) and portfolio flows) as well as ongoing declines in overseas development assistance and remittances.

The empirical literature that estimates the determinants of savings falls into one of two types: cross-country regressions and country studies. The cross-country literature postulates various factors as determinants of cross-country private and gross savings, including (i) economic factors such as gross domestic product (GDP) per capita, economic growth, and household incomes (Athukorala and Sen 2004; Athukorala and Suanin 2024); (ii) financial sector variables such as interest rates, broad money (i.e. money supply), and domestic credit to the private sector (Loayza et al. 2000; Kelly and Mavrotas 2008; Nagawa et al. 2020); (iii) macroeconomic variables such as inflation, terms of trade shocks, and remittances (Ang and Sen 2011; Chowdhury 2015); and (iv) institutional variables such as trust in

*The authors thank Kunal Sen and Kenya Institute for Public Policy Research and Analysis (KIPPRA) for comments and discussions on this chapter. The authors also thank participants at the United Nations University (UNU)-World Institute for Public Policy Research and Analysis (WIDER) Workshop on Domestic Savings (March 2022) and participants at the UNU-WIDER Conference on 'Revving Up Revenue for Development—the Role of Domestic Resource Mobilization' (Oslo, 6–8 September 2023) for comments. Any errors are ours.

Abrams Tagem and Desiree Sama-Lang, *The determinants of domestic savings in Cameroon*. In: *The Domestic Savings Shortfall in Sub-Saharan Africa*. Edited by: Rose Ngugi and Kunal Sen, Oxford University Press. © UNU-WIDER (2025). DOI: 10.1093/oso/9780198932482.003.0012 public institutions, corruption, government effectiveness, and government stability (Swaleheen 2008; Freytag and Voll 2013; Boateng et al. 2019). While the above have been shown to be standard determinants of private and gross savings within and across countries, research also shows that there are idiosyncratic (context-specific) determinants of private savings that differ from those of government savings.

Financial-sector policies targeted at promoting incentives to save (e.g. financial-sector liberalization episodes, the adoption of fintech, and the development of long-term capital markets) are what drive private savings, while the overarching involvement of the state (i.e. domestic political economy factors) is most crucial for gross savings. These context-specific factors (which are the result of reforms implemented in different ways, at varying speeds, and with varying levels of political commitment) are more easily incorporated into country studies. This chapter is linked to this group of studies. The chapter contributes to the literature by estimating the robust determinants of private and gross savings in Cameroon over the period from 1980 to 2018, distinguishing between the standard and idiosyncratic determinants that are important in the Cameroonian context.

We focus on Cameroon for three reasons. First, Cameroon has a high level of savings but low growth in savings. Second, Cameroon is a resource-rich country that has historically depended on the production and exports of primary commodities for foreign exchange and government revenue. The performance of these primary commodities—whose prices are determined on international markets—are susceptible to the vagaries of international movements and leave the countries vulnerable to external shocks (especially terms of trade shocks). This can impact savings if economic agents smooth their consumption to guard against volatile commodity prices, or if changes in governments' fortunes alter public savings ratios (as expected). Third, institutional quality in Cameroon is low compared to peer countries. The country characteristically ranks badly in various rankings of institutional quality. For example, in 2022, Cameroon ranked 142nd out of 180 countries (up from 144th in 2021) in Transparency International's (TI) corruption perceptions index (CPI). For 2022, the Varieties of Democracy (V-Dem) regime corruption index puts Cameroon at 0.926 (for context, Denmark, which ranked first on TI's CPI, has 0.002) and the rule of law index at 0.103 (0.998 for Denmark).

There are three elements to the analysis. First, we employ the autoregressive distributed lag (ARDL) estimation method to ascertain the impact of various economic, financial-sector, macroeconomic, and institutional variables on savings aggregates in Cameroon. The ARDL method is attractive as it permits estimation of a long-run equilibrium (i.e. cointegrating) relationship between savings aggregates and their determinants and a distinction between long-run and short-run effects (by estimating an error correction model), while being theoretically agnostic about the order of integration of key variables, and it permits analysis of the dynamics of the error correction term. Our primary findings show that there is a cointegrating relationship between both savings aggregates and their determinants. In addition, both long-run and short-run effects match a priori expectations. Second, we incorporate various measures of institutional quality to gauge their direct impacts on savings aggregates. We find that the primary measure of corruption (i.e. the political corruption index) reduces savings aggregates, while the rule of law index is associated with higher savings. Third, we attempt to isolate the impact on savings aggregates of various global shocks and specific financial sector reforms, specifically the oil price hike of the early 1980s, the devaluation of the CFA franc in 1994, the 2008 global financial crisis, and the introduction of mobile money in 2012. We find the shock variables not to be particularly important (the oil price hike was associated with higher private savings), and we find a significant impact of the oil price hike on savings through its impact on terms of trade shocks. The CFA devaluation, the global financial crisis, and the introduction of mobile money all have no discernible impact on savings aggregates.

The rest of the chapter is organized as follows. Section 2 describes the policy context that underpins the evolution of savings in Cameroon, distinguishing between macroeconomic and financial sector policies. Section 3 discusses the analytical framework that underpins the economic analysis and the data and introduces the empirical specification. Section 4 presents findings on the time-series properties of the data, focusing on unit roots and cointegration tests. Section 5 presents the main results and some robustness checks and extensions. Section 6 summarizes the findings and concludes.

2. Policy context: Evolution of savings and associated performance in Cameroon

2.1 Macroeconomic policy context

The oil sector was the main source of foreign exchange in the early 1980s, contributing most to the country's foreign exchange (Khan 2011). Nevertheless, agriculture was still a fundamental cornerstone of the economy, specifically through foreign exchange earnings from primary crops like cotton, cocoa, and coffee. The increase in oil prices from the late 1970s resulted in the oil sector contributing significantly more to government revenue (through a threefold increase in export revenue), with the sector's contribution rising from 9% in 1980 to 41% in 1985 (Khan 2011). The increased oil revenues in the country mostly reflected the strong increase in foreign investment during that period, as most foreign investment was directed towards the booming natural resource sector. The surge in oil revenues contributed to an expansionary fiscal policy during that period, with government investment—especially in physical infrastructure and the manufacturing sector—increasing significantly and also as part of an import-substitution industrialization strategy. This was achieved through increased spending on the manufacturing and agro-industrial sectors, regularly supported by government subsidies.

The prices of primary commodity exports slumped considerably after 1986, resulting in a deterioration in terms of trade (export earnings dropped considerably), which plunged the country into a crisis. The economic effects were dire: export earnings, economic activity, and consequently economic growth shrank (the latter dropped by about 4%), FDI and other private capital flows plummeted, production of major cash crops dropped, and the real effective exchange rate appreciated (IMF 1996; Khan 2011). The drop in government revenues, coupled with the procyclical increase in spending during the oil boom years, resulted in huge fiscal deficits, which were ultimately financed by government loans (i.e. external and domestic borrowing). While these debts reduced the fiscal deficit, the loans invariably increased the debt stock, and the interest rates on the loans increased debt service costs, resulting in huge domestic and external arrears as well as depleted foreign exchange reserves. This economic condition underscored Cameroon's rapprochement with the International Monetary Fund (IMF) and World Bank, ultimately attracting a special drawing right worth US$62 million and a structural adjustment loan worth US$150 million.[1]

The economic crises that had dampened the external competitiveness of the country and contributed to an overappreciated exchange rate ultimately culminated in the devaluation of the CFA franc in 1994. The devaluation—accompanied by financial assistance, especially from multilateral donors—produced major upturns in economic activity in Cameroon, primarily through increased external competitiveness in export-orientated and import-substitution sectors, and hence improved terms of trade and economic growth (IMF 1996). Domestic demand increased following the devaluation, reflecting steady increases in both domestic consumption and investment. The containment of inflation, aided by the abundance of goods and services in the country and a containment of unit labour costs, also contributed to the upturn. Due to budget constraints, and as part of the structural adjustment programme, public investment and consumption declined while private-sector investment and consumption increased. The private sector thus contributed more to the expansion of domestic investment during the post-devaluation period.

The fiscal deficit was ultimately reversed to a surplus, with total government revenue increasing while total expenditure declined (IMF 1996). In the wake of the devaluation, and despite widespread tax evasion and the granting of discretionary tax exemptions, the government introduced several indirect tax reforms, which

[1] The loan was preceded by a debt-rescheduling episode involving the national authorities and Paris Club creditors.

contributed to boosting non-oil domestic revenues.[2] The rebound in non-oil exports—buttressed by the enhanced external competitiveness in the country and improved world prices—also contributed significantly to the increase in non-oil revenue mobilization. Timber played a dominant role, while export receipts from the primary commodity exports (i.e. cocoa, coffee, and cotton) also increased. Total oil revenue also increased, driven by two factors: the total surplus from the national oil company (SNH) was transferred to the central government budget, and there was a mild upturn in oil prices. Unstable non-interest expenditures, including civil servants' salaries and higher defence spending, created rigidity in government spending, albeit not enough to countervail the overall stability of government spending.

The devaluation, however, did not significantly alter the burden of debt (especially external debt) as debt soared considerably during that period. By the end of June 1999, total external debt amounted to US$7.8 billion—the present value of the debt-to-exports ratio exceeded 150%, while the present value of the debt-to-revenue ratio exceeded 250% (Khan 2011). This huge debt burden forced the country's admission into the Heavily Indebted Poor Country (HIPC) initiative in 2000. The government implemented economic reforms to stabilize the economy, albeit with recurrent slippages due to governance-related drawbacks, and ultimately reached the HIPC completion point in 2006. Reaching the HIPC completion point made the country automatically eligible for the Multilateral Debt Relief Initiative. The completion point was important as the debt relief opened up significant fiscal space, which the government could use to boost investment, increase civil servants' wages, and expand other social-sector spending to alleviate cost-of-living pressures, which had started to take hold (IMF 2007; Khan 2011). The additional fiscal space was, nonetheless, badly managed and the sustained increase in the cost of living (itself fuelled by increases in commodity prices, hence food inflation) resulted in demonstrations in February 2008. The government ultimately quelled the demonstrations by promoting economic measures such as reductions in prices of essential goods and increases in civil servants' salaries (IMF 2009).

The security situation in some regions of Cameroon has become progressively more precarious, resulting in deteriorating economic outcomes and widening fiscal deficits (mostly driven by increased social-sector and security spending). Terrorist or insurgent activities in the Lake Chad basin, perpetuated by the scourge of Boko Haram, and increasing insecurity in the Central African Republic have led to a surge in the number of refugees and internally displaced persons. Relatively recently, the crisis in the two anglophone regions has intensified, compounding

[2] The reforms included (IMF 1996): the creation of two large taxpayer units in Douala and Yaoundé, an increased turnover rate from 12.5 to 15%, and extension of the common tax or tariff regime to include public enterprises.

the significant security challenges already faced in other regions (IMF 2018a, 2019). The social unrest, which occasionally evolves into violent clashes between the government and splintered separatist groups, disrupts economic activity and weakens growth. This also makes it more difficult to collect taxes from obvious tax bases, while the government's legitimacy in the restive anglophone regions is eroded, contributing to low tax compliance. There has also been a huge increase in military spending to counter the impact of insurgents in the restive regions (thus diverting scarce government finances from where they may be most needed) as well as increases in social spending to deal with spiking internally displaced populations.

2.2 Financial-sector policy context

Cameroon's financial system is the largest in the Economic Community of Central African States (CEMAC) and accounts for more than one-half of the region's financial assets (IMF 2014). The financial system is dominated by commercial banks—total bank assets accounted for 70% of total financial-sector assets and 27% of GDP in 2017—although the system is highly concentrated and ultimately prone to concentration-related vulnerabilities. As of 2017, the four largest banks accounted for 59% of the total market share, and the two largest cities, Yaoundé and Douala, generated up to 90% of total bank credits and deposits (IMF 2018b).[3] The banking system remains shallow, with private-sector credit to GDP considerably lower when compared to peer countries.

The financial sector was not detached from the economic crisis that gripped the Cameroonian economy in the 1980s. Financial repression by the government, through huge government interference in banks' lending policies and the government's (majority) ownership of banks, added to weak supervisory frameworks, poor management, and excessive risk concentration, and a weak judicial system contributed to the crisis in the financial sector (IMF 2007; Khan 2011). This resulted in liquidity and solvency problems in the sector, which affected commercial banks (e.g. huge undercapitalization of banks) as well as non-bank financial institutions (IMF 2007). Structural adjustment programme (SAP) reforms also extended to the financial sector, specifically through measures focused on

[3] The financial sector also includes insurance companies, microfinance institutions, a stock exchange (i.e. the Douala Stock Exchange), government-owned specialized financial institutions, and non-banking financial institutions or informal services, the most popular of which are the *njangui*. In addition, a large proportion of the commercial banks are foreign-owned, e.g. CitiBank, ECOBANK, and United Bank of Africa, most of which are better capitalized (with higher capital adequacy ratios than domestic-owned banks, typically above 8%) than domestically owned banks. Most other financial sector entities suffer from chronically weak governance and oversight and operating losses. These include the Cameroonian Postal Service (CAMPOST) and the state-owned mortgage institution, Crédit Foncier du Cameroun, both of which have non-performing loans more than one-quarter of their total assets.

reducing the government's share in the capital of financial institutions (and withdrawing altogether from their management), liquidation of banks, restructuring (with higher branch concentration in major cities), privatization of non-performing institutions, and the issuance of government securities to commercial banks. The creation of the Central African Banking Commission (COBAC) was instrumental in the reform of the financial sector, with the institution tasked with enforcing the regulatory dispositions put in place.[4]

The microfinance sector has increasingly contributed more to the financial system's assets in Cameroon, rising from less than 5% in 2005 (Khan 2011). Their increased activity reflected commercial banks' inability or unwillingness to provide credit to the poor and micro, small, and medium-sized enterprises (MSMEs) and an increasingly rich middle class, as well as a decline in bank penetration, which resulted from the structural adjustment. However, the surge in microfinance institutions is not without structural and regulatory drawbacks, such as low capitalization and its limited ability to finance long-term development, weak credit risk assessment, poor governance (owner interventionism is endemic), and fragmented regulatory frameworks (limited supervision). In addition, and because of their lack of supervision, lending rates in microfinance institutions are very high, while their deposit rates are considerably low relative to commercial banks. These large interest rate differentials point to low financial intermediation in the financial sector (IMF 2009).[5]

Low financial inclusion also results from the prevalence of informal financing institutions, which can be distinguished between commercial and non-commercial financial institutions (Nissanke and Aryeetey 2008). The former are transactions conducted by traders, money lenders, and estate collectors; the non-commercial transactions are those between relatives, friends, and other small-scale groups. The most popular non-commercial informal financial service is the *njangui*, a community-based system of saving and lending money at concessional interest rates (i.e. rates lower than the market rates) with little or no collateral requirements.[6] While these informal institutions tend to offset low access to formal finance, they perpetuate the use of cash transactions as they are mostly unknown to the authorities and ultimately play a key financial intermediary role in the sector.

[4] One of the most significant changes introduced by COBAC was the abolition of the maximum lending rate by banks (which stood at 15%), which was considered insufficient to countervail perceived risks of lending (particularly to small and medium-sized enterprises).

[5] The Cameroonian government, upon suggestion from COBAC, set up a new bank for MSMEs in 2014. The bank was set up to cater to specific needs of MSMEs and its seed capital of CFAF10 billion was totally subscribed by the Cameroonian government (IMF 2014). It is unclear what impact, if any, this bank has had in galvanizing credit to the specific target group.

[6] These *njanguis* offer three types of financial instrument (IMF 2018b): periodic contributions (typically monthly), savings and loans, and solidarity funds. The *njanguis* are not without challenges, with elevated costs (interest rates on loans tend to be very high with short maturity periods), lack of regulation, small credit size, and susceptibility to insecurity.

Digital finance can contribute significantly to financial inclusion and intermediation under the right environment. Mobile banking was initiated in 2012, and its uptake has been huge: the number of mobile money accounts grew from 9% of adults in 2012 to 20% in 2020; the average number of active agents per km^2 increased from 4 in 2014 to 230 in 2020; and the number of mobile agent outlets per capita increased from 35 agents in 2014 to 709 in 2020 (IMF 2018b, 2022). The huge uptake can be attributed, in part, to the vast array of services they cover (e.g. money transfer, payment for purchases and shipments, payment of bills, and taxes). Nevertheless, digital financial inclusion is still low in Cameroon, and mobile money is used primarily as a means of transaction, not saving. Additionally, IMF (2022) shows a significant negative relationship between mobile banking activity and microfinance institution lending activities, suggesting that both substitute for, rather than complement, each other.

The financial system, however, is still fraught with challenges and vulnerabilities, which muddle its contribution to financial inclusion and intermediation. Despite its bank-dominated financial system, access to finance in Cameroon is very low and unevenly distributed (IMF 2018b). In 2021, bank account ownership was only 9% compared to 14% on average in sub-Saharan Africa (SSA). There has been a decline in bank penetration, and there are inefficiencies in the operating environment and difficulties in assessing credit risk. Financial intermediation, which has been shown to contribute to more efficient resource allocation and ultimately economic growth, is low in Cameroon. This has contributed to largely unsuccessful financial-sector liberalization in Cameroon. While the level of financial intermediation compares favourably with other CEMAC countries, it is lower than in other peers in SSA (IMF 2007, 2009). Key indicators of financial intermediation (i.e. broad money, deposits to GDP, and domestic credit to the private sector) compare unfavourably to SSA peers.

3. Data and empirical specification

3.1 Analytical framework and data

The life-cycle model (LCM) of savings underpins our empirical analysis. The theory posits that the primary reason for saving is to accumulate capital for retirement (Ando and Modigliani 1963); that is, the model is premised on the spending and saving habits of economic agents over the course of their lifetimes, incorporating their future incomes. Economic agents, through their consumption or saving behaviour, aim to maximize the net present value of their lifetime utility, subject to a budget constraint that equals the current net worth plus the present value of the expected labour income of the economic agent over their remaining working life. Assuming perfect capital markets and perfect foresight of the agent about the true income-generating process, the LCM theory is able to predict that consumption in a particular period depends on expectations of lifetime incomes (Athukorala and Sen 2004). As the agent's lifetime income fluctuates, their saving behaviour is crucially determined by what stage they are at in their life cycle: during the working years, the agent is a net saver but during retirement years becomes a dis-saver.

Modigliani (1993) extends the model to include the economic growth rate and demographic dynamics (i.e. age structure) as main determinants of gross savings, while Athukorala and Sen (2004) extend the model even further to include other variables (discussed below). The Keynesian model postulates that economic growth has predictive power on savings behaviour: higher growth rates can increase disposable income through increased production and productivity, which allows individuals to increase both consumption and savings simultaneously. The population growth rate is used as a proxy for demographic dynamics in a country (Modigliani 1986). The model postulates that population growth caused by increases in age-specific fertility rates increases the number of savers relative to the number of dis-savers. Nevertheless, there can be a theoretically ambiguous effect when an increase in the population growth rate increases not only the number of economically active individuals relative to those retired but also the share of the younger population (as both the young and retired consume more than they earn).

Other determinants of savings include economic, macroeconomic, financial-sector, and institutional variables (Masson et al. 1998; Freytag and Voll 2013; Sahoo and Dash 2013; Chowdhury 2015; Grigoli et al 2017, 2018; Boateng et al 2019). The economic variables include GDP per capita and GDP per capita growth. We expect a positive relationship between per capita GDP and savings behaviour, with steady improvements in development levels linked to increases in production and productivity, hence higher disposable incomes and savings rates. In addition, GDP per capita can be seen as a proxy for agents' capacity to accumulate capital and save. Likewise, per capita growth is expected to increase savings through economic expansion and its attendant benefits.

The macroeconomic variables include the terms of trade index and inflation (percentage change in the consumer price index). The terms of trade index serves as a useful proxy for macroeconomic uncertainty (Chowdhury 2015). Strong fluctuations in tradable commodity prices (especially for natural resource and primary agricultural products, prices of which are determined on international markets) result in volatility in trade balances and government revenues, and potentially impact disposable income and savings behaviour. The net effect, however, depends on the perception of the duration of changes in the terms of trade index, that is whether the changes are temporary or permanent. The relationship between private consumption and domestic savings is straightforward: increases in household consumption reduce disposable income that can otherwise be saved, resulting in reduced savings rates. Inflation is a good proxy for the prevailing macroeconomic conditions within an economy, with high inflation implying that people get to spend more of their disposable income, hence they have less savings.

Inflation can also reduce savings by increasing the uncertainty about the future value of accumulated savings (which will ultimately be eroded as savings are not indexed to changes in incomes or prices). Conversely, inflation can create uncertainty about future income streams, causing savings to increase on a precautionary or pre-emptive basis (Athukorala and Sen 2004).

Financial-sector variables include broad money (% GDP), domestic credit to the private sector (% GDP), and the deposit interest rate.[7] Broad money, a proxy for money supply or financial intermediation depth across countries, increases the willingness of households to save. Domestic credit to the private sector, a proxy for financial depth across countries, measures financial resources provided to the private sector by financial corporations (e.g. through loans, trade credits, and other purchases). Increased credit permits greater investment and expansion of economic activity, resulting in higher (disposable) income, hence more saving.

Institutions are also expected to have a significant impact on private and gross domestic savings. Various proxies for institutional quality are expected to impact savings through different mechanisms, with better institutional quality associated with deeper financial markets across countries. For example, poor rule of law creates weak law enforcement of contracts, which reduces bank credit and increases the cost of financial intermediation. Poor regulatory quality exacerbates the fragmentation of financial markets and products, inflating transaction costs. Conversely, high regulatory quality eases credit constraints, which reduces the cost of doing business in the economy (Feng and Yu 2021). Furthermore, corruption is anathema to all development outcomes as it causes inefficiencies and diversion of resources from productive instruments, increases the cost of doing business, limits access to financial resources and markets, and discourages entrepreneurs from investing (Freytag and Voll, 2013; Sahoo and Dash 2013; Sanga and Aziakpono 2022). In this chapter, we obtain data from the International Country Risk Guide (ICRG) data set (ICRG 2018), the World Governance Indicators (WGI) database (World Bank 2024), and the V-Dem data set (Coppedge et al. 2023). From the ICRG data set, we obtain data on bureaucratic quality; from the WGI database, we obtain data on all measures of institutions; and from the V-Dem data set, we collect data on the political corruption index and the rule of law index.[8]

3.2 Empirical specification

Guided by the theoretical considerations above, we intend to estimate two savings equations using the same set of regressors. The first equation posits the determinants of private savings (*SPV*) as follows:

[7] Due to unavailability of data, none of the interest rate variables were included.

[8] The WGI includes six measures of institutions: voice and accountability, government effectiveness, rule of law, political stability, regulatory quality, and control of corruption.

$$SPRV = f(SPB, GY, GPOP, TOT, FIN, INF, INS, W, GPOP, RID, LY) \quad (1)$$

The second equation posits the determinants of gross national savings (*SNAT*) as follows:

$$SNAT = f(GY, GPOP, TOT, FIN, INF, INS, W, GPOP, RID, LY) \quad (2)$$

where *SPRV*, *SNAT*, and *SPB* are, respectively, the private savings, gross national savings, and public savings ratios (all expressed as a percentage of GDP). The public savings ratio is calculated as the difference between government revenue and government final consumption expenditure (i.e. general government consumption), while private savings is calculated as the difference between gross savings and public savings. *GY* represents the per capita GDP growth rate, while *GPOP* denotes the population growth rate. *LY* is the log of GDP per capita, *ToT* is the terms of trade index, *RID* is the real interest rate, *W* is broad money (a proxy for financial intermediation), *INF* is the rate of inflation (i.e. the percentage change in the consumer price index), *FIN* is domestic credit to the private sector, and *INS* represents measures of institutional quality. All variables are obtained from the World Development Indicators (WDI) database (World Bank 2023), covering the period from 1980 to 2018.

To estimate equations (1) and (2) above, we employ the ARDL method (Pesaran et al. 2001).[9] The method is suitable for linear time-series modelling, particularly given our interest in establishing a long-run relationship between savings aggregates and other macroeconomic and institutional variables. The ARDL method suits our analysis in two key dimensions: first, it is possible to include a mixture of variables with different orders of integration—specifically I(0) and I(1)—in the same model and, second, it permits distinguishing between the long-run and short-run effects of independent variables on savings rates.

The generalized ARDL (*p*, *q*) model with *k* explanatory variables is specified thus:

$$SPRV_t = \gamma_0 + \beta_1 SPRV_{t-1} + \ldots + \beta_p SPRV_{t-p} + \alpha_0 X_t + \alpha_1 X_{t-1} + \ldots + \alpha_q X_{t-q} + \varepsilon_t \quad (3)$$

$$SNAT_t = \gamma_0 + \beta_1 SNAT_{t-1} + \ldots + \beta_p SNAT_{t-p} + \alpha_0 X_t + \alpha_1 X_{t-1} + \ldots + \alpha_q X_{t-q} + \varepsilon_t \quad (4)$$

where the dependent variables and their lags are defined as above, X_t is a $(kx1)$ matrix of independent variables described above, γ_0 is the constant term, and

[9] See Musamali et al. (2022), Were and Joseph (2022), and Ackah and Lambon-Quayefio (2023) for similar analysis focusing on Kenya, Tanzania, and Ghana, respectively.

ε_t is the error term with standard *i.i.d* properties. The dependent variables are explained by lags of themselves (the autoregressive component, included up to lag order p), as well as by current and lagged values of independent variables (up to q lags). In the presence of cointegration, equations (3) and (4) can be compressed and re-parameterized into an unrestricted error correction model (ECM) of the form:

$$\Delta Y_t = \gamma_0 + \sum_{i=1}^{p} \delta_i \Delta Y_{t-i} + \sum_{i=0}^{q} \delta_i \Delta X_{t-i} + \lambda (Y_t - \theta X_t) + \varepsilon_t \qquad (5)$$

where $\lambda = \left(1 - \sum_{i=1}^{p} \delta_i\right)$ is the speed of adjustment to equilibrium, the expression in brackets is the long-run (cointegrating) relationship between variables, and $\theta = \frac{\sum_{i=0}^{q} \pi_i}{\left(1 - \sum_{i=1}^{p} \delta_i\right)}$ is the long-run parameter.[10] If $\lambda = 0$, then there is no evidence of a long-run relationship between savings (both private and gross) and their respective determinants. The parameter is expected to be significantly negative under the prior assumption that, following a deviation, the variables return to their long-run equilibrium (cointegration). In addition to the above, the method is more efficient for samples with small-to-moderate time-series properties and allows for post-estimation diagnostics to be carried out.[11]

The unrestricted ECM formulation has the following advantages over other dynamic panel methods. First, it permits differentiation between long-run and short-run effects. The intuition is that while short-run deviations may exist (such deviations may result from domestic fiscal policy and financial sector reforms, as well as from the influence of donors through foreign aid disbursements and structural adjustment loans), the variables are expected to co-evolve in the long run. Second, it permits testing for cointegration by analysis of the adjustment coefficient. Third, it allows analysis of the EC term and the speed of adjustment for the economy to the long-run equilibrium.

4. Time-series properties of the data

4.1 Tests for stationarity

Time-series data is typically characterized by trends (either upwards or downwards) linked to their order of integration, and including variables of different

[10] The presence of a cointegrating relationship (i.e. an equilibrium long-term relationship) between the dependent and independent variables is a prerequisite for this re-parameterization.

[11] Standard post-estimation diagnostics include normality tests, first- and second-order serial correlation, heteroskedasticity, model misspecification, and model stability tests (see Cameron and Trivedi 2010 for details).

orders of integration in one regression inevitably results in spurious econometric analysis. The ARDL model inherently deals with this issue by permitting a mixture of (at most) I(0) and I(1) variables, that is variables stationary in levels or, at most, first-differenced stationary, respectively.[12] To assess the order of integration of the variables, we employ the augmented Dickey–Fuller (ADF) and Phillips–Perron (PP) tests. Both tests are for the null hypothesis that the variable series has a unit root (i.e. the variable is non-stationary) against the alternative that the variable is a stationary process. See Tagem and Sama-Lang (2024: Tables 1a and 1b) for stationarity tests for variables in levels and first differences, respectively. The null hypothesis can be rejected (or not) at standard levels of significance or if the absolute value of the test statistic is larger than the critical values at conventional levels of significance. Even after including lags and a trend, some variables are stationary in levels while others are non-stationary (first differencing these non-stationary variables renders them stationary). We conclude that we have a mixture of I(0) and I(1) variables, so the ARDL model is suitable.

4.2 Tests for cointegration

As our variable series are a mixture of I(0) and I(1) processes, the most suitable technique to test for the presence of a long-run relationship amongst the variables is the bounds test for cointegration (Pesaran et al. 2001). The test, which generates an *F*-statistic that is compared with critical value bounds at standard levels of significance, is for a null hypothesis of no long-run (cointegrating) relationship between variables. The test reports lower and upper bounds, i.e. I(0) and I(1), respectively. The decision rule is to reject the null hypothesis if the *F*-statistic is greater than the critical value for I(1) regressors at given levels of significance (see Tagem and Sama-Lang 2024: Table 2).[13] Columns (2) and (3) present the results for private savings, while columns (4) and (5) present the results for gross savings. Both panels show that across various levels of significance, the *F*- statistic is greater than the critical value for I(1) regressors, so we can comfortably reject the null hypothesis of no long-run relationship between the savings aggregates and their respective determinants. This allows us to re-parameterize the ARDL model and estimate it as an ECM.

[12] It is important that the variables be, at most, first-difference stationary (i.e. I(1)). In the presence of higher-order levels of integration (e.g. I(2)), the critical values of the stationarity tests become invalid.

[13] The bounds test also generates a t-statistic which is compared with the critical value bounds. The decision rule is to reject the null hypothesis if the t-statistic is less than the critical value of I(1) regressors at given levels of significance. See Tagem and Sama-Lang (2024: Appendix Table A1) for the cointegration test results with the t-statistic.

5. Results

5.1 Baseline results

5.1.1 ECM analysis for private savings

It is necessary to ascertain the validity of an empirical time-series model: a valid model is expected to be normal and have no autocorrelation and heteroskedasticity, and the coefficients must be structurally stable. Diagnostic tests to ascertain the viability of the ARDL model are reported in panel B of Table 12.1. The Breusch–Godfrey Lagrange Multiplier (LM) test confirms the absence of serial correlation across models, the Breusch–Pagan/Cook–Weisberg test confirms that the models are homoscedastic, and the Jarque–Bera test confirms normality across models. As one can never assume against structural breaks in time-series analysis (especially assumptions concerning specific break dates), we check for stability of estimates using the cumulate sum (CUSUM) and cumulative sum of squares (CUSUMSQ) tests. Both plots fall within the boundaries of the 5% significance level, suggesting that the primary model is stable (see Tagem and Sama-Lang 2024: Appendix Figure A1).

Panel A of Table 12.1 shows that in the long run, public savings, GDP per capita growth, terms of trade, domestic credit to the private sector, and inflation are the robust determinants of private savings (column 1). Public savings have a negative impact on private savings, suggesting that in the Cameroonian context, public savings crowd out private savings (see Athukorala and Sen 2004 and Freytag and Voll 2013 for similar findings). This negative relationship can be attributed to the large fiscal deficits that have characterized the Cameroonian economy during the period under review. Strong economic growth reinforces capital accumulation, which expands the amount of credit available for lending to individuals (in addition to other attendant benefits), an effect that can be reinforced by individuals saving more when they know they can easily have access to credit. Also consistent with the life-cycle hypothesis theory, an increase in GDP per capita growth is associated with increased private savings through higher income per capita permitting increased savings and consumption.

The terms of trade index has a negative relationship with private savings, suggesting that agents increase their savings in response to a terms of trade deterioration; that is, when the terms of trade increases (a deterioration), agents increase their savings to forestall, or at least countervail, the negative impact of the terms of trade increase. Domestic credit to the private sector has a positive relationship with private savings, consistent with the fact that as the financial system improves (i.e. through high levels of private-sector increasing growth), it motivates private individuals to save more. Inflation is positively associated with private savings,

Table 12.1 Long-run analysis for private savings

	(1)	(2)	(3)	(4)	(5)	(6)	(7)
				Panel A: Long-run coefficients			
SPB	−1.227*** (0.284)	−1.088*** (0.250)	−1.127*** (0.214)	−1.253*** (0.259)	−0.587*** (0.099)	−1.212*** (0.299)	−2.078*** (0.486)
Log GDP per capita	3.298 (2.821)	5.310* (2.677)	2.589 (3.066)	2.695 (2.559)	0.604 (0.999)	3.426 (3.131)	−7.764 (4.876)
Domestic credit	0.233*** (0.077)	—	0.338*** (0.095)	0.151* (0.076)	−0.059 (0.035)	0.230*** (0.081)	0.164** (0.069)
ToT	−0.117** (0.043)	−0.180*** (0.034)	−0.093** (0.044)	−0.050 (0.058)	− 0.054*** (0.019)	−0.116** (0.048)	−0.123*** (0.041)
GDP growth	0.383** (0.158)	0.324** (0.148)	0.330** (0.128)	0.385** (0.142)	−0.024 (0.070)	0.386** (0.162)	0.642*** (0.199)
Inflation	0.357*** (0.078)	0.350*** (0.073)	0.334*** (0.066)	0.290*** (0.076)	0.115** (0.051)	0.354*** (0.086)	0.393*** (0.079)
Broad money	—	0.366** (0.132)	—	—	—	—	—
Population growth	—	—	−5.466 (3.782)	—	—	—	—
Urban population	—	—	—	−0.262 (0.155)	—	—	—
Household consumption	—	—	—	—	−0.804*** (0.119)	—	—
Remittances	—	—	—	—	—	−0.353 (3.464)	—
Debt	—	—	—	—	—	—	−0.123** (0.045)
Adjustment term	−0.644*** (0.126)	−0.701*** (0.126)	−0.731*** (0.116)	−0.692*** (0.125)	−0.637*** (0.130)	−0.648*** (0.133)	−0.537*** (0.104)

Continued

Table 12.1 *Continued*

	(1)	(2)	(3)	(4)	(5)	(6)	(7)
				Panel B: Diagnostic tests			
R-squared	0.867	0.840	0.890	0.882	0.984	0.867	0.919
LM *p*-value	0.387	0.932	0.163	0.537	0.994	0.364	0.826
BP *p*-value	0.420	0.269	0.313	0.176	0.607	0.229	0.323
JB *p*-value	0.926	0.891	0.989	0.911	0.618	0.931	0.989
Observations	35	35	35	35	35	35	35

Note: panel A reports long-run results from estimating the ARDL with private savings as dependent variable, with column (1) representing the baseline model. Standard errors are reported in parentheses (***$p \leq 0.01$, **$p \leq 0.05$, *$p \leq 0.1$). SPB is the public savings ratio and ToT is the terms of trade index. Panel B reports the diagnostic tests for the various models from columns (1)–(7) (see Cameron and Trivedi 2010 for details). LM *p*-value is for the Breusch–Godfrey LM test for autocorrelation (null hypothesis is no serial correlation), BP *p*-value is for the Breusch–Pagan/Cook–Weisberg test for heteroskedasticity (null hypothesis is homoskedasticity), and JB *p*-value is for the Jarque–Bera normality test (null hypothesis of normality).

Source: authors' construction.

suggesting that pre-emptive increases in private savings in response to inflation are common in the Cameroonian context.

Institutional variables were introduced independently, and the results can be summarized thus (see Tagem and Sama-Lang 2024: Table 4). First, the ICRG variable (bureaucratic quality) was positive but insignificant. Second, the V-Dem variables (political corruption, rule of law, and vertical accountability) were insignificant. Third, all institutional variables from the WGI database were also insignificant. Columns (2)–(7) of Table 12.1 report the results for additional determinants of private savings.[14]

The short-run results show that only private savings, terms of trade, and inflation have significant effects on private savings (see the appendix at Table 12.A1). The lagged change in private savings is associated with lower private savings, while terms of trade has an uncertain impact on private savings as both effects are at play. The immediate short-run effect of terms of trade is positive (which shows that a deterioration of terms of trade results in lower savings if agents are hugely affected by lower commodity prices), while the lagged short-term effect is negative (again, suggesting that agents increase their savings to countervail the effects of terms of trade deteriorations). Inflation also has a negative short-run impact on private savings, suggesting that, in the short run, the opportunity cost of holding liquid assets is higher, resulting in reduced savings. The negative effect may also reflect individuals' inability to adjust to increased costs of living in the short run (changes in cost of living have a huge unexplained component to them).

5.1.2 ECM analysis for gross savings

The diagnostic tests ascertain the suitability of our model with gross savings (panel B of Table 12.2): none of the diagnostic tests can reject the respective null hypotheses of normality and heteroskedasticity, and both CUSUM and CUSUMSQ plots fall within the boundaries of the 5% significance level (see Tagem and Sama-Lang 2024: Appendix Figure A2). The diagnostics, however, reject the null hypothesis of no serial correlation.

Panel A of Table 12.2 shows that the main determinants of gross savings are GDP per capita, domestic credit to the private sector, terms of trade, and inflation (column 1). GDP per capita is positive and significant, consistent with the literature, which suggests that higher output per capita is associated with higher savings through increases in production and productivity, which ultimately increase disposable incomes (Athukorala and Sen 2004; Were and Joseph 2022). In addition, for countries with comparatively lower income levels, a small increase in economic

[14] Other economic variables are included to ascertain (i) their direct impacts on private savings and (ii) the robustness of the primary variables to the inclusion of these additional controls (see Tagem and Sama-Lang 2024: s. 5.2 for a discussion).

Table 12.2 Long-run analysis for gross savings

	(1)	(2)	(3)	(4)	(5)	(6)	(7)
			Panel A: Long-run coefficients				
Log GDP per capita	7.662** (3.032)	7.460 (5.677)	11.290*** (3.441)	7.732*** (2.738)	1.561 (3.206)	6.452* (3.401)	14.079*** (3.629)
Domestic credit	0.150*** (0.047)		0.158*** (0.047)	0.017 (0.067)	0.022 (0.068)	0.147*** (0.049)	0.096* (0.052)
ToT	−0.103** (0.044)	−0.101 (0.073)	−0.131*** (0.045)	−0.008 (0.057)	0.069 (0.060)	−0.134** (0.054)	−0.215*** (0.031)
GDP growth	0.438*** (0.124)	0.229 (0.228)	0.415*** (0.124)	0.422*** (0.112)	0.129 (0.163)	0.372** (0.143)	0.516*** (0.093)
Inflation	0.388*** (0.081)	0.497*** (0.162)	0.431*** (0.085)	0.299*** (0.079)	0.149* (0.087)	0.422*** (0.092)	0.471*** (0.025)
Broad money	—	0.187 (0.192)	—	—	—	—	—
Population growth	—	—	−5.540* (2.719)	—	—	—	—
Urban population	—	—	—	−0.409** (0.166)	—	—	—
Household consumption	—	—	—	—	−0.958*** (0.280)	—	—
Remittances	—	—	—	—	—	4.173 (4.019)	—
Debt	—	—	—	—	—	—	−0.023 (0.025)
Adjustment term	−0.749*** (0.103)	−0.480*** (0.098)	−0.699*** (0.099)	−0.754*** (0.094)	−0.548*** (0.116)	−0.714*** (0.107)	−0.864*** (0.071)

			Panel B: Diagnostic tests				
R-squared	0.832	0.678	0.860	0.866	0.899	0.839	0.934
LM *p*-value	0.006	0.760	0.189	0.029	0.699	0.008	0.625
BP *p*-value	0.983	0.000	0.949	0.612	0.458	0.562	0.384
JB *p*-value	0.448	0.770	0.613	0.817	0.511	0.758	0.823
Observations	37	38	37	37	37	37	37

Note: panel A reports long-run results from estimating the ARDL with gross savings as dependent variable, with column (1) representing the baseline model. Standard errors are reported in parentheses (***$p \leq 0.01$, **$p \leq 0.05$, *$p \leq 0.1$). ToT is the terms of trade index. Panel B reports the diagnostic tests for the various models from columns (1)–(7) (see Cameron and Trivedi 2010 for details). LM *p*-value is for the Breusch–Godfrey LM test for autocorrelation (null hypothesis is no serial correlation), BP *p*-value is for the Breusch–Pagan/Cook–Weisberg test for heteroskedasticity (null hypothesis is homoskedasticity), and JB *p*-value is for the Jarque–Bera normality test (null hypothesis of normality).

Source: authors' construction.

expansion is associated with a higher marginal propensity to save, boosting gross savings (i.e. both private and public savings) in the country. Domestic credit to the private sector has a positive relationship with gross savings. While standard models of saving behaviour postulate a precautionary saving motive by which total savings fall when access to credit improves, the positive relationship here suggests that individuals or businesses will find it safer to keep their financial assets in financial institutions and still have access to credit. It may also be the case that excess credit contributes to an expansion of the economy, which then encourages both consumption and saving.

We find a strong negative relationship between gross savings and the terms of trade index, suggesting that adverse shocks to commodity prices (i.e. a terms of trade deterioration) are associated with attempts to smooth consumption in the face of such shocks, hence increased gross savings (similar to the results above with private savings). This finding is unsurprising given Cameroon's strong dependence on primary commodity exports, the prices of which are susceptible to unpredictable changes (see section 2.1). In the long run, higher inflation is associated with higher domestic savings. While higher inflation increases the opportunity cost of holding liquid assets in comparison with spending, it also creates uncertainty about future income streams, which incentivizes an increase in (precautionary or pre-emptive) savings.

Measures of institutions were introduced analogously to the model with private savings (Table 12.3). The ICRG and WGI variables are all insignificant, while the V-Dem variables (political corruption and rule of law) are significant. The political corruption index has a strong negative impact on gross savings, which may result from increased costs of doing business and limited access to financial resources and markets. Swaleheen (2008) shows that corruption adversely affects savings by encouraging capital flight. Freytag and Voll (2013) show that better economic institutions (but not necessarily better political institutions) increase private savings. Facchini et al. (2024) show that, while institutions themselves do not impact private savings, trust in political institutions—specifically institutions at the higher level (politicians) and institutions responsible for passing laws (parliament)—is a significant driver of private savings in Organisation for Economic Co-operation and Development (OECD) countries. As the political corruption index measures different types of corruption ranging from petty to grand corruption, bribery, and theft as well as to corruption aimed at influencing law-making and policy, the specific effect that drives the negative effect on savings is difficult to decipher. The rule of law index has a positive relationship with gross savings, meaning that strong enforcement of credit contracts has a strong effect on gross savings, potentially through increased bank credit (hence more loans) and reduced costs of financial intermediation.

Table 12.3 Long-run analysis of gross savings, institutions

	(1)	(2)	(3)
		Panel A: Long-run coefficients	
Log GDP per capita	4.530 (3.511)	7.889** (2.782)	11.936*** (3.306)
Domestic credit	0.181* (0.092)	−0.028 (0.095)	−0.453*** (0.153)
ToT	−0.143*** (0.045)	−0.072 (0.044)	−0.055 (0.048)
GDP growth	0.342** (0.151)	0.372*** (0.117)	0.494*** (0.138)
Inflation	0.277** (0.109)	0.281*** (0.073)	0.276*** (0.069)
Bureaucratic quality	0.556 (0.971)	—	—
Rule of law index	—	0.564** (0.274)	—
Political corruption index	—	—	−0.607*** (0.151)
Adjustment term	−0.748*** (0.157)	−0.770*** (0.098)	−0.762*** (0.088)
		Panel B: Diagnostic tests	
R-squared	0.866	0.908	0.910
LM *p*-value	0.241	0.444	0.297
BP *p*-value	0.723	0.207	0.629
JB *p*-value	0.883	0.676	0.831
Observations	33	35	37

Note: panel A reports long-run results from estimating the ARDL with gross savings as dependent variable, with column (1) representing the baseline model. Standard errors are reported in parentheses (***p ≤ 0.01, **p ≤ 0.05, *p ≤ 0.1). SPB is the public savings ratio, and ToT is the terms of trade index. Panel B reports the diagnostic tests for the various models from columns (1)–(7) (see Cameron and Trivedi 2010 for details). LM *p*-value is for the Breusch–Godfrey LM test for autocorrelation (null hypothesis is no serial correlation), BP *p*-value is for the Breusch–Pagan/Cook–Weisberg test for heteroskedasticity (null hypothesis is homoskedasticity), and JB *p*-value is for the Jarque–Bera normality test (null hypothesis of normality).
Source: authors' construction.

The short-run effects mirror those from the private savings model, with terms of trade mostly displaying significant negative effects (see the appendix at Table 12.A2).

5.2 Robustness analysis

5.2.1 Crisis variables

We introduce dummy variables to ascertain the robustness of our results to the following global and country-specific events: the oil price hike of the late 1970s to early 1980s, the devaluation of the CFA franc in 1994, the effects of the global financial crisis, and the introduction of mobile money (digital finance) in 2012. See

Tagem and Sama-Lang (2024: Tables 7–8) for the findings on private savings and gross savings, respectively, and section 5.3 (Tagem and Sama-Lang 2024: 18–20) for a more in-depth discussion of the results.

First, we incorporate the sustained oil price hike in the early 1980s. Given that oil was the main source of export revenue (hence domestic revenue) in the 1980s, we ascertain whether the constant high price between 1980 and 1986 had an impact on savings aggregates. We create a dummy variable, which equals one for the periods of elevated oil prices (i.e. over 1980–86_ and zero otherwise. We find a strong positive relationship between the dummy variable and private savings. Second, we attempt to ascertain the impact of the 1994 devaluation of the CFA franc. We create a dummy variable, which takes the value of one in the year of the devaluation and zero otherwise. The dummy variable is positive but insignificant. Third, we incorporate the impact of the global financial crisis during 2008–09. We create a dummy variable, which equals one for the years 2008 and 2009 and zero otherwise. The dummy variable, while negative, is also insignificant. Fourth, we try to isolate the impact of the introduction and usage of digital finance, that is mobile money. We create a dummy variable, which equals one from the year of introduction to the final year of the sample (i.e. from 2012 to 2018) and zero otherwise. We find the variable to be negative and insignificant. The negative effect may not be surprising as digital money is mostly used to cover other services (e.g. payment of bills) rather than as a means of savings.

We carry out similar analysis of crisis variables on gross savings and summarize the results below. First, the oil price dummy variable is strongly significant, suggesting that the period of elevated oil prices that contributed to significant government revenues also had a positive impact on gross savings through higher public savings. Second, all the other dummy variables (i.e. devaluation, global financial crisis, and mobile money) are insignificant.

6. Conclusion

Domestic resource mobilization (DRM) has been reiterated as a fundamental tenet in the post-COVID-19 pandemic recovery across developing countries. While much of the DRM discussion has aptly focused on expanding tax revenue mobilization, less is known about the potential galvanizing impact of domestic savings on the DRM process. For this, it is important to understand the factors that cause savings rates to differ across countries (and possibly regions) and over time. This chapter filled that gap by estimating the determinants of savings rates, both private and gross, in Cameroon over the period from 1980 to 2018. Applying the ARDL method to distinguish between long-run and short-run effects, we found that our empirical analysis matched predictions from the life-cycle model of savings: the findings showed that income growth is a core determinant of savings.

Two key findings are highlighted. First, we found strong similarities between the determinants of private and gross savings (e.g. economic growth, domestic credit to private sector, terms of trade, and inflation influence both savings aggregates). We showed that the terms of trade index has a positive relationship with gross savings, indicating that adverse shocks to commodity prices are associated with increased savings through agents' attempts to smooth consumption in the face of such shocks. We showed that public savings erode private savings, which is unsurprising given the dampening effects that persistent fiscal deficits ultimately have on economic outcomes. Second, we sought to isolate the impact of various global and country-specific shocks and policy reforms, specifically the sustained oil price increases in the 1980s, the 1994 devaluation of the CFA franc, the 2008–09 global financial crisis, and the introduction (and continued usage) of mobile money from 2012. With the exception of the oil price dummy variable, which is occasionally significant, all other dummy variables are consistently insignificant.

While these findings are highly context-specific, hence not generalizable, some policy implications can be gleaned from them. The obvious starting point will be to incorporate specific (quantitative) targets for private and gross savings into national development plans and DRM strategies. This will ensure that targets are grounded in sound economic analysis and that targeted policies to improve domestic savings are not arbitrary but are enshrined in legislation, which lends them more credibility. Furthermore, policies that encourage financial inclusion and deepening should be fostered.

Appendix

Table 12.A1 Short-run model for private savings

	(1)	(2)	(3)	(4)	(5)	(6)	(7)
L. ΔPrivate savings	−0.267** (0.112)	−0.284** (0.124)	−0.220* (0.108)	−0.223* (0.111)	0.121** (0.049)	−0.264** (0.117)	−0.305*** (0.090)
ΔToT	0.097*** (0.028)	0.137*** (0.025)	0.098*** (0.031)	0.076** (0.030)	—	0.096*** (0.031)	0.110*** (0.023)
L1. ΔToT	−0.045* (0.025)	—	—	−0.055** (0.025)	—	−0.045* (0.026)	−0.043** (0.020)
ΔInflation	−0.102*** (0.035)	−0.120*** (0.037)	−0.124*** (0.033)	−0.089** (0.035)	−0.065*** (0.015)	−0.102** (0.036)	0.100*** (0.028)
ΔDomestic credit	—	—	−0.078 (0.089)	—	—	—	—
L1. ΔDomestic credit	—	—	−0.225** (0.106)	—	—	—	—
L. ΔPublic savings	—	—	—	—	−0.343*** (0.114)	—	—
ΔGrowth	—	—	—	—	0.017 (0.036)	—	—
L. ΔGrowth	—	—	—	—	−0.080** (0.032)	—	—
ΔHousehold consumption	—	—	—	—	−0.499*** (0.139)	—	—

Note: diagnostic tests same as from Table 12.1 (unreported).

Source: authors' construction.

Table 12.A2 Short-run model for gross savings

	(1)	(2)	(3)	(4)	(5)	(6)	(7)
L. ΔGross savings	—	—	—	—	0.444***	—	—
					(0.149)		
Δ Log GDP per capita	—	—	—	—	—	—	−9.619***
							(2.820)
L. Δ Log GDP per capita	—	—	—	—	—	—	−5.439*
							(2.796)
ΔToT	0.090***	0.139***	0.093***	0.048	—	0.110***	0.165***
	(0.032)	(0.035)	(0.030)	(0.033)		(0.036)	(0.021)
L1. ΔToT	−0.059*	−0.077**	—	−0.076**		−0.055*	—
	(0.029)	(0.028)		(0.028)		(0.029)	
ΔInflation	−0.140***	−0.135***	−0.124***	−0.104**	—	−0.152***	−0.236***
	(0.042)	(0.039)	(0.033)	(0.041)		(0.044)	(0.047)
ΔDebt	—	—	—	—	—	—	−0.091**
							(0.033)
L1. ΔDebt	—	—	—	—	—	—	−0.090**
							(0.038)
ΔHousehold consumption	—	—	—	—	−0.049	—	—
					(0.239)		
L. ΔHousehold consumption	—	—	—	—	0.795***	—	—
					(0.211)		

Note: diagnostic tests same as from Table 12.2 (unreported).

Source: authors' construction.

References

Ackah, C., and M. Lambon-Quayefio (2023). 'Domestic Savings in Sub-Saharan Africa: The Case of Ghana'. WIDER Working Paper 2023/38. Helsinki: United Nations University (UNU)-World Institute for Public Policy Research and Analysis (WIDER). https://doi.org/10.35188/UNU-WIDER/2023/346-8.

Ando, A., and F. Modigliani (1963). 'The "Life Cycle" Hypothesis of Saving: Aggregate Implications and Tests'. *American Economic Review*, 53(1): 55–84.

Ang, J. B., and K. Sen (2011). 'Private Saving in India and Malaysia Compared: The Roles of Financial Liberalization and Expected Pension Benefits'. *Empirical Economics*, 41: 247–67. https://doi.org/10.1007/s00181-010-0386-3.

Athukorala, P. C., and K. Sen (2004). 'The Determinants of Private Saving in India'. *World Development*, 32(3): 491–503. https://doi.org/10.1016/j.worlddev.2003.07.008.

Athukorala, P. C., and W. Suanin (2024). 'Saving Transition in Asia'. *Journal of Development Studies*, 60(8): 1–16. https://doi.org/10.1080/00220388.2024.2328033.

Boateng, E., F. W. Agbola, and A. Mahmood (2019). 'Does the Quality of Institutions Enhance Savings? The Case of Sub-Saharan Africa'. *Applied Economics*, 51(58): 6235–63. https://doi.org/10.1080/00036846.2019.1616066.

Cameron, A. C., and P. K. Trivedi (2010). *Microeconometrics Using Stata*, Vol. 2. College Station, TX: Stata Press.

Chowdhury, A. (2015). 'Terms of Trade Shocks and Private Savings in the Developing Countries'. *Journal of Comparative Economics*, 43(4): 1122–34. https://doi.org/10.1016/j.jce.2015.02.006.

Coppedge, M., J. Gerring, C. H. Knutsen, S. I. Lindberg, J. Teorell, D. Altman, M. Bernhard, M. S. Fish, A. Glynn, A. Hicken, A. Lührmann, K. L. Marquardt, K. McMann, P. Paxton, D. Pemstein, B. Seim, R. Sigman, S. E. Skaaning, J. Staton, A. Cornell, L. Gastaldi, H. Gjerløw, V. Mechkova, J. von Römer, A. Sundtröm, E. Tzelgov, L. Uberti, Y. Wang, T. Wig, and D. Ziblatt (2023). *V-Dem Codebook v13*. University of Gothenburg Varieties of Democracy (V-Dem) Project. Gothenburg: University of Gothenburg.

Elbadawi, I. A., and F. M. Mwega (2000). 'Can Africa's Saving Collapse Be Reversed?' *World Bank Economic Review*, 14(3): 415–43. https://doi.org/10.1093/wber/14.3.415.

Facchini, F., S. Massin, and K. Brookes (2024). 'The Relationship between Institutional Quality, Trust and Private Savings'. *Journal of Institutional Economics*, 20: e8. https://doi.org/10.1017/S1744137423000346.

Feng, Y., and X. Yu (2021). 'The Impact of Institutions on Financial Development: Evidence from East Asian Countries'. *Australian Economic Papers*, 60(1): 122–37. https://doi.org/10.1111/1467-8454.12196.

Freytag, A., and S. Voll (2013). 'Institutions and Savings in Developing and Emerging Economies'. *Public Choice*, 157: 475–509. https://doi.org/10.1007/s11127-013-0121-7.

Grigoli, F., A. Herman, and K. Schmidt-Hebbel (2017). 'Is Private Saving in Latin America and the Caribbean Different?' *Review of Development Economics*, 21(4): 1255–80. https://doi.org/10.1111/rode.12306.

Grigoli, F., A. Herman, and K. Schmidt-Hebbel (2018). 'Saving in the World'. *World Development*, 104: 257–70. https://doi.org/10.1016/j.worlddev.2017.11.022.

ICRG (International Country Risk Guide) (2018). *IRIS Database*, 5th edn. Syracuse NY: The Political Risk Services Group.

IMF (International Monetary Fund) (1996). 'Cameroon—Selected Issues and Statistical Appendix'. IMF Country Report 96/125. Washington, DC: IMF. https://doi.org/10.5089/9781451807998.002.

IMF (2007). 'Cameroon Selected Issues'. IMF Country Report 07/287. Washington, DC: IMF. https://doi.org/10.5089/9781451808230.002.

IMF (2009). 'Cameroon: Financial System Stability Assessment—Update'. IMF Country Report 09/051. Washington, DC: IMF. https://doi.org/10.5089/9781451808285.002.

IMF (2014). 'Cameroon Selected Issues'. IMF Country Report 14/213. Washington, DC: IMF. https://doi.org/10.5089/9781498396011.002.

IMF (2018a). '2018 Article IV Consultation, Second Review under the Extended Credit Facility Arrangement, Requests for Waivers of Nonobservance of Performance Criteria and Modification of Performance Criteria'. IMF Country Report 18/235. Washington, DC: IMF.

IMF (2018b). 'Cameroon Selected Issues'. IMF Country Report 18/256. Washington, DC: IMF. https://doi.org/10.5089/9781484373378.002.

IMF (2019). 'Fourth Review under the Extended Credit Facility Arrangement and Requests for Waivers of Nonobservance of Performance Criteria and Modification of Performance Criteria'. IMF Country Report 19/247. Washington, DC: IMF.

IMF (2022). 'Cameroon Selected Issues'. IMF Country Report 22/076. Washington, DC: IMF. https://doi.org/10.5089/9798400204074.002.

Kelly, R., and G. Mavrotas (2008). 'Savings and Financial Sector Development: Panel Cointegration Evidence from Africa'. *European Journal of Finance*, 14(7): 563–81. https://doi.org/10.1080/13518470801890602.

Khan, S. A. (2011). 'Volatility of Resource Inflows and Domestic Investment in Cameroon'. AERC Research Paper 221. Yaoundé: African Economic Research Consortium.

Loayza, N., K. Schmidt-Hebbel, and L. Servén (2000). 'Saving in Developing Countries: An Overview'. *World Bank Economic Review*, 14(3): 393–414. https://doi.org/10.1093/wber/14.3.393.

Masson, P. R., T. Bayoumi, and H. Samiei (1998). 'International Evidence on the Determinants of Private Saving'. *World Bank Economic Review*, 12(3): 483–501.

Modigliani, F. (1986). 'Life Cycle, Individual Thrift, and the Wealth of Nations'. *Science*, 234(4777): 704–12. https://doi.org/10.1126/science.234.4777.704.

Modigliani, F. (1993). 'Recent Declines in the Savings Rate: A Life Cycle Perspective'. In M. Baldassarri, L. Paganetto, and E. S. Phelps (eds), *World Saving, Prosperity and Growth*,249–86. London: Palgrave Macmillan.

Musamali, R., C. Mutia, and R. Ngugi (2022). 'The Determinants of Domestic Savings in Kenya'. WIDER Working Paper 2022/166. Helsinki: UNU-WIDER. https://doi.org/10.35188/UNU-WIDER/2022/265-2.

Nagawa, V., F. Wasswa, and E. Bbaale (2020). 'Determinants of Gross Domestic Savings in Uganda: An Autoregressive Distributed Lag (ARDL) Approach to Cointegration'. *Journal of Economic Structures*, 9(1): 1–19. https://doi.org/10.1186/s40008-020-00209-1.

Nissanke, M., and E. Aryeetey (2008). 'Institutional Analysis of Financial Market Fragmentation in Sub-Saharan Africa: A Risk-Cost Configuration Approach'. In Mavrotas, G. eds., *Domestic Resource Mobilization and Financial Development. Studies in Development Economics and Policy*, 112–45. London: Palgrave Macmillan. https://doi.org/10.1057/9780230594012_6.

Pesaran, M. H., Y. Shin, and R. J. Smith (2001). 'Bounds Testing Approaches to the Analysis of Level Relationships'. *Journal of Applied Econometrics*, 16(3): 289–326. https://doi.org/10.1002/jae.616.

Sahoo, P., and R. K. Dash (2013). 'Financial Sector Development and Domestic Savings in South Asia'. *Economic Modelling*, 33: 388–97. https://doi.org/10.1016/j.econmod.2013.04.018.

Sanga, B., and M. Aziakpono (2022). 'The Effect of Institutional Factors on Financial Deepening: Evidence from 50 African Countries'. *Journal of Business and Socio-economic Development*, 3(2): 150–65. https://doi.org/10.1108/JBSED-12-2021-0175.

Sen, K. (2023). 'The Drivers of Investment and Savings Rates: An Exploratory Note'. *Transnational Corporations Journal*, 30(3): 91–9. https://doi.org/10.18356/2076099x-30-3-5.

Swaleheen, M. (2008). 'Corruption and Saving in a Panel of Countries'. *Journal of Macroeconomics*, 30(3): 1285–301.

Tagem, A. M., and D. Sama-Lang (2024). 'The Determinants of Domestic Savings in Cameroon: What Role for Institutions'. WIDER Working Paper 2024/42. Helsinki: UNU-WIDER. https://doi.org/10.35188/UNU-WIDER/2024/504-2.

Were, M., and C. Joseph (2022). 'Determinants of Domestic Savings in Tanzania: Empirical Evidence'. WIDER Working Paper 2022/166. Helsinki: UNU-WIDER. https://doi.org/10.35188/UNU-WIDER/2022/299-7.

World Bank (2023). 'World Development Indicators'. Washington, DC: World Bank. Available at: https://databank.worldbank.org/source/world-development-indicators (accessed 18 September 2023).

World Bank (2024). 'World Governance Indicators'. Washington, DC: World Bank. Available at: https://www.worldbank.org/en/publication/worldwide-governance-indicators (accessed 27 January 2024).

PART IV
CONCLUSION

13
Conclusions and policy implications

Rose Ngugi and Kunal Sen

In this chapter, we briefly discuss the main conclusions of the book and key policy implications.

1. Key findings

One important development in developing countries in the past two decades has been the way technology and innovation have revolutionized financial markets. Financial technology (fintech) has changed provision of banking services, the way banks work, how capital is raised, and how payments—including retail payments—are conducted. Chapter 2 traces the development of fintech in sub-Saharan Africa, and how this may have led to financial inclusion for underserved and unserved parts of the population in the continent. The chapter observes that fintech has vast potential to mobilize financial savings in sub-Saharan Africa and suggests options for policymakers to take to increase the rapid uptake of fintech products.

A particular challenge that policymakers in Africa face is mobilizing long-term capital for investment needs given the underdeveloped nature of stock and bond markets in the continent. Chapter 3 reviews the state of progress in the development of capital markets in sub-Saharan Africa. It argues that policymakers need to stabilize capital markets in the continent by building investor confidence through strict enforcement of rules and regulations, having a stable macroeconomic environment, and supporting the growth of micro, small, and medium enterprises to enhance their attractiveness for listing in bond and stock markets.

Pension systems are also a potential source of long-term investible funds, as is clear from the East Asian experience. Pensions also provide an important form of social protection for the elderly. Chapter 4 discusses the experience with pension funds in sub-Saharan Africa (SSA), noting low coverage and excessive costs of joining pension schemes and that these schemes mostly cover formal-sector employees. The chapter argues for a targeted universal pension system funded by public resources and that the move to universal coverage needs to be gradual so as not to lead to fiscal strain.

Rose Ngugi and Kunal Sen, *Conclusions and policy implications*. In: *The Domestic Savings Shortfall in Sub-Saharan Africa*. Edited by: Rose Ngugi and Kunal Sen, Oxford University Press. © UNU-WIDER (2025).
DOI: 10.1093/oso/9780198932482.003.0013

In many developed (as well as developing) countries, sovereign wealth funds (SWFs) play an increasingly significant role in fiscal stabilization, productive investment, and intergenerational saving. Chapter 5 assesses the potential role that SWFs can play in Africa in mobilizing savings for investment. African SWFs hold US$8 trillion in assets, making them global financial players. The chapter argues that in addition to fiscal stabilization and intergenerational savings roles, African SWFs should act as development funds in financing productive investment in long-term structural transformation.

In recent years, many countries in SSA had to borrow from external markets to make for the shortfall in domestic savings to finance public investment projects. This has led to an increased prevalence of debt distress on the continent, as financial conditions in the international market have tightened with elevated world interest rates and depreciated exchange rates. Chapter 6 assesses the emerging public debt challenges that African countries face, especially considering the uncertain global environment and constrained fiscal space at a time when most sub-Saharan African economies have not fully recovered from the aftermaths of the COVID-19 pandemic. The chapter finds that a considerable proportion of low-income countries in SSA are either in debt distress or at substantial risk of debt distress. Furthermore, debt sustainability risk for the Heavily Indebted Poor Countries (HIPC), traditionally known to be at minimal risk of debt distress before the pandemic, has since increased from low to moderate.

Many countries in Africa implemented financial-sector reforms as part of the structural adjustment programmes in the 1980s and 1990s. The debate on whether financial liberalization leads to an increase or decline in savings is unresolved in the African context. Chapter 7 assesses the impact of financial liberalization on private savings in SSA using cross-country panel data and finds no discernible effect of financial reforms on private savings in the continent.

Chapter 8 examines the Asian experience with domestic savings, where the region has done better than other developing regions in having high savings rates. The chapter notes the differences in savings behaviour both across countries in Asia and over time. The chapter argues that there is no evidence that a prior phase of promoting savings through specific policy initiatives was critical to Asia's success in mobilizing savings, and rapid economic growth was a primary factor in initiating the savings transition in the region.

Chapters 9–12 analyse case studies for four countries—Kenya, Tanzania, Ghana, and Cameroon. Chapter 9 covers the key drivers of domestic saving in Kenya. The study also draws lessons from Kenya on exploiting fintech as an alternative channel for savings mobilization. Per capita income growth rate, inflation, and age–dependency ratio significantly influence private savings in the long run. Also, in the long run, the national saving is positively and significantly influenced by the per capita income growth rate, inflation, and private-sector credit growth rates.

Chapter 10 analyses the trends and determinants of gross domestic savings in Tanzania. Using data for the period 1990–2020, the study reveals that in the long run, per capita income, public saving, and the ratio of broad money to gross domestic product as a proxy for financial deepening significantly determine private savings. The per capita income, real deposit rate, and broad money influence the gross domestic savings.

The country case study for Ghana, in Chapter 11, uses data from 1980 to 2019 to explore the determinants of savings in Ghana. The analysis finds no evidence supporting a long-run relationship between private savings and independent variables. However, in the short run, per capita income, per capita squared, and money supply significantly increase savings.

Finally, Chapter 12 provides the case study of Cameroon. The empirical analysis uses annual data over the period 1980–2018. The chapter finds that per capita income, income growth, and domestic credit to the private sector are associated with increases in both savings aggregates. Further, institutions, specifically measures of corruption and rule of law, are significant determinants of savings.

Overall, we find that per capita income and financial deepening (as captured by M2/GDP) are common determinants of savings across all country studies. This suggests that economic growth along with financial sector policies are key factors that explain the variation in savings rate across the four countries—Kenya, Tanzania, Ghana, and Cameroon.

2. Policy implications

To harness the vast potential of fintech in mobilizing financial savings in SSA, there is need to create a competitive ecosystem and infrastructure that facilitate entry and robust consumer protection regulations to provide an enabling and innovative environment; also to build capacity to monitor and prevent cybercrime, especially in terms of office-level surveillance. Addressing the key enablers of mobile and internet connectivity infrastructure, affordability, consumer readiness, and content—particularly around network quality, affordability for low-income users, digital skills, and the creation of content in more local languages—is also critical. Also, devising a system of leasing will enhance mobile network operators' and mobile virtual network operators' interoperability, agent network interoperability, and regional payments interoperability across Africa. Further, leveraging on digital technology can improve the personal identity system (e-ID system) and thus facilitate coping with market innovations and securing the market. Finally, enhancing research and capacity in the technology of artificial intelligence across SSA to increase the uptake of fintech products and encourage innovation is necessary.

Interventions to accelerate capital market development include sustaining efforts to ensure stability of the capital markets to build investor confidence through strict enforcement of the laws, regulations, and rules governing them; having a constant stable and conducive macroeconomic environment to incentivize investments; developing and implementing focused policies to support the growth of micro, small, and medium-sized enterprises to enhance their listing attractiveness; having prudent and comprehensive policies that support the development of capital markets and their timely review; and growing a vibrant private sector necessary to support the development of capital markets by designing effective approaches to exploit the anticipated benefits from trade agreements.

To grow and develop pension systems in SSA, necessary interventions include putting in place a universal non-contributory pension scheme that meets the needs of unemployed among the working-age population and those in the informal sector; offering incentives such as a matching contributions, or some guaranteed insurance cover if a certain level of contribution is reached by a member in a given period to motivate members to save more for old age; and instituting a well-structured legal and regulatory framework to streamline pension fund management and minimize administration cost, particularly for private pensions.

In the African context, fiscal stabilization funds are often necessary but entail considerable opportunity costs. In the absence of a strong framework of multilateral financial assistance that would reduce 'self-insurance' needs, paying down sovereign debt during times of revenue windfalls may constitute a better option as the cost of debt servicing usually exceeds the rate of return on financial investments. Further, investing in human capital and infrastructure has higher developmental returns than the returns on financial assets in intergenerational SWFs. Finally, it is preferable to capitalize development funds or national development banks to effectively finance productive investments for long-term structural transformation, provided they have clear mandates and strong governance. Such development funds, either sovereign development funds (SDFs) or national development banks (NDBs) need full transparency, strong governance, and the necessary analytical capacity to ensure that their investments contribute to structural transformation.

Though there are no quick fixes or a one-size-fits-all solution to SSA's rising debt burden, sustainable long-term solutions require a concerted multi-pronged approach. Hence, various stakeholders both at domestic and international level have a critical role to play. A debt-relief programme—currently missing in global public-debt-related initiatives and debates—is critical. The G20 Common Framework should be made more effective in addressing SSA's public debt burden, including timely and orderly debt restructuring. There is also need for the international community to enhance the availability and predictability of long-term international finance in the form of concessions. At domestic level, fiscal consolidation is key and complemented by domestic resource mobilization through the widening of the tax base, digitalization, financial deepening, and capital market development. SSA's long-term sustainability of public debt also requires economic transformation, for example through export-led growth for increased access to global markets and value chains and leveraging on the African Continental Free Trade Area.

Though the factors that drive private savings in the SSA region are like those in other developing regions, SSA countries need to implement more aggressive policies than other developing countries to realize similar positive effects. Further, implementing policies that raise long-term growth such as promoting good institutions and investing in human capital, physical capital, and technology will boost private savings. This means that improving institutional quality in the SSA region may facilitate higher growth and thereby promote private savings. Finally, it would be beneficial for SSA governments to sustain fiscal consolidation to increase national savings.

To inform the policy debate in SSA countries, the Asian experience with domestic savings provides some lessons. A policy regime shift in favour of an outward-orientated development strategy has underpinned the time patterns of savings behaviour in Asia. Export orientation therefore has contributed to higher private savings both by its direct contribution and by compounding the impact of the rate of income growth on the savings rate. Foreign capital inflows are complementary to domestic savings. The private sector drives the trends and patterns of saving in Asia—the emergence of the corporate sector has been the prime mover of national savings.

To grow savings in Kenya, efforts to encourage growth in income—including the creation of decent employment—and to manage the erosion of real value are critical. Also, measures to enhance financial development need to be sustained with a focus on savings mobilization. A continued focus on creating an enabling environment for the private sector to thrive is necessary. Further, a persistent policy environment that insists on savings mobilization, with tangible closely monitored outcomes, needs to be maintained in the medium-to-long term if it is to yield the desired results. It is also important to prioritize fiscal stability to boost public saving. Finally, the window of opportunity provided by fintech developments, such as mobile money mainly used for transactions, can be exploited to encourage saving.

To promote domestic savings in Tanzania, pursuing growth-enhancing policies and development strategies geared towards increasing incomes is critical. Further, measures aimed at enhancing financial deepening and financial sector development are a priority. These include the expansion of access to financial services to rural areas and measures to enhance financial intermediation, including reducing market fragmentation and interest rate spreads, plus the adoption of technology to improve the efficiency of the financial sector. A stable macroeconomic environment, including price stability, is equally crucial for promoting savings and the growth of the economy. Finally, measures such as expanding exports through increased value addition can improve terms of trade (ToT), and therefore reduce the adverse effects of ToT on domestic savings.

To trigger savings in Ghana, it is critical to continue to pursue policies aimed at keeping households' income high, as well as to promote financial deepening to support savings mobilization. Additionally, enhancing financial inclusion can effectively increase savings. Finally, it is recommended to pursue sound monetary and fiscal policies to encourage savings mobilization.

To grow savings in Cameroon, it is important to incorporate specific targets for private savings into national development plans and domestic resource mobilization strategies. This will ensure that targets are not arbitrary but based on sound economic analysis and enshrined in legislations for credibility. It also critical to institute policies that foster financial inclusion and deepening.

Overall, the volume highlights that concerted policies promoting financial deepening, macroeconomic stability, and public savings are essential to foster growth, increase the savings rate in SSA, and close the continent's savings gap with East and South Asia.

Index

For the benefit of digital users, indexed terms that span two pages (e.g., 52–53) may, on occasion, appear on only one of those pages.

Note: Many of the main entries can also be found as sub-entries under the case study chapters of Asia, Cameroon, Ghana, Kenya and Tanzania.